Courts of Chivalry and Admiralty
in Late Medieval Europe

Courts of Chivalry and Admiralty in Late Medieval Europe

Edited by
Anthony Musson and Nigel Ramsay

THE BOYDELL PRESS

First published 2018
The Boydell Press, Woodbridge

ISBN 978 1 78327 217 4

The Boydell Press is an imprint of Boydell & Brewer Ltd
PO Box 9, Woodbridge, Suffolk IP12 3DF, UK
and of Boydell & Brewer Inc.
668 Mt Hope Avenue, Rochester, NY 14620–2731, USA
website: www.boydellandbrewer.com

A CIP catalogue record for this book is available
from the British Library

The publisher has no responsibility for the continued existence or accuracy of
URLs for external or third-party internet websites referred to in this book, and
does not guarantee that any content on such websites is, or will remain, accurate
or appropriate

This publication is printed on acid-free paper

Printed and bound in Great Britain by
TJ International Ltd, Padstow, Cornwall

CONTENTS

Contents

vi

ILLUSTRATIONS

Plates
(between pages 114 and 115)

Figures

Table

The editors, contributors and publishers are grateful to all the institutions and persons listed for permission to reproduce the materials in which they hold copyright. Every effort has been made to trace the copyright holders; apologies are offered for any omission, and the publishers will be pleased to add any necessary acknowledgement in subsequent editions.

NOTES ON CONTRIBUTORS

Andrew Ayton works principally on the military and maritime communities of late medieval England, and on the organisation and conduct of the king's wars in Scotland, France and at sea. He is Honorary Senior Research Fellow in History at the University of Hull (where he lectured for thirty years prior to his retirement in 2015) and Honorary Senior Research Fellow at Keele University.

Richard Barber has written widely on medieval literature and history; major titles include *The Holy Grail: The History of a Legend, Henry II* in the Penguin English Monarchs series, and the award-winning *The Knight and Chivalry*. His recent book *Edward III and the Triumph of England* made extensive use of the evidence given in the Court of Chivalry. He founded and directed Boydell & Brewer Ltd for forty years, and was made a Doctor of the University by the University of York in 2014.

John Ford is the Professor of Civil Law at the University of Aberdeen. He works mostly on the legal history of early modern Scotland, but recently he has been pursuing an interest in the development of maritime law. He is currently writing a book about the emergence of privateering.

Laurent Hablot is a Director of Studies at the École Pratique des Hautes Études in Paris, holding the chair of Emblematic Studies. After completing a Ph.D. on badges, he is now working on heraldic practices in the Middle Ages (online database ARMMA (ARmorial Monumental du Moyen-Âge)) and on medieval seals (SIGILLA (Base numérique des sceaux conservés en France)).

Thomas K. Heebøll-Holm is Assistant Professor in Medieval History at the Centre for Medieval Literature, University of Southern Denmark. His main research areas are conflict and crime at sea, *c.* 1200–*c.* 1500, and Danish connections with Europe in the High Middle Ages.

Julian Luxford is a Reader in Art History at the University of St Andrews. He has written widely on the art and architecture of the Benedictine and Carthusian monastic orders, and is currently working on a book about medieval drawings in England, Scotland and Wales.

Ralph Moffat is Curator of European Arms and Armour at Glasgow Museums, and is responsible for the care, study and dissemination of knowledge of the collection. He is interested in the interpretation of original source material in order to gain a better understanding of the construction and use of medieval weapons and armour.

Philip Morgan is Senior Lecturer in History at Keele University. He writes on the social context of medieval warfare and on social rank, especially the gentry, and on chronicles in the later Middle Ages. He was co-director of a Leverhulme-funded project to produce an online digital edition of the Gascon Rolls (1360–1468), the records of English administration in south-west France.

Anthony Musson is currently Head of Research at Historic Royal Palaces. He was previously Professor of Legal History and Director of the Bracton Centre for Legal History Research at the University of Exeter. He has published on the medieval legal profession, the visual culture of the law and criminal justice, and was principal investigator on *Law and Arms: The Medieval English Court of Chivalry*, a recent research project funded by the Leverhulme Trust.

Nigel Ramsay is an Honorary Senior Research Associate of the History Department, University College London; he was until recently also a Senior Research Fellow in the History Faculty, University of Oxford. He is at present preparing an edition of all the extant medieval records of the (English) Court of Chivalry for publication by the Selden Society.

Bertrand Schnerb is Professor of Medieval History at the University of Lille. His academic work focuses on Burgundian State, nobility and war at the end of the Middle Ages. He is author of *Enguerrand de Bournonville et les siens: Un lignage noble du Boulonnais aux XIVe et XVe siècles* (1997), *L'État bourguignon, 1363–1477* (1999), *"L'honneur de la maréchaussée". Maréchaux et maréchalat en Bourgogne des origines à la fin du Moyen Age* (2000), and *Jean sans Peur. Le prince meurtrier* (2005). He is currently working on a book about the Saveuse family (of Picardy) at the end of the Middle Ages.

Anne F. Sutton is the former Archivist of the Mercers' Company of London. She is author of *The Mercery of London: Trade, Goods and People, 1130s–1578* (2005), *Wives and Widows of Medieval London* (2017), and many articles on fifteenth-century London; she is also the co-editor and author of *The Coronation of Richard III* (1983), *The Hours of Richard III* (1990), *Richard III's Books* (1997), and *The Privileges of the Merchant Adventurers of England, 1296–1483* (2009).

Lorenzo Tanzini is Associate Professor of Medieval History at the University of Cagliari. His research interests are focused on the institutional history of Italian towns of the Middle Ages and the relations between law, politics and economic practices in late medieval Italy. His main publications are *Alle origini della Toscana moderna* (2007), *A consiglio: La vita politica nell'Italia dei comuni* (2014) and *La mobilità sociale nel medioevo italiano, 1: Competenze, conoscenze e saperi tra professioni e ruoli sociali (secc. XII–XV)*, edited with S. Tognetti (2016).

PREFACE

This volume of papers arises from a two-day symposium entitled 'Heraldry and Piracy in an Age of Chivalry: The Jurisdiction of the Constable and Marshal(s) and of the Admiralty in Later Medieval England and France' which was held in Exeter's Royal Albert Memorial Museum and Gallery on 4–5 June 2015. It forms part of a project specifically on the medieval English Court of Chivalry undertaken by the editors, which was funded by the Leverhulme Trust. We are most grateful to the College of Social Sciences and International Studies, University of Exeter, and to the Royal Albert Memorial Museum and Gallery for enabling us to hold the symposium, and to the Leverhulme Trust for its contribution towards the production of this book.

A NOTE ON EDITORIAL PRACTICE

Some degree of modernisation has been applied to medieval texts that are printed or excerpted in this volume. Abbreviations and contractions have been expanded (e.g., 'y^e' to 'the'), 'u' and 'v' have been altered to 'v' and 'u' to conform to present-day practice, and a degree of modern punctuation has been introduced when necessary to make sense of the text. References to folios of manuscripts are to be assumed to be to the recto unless the verso is specifically indicated.

ABBREVIATIONS

BL	British Library, Dept of Manuscripts
Cal. Close R.	*Calendars of Close Rolls, 1227–1509,* 61 vols (London, 1892–1963)
Cal. Fine R.	*Calendars of Fine Rolls, 1272–1509,* 22 vols (London, 1911–62)
Cal. I.P.M.	*Calendars of Inquisitions Post Mortem, Henry III – 1485,* 26 vols (London, 1904–2009)
Cal. Pat. R.	*Calendars of Patent Rolls, 1232–1509,* 52 vols (London, 1893–1916)
Emden, *Biog. Reg. Univ. Oxford*	A.B. Emden, *Biographical Register of the University of Oxford to A.D. 1500,* 3 vols (Oxford, 1957–9)
Eng. Hist. Rev.	*English Historical Review*
GEC, *Complete Peerage*	G.E. C[okayne], *The Complete Peerage,* ed. V. Gibbs et al., 14 vols (London, 1910–98)
Given-Wilson, *PROME*	*Parliament Rolls of Medieval England, 1275–1504,* general editor C. Given-Wilson, 16 vols (Woodbridge and London, 2005)
Jnl	*Journal*
Nicolas, *Scrope and Grosvenor Controversy*	*The Scrope and Grosvenor Controversy: De Controversia in Curia Militari inter Ricardum Le Scrope et Robertum Grosvenor Milites,* ed. Nicholas Harris Nicolas, 2 vols (privately printed, [1832]).
ODNB	*Oxford Dictionary of National Biography,* ed. H.C.G. Matthew and Brian Harrison, 60 vols (Oxford, 2004); updated online
PCM	College of Arms, London, MS Processus in Curia Marescalli, 2 vols
PRO	Public Record Office (now absorbed into the National Archives or TNA, q.v.)
Rymer, *Foedera*	T. Rymer and R. Sanderson, compiled, *Foedera, Conventiones, Litterae et Cuiuscunque Generis Acta Publica,* ed. T. Rymer and R. Sanderson, 20 vols (London, 1704–35); revised edition, 1066–1383, 4 vols in 7 parts (Record Commission, 1816–69); cited from the latter edition down to 1383 and thereafter from the original edition

Ser.	Series
Soc.	Society
Statutes of the Realm	*Statutes of the Realm*, ed. Alexander Luders et al., 11 vols in 12 (London, 1810–28)
TNA	The National Archives
Twiss, *Black Book of the Admiralty*	*The Black Book of the Admiralty*, ed. T. Twiss, 4 vols (Rolls Ser., 55, 1871–6)

INTRODUCTION

Anthony Musson and Nigel Ramsay

The wars waged by the English in France during the fourteenth and fifteenth centuries led to the need for judicial agencies that could deal with disputes that arose on land or sea, beyond the reach of indigenous laws. While much has been written on the culture of chivalry,[1] to date the jurisdictional development of these Courts has attracted comparatively little scholarly attention.[2] The court of the English Admiral in the medieval period has received significantly less.[3] This volume explores the Courts of Chivalry and Admiralty, their officers and the wider cultural and political context in which they had jurisdiction and operated in later medieval Western Europe. Combining law with military and maritime history, and discussing the art and material culture of chivalric disputes as well as their associated heraldry, each chapter builds on recent work in the field and provides a valuable multidisciplinary outlook on an important area of medieval life and culture.

Established during Edward III's reign under the presidency of the Constable and Marshal of England, the Court of Chivalry heard cases that arose out of

---

[1] For example: Malcolm Vale, *War and Chivalry. Warfare and Aristocratic Culture in England, France and Burgundy at the End of the Middle Ages* (London, 1981); Nigel Saul, *For Honour and Fame: Chivalry in England, 1066–1500* (London, 2011); C. Taylor, *Chivalry and the Ideals of Knighthood in France during the Hundred Years War* (Cambridge, 2013).

[2] A general account of the entire history of the English Court of Chivalry was published by G.D. Squibb, *The High Court of Chivalry: A Study of the Civil Law in England* (Oxford, 1959), but its focus is primarily on the post-medieval period. The medieval history of the Court has principally been examined to date by the late Maurice Keen, in his *The Laws of War in the Later Middle Ages* (London, 1965), and 'The Jurisdiction and Origins of the Constable's Court', in *War and Government in the Middle Ages. Essays in Honour of J.O. Prestwich*, ed. J. Gillingham and J.C. Holt (Cambridge, 1984), pp. 159–69 (reprinted in M. Keen, *Nobles, Knights and Men at Arms in the Middle Ages* (London and Rio Grande, Ohio, 1996), pp. 135–48). For a comprehensive study of the origins and jurisdiction of the Court see: Anthony Musson and Nigel Ramsay, *Law and Arms: The Medieval English Court of Chivalry* (forthcoming).

[3] R. Ward, 'The Shipmaster and the Rise and Fall of the Admirals' Courts', in *idem*, *The World of the Medieval Shipmaster: Law, Business and the Sea, c. 1350 – c. 1450* (Woodbridge, 2009), pp. 27–47; D. Simpkin, 'Keeping the Seas: England's Admirals, 1369–1389', in *Roles of the Sea in Medieval England*, ed. R. Gorski (Woodbridge, 2012), pp. 79–101.

acts of war, including disputes over rights in prisoners and their ransoms as well as about rights to particular coats of arms. It also took cognisance of appeals of treason, in which battle was offered by the appellant. Around the same period, the Court of the Admiralty, under the titular presidency of the Admiral of England, claimed jurisdiction over the waters surrounding the English king's territories and heard cases under maritime law involving a broad remit of issues, including naval discipline and administration, coastal defence, threats to shipping, disputes over prizes, wrecks and the depredations of pirates. Both courts were distinct from the other central courts in employing the civil law procedures of the Continental *ius commune* system rather than the English common law.

The developing European cult of chivalry gave greater prominence to the Prince's position as head of an apparatus that would resolve disputes between members of the noble and knightly ranks, particularly over coats of arms, as well as over military discipline and military and maritime perquisites such as ransoms and prizes. Jurisdictions comparable to the Courts of Chivalry and Admiralty in England accordingly also developed in France, under the Constable and Marshals of the kingdom and certain of its duchies as well as under the Admiral of France. While French admirals were primarily concerned with the navy and the regulation of prizes, admirals in Mediterranean states possessed wider legal prerogatives with competence to deal with commercial matters.

Although scholars have rightly pointed to precursors of the Courts of Chivalry and Admiralty operating in the thirteenth century, the second half of the fourteenth century was a key period in their jurisdictional development in various regions. Both England and France witnessed royal clarifications of the competences of Chivalry and Admiralty courts and their officers through the promulgation of important statutes and ordinances. The lead seems to have been taken in France during the 1370s and 1380s with edicts affecting the judicial authority of both the Constable and Marshal and the Admiral. In England, royal statutes of 1389–92 provided significant clarification of the powers of the Courts of Chivalry and Admiralty, particularly with regard to their relationship with the common law courts.[4]

*

The main chronological focus of the book is on the fourteenth and fifteenth centuries. Within this framework, it adopts a thematic approach. The initial chapters concentrate on the role of heralds in the chivalric arena. In their examination of heralds and heraldry, Richard Barber and Laurent Hablot respectively offer a revisionist view on when heralds can be regarded as

---

[4] For an examination of the Scottish experience, see Katie Stevenson, *Chivalry and Knighthood in Scotland, 1424–1513* (Woodbridge, 2006), pp. 1–12.

professionals in their sphere and on the discrepancies between the theory and practice relating to the law of arms. Barber evaluates sources for the early history of heralds and shows how historians should not imbue their title with too much significance nor infer responsibilities based on the later expansion of their role. Hablot pursues the role of heralds in disputes about coats of arms on the wider European stage and assesses the political and legal significance of these confrontations. In particular, he highlights the growing monopoly of the sovereign – not only to grant arms and authorise transfers, but also to check on their use (via heralds) and even to degrade coats of arms or prohibit their display.

Chapters by Julian Luxford, Philip Morgan and Andrew Ayton are based specifically on evidence presented in the Court of Chivalry by witnesses to the bearing of particular coats of arms. As Ayton explains, the depositions that make up much of the surviving Court of Chivalry material – recollections of veterans from numerous foreign campaigns – 'can add a precise and structured martial dimension to an all-too-often shadowy life story'. Using the rich witness testimony, he is able to set the career of Nicholas Sabraham within the military and social contexts that shaped his professional life. Morgan examines the statements in the context of contemporary gentry culture and in particular the use made of them by the parties in defining their own history and lineage through the fortunes of Sir Robert Grosvenor and his family. He contends that even though the verdict in the Scrope *v.* Grosvenor suit in the Court of Chivalry contributed to Grosvenor's relative impoverishment, his presence in the case 'affirmed his own part and power in regional society' as well as bringing him 'to the notice of a wider chivalric society'. By contrast, Luxford analyses the depositions in terms of their value as visual evidence and the use to which this was put by the parties and by the Court, which clearly built consideration of material culture into its investigative methodology from the outset. He assesses the value placed by contemporaries on the validity of forensic evidence, the widespread knowledge of 'the material and heraldic apparatus' and the process of gathering what was considered significant for its antiquity and authenticity. As his chapter demonstrates, the importance of being able to discern medieval attitudes towards material objects lies not only in their association of objects with particular historical circumstances (whether real or conflated), but in the fact that they also display their ignorance of the chronological specificity that we take for granted.

Ralph Moffat combines the artistic and military in his discussion and edition of John Hill's treatise about arming for a judicial duel. In addition to providing explanations of the various pieces of armour and the advantages that they brought to combat, he presents relevant sections of the text in modern English and supplies for the first time a fully transcribed version of the original. As a foil to their better known English equivalents, Bertrand Schnerb explores the importance and judicial competence of the Constable and Marshals of France. In doing so he also provides comparative evidence

3

of the officials operating in great lordships such as the duchies of Savoy and Burgundy and gives insight into some of the opposition to their authority encountered from other senior military officers (such as the Master of Crossbowmen).

The law of the sea and its significance for international relations are highlighted by Thomas Heebøll-Holm and Lorenzo Tanzini. The former charts the rise of the Court of Admiralty, the counterpart to the Court of Chivalry, arguing that its jurisdictional growth reflects pragmatic assertion of English maritime supremacy following the peace of Brétigny in 1360. Indeed, it is Heebøll-Holm's contention, in contrast to previous studies, that this was 'the defining moment', the time from when its establishment should properly be dated. The *Llibre del Consolat de mar*, the influential text on the law of the sea, is discussed by Tanzini, who sees its use and circulation as reflecting economic, political and cultural prestige among Mediterranean sea-faring powers. The editors of the text's various editions selected what they regarded as the most appropriate rules and customs for the arena in which they were operating. Consequently, as Tanzini emphasises, local and regional politics lie at the heart of its compilation, more so than maritime practice, thereby also reflecting the value of the text to merchant–municipal elites as a symbol of autonomy.

The final two papers straddle both military and maritime worlds. Anne Sutton's contribution, focusing on the future Richard III's tenure of office as Constable and Admiral, considers the significance of his personal input and, more generally, the influence of officialdom in these areas. She reveals that the authority to deal with treason was a significant aspect of the Constable of England's purview. The large number of treason cases occurring between the 1460s and 1480s and the harsh punishment meted out probably reflect the unsettled political times and underlines the politically charged nature of the office. As well as treason trials, she highlights notable royal interest in protecting shipping and trade convoys as well as in formalising the institutional shape of what later became the College of Arms. John Ford provides a reassessment of the overlap between the law of arms and the law of prize, the acquisition of ownership of ships or goods from enemies, contending that piracy will only be studied reliably by historians if they know how to distinguish the different situations in which it was thought legitimate for ships or goods to be seized. He also emphasises the need to consider the subject in relation to the 'learned laws' of the university law schools, a juridical context which seems to have been neglected in most examinations of the English experience.

Sources

The absence of tangible written evidence and deliberate obfuscation are problems facing anyone trying to establish the origins or activities of these courts before the later thirteenth century. While the Constable and Marshals of the French chivalric tradition are evident as official posts from the end of the twelfth century, it is not until the beginning of the fourteenth century that there is any specific documentation of their military jurisdiction. Similarly, the offices of the Constable and Marshal in England date back to Henry I, but there is at first nothing to link the posts with their later competence to deal with judicial matters. It is equally unclear at what point heralds acquired authority over coats of arms. There are scattered mentions and some records of disputes over devices worn by knights from the mid thirteenth century onwards, but it is difficult to tell without detailed cases precisely when identification and recording of devices became administration and control.

When it comes to military service and the laws of the sea, the problem is that of separating fact from fiction. As Luxford points out, witnesses were following officially set parameters, which encouraged them to locate ancient items of visual or material culture to back up their claims, but some of the testimony about heraldry containing arms 'savours of hearsay', or at least the object's antiquity (to modern understanding at least) does not in itself back up the claimed antiquity of the coat of arms. Morgan, too, asserts that the veracity of the depositions by witnesses in the Court of Chivalry needs to be questioned and the reliability of the soldiers' memories mistrusted. He regards some of the misleading evidence, however, as foundation myths especially created for the litigants (in collaboration with the evidence of chronicles and charters possessed by monastic foundations) to provide them with a suitable lineage. In this respect, as Tanzini explains, the *Llibre del Consolat de mar* (in Italian, *Libro del Consolato del Mar*) equally has a pretended genealogy, one deliberately claimed by towns in the Mediterranean region as being of ancient origin (or dating from at least the eleventh or twelfth centuries) in order to promote its effectiveness. Attitudes towards evidence and history are thus inextricably linked with personal and political agendas.

The judicial records of the various courts survive in disproportionate numbers and for fleetingly brief chronological runs.[5] Schnerb highlights the scarcity of judicial records relating to French military jurisdiction before the sixteenth century. Aside from two mid-fourteenth-century texts (*Les droiz du connétable* and *Ce sont les droits que le connestable doit avoir pour cause de sa connestablie*) – which set out the military power and financial rights of the constable, but reveal nothing of his judicial authority – and some

---

[5] Some of the proceedings of the Court of Chivalry have appeared in printed editions, as have early cases appearing in the Court of Admiralty, for example: Sir Nicholas Harris Nicolas, *The Scrope and Grosvenor Controversy: De Controversia in Curia Militari inter Ricardum le Scrope et Robertum Grosvenor, 1385–90*, 2 vols (1832); *Select Pleas in the Court of Admiralty*, ed. R.G. Marsden, 2 vols (Selden Soc., 6 and 11, 1894–7). Nigel Ramsay is currently preparing an edition of surviving proceedings from the medieval Court of Chivalry for publication by the Selden Society.

early-fifteenth-century royal ordinances, references to the Constable and Marshals of France are diffusely scattered. Yet there is just enough when pulled together to testify to the nature of their activities. Similarly, the lack of judicial records of the mercantile courts in Valencia and Barcelona means that it is difficult to assess their practical application in the courts and thus the impact of the written customs on real life. In spite of the generally poor survival rate of records of proceedings in the Courts of Chivalry and Admiralty during the fifteenth century, a few judicial records for both are extant for brief periods: for example, cases and court documents relating to the period 1443–6, when John Holland, duke of Exeter, was in office as Admiral, were included in the *Black Book of the Admiralty*. Again, although the only surviving records of the Constable's Court for this period are a series of appeals of 1469–76, the lack of documentation should not be taken to imply that it had ceased to be effective judicially. The number of appointments made by the Crown to commissions to hear appeals at this time demonstrates that it was not a moribund jurisdiction.

In spite of the caveats about using witness testimony from the surviving records of the English Court of Chivalry, the contributors are definite about the advantages that it can bring. The problem of invisibility in the records with regard to family and socio-economic background is countered by the family connections, status or social aspirations revealed in witness testimony. It can also provide opportunities for comparisons with other data and for a broader prosopographical study of military personnel. Luxford is especially enthusiastic about its possibilities for understanding attitudes towards material objects, and underlines its value as recording objects no longer in existence or interiors and landscapes that have long since vanished. The description of the tomb of Philip Burnell in the church of the Austin friars in Oxford, for example, 'has a fundamental art historical value' as it records a monument, otherwise undocumented, in a church that was itself at one time of importance to Oxford University but that is also practically unknown.

The research in this volume reveals that this is a subject that not only relies on the somewhat capricious survival of judicial records, but also offers access to the theoretical understanding underlying both the practice of the law in the areas covered by the jurisdiction of the courts and the practice of heraldry. Researchers are faced with either very little to go on or conversely an abundance of different versions. John Hill's treatise describing the arming process for judicial combat in fifteenth-century England, elaborated upon by Moffat, survives only in two almost identical seventeenth-century copies (one in Lincoln's Inn Library, the other in the Bodleian Library at Oxford). A problem of a rather different order is faced by anyone studying the *Llibre del Consolat de mar*. While the earliest version dates from the fourteenth century, manuscript copies were textually different and circulated in several regions before they were first consolidated in an edition of 1484 and thereafter went through numerous printed editions in Italian and Catalan during the late fifteenth and early sixteenth centuries. Researchers are also reliant on individuals providing what we now regard as vital and otherwise unknowable details which would otherwise be lost. The king of the heralds of the Rhine, Claes Heynenzoon (d. 1414), for example, served with the duke of Guelders before his appointment to the household of the duke of Bavaria and composed two significant armorial collections (the *Wapenboek Gelre* or *Book of Arms of Guelders* and *Wapenboek Beyeren* or *Book of Arms of Bavaria*) as well as penning poetic portraits of the flower of chivalry of the time (*Lobdichten*).

Schnerb and Hablot both highlight the importance of the fifteenth-century treatise by Honoré Bouvet, *L'Arbre des batailles*, regarded as the highest authority on matters of military justice in the early sixteenth century, although it was in fact largely a French translation of the work of the great Bolognese jurist John of Legnano, *De bello, de represaliis, et de duello*.[6] The problem for the historian, however, is the extent to which the treatises provide evidence of contemporary practice by interpolating real cases from the author's experience, or whether they simply rely on the examples set out in their earlier models. As both authors point out, Bouvet's heraldic discussion and practical questions are clearly drawn from Bartolo da Sassoferrato's *Tractatus de Insigniis et Armis*, whose ideas were also adapted in *Le songe du vergier* by Evrard of Trémaugon and *Le livre des faits d'armes et de chevalerie* by Christine de Pizan. In Bouvet's case, however, as Hablot demonstrates, the solutions he offers to disputes over the use of identical or homonymous coats of arms (one of the recurring themes of treatises of heraldic law) not only are different to those of his exemplar, but also are found documented in the legal practice of the period.

People

This volume offers important insights into the wide spectrum of people connected with these tribunals: from the litigants whose disputes provided their lifeblood, to the witnesses who gave such eloquent testimony on their behalf, and to the judges, commissioners, lawyers and other officials responsible for their functioning and legal remedies. It also includes those who were technically outside the legal institutions but whose professional work was intimately connected with the theatre of law: the heralds and armourers.

The Constable and Marshal (and above them the king in parliament) entertained grievances from all those connected with the army, not only the obvious petitioners, knights and men at arms, but also the non-combatants vital for keeping it marching: 'artificers, camp laundresses and cooks'. It is the more

---

[6] John of Legnano's *Tractatus de bello* was ed. T.E. Holland (Oxford, 1917); for its use by Bouvet, see G.W. Coopland, *The Tree of Battles of Honoré Bonet* (Liverpool. 1949), pp. 25–34.

high-profile or higher status litigants, however, for whom detailed records of their cases survive and with whom writers are generally concerned. Philip Morgan's paper adopts an interesting stance by considering the after-effects of the Scrope *v.* Grosvenor dispute on the Grosvenor family's fortunes and especially the estate left by Sir Robert Grosvenor (d. 1465), the grandson of his namesake who has been immortalised by the case brought against him in the Court of Chivalry by Sir Richard le Scrope. Grosvenor's outlook is compared with that of the Scropes and, correspondingly, the attitudes of the Cheshire gentry and clergy towards the two families at the time of the great armorial controversy and subsequently. Morgan uncovers some very human features, including a conspiracy and sibling rivalry over inheritance (experienced by the Grosvenors); and an unsettling anxiety about appearances on the part of the Scropes, who feared coming across as too lawyerly and unwarlike.

For Andrew Ayton, similarly, the Court of Chivalry material provides a springboard for a broader assessment of military culture. Focusing on the testimony of Nicholas Sabraham, one of the witnesses in the Scrope *v.* Grosvenor case, Sabraham's career is (in Ayton's words) 'tentatively reconstructed' and shown to reflect the experiences of similar young men embarking on a military career, while at the same time crystallising some of the difficulties encountered by historians in attempting to re-imagine their lives in the circumstances of the time. It gives insight into contemporary military life through the dynamics of recruitment and the relationships formed within military communities, locally and regionally, that were to influence particular stages of his life. Comradeship and the shared experience of warfare presented him with advantages and opportunities, not only in social and economic terms (wealth, status, marriage and political service), but also for further 'professional' employment as a mercenary. As Morgan recounts, too, the 'bonds of bands of brothers' were strong and witness-testimony was supplied by men who had not only served in the past, but were actually going to war (in some cases) at the very time when they were relaying their understanding and experiences to the commissioners.

Commissions hearing cases delegated to them by the king or the Court of Chivalry comprised well-balanced panels of lay and legal experts, including a mixture of nobles, royal councillors and leading knights. The judges and commissioners themselves were often people with considerable military experience who could thus both command respect and apply their own knowledge of the practical aspects. Some – like the commissioners hearing depositions of witnesses in the Scrope *v.* Grosvenor dispute while the Court was sitting in Cheshire – were local men, a mixture of gentry (including Sir Nicholas Vernon and Sir John Butler, 'baron' of Warrington) and ecclesiastics (such as William Bromburgh, parson of Aldford, and Thomas Stretton, a canon of Lichfield).

Not surprisingly, lawyers played an important role in interpreting and implementing both the law of arms and the law of the sea. Unusually for

English secular courts, men highly trained in Roman civil law were employed as commissioners/judges as well as proctors/advocates in the Courts of Chivalry and Admiralty. In France, likewise, professional lawyers acted as lieutenants of both the Constable and Marshals and deputised for hearings at the Marble Table in Paris. Interestingly, in England at least, as Anne Sutton illustrates, there was sometimes an overlap in personnel, and therefore in expertise, between the two. During the second half of the fifteenth century, for example, William Goodyer, John Aleyn and Robert Rydon, as deputies and judges, were involved in cases in both the Admiral's and the Constable's courts.

Underpinning the entire operation of the Courts of Chivalry and Admiralty and their precursors were their most senior figures, the Constable and Marshal on the one hand, and on the other, the Admiral. While their English counterparts have already been the subject of detailed study, Bertrand Schnerb examines the lesser known role of the French chivalric judges, demonstrating the expanding competence of these officers over the course of the second half of the fourteenth century and the gradual consolidation of their powers in the fifteenth century. He outlines the hierarchical nature of these positions, contrasting those who held office as Constable of France, among whom were Bertrand du Guesclin, Robert de Fiennes and Arthur de Richemont, with their subordinates, Marshals of France, soldiers like Jean le Maingre (Boucicaut) and Mouton de Blainville, and a bevy of provost marshals.

Anne Sutton's chapter traces the role and influence of various English Constables and Admirals in their separate spheres during the fifteenth century, but focuses in particular on Richard, duke of Gloucester's tenure as both Constable and Admiral, which uniquely concentrated the authority of both key offices in the hands of the same person. As Richard III, he continued to have a keen interest in the legal and political implications of the office and was very much responsible for the centralisation and re-organisation of military and maritime judicial business. It was he, too, who granted a royal charter and property in the city of London to the heralds of England in 1484, recognising their professional armorial skills. Heebøll-Holm points out another important unification of responsibilities, one previously overlooked by historians, namely that of Admiral of the Fleet and Warden-Constable of the Cinque Ports. First combined in the person of Admiral John Beauchamp in the 1350s, the unified post greatly assisted claims to English sovereignty over the sea both legally and politically by strengthening the power and independence of the Admiralty Court and tightening control over a maritime community which was prone to engagement in piracy and yet also assertive of its immunities.

Heralds and armourers both had a vital part to play in visual spectacles, whether jousts and tournaments or real battles. There was also a particular role for armourers in the legal arena. Proof in treason trials, or in accusations of *lèse-majesté*, was provided by duel or judicial combat in the Court of Chivalry as it was, too, in the court of the Marshals of France. As royal armourer and serjeant of the armoury of Henry V, John Hill's credentials for writing a treatise on the arming process for trial by combat were impeccable. Moreover, as Moffat's paper shows, in describing the process Hill actually enters into the psychology of the duel by revealing in his description of the requisite clothing that it not only vitally protects, but by its red colouring disguises loss of blood, thus ingeniously obscuring signs that might otherwise have potentially signalled victory or defeat.

Heralds feature not only in the courtly literature, but also in accounts of military activities, and were by the fifteenth century the undisputed experts on heraldic display, notably in the identification of 'cotearmures'. As Barber demonstrates, they may have been employed as musicians or messengers, but they also played an important part at tournaments as the equivalent of today's public announcers or commentators, using their expertise to identify the participants. On some occasions they gave knights directions, delivered the challenge or simply acted as 'cheerleaders'. They gained nicknames and had some regional identification, but until the mid-fourteenth century were only organised in a very rudimentary fashion. The leading heralds, termed kings of arms, when they were not festive kings ('king of the ribalds'), were more seriously found organising festivals and the attendant minstrels. Critically, although men such as Andrew Clarenceux and William Volaunt were paid during Edward III's reign as heralds and kings of arms in England, there is little indication as to what role they actually performed at this time. In spite of the significant lawsuits on armorial bearings raging in the Court of Chivalry during the later fourteenth century, it was not until the early fifteenth century that the sovereigns of France and England (following in the French king's coat-tails) formally conferred on heralds responsibility for registering and administering grants of arms.

European Dimension

The chapters in this volume are united in having a broad European dimension. They reveal similarities in personnel, institutions and outlook, as well as in the issues confronting rulers in territories across Europe. Assertions of sovereignty and challenges to judicial competence were inextricably linked to complex political agendas. Military or naval conflict between nations naturally had ramifications for both the people involved and items located within the territory being fought over. Shifting alliances and boundaries blurred the lines between legitimate actions and illegality, between what was countenanced by a sovereign lord and what was simply a piece of private enterprise. There was also a fine line between what occurred in war and what otherwise amounted to buccaneering or piracy: there were legal repercussions from attacking, capturing or inflicting damage on the crew and cargo of foreign ships during peacetime.

The complexity underlying the jurisdictional competence of the Constables and Admirals is a feature that they all seem to have had in common. Indeed, all of these special military and maritime tribunals experienced overlap and conflict with their native 'ordinary' jurisdictions, particularly where they were dealing with disputes over debts, contracts or criminal matters. Indeed, the question of how to deal with piracy and whether it was best considered as a civil matter (in terms of restitution or debt) or a criminal one was a keen practical issue as well as an academic one, especially in light of problems of enforcement. Knowledge of the laws of different regions was evident in the 'forum shopping' that took place in the Mediterranean consulates, just as much as in the English courts, where familiarity with what happened in other jurisdictions led to the assertion of rights that were in conflict with what was understood as the approach under the common law. In some Italian city-states the Catalan-inspired *Llibre del Consolat de mar* was translated and transposed into a different legal context (as in Rome and Florence), and yet in others it was received and ignored (for example, in Venice) simply because it came from a very different institutional background.

That is not to say that there was not co-operation and compromise on occasion. Although exemptions were sought from the English admirals by various ports (including Southampton, Bristol, Rochester and Ipswich), co-operation between the ports and the Admiral was not unknown and there were distinct advantages for litigants in choosing those areas exercising local admiralty jurisdiction, in that they provided swift justice locally (when time may have been of the essence) rather than in the Admiralty Court in London. Moreover, on a broader scale, there is evidence of the Admiral of England and Admiral of Scotland presiding over infringements of truces at sea, and it is also documented that Anglo-Scottish border relations during time of war were policed by Wardens of the Western March with regular court sessions or 'lovedays' being held, backed up by consistent support from both English and Scottish kings.[7] Ultimately, where the dispute was between the subjects of different nations and if redress was not forthcoming in the courts there, it was open to a litigant to ask his own ruler to intervene. The seizure of foreign ships from offending towns in retaliation until a suitable sum had been paid in compensation could, however, be an unsatisfactory and lengthy process.

The law of arms comprised customs and usages that were international in flavour. Indeed, its principles were recognised and applied in different

---

[7] Cynthia J. Neville, 'The Keeping of the Peace in the Northern Marches in the Later Middle Ages', *Eng. Hist. Rev.*, 109 (1994), pp. 1–25; Jean-Philippe Genet, 'Scotland in the Later Middle Ages: A Province or a Foreign Kingdom for the English?', in *Contact and Exchange in Medieval Europe: Essays in Honour of Malcolm Vale*, ed. Hannah Skoda, Patrick Lantschner and Robert Shaw (Woodbridge, 2012), pp. 132–42.

tribunals across Europe precisely because they operated in accordance with and were underpinned by the procedures and doctrines of Continental civil law (the *ius commune*) expounded by legal theorists in universities across Western Christendom. Similarly, the law of the sea, by its very nature, contained provisions that were understood and accepted by different states across Europe; it was closely linked with the law merchant, with which it shared trans-national elements. While the Atlantic seafarers claimed to be governed by the Laws of Oléron, another body of maritime laws was in use in the Mediterranean region. By incorporating the maritime customary laws of different mercantile cities, the text called the *Llibre del Consolat de Mar* provides insight into the institutional rules and history of the various regional courts that used it right across the Mediterranean. Its broader international aspirations, however, were clear. As part of a bid to expand Italian mercantile interests, publication of the book itself was justified by the Pope as providing the tools to solve *any* maritime controversy and as being 'useful for the whole world'.

Comparably, the accounts of campaigns by veterans and soldiers of the time reveal military service in a panorama of theatres of war that took them not only to the further reaches of the British Isles, but right across Continental Europe into the Mediterranean and, for some of them, even beyond (into Hungary and the Black Sea region). They recall events that locate them in a world of military and naval combat that is geographically widespread, but based in reality, and not as remote and fantastical as might seem from the imaginative literature of the period. Heralds were equally in evidence in the theatres of war across Europe. Serving in representative and quasi-legal capacities in royal and noble households within the sprawling Holy Roman Empire, their knowledge and skill enabled kings of arms (the most senior heralds) to move with ease from one influential patron to another and witness at first hand the heraldic symbols deployed on banners and armour in campaigns as well as on buildings and material objects. Given the sheer size of Continental Europe and the fact that no single country could possibly keep abreast of its existing 'stock' of coats of arms in this period, cases of heraldic homonymies (where the same coat of arms was borne by two unrelated people) were inevitable.

This volume encapsulates the medieval experience of, and resort to, tribunals of military and maritime law whose futures lay in quite different directions. While courts martial have been retained up to the present day to deal with matters of military discipline, by the end of the fifteenth century the Court of Chivalry as an all-encompassing tribunal had more-or-less ceased to be formally convened until its brief resurrection as a court of law in the seventeenth century (1634–40).[8] As an institution for adjudicating honour-

---

[8] Cf. *Cases in the High Court of Chivalry, 1634–1640*, ed. Richard P. Cust and A.J. Hopper (Harleian Soc., new ser., 18, 2006); there are expanded versions at: www.court-of-chivalry.bham.ac.uk and www.british-history.ac.uk/no-series/court-of-chivalry.

related disputes it had proved only an interim solution: such matters were increasingly taken over – in France, as in England – by the Crown, which along with its hold over what constituted treason had gradually also gained a monopoly of control over heraldic capacity. Courts of Admiralty, on the other hand, had a long future ahead of them as a result of increased naval warfare and the expansion of commerce. The English tribunal in particular flourished with the country's imperial ambitions. Incorporated as a specialist division within the High Court of Justice, it survived the reforms of the late nineteenth century and although today subsumed within the Queen's Bench Division, nevertheless still maintains its civil jurisdiction over shipping and maritime disputes. Both courts, however, were significant in the medieval period in having a jurisdiction that stretched beyond the British Isles, in requiring their judges and practitioners to have an understanding of codes of international law, and in sharing an international stage.

CHAPTER 1

Heralds and the Court of Chivalry: From Collective Memory to Formal Institutions

Richard Barber

The Court of Chivalry lies at the heart of the present volume, and two cases among the relatively few of which we have record stand out. They are Scrope *v.* Grosvenor and Lovell *v.* Morley, which, as Maurice Keen pointed out long ago, give us a real insight into the thought processes and attitudes of the knights of the period, as well as a vivid sense of how heraldry was much more ubiquitous than we had perhaps imagined. They have been much studied, but there are still surprises to be found. When I discovered that Nigel Ramsay was working on the cases in the Court of Chivalry, I sent him some transcripts I had commissioned, and got the following email back:

> You will be tickled when I say that last week, when out at Kew checking the section that you commissioned and so very kindly sent me, of the proceedings in the case Lovell v. Morley, I noticed that a contemporary marginal annotator (presumably one of the commissioners who was assessing each deponent's value) had put beside the paragraph with the statement of John Suffolk herald the damning comment: 'no[n] ho[mo] gent[ilis]'!

'Not a gentleman!' There is a wonderful Victorian snobbery about the remark, as if John Suffolk had been put up for a London club; one can see the author of this remark quizzing the list of candidates through his monocle, and letting it fall in horror at the discovery. And it is made all the more powerful by the fact that John Suffolk is the only herald recorded as testifying in the Court of Chivalry before 1400.

The early status of heralds

Seriously, however, it is useful confirmation of something that I think needs to be revisited, namely the question of the early status of heralds and the point at which they actually acquire authority over armorial matters. With all due respect to historians of heraldry before 1400, I think we have perhaps overvalued the status of heralds from the twelfth to the fourteenth centuries. Anthony Wagner, the doyen of such studies, is indeed very cautious about what we can know,[1] as is Noël Denholm-Young with regard to the heralds' authority to adjudicate in disputes over arms or even over subordinate heralds and minstrels.[2] Nonetheless, it is very difficult to read such discussions without subconsciously conferring the image of the modern herald, member of a college with a royal charter, and appointed by writ under the Great Seal, on the medieval heralds about whom they write.

It is fair to say that before the fifteenth century there is very little evidence of a permanent official role for heralds, and the evolution of the 'king at arms' is even more obscure. What the early records reveal is that 'herald' in the thirteenth and fourteenth centuries means little more than a man who is a public announcer. The Latin equivalent is *praeco*, a crier in courts of justice or auctions, used pejoratively of a loudmouth. The herald may also be a messenger. If he is expert in heraldic identification he may be called a 'herald at arms'. He may well earn his living as a minstrel or musician, or even, in one instance, as a barber. The place where these announcers enter the world of blazon and insignia, which is the origin of modern heraldry, is at tournaments from the twelfth century onwards. If we think of the heralds at these occasions as commentators, and the kings of arms as the men who organise festivals, we begin to make sense of their status. One of the necessary skills for the success of such an occasion was the ability to identify knights by their arms, and it is from this that their expertise in heraldry arises. The main action of early tournaments was the mêlée, in which all the knights were involved at once – jousting one to one comes much later – and the onlookers needed help. The heralds called out the names of the contestants to the audience, and perhaps added comments. In the biography of William Marshal, who rose to fame in the early thirteenth century through his prowess in tournaments, the waiting crowd at a tournament was entertained by 'a singer who was a new herald of arms',[3] implying that there was some kind of recognition of his expertise in identifying the participants. Other references in the biography tell us that heralds were also messengers at an early date.

However, these men were freelances with no actual appointment. They were, if you like, travelling players who turned up and found employment when a tournament was announced, and were valued for their skills. Like other medieval tradesmen they may have formed themselves into loose organisations by the thirteenth century, when we find a legal document in 1276 in which 'Peter king of the heralds beyond the Trent on the northern side' acknowledges a payment from a knight in payment of everything 'owed

---

[1] Anthony Richard Wagner, *Heralds and Heraldry in the Middle Ages*, 2nd edn (London, 1956), pp. 25–45.
[2] N. Denholm-Young, *History and Heraldry, 1254–1310* (Oxford, 1965), p. 6.
[3] *The History of William Marshal*, transl. Nigel Bryant (Woodbridge, 2016), p. 63.

to him from the beginning of the world down to 18 March 1276',[4] a curious phrase which reflects the legal fiction of 'time immemorial' enshrined in the Statute of Westminster of the previous year. At the beginning of the fourteenth century, we encounter Walter, called 'le Rey Marchys' or king of arms of the Welsh marches, acknowledging a debt of 100 marks to a minstrel in 1310.[5]

There are traces of some kind of loose organisation, perhaps that of a mutual guild of performers choosing a spokesman, in the thirteenth century. There are records naming a minstrel or herald as king of a region, but this has nothing to do with any royal warrant. The name Norrois ('of the North') might link to 'Peter king of the heralds beyond the Trent', or to William de Morley, king's minstrel, called 'Roi de North' in 1322.[6] Their successor, judging by his name, was one Andrew 'Norrois' a century later. His name is believed to be the origin of today's Norroy herald at the College of Arms. Another apparent herald, Henry 'le Norrois', is described in *The History of William the Marshal* as following him around crying 'This way! Over here! God save the Marshal': but from the context he is actually in the thick of the fighting, and is therefore a knight, not a bystander.[7]

Prominent heralds had nicknames: a certain Bruiant appears as a herald in the Marshal's biography, at the end of the twelfth century, and there is another in a poem about the tournament at Chauvency in 1285, and again in the accounts of Edward II; and 'bruyant' means loud or noisy: in modern French, 'un homme bruyant' is a loud talker.[8] We are back to the Latin *praeco* as a loudmouth. This, and the comment – again from the Marshal's biography – that knights have to have three or four heralds in tow seems to suggest that heralds acted as cheerleaders. But 'bruyant' is on the face of it unlikely to be a title of any kind. On the other hand, the leader of the northern heralds, and therefore a kind of rudimentary organisation, may indeed go back to the late thirteenth century.

'Kings' of heralds

The so-called 'kings' of this period, whether of minstrels or heralds, are forerunners of the modern kings of arms in name only. Sometimes they are festive kings, like the familiar *rex fabe*, king of the bean, at a medieval

[4] London, BL, Harley Charter 54 G. 44; the same phrase occurs in relation to debts elsewhere, e.g. the Annals of Dunstable, in *Annales Monastici*, ed. H.R. Luard, 5 vols (Rolls Ser., 36, 1864–9), III, p. 255, *s.a.*1272.
[5] Kew, TNA, Chancery: Certificates of Statute Merchant & Statute Staple, C 241/69/259.
[6] Constance Bullock-Davies, *Menestrellorum Multitudo* (Cardiff, 1978), pp. 74–5.
[7] *History of William the Marshal*, transl. Bryant, p. 82.
[8] Jacques Bretel, *Le tournoi de Chauvency*, ed. Maurice Delbouille (Liège and Paris, 1932), l. 305; Bullock-Davies, *Menestrellorum Multitudo*, pp. 74–6.

Christmas (hence our bean-feast); or the similar king of fools. More often, they are kings in the sense that they keep unruly followers in order, whether minstrels, heralds, or, at a lower level, 'ribalds' – the vagrants and prostitutes found as hangers-on at the royal court. The French kings from the early thirteenth century had an official called *rex ribaldorum* or *roi des ribauds*, with jurisdiction over crimes committed at court, vagrants found there and brothels and gaming-houses in its neighbourhood. In 1317, the household ordinance of Philip V states that 'Fat Joe (*Grasse-Joe*) king of the ribalds is not to eat at court but shall have sixpence worth of bread ... a horse from the royal stable, and shall always be outside the door to see that only those enter who ought to be there'. [9]

In this context, it is easier to understand a satirical poem by Bertran de Born describing Eleanor of Aquitaine as sending a tax receipt on the torn-up tabard of a 'king of arms'. This is a joking reference, and does not mean that the king of arms was an official in her household. The point was that the queen's receipt was worthless, written on a scrap from a mere minstrel's clothing. Indeed, the poet points out that it did not save the taxpayer from the knives of his creditors.[10]

At the English court between 1272 and 1307, we have the names of at least fifteen possible kings of heralds. Typically, they appear to be in charge of a group of minstrels, or of all the minstrels at a particular occasion; 'king Baisescu' and 'king Caupeny' share out royal gifts between the minstrels at the great feast for the knighting of Edward II when prince of Wales in 1306. Such men are recognised leaders of minstrels, but as *primus inter pares*: in the same year 'king Caupenny' is paid with other minstrels 'for performing plays and making their minstrelsies in the presence of the Queen'. 'Caupenny' was from Scotland, and is given the title 'king Caupenny of Scotland': we also hear of the 'king of Champagne', the leader of the minstrels from Champagne.[11] In 1318, Bois Robert, king of heralds of France, distributed 100 livres among the minstrels who played at the wedding of princess Jeanne of France and the duke of Burgundy.[12]

A king of heralds is paid for making a proclamation about the prohibition of tournaments in England at Northampton on Christmas Day 1300,

---

[9] Charles du Fresne, Sieur du Cange, *Glossarium mediae et infimae Latinitatis*, ed. G.A.L. Henschel, 7 vols (Paris, 1840–50), V, p. 766.

[10] David Crouch, 'The Court of Henry II of England in the 1180s, and the Office of King of Arms', *The Coat of Arms: Jnl of the Heraldry Soc.*, 3rd Ser., vi (2010), pp. 47–55, takes this episode as serious evidence for the existence of an official king of arms at the Plantagenet court.

[11] Bullock-Davies, *Menestrellorum Multitudo*, pp. 77–9 (Caupenny), 72–3 (Baisescu) and 80 (Champagne).

[12] P. Adam-Even, 'Les fonctions militaires des hérauts d'armes: Leur influence sur le développement de l'héraldique', *Archives héraldiques suisses*, lxxi (1957), pp. 2–33, at 4.

underlining the idea that one of his functions was as public crier.[13] This role certainly continued in Holland and Germany well into the fifteenth century: in the accounts of the count of Katzellenbogen for 1400 and 1401 the same man is called 'herald' and 'speaker' in successive years.[14] Heralds appear as public criers at the feast held in Bruges by Philip the Good on the occasion of his marriage in 1430, where they are found in the gallery with the minstrels, announcing the different stages of the feast.[15]

By Edward I's time we find three 'kings of heralds' appearing on the royal payroll: Robert Little and Nicholas Morel, who span the years 1282 to 1300.[16] Andrew Norrois, apparently Nicholas Morel's successor, drew war wages in 1311–12, and was still at court in 1338.[17] What has changed is that tournaments, which took place almost entirely outside the royal court, are now part of the court entertainments, Edward I himself being a keen jouster. So the men skilled in organising them are now part of the establishment. They received summer and winter liveries with the rest of the court servants, presumably with a permanent responsibility for the minstrels at court. They were clearly minstrels themselves, as Robert is paid for 'making his minstrelsy' on New Year's Day 1303, and is probably the same as 'Robert the king's trumpeter' on the Scottish campaign of 1301.

It is only gradually, during the following century, that heralds begin to acquire a more general authority in what was to become their speciality: questions of coats of arms. Visual collections of coats of arms begin in *c.* 1244 with the famous shields in Matthew Paris's great chronicle; the first known English roll of arms, Glover's roll, dates from about 1255.[18] The oldest French roll is the Bigot roll of 1254.[19] Many rolls of arms are clearly intended as a record of knights' arms which is to be used to identify shields, and the earliest examples – such as Glover's roll – often survive only in copies, the originals presumably having been worn out with use. It is at the end of the thirteenth century that we find these rolls of arms being created as records of the knights present at a given military event: after the battle of Falkirk in 1298, a roll was created recording 'the great lords with banners who king Edward the first since the conquest had with him in Scotland in the twenty-sixth year

---

[13] Bullock-Davies, *Menestrellorum Multitudo*, p. 43.

[14] Ursula Peters, 'Herolde und Sprecher in mittelalterlichen Rechnungsbüchern', *Zeitschrift für deutsches Altertum und deutsche Literatur*, 105 (1976), pp. 233–50, at 247.

[15] *Chronique de Jean Le Fèvre, seigneur de Saint-Remy*, ed. François Morand, 2 vols (Paris, 1876–81), II, p. 61.

[16] Robert Little (or *Parvus*): *ibid.*, pp. 159–62. Nicholas Morel: Wagner, *Heralds and Heraldry* (cit. in n. 1), p. 34.

[17] *Ibid.*, p. 35.

[18] A.R. Wagner, *A Catalogue of English Mediaeval Rolls of Arms* (London, 1950), pp. 3–7.

[19] Robert Nussard, *Le rôle d'armes Bigot*, Documents d'héraldique médiéval 2 (Paris, 1985).

of his reign at the battle of Falkirk on St Mary Magdalene's day'.[20] Similar documents exist for the siege of Caerlaverock near Dumfries in 1300, for an expedition into Galloway in the same year, and for the siege of Stirling in 1304. Only the Caerlaverock roll survives in the original, so we cannot tell whether these were all the work of the same herald travelling with the army or not.[21]

The emergence of heralds as experts in armorial matters

There is no doubt, however, that this is firm evidence that men with heraldic knowledge were now part of the real military world, as opposed to figures in the mock warfare of the tournament. But they were not employed as royal officials, with annual fees: they were still freelancers who had other parts to play in the army, as in the case of Robert Little. The correct identification of banners could be critical; at the battle of Evesham in 1265, Simon de Montfort's barber, Nicholas, 'a man expert in the recognition of arms', was deceived by a stratagem of the Lord Edward into identifying the enemy's troops as those of Montfort, with disastrous consequences.[22] Rolls of arms would help to avoid such errors, and it is possible that they were shown to the knights so that they could identify their friends in battle. But they are unlikely to have been the work of specialists whose sole job was to deal with heraldic matters: they are much more akin to the paintings done by friar Walter atte More in the course of his diplomatic mission to Hungary in 1346. Walter atte More was not a herald, but he recognised the usefulness of the heraldic information and either painted it himself or, more probably, commissioned someone else to do it.[23]

Heralds are first clearly documented in a military context from 1306 onwards, when an ordinance of Philip IV of France specified them as the messengers who deliver a challenge to battle. This might be the reason for the wages paid in 1347 by John, duke of Normandy and heir to the French throne, to four kings of arms of France, the king of arms of Normandy, and twenty-one heralds. In 1355, he pays the king of heralds of Champagne for his service 'in the present wars' and for compensation for horses he has lost.[24]

---

[20] Wagner, *Catalogue of English Mediaeval Rolls of Arms*, pp. 27–8.

[21] *Ibid.*, pp. 29–34.

[22] Edward displayed banners captured earlier at Kenilworth from Montfort's army: *The Chronicle of Walter of Guisborough*, ed. Harry Rothwell, Camden 3rd Ser., lxxxix (Royal Historical Soc., 1957), p. 200.

[23] Richard Barber, *Edward III and the Triumph of England* (London, 2013), p. 349.

[24] Adam-Even, 'Les fonctions militaires' (cit. in n. 12), p. 4. Adam-Even quotes an ordinance of 1309 on the role of the constable of the army which envisages a grouping of kings of arms, heralds and pursuivants around the bearer of the royal standard, taken from G. Vuatrin, *Étude historique sur le Connétable* (Paris, 1905),

The status of the heralds is still that of a profession, but not yet an office, at the beginning of Edward III's reign.[25] There are payments to William Volaunt, king of heralds, in 1354. Andrew Clarenceux is entitled herald and king of arms in a wardrobe account of 1334, in his capacity as leader of a group of minstrels playing to the king on the day that the king of Scotland did homage. John Musshon, herald, was in the service of the prince of Wales in 1353, and appears several times in the prince's household records: he is given quite substantial sums, but what his actual role was does not emerge.[26] John Suffolk, herald, whom we have already met, was in the service of Robert Ufford, earl of Suffolk, from at least 1340 to after 1359. After 1350, an increasing number of personal heralds appear, and even the *routier* captains had their own pursuivants. Heralds were sent out by Edward in their traditional role as criers of public events in January 1344 to announce the great tournament at Windsor.[27] The accounts of the count of Holland show heralds coming and going in the 1330s, from the king of Cyprus or conveying invitations from neighbouring princes; but actual records of heralds on messenger or diplomatic service are relatively scarce until the fifteenth century. Hereford herald was employed from the end of Edward III's reign and in the first decade of that of Richard II, on journeys to Flanders and elsewhere.[28]

The scattered mentions, taken together, seem to indicate that it is in the later 1340s that heralds acquire a more distinguished status and a definite place in royal and baronial households, but they are still largely messengers, conveying information by letters from their masters or by word of mouth. As such, they enjoyed immunity from war, in the same way as men in holy orders, and this immunity seems to have been invariably respected in the fourteenth century. A letter from Henry of Grosmont describing his raid into Normandy in 1356 describes how two heralds were sent on 8 July by John II to challenge him to a battle at Verneuil.[29] They are still most in evidence at feasts, as masters of ceremonies organising the entertainments and controlling the possibly unruly performers. Edward increased the number of his heralds in the 1350s for the long series of Garter feasts in the latter part of his reign.

When it comes to written records, such as the list of the dead after Crécy, such items were far more likely to be the work of clerks in the army's

pp. 78 ff.; but this is from a modern copy of a medieval record which F. Lot, *L'Art militaire et les armées au Moyen Âge en Europe et dans le Proche Orient*, 2 vols (Paris, 1946), I, p. 222, dates to the 1380s, when it would make much more sense.

[25] Wagner, *Heralds and Heraldry* (cit. in n. 1), p. 35.

[26] *Register of Edward the Black Prince*, 4 vols (London: Public Record Office, 1930–3), IV, pp. 100, 108, 157, 163, 167, 253.

[27] Barber, *Edward III and the Triumph of England* (cit. in n. 23), p. 477.

[28] Kew, TNA, King's Remembrancer: Exchequer Accounts Various, E 101/317/12, 318/11 and 318/18.

[29] *Adae Murimuth, Continuatio Chronicarum. Robertus de Avesbury, De Gestis Mirabilibus Regis Edwardi Tertii*, ed. E.M. Thompson (Rolls Ser., 93, 1889), p. 464.

administration; the freelance heralds were called in to help with the identi-fication of arms, and indeed there is no reason why the clerks themselves would not have had some knowledge of heraldry. Le Bel tells us that Reginald Cobham was told by the king to take with him 'a herald who knew arms' to seek out the dead French nobles at Crécy, implying that not all heralds were expert in the subject.[30]

The critical evidence for the heralds' lack of official recognition as authorities on coats of arms in the mid-fourteenth century comes from the proceedings of the Court of Chivalry which we discussed earlier. The evidence, carefully and laboriously assembled both in the court itself and by commissioners sent to obtain statements from outside the capital, who spent a good deal of time and energy on the process, never once involves a herald. If the court's proceedings had been informal and verbal, we might argue that the records merely failed to mention the heralds' evidence. However, it is absolutely clear that only the evidence of fellow knights and sometimes of clergy of similar standing is admissible. Written records such as the rolls of arms are never referred to, though painted heraldry in tombs, churches and great houses is endlessly cited. The knights themselves sometimes recall their training in heraldry, as in the case of Robert Laton, giving evidence in the Court of Chivalry in 1386, who testified that his father taught him to write down in a schedule (probably meaning a roll) all the arms that he had learnt from his ancestors.[31]

Towards the end of the fourteenth century, Froissart could call heralds 'rightly the investigators and reporters of such affairs, and I believe that their honour is such that they would not dare to lie'. He places a herald at the centre of the scene which is effectively the opening of the Hundred Years' War: the much-travelled Carlisle herald returns to Edward III's court at Westminster in April 1338 after five years wandering abroad, coming post-haste with letters from the Anglophile lords of Gascony reporting that war had broken out with the French in their region, which he supplements with a verbal report. Unfortunately, there are a lot of problems with the historical background and details of this, and it is probably pure fiction: what Froissart is doing is recreating the scene as he thought it should have happened, looking back from the 1370s; heralds had gained considerably in stature in the intervening forty years.[32] It is a neat way of outlining the beginning of hostilities to his audience, by providing a setting with which they would have been familiar. His declaration that he had got much of his information from heralds is certainly true, but that does not mean – particularly in the first book of the chronicle – that every scene containing a herald is genuine. Froissart often succumbs to the temptation to create his Technicolor vision of heralds and heroes, a history seen through a prism of shining deeds and brilliant colours.

---

[30] *Chronique de Jean le Bel*, ed. J. Viard and E. Déprez, 2 vols (Paris, 1904–5), II, p. 108.

[31] Nicolas, *Scrope and Grosvenor Controversy*, I, p. 111.

[32] *Oeuvres de Froissart*, ed. Kervyn de Lettenhove, 29 vols (Paris, 1867–77), I, p. 394.

How does the herald's role pass from the identification and recording of arms to the administration and control of the use of armorial insignia? Without such records, there was always the possibility that two knights might choose the same arms, and from the mid-thirteenth century onwards we have evidence of disputes and settlements of disputes over the use of particular devices. First of all, a recognised vocabulary for describing arms needed to be evolved, and this began to emerge in the late twelfth century; the first evidence for it is found in the romances, notably the highly influential works of Chrétien de Troyes. The shields of his Arthurian heroes are to be found in many medieval rolls of arms, down to the fifteenth century. As we have seen, these rolls of arms survive from the mid-thirteenth century onwards; they sometimes show two knights as bearing the same arms, without comment.[33] There is evidence of disputes in 1300, when Brian Fitzalan and Hugh Poyntz displayed identical banners of *barry or and gules* at the siege of Caerlaverock. How the dispute was settled we do not know.

The inheritance of arms by members of a family indicated that arms were regarded as a kind of property. One of the earliest surviving legal documents concerning arms was an agreement as to how a family banner should be inherited; this comes from Alsace in 1267–76.[34] Grants of the right to use a personal crest are found in 1286 and 1293 from South Tirol and from Bavaria. The right to the use of arms is linked to two English land transactions in 1317 and 1324, while in 1347 Sir Michael Poynings granted Sir Stephen de Valoynes 'a crest of a dragon's head with two wings extended'. This does not seem to have been Poynings's own crest, and another record concerns the ceding of an inherited right to use specific arms to someone who is not a member of the family concerned: in 1348 Robert Lord Morley gave Robert Corby the arms he had inherited from Sir Baldwin de Manners. The idea that arms were owned in some way seems to have been well established by the mid-fourteenth century, but there was no formal structure or case law concerning the use and disposal of arms.

Heraldry and the law

It is at this point that the Court of Chivalry makes its first appearance. Sir Anthony Wagner argued that the cases heard at Calais during the siege there in 1347 were heard by deputies of the Constable and Marshal of England, who had jurisdiction over the army in the field. However, a charter – known only through an engraving made in 1729[35] – relating to one of the cases makes it clear that these are commissioners appointed by the king. According to a

---

[33] Wagner, *Heralds and Heraldry* (cit. in n. 1), p. 18.
[34] *Ibid.*, p. 19.
[35] Oxford, Bodleian Library, MS Ashmole 1137, f. 144: reproduced in M.H Keen,

witness forty years later, the other case was indeed heard by the Constable and Marshal, but the king intervened because the dispute might lead to conflict within the camp. It may be that this episode, undated but certainly at the siege of Calais, was what led Edward to establish his jurisdiction in such matters. The same witness remembers a herald called Lancaster taking part in the proceedings: but this was only in his role as public crier, in proclaiming the result of the adjudication.[36]

The idea that heraldry could be subject to legal supervision was first properly formulated by Bartolo di Sassoferrato, one of the most influential jurists of the fourteenth century and a professor at the University of Padua.[37] He is credited with founding many of the principles of civil law, and was therefore hugely influential. He does not actually produce any kind of code of law applicable to arms, but simply discusses the legal status of arms; there is no exclusivity, and two people can bear the same arms provided that this does not lead to conflict or injury. He presents the hypothetical case of a German who goes to Rome on pilgrimage, and finds someone bearing his arms; his complaint is refused because they live too far apart. Such a ruling would have applied to Lovell *v.* Morley; it was only in the armies raised for the French campaigns that the two families encountered each other, and a genuine conflict arose. If someone discovers that there is an intention to adopt his arms by another, then he is within his rights to try to prevent it.

Sassoferrato himself was granted a coat of arms by a writ of the emperor Charles IV, and the idea of royal grants of arms seems to originate in the empire and in Hungary. The earliest royal grants connected with arms I have been able to trace are, curiously, from Hungary. As Charles of Anjou had been brought up in the French court before he inherited the kingdom, these probably derive from French practice, despite the absence of French records on the subject. In 1332, Charles made a formal grant to Colus son of Colus giving him the right to bear a crest on his helmet, though the form of the crest is not named.[38] Edward III's grant of a crest (*timbre*) to William Montagu, his closest friend, in 1335, is somewhat different, as it is better described as permission to use his personal royal crest of an eagle.[39] A grant of 1338 from the emperor Louis IV the Bavarian is similar in form in that he rewards two brothers for their good service with the right to add a 'crown of the arms of our duchy of Bavaria' to the yellow lion on their inherited arms.

Origins of the English Gentleman: Heraldry, Chivalry and Gentility in Medieval England, c. 1300–c. 1500 (Stroud, 2002), p. 40.

[36] Wagner, *Heralds and Heraldry*, p. 22.

[37] *Ibid.*, pp. 68, 66.

[38] 'A Kolos Család Czímeres Levele 1332–Ból', *Turul*, 5 (1888), pp. 156–8.

[39] *Calendar of Documents Relating to Scotland*, ed. J. Bain et al., 5 vols (Edinburgh, 1881–1986), III, p. 211, no. 1166.

Institutional heraldry

Official heraldry is based around the sovereign, as the fount of honour; the heralds are grouped by nations, not by principalities, and so the French heralds had jurisdiction in Burgundy and the French parts of the Low Countries. In Burgundy particularly, if the structure had not been sovereign, one would have expected to find a Burgundian college of arms, and control of Burgundian heraldry from the college of arms founded in Paris was a reminder to the dukes that, for all their splendour, they were subjects of the French king. Similarly, a system of imperial heraldry was a symbol of the emperor's sovereignty over the German states.

On 1 January 1407, Charles VI founded a chapel for the kings of arms and heralds of the kingdom of France in a church next to the hôtel Saint-Pol, one of his favourite royal residences in Paris. They were to have a chapel in which to hear masses, to be furnished with chairs and chests, and were to have the right to be buried there. It was in effect a religious college, and it had been preceded by earlier royal appointments of kings of arms, notably that of a herald named Charlot, who became Montjoy king of arms, named after the battle-cry of France ('Montjoie, Saint Denis!') about 1389. The year after the foundation of the college, Montjoie and his fellow kings of arms petitioned the king for the regulation of the appointment of heralds. They defined the duties of heralds as 'to view, know and loyally report, without the least favour or fiction, excepting nobody, the attribution of victory and praise of deeds of arms and chivalry to those who, by their glorious deeds, prowess and merits, deserve it'.[40] To ensure that standards were maintained, a formal system for the investiture of suitably qualified persons as heralds was needed, with an appropriate progression first to pursuivant, and then to king at arms. As things stood, any herald could go round the local lords and collect their seals, and present them to the prince, who would glance at them cursorily and appoint him to the desired office.

In England, the key moment when heraldry becomes a royal office is the appointment of William Bruges as Garter Principal King of Arms of Englishmen by Henry V in 1415, and the subsequent writ of 1417 which made the use of arms subject to royal control.[41] This is an instructive document, because once again, it shows that authority in matters armorial is still not given to the heralds. It is a writ addressed to the sheriffs of southern England which recites how 'many persons had taken to themselves arms and tunics of arms called "Cotearmures", when neither they nor their ancestors had used such in times past', and it orders that everyone 'except those who had borne arms with the king at Agincourt' should declare their arms and by whose

---

[40] Philippe Contamine, 'Office d'armes et noblesse dans la France de la fin du Moyen Âge', *Bulletin de la Société nationale des Antiquaires de France*, 1994, pp. 310–21, at 310–12.
[41] For what follows see Wagner, *Heralds and Heraldry* (cit. in n. 1), pp. 58–64.

grant they had them to 'persons named or to be named for the purpose'. If they failed to do so, they were to be dismissed from the expedition which was about to sail for France, forfeit their wages, and have their arms defaced.

The critical concept here is the 'grant of arms', and the implication, if we think about it for a moment, is that it was widespread, as everyone who bears arms is expected to have such a grant. But this cuts clean across what we learn from the two famous cases in the fourteenth century Court of Chivalry: there are no grants of arms mentioned in the evidence – unless I have missed something – and everything is down to the collective memory of the knights and squires of England. Grants of arms certainly existed, but seem to have been very much the exception rather than the rule. And not all the knights who had used arms from time immemorial would have served with Henry at Agincourt. But even allowing for the evidence of increasing use of grants in the late fourteenth century, the implication in the writ that such things were widespread looks like the work of a Chancery clerk who cannot imagine that matters like this could still be outside the written record.

A further element is the destruction of such records during the Peasants' Revolt in 1381, and the frequent neglect of deeds other than those concerned with property. The Garter records seem to have virtually disappeared by the end of the fourteenth century, and had to be consciously recreated under Henry IV. And although arms were beginning to be treated as property from the late thirteenth century onwards, they were not the subject of lawsuits until around 1350, and records were therefore not called into question. In effect, the procedures of the Court of Chivalry were deemed to be too cumbersome for practical purposes. Henry V replaced it by officials wielding royal authority and maintaining a system of records.

The writ of 1417 was followed by further royal regulations, and by ordinances issued by Thomas, duke of Clarence, as Constable, at some time between 1419 and 1421. These effectively put the registration and admin-istration of matters concerned with the bearing of heraldic arms under the jurisdiction of Garter King of Arms and his fellow kings of arms. There is to be a general chapter held by Garter and local chapters held by the relevant king of arms, and the kings of arms are to ensure to the best of their ability that they know all the noblemen and gentlemen of their march, and they are to register their arms. These registers are henceforth to be the written authority on which the system of heraldic arms is based. The oral testimony of the Court of Chivalry is superseded, and the Court itself falls into abeyance as far as such matters are concerned.

Perhaps the best example of the new professional heralds who emerge at the beginning of the fifteenth century is Claes Heynenzoon,[42] who had begun

---

[42] He was king of heralds of the Rhine, and thus overlaps the old and new structure of heraldic employment.

as herald of the duke of Guelders and was later herald to the duke of Bavaria. His activities were wide-ranging, and he left us two splendid armorials, *The Book of Arms of Guelders* and *The Book of Arms of Bavaria*, as well as his *Lobdichten*, poetic portraits of the great knights of his time. These volumes, as well as the extensive depictions of arms by skilled artists, include historical texts, among them two chronicles. The arms are arranged systematically by rank, beginning with the German emperor and working through the kings of Europe, each with the arms of those who owed allegiance to them. And while he was employed by William I of Guelders, Heynenzoon was responsible for buying heraldic flags when the duke sailed to England. In the first quarter of the fifteenth century, the herald is increasingly the representative of the person whose name he bears: his status moves from that of a freelance whose skills are rewarded with the occasional gift to someone who has a definite diplomatic, legal and armorial function. The modern herald has arrived.

CHAPTER 2

French Armorial Disputes and Controls

Laurent Hablot

Fourteenth- and fifteenth-century sources reveal a strikingly large number of conflicts that resulted from the disputed use of coats of arms. The collection and analysis of these examples allow us to understand the nature of these conflicts and more particularly to see how and by whom these heraldic quarrels could be resolved. These documents call for clarification, to explain, justify or revise the role of certain actors, such as the agents of seigneurial or royal justice, the heralds, and the court of the Marshals, to highlight the social, legal and political stakes that these confrontations then assumed.

The reasons for heraldic disputes in the Middle Ages

The reasons which might give rise in the Middle Ages to a dispute between two physical (individual) or legal persons about heraldic insignia were quite diverse, and their nature and context would often decide the form of resolution that was made.

The first ground of conflict was often the use by two parties of an identical coat of arms, whether intentionally or by accident. But there were other possible causes of the antagonism, in particular the wrongful public display of a coat of arms: either the overstepping of acquired privileges or the enunciation of unsustainable rights and claims; or punitive or defamatory actions against heraldic insignia for some political, military or social reason. Let us consider these different cases.

The use of identical or homonymous coats of arms was a recurrent theme of the various treatises that considered heraldic law – proof that the question remained problematic, as illustrated by several documented heraldic conflicts. This homonymy was, moreover, a consequence of the very principles of the medieval heraldic system.

In the first place, blazon – the set of rules that governs the composition of coats of arms – also includes the very precise design of any heraldic symbol, and in fact multiplies the risk of the same coat of arms being created again and again.[1] Moreover, until the eighteenth century, no Continental European country could claim to maintain an up-to-date and comprehensive catalogue of its existing coats of arms, especially if this stock extended to all social categories. Cases of heraldic homonymies were therefore inevitable and far from rare on the scale of Europe and even just on that of a large region. At the very origin of the coat of arms, the practice of forming groups of similar coats of arms which indicated members of the same blood-lineage, sometimes very large or ancient, also tended to result in homonymy. On the other hand, within the same lineage or family, the variation by cadets of the heraldic prototype that belonged to the elder son or heir – the undifferentiated arms – by means of marks of cadency was not always applied in practice. It might be the case either that local heraldic practice did not favour it, since certain regions or social groups were unfamiliar with marks of cadency, or else that the cadets knowingly abandoned this potentially devaluing mark. Moreover, the vagaries of succession and inheritance could themselves provoke such instances of homonymy.[2] Such similarities might then even be considered as adding extra lustre to the *fama* of the families concerned.[3]

Subsequently, medieval custom established, almost throughout the medieval West, the principle of free assumption, according to which anyone – without distinction of gender, status or rank – could freely choose a new coat of arms, on the sole condition that it did not usurp that of another. This principle, with that one reservation of uniqueness, naturally offered no means of guarantee, other than a good heraldic upbringing and sense of respect on the part of the new bearer or the designer of the arms. All the writers of the Middle Ages, such as Honoré Bouvet, Nicholas Upton or Diego de Valera, nevertheless agree on this principle, which apparently was first stated by the Bolognese jurist Bartolus de Sassoferrato in around 1355 in his *De insigniis et armis*.[4] Indeed, the practice of free assumption seems to have prevailed

---

[1] In reality the system allows an infinity of combinations, but it is also necessary to understand its content and subtleties. The coats of arms created by amateurs all tend spontaneously to reproduce coats of arms that they have already seen.

[2] A few years ago, Inès Villela-Petit re-examined a surprising and unintended case of heraldic homonymy between two distant cousins; see her 'Béraud III, dauphin d'Auvergne, ou Guichard II Dauphin? Un cas d'homonymie héraldique', *Revue Française d'Héraldique et de Sigillographie*, 71–2 (2004, for 2001–2), pp. 53–72.

[3] This is the case, for example, with the heraldic homonymy between the Orsini of Rome and the Jouvenel des Ursins from Paris. See especially Paul Durrieu, 'Le nom, le blason et l'origine de la famille de l'historien Juvenal des Ursins', *Annuaire Bulletin de la Société de l'Histoire de France*, 29 (1892), pp. 193–221, and the forthcoming book by Werner Paravicini, *Colonna and Orsini: The Imaginary Origins of the European Nobility at the End of the Middle Ages*.

[4] Bartolo da Sassoferrato, *De Insigniis et Armis*, ch. 4: 'Some people assume coats of arms and insignia on their own initiative: and we should consider whether they are permitted to do it. I think that they are permitted … everyone has the right to wear

throughout Europe until the beginning of the modern era, although it would be necessary to analyse its application more precisely and to distinguish the categories of individuals who actually used the right.[5] This legal definition of the right to arms comes at almost the same time, the early fourteenth century, as the first appearance of grants of arms in Europe[6] – a practice which ultimately ended with the taking over of heraldic law by the prince or sovereign authority.[7]

Perhaps unsurprisingly, then, the medieval treatises of heraldry make this problem of similarity of coats of arms into a case study, which subsequently we find to have been reiterated frequently. We will see the regulatory solutions that they proposed, and the echoes that these texts found in practice.

But the many potential causes of heraldic conflict far outnumbered these few cases about identical coats of arms. The role played by heraldry in the public and legal expression of social, political and financial prerogatives in the thirteenth century in effect encouraged the numerous disputes arising from coats' display, including disputes over the actual wearing or use of coats of arms by individuals who were allegedly exceeding their rank or entitlement. These conflicts developed clearly in the last centuries of the Middle Ages, directly in line with the strengthening of sovereign power, whether of the

insignia and put them on their own belongings' ('Quidam tamen arma seu insignia sua propria auctoritate assumunt sibi, et istis an liceat videndum est. Et puto quod liceat. Sicut enim nomina inventa sunt ad recognoscendum homines ... Ita et ista insignia inventa sunt. ... Ita ista insignia cuilibet licet portare et depingere in suo tantum, non in alieno ...'). Printed in *A Grammar of Signs: Bartolo da Sassoferrato's Tract on Insignia and Coats of Arms*, ed. O. Cavallar, S. Degenring and J. Kirshner (Berkeley, Calif. [1994]), pp. 110, 145–6 (English translation). On this treatise, see also *Medieval Heraldry: Some Fourteenth Century Heraldic Works*, ed. E.J. Jones (Cardiff, 1943), and Bartolo da Sassoferrato, *De Insigniis et Armis*, ed. Mario Cignoni (Florence, 1998).

[5] For a synthesis, see my article: 'Les armoiries, un marqueur du rang dans les sociétés médiévales?', in *Rank and Order: The Formation of Aristocratic Elites in Western and Central Europe, 500–1500*, ed. J. Peltzer (Memmingen, 2015), pp. 245–70.

[6] That is to say, the coat of arms with all or part of the donor's arms. See Adrian Ailes, 'Medieval Grants of Arms, 1300–1461', MA thesis, University of Reading, 1997; his 'Royal Grants of Arms in England before 1484', in *Soldiers, Nobles and Gentlemen: Essays in Honour of Maurice Keen*, ed. P. Coss and C. Tyerman (Woodbridge, 2009), pp. 85–96; and his 'The Granting of Arms to Individuals', in *Partages héraldiques*, ed. L. Hablot, forthcoming, as well as my own 'habilitation thesis', 'Affinités héraldiques: Concessions, augmentations et partages d'armoiries, XIIe–XVIe siècle', presented at the École pratique des hautes études, Paris, in December 2015.

[7] See my article, 'Le roi fontaine de justice héraldique La captation royale de l'expression emblématique à la fin du Moyen Age', in *Le roi, fontaine de justice: Pouvoir justicier et pouvoir royal au Moyen Âge et à la Renaissance*, ed. S. Menegaldo and B. Ribémont ([Paris], 2012), pp. 223–40.

prince or, occasionally, of the Commune.[8] This will to control individuals' heraldic expression could be applied in a range of different contexts, often linked with political dependence, property, lineage or rank: the public but contested display of coats of arms supporting seigneurial rights or patronage in either a private or a public location; the public use of full arms (without marks of cadency) expressing a claim as being of the lineage and with the rights of the eldest; and the use of heraldic or paraheraldic insignia (coat of arms or coronet, crest, or collar of chivalric order) presented as an unwarranted and unlawful expression of social pretension and so forth.

This right of oversight of the use of coats of arms, claimed by the State, often contradicted the principle of free adoption or assumption that has been mentioned above, but it was in conformity with the customary law that had progressively developed around the actions of setting up and displaying coats of arms. All over Europe, in fact, these public displays of matters of honour were being brought within the purview of governmental authorities, whether sovereign ordinances or the deliberations of municipal authorities. The Crown's will to control was slowly evolving from a bundle of sovereign claims, some unprecedented or improper; such were the gaining of the right to grant new arms, the imposition of sumptuary laws, and the making of legal and sovereign definitions of ranks and status.[9] By claiming to be the only authority able to grant nobility or new arms, authorise transfers of coats of arms or crests, or list and verify the heraldic emblems in use, the sovereign authority gradually gained a monopoly of control of heraldic capacity and assumed the right to dispute the use of a given design, to destroy representations of it and to prohibit its use.

Finally, the symbolic potential that attached to these emblematic signs, each a veritable blending together of a lineage's honour and prestige, as well as being the identity card of the individual bearer, inevitably made them the focal point of public displays of both honour and, at times, condemnation. The development of a specific judicial practice, the *subversio armorum* – the public defamation of the coat of arms by the display of the armorial shield upside down – applied by sovereign or military authority to perjurers and traitors, also generated important heraldic disputes. As early as the end of the thirteenth century, sources document this ritual of overthrowing the

---

[8] For example, the well-documented case of Florence during the reintegration of the Magnati who had been banned from the city in the Popolo after the Ordonnanze di justicia. See M. Pastoureau, 'Comment change-t-on d'armoiries? Centdix exemples florentins du XIVe siècle', in *Brisures, augmentations et changements d'armoiries: Actes du 5e colloque d'héraldique, Spolète, 12–16 octobre 1987* (Brussels, 1988), pp. 231–50.

[9] See on this subject my articles: 'Le roi, fontaine de justice' (cit. in n. 7); and 'Les armoiries, un marqueur du rang dans les sociétés médiévales?' (cit. in n. 5).

shield, descended in part from ancient funerary rituals and also from the iconography of chivalric death.[10] The reasons for applying this sanction were varied, but most often it was to punish a word of honour or promise that had not been kept, especially in the context of unpaid war ransoms.[11] Recorded instances of the practice, collected from all parts of Europe, are relatively numerous: it is evident that the mere threat of this sanction became a guarantee of such promises. The defamatory ritual was also associated in some cases with the condemnation in effigy, in which the culprit and his arms were displayed side by side, the shield of arms hung upside down. But the coat of arms might also be broken, soiled or dragged, to emphasise the humiliation of the guilty party.[12]

Examples, solutions and regulation

Most of the cases that may be cited show various different sorts of dispute and different ways in which they might be regulated.

Let us first return to the cases of heraldic homonymies and the theoretical conditions for the resolution of these conflicts – that is to say, the conditions that were presented by heraldic writers. I will leave to one side the famous example of the Scrope *v.* Grosvenor lawsuit,[13] a classic case discussed

---

[10] See Francesca Español Bertrán, 'El «córrer les armes»: Un aparte caballeresco en las exequias medievales hispanas', *Anuario de Estudios Medievales*, 37 (2007), pp. 867–905.

[11] On this practice see L. Hablot, '"Sens dessoubz dessus": Le blason de la trahison au Moyen Âge', in *La trahison au Moyen Age: De la monstruosité au crime politique (Ve–XVe siècle)*, ed. Maïté Billoré and Myriam Soria (Rennes, 2009), pp. 331–47; and 'Corps ravagés, emblèmes outragés: L'utilisation de l'emblématique dans les châtiments à la fin du Moyen Âge', in *Corps outragés, corps ravagés*, ed. M. Billoré and M. Soria (Rennes, 2010), pp. 139–54. See also M. Strickland, '"All Brought to Nought and Thy State Undone": Treason, Disinvestiture and the Disgracing of Arms under Edward II', in *Soldiers, Nobles and Gentlemen: Essays in Honour of Maurice Keen*, ed. P. Coss and C. Tyerman (Woodbridge, 2009), pp. 279–304.

[12] These infamous rituals were enacted during the siege of Moncontour in 1371, against Bertrand du Guesclin's coat of arms, and in 1412, in the town of Neufchateau, on the border of Lorraine, against the royal arms. On these examples see Hablot, 'Le blason de la trahison' and 'Corps ravagés, emblèmes outragés'.

[13] Cf. Nicolas, *Scrope and Grosvenor Controversy*; and see Philip Morgan below, chapter 4. This famous conflict was waged between two English families, Scrope and Grosvenor, between 1385 and 1391, over the right to use identical coats of arms, *Azure a bend or*. The case also brought into play the argument of the imaginary grant, at least to explain the antiquity of the coat of arms. Robert Grosvenor was the first to assert pre-eminence, on the grounds that his family had been bearing arms since the time of William I, whom his ancestor had accompanied in the Conquest. The quarrel extended to a third family, of Carminow, of Cornwall, who also bore the very same coat – according to them, since the time of King Arthur. This

elsewhere in this volume, in order to concentrate on French examples and the study of the gap between practice and reality. As has been mentioned above, this question was the subject of much theoretical discussion (albeit without much originality) in the heraldic treatises of the late Middle Ages.

It was Bartolus who first reviewed the question of homonymy by enunciating the principle of free assumption, alongside the new possibility of formal grant or concession. He proposed a hierarchy that depended upon the different origins of coats of arms:

> What are the advantages of having a coat of arms by imperial grant? There are several. First, they are of greater dignity [...]. Secondly, one cannot be prohibited by another from bearing such a coat – confirmation for us that the practice then existed, although we do not know who might have been able to prohibit a particular coat of arms in mid-fourteenth-century Bologna! – Thirdly, if two persons bear the same coat of arms and it is not clear who had it first, then the one that bears the arms by grant of the prince will be preferred. Fourthly, if a question of precedence arises on the battlefield or elsewhere, the coat of arms granted by the prince must take precedence (this being so on the basis that the bearers of the coats are of equal rank; if not, the arms of the person of higher rank will have precedence).[14]

Here we find the main causes of disputes about coats of arms: issues about rank, homonymy or identicality, and circumstances of display. But it also contains most of the areas of argument advanced in conflicts about heraldic homonymies: priority of use, princely grant and social rank.

Bartolus then sets out two specific types of dispute which might or might not justify recourse to the law: first, the case of an Italian who wants to bring to justice a German traveller who has come to Rome to celebrate the Jubilee, the Italian having found that the German bears arms identical to his own. This is a situation which, according to the jurist, does not merit a trial because of the physical distance between the residences of these men, who therefore

---

heraldic homonymy had already opposed them to the Scropes, but the argument of geographic distance between the two families was then raised and their respective rights to the coat preserved. In the Scrope–Grosvenor conflict, on the basis of the testimony received and the political backing of each party, the Court of Chivalry ordered the Grosvenors to alter their arms by the addition of a silver border. Appealing to Richard II against this decision, Robert Grosvenor was advised by him to change arms altogether and adopt *Azure a wheat sheaf or*, a coat that was clearly inspired by the ancient arms of the earls of Chester, whose family had been of his native Cheshire. This heraldic design was associated with one of the titles borne at that time by the Prince of Wales and appears to have been part of the stock of coats of arms kept 'in reserve' by the prince – like the arms of Edward the Confessor and King Arthur and those of Winchester and Richmond, likewise granted by the sovereign.

[14] *A Grammar of Signs*, ed. Cavallar, Degenring and Kirshner, pp. 112, 147–8 (English translation).

cannot be troubled by the heraldic homonymy. Secondly, Bartolus considers the case of a peaceful man who shares his coat of arms with a man who is a threat to public order. The peaceful man, who is in effect threatened by this homonymy, may seek out a judge 'whose concern is the peace of the people'. The identity of this judge and the court over which he presides are not, however, specified by our Bolognese jurist.[15]

Let us note that these developments were taken up and adapted in the treatises on the law of arms of the late fourteenth and early fifteenth centuries, *Le songe du vergier* of Évrart de Trémaugon,[16] *L'arbre des batailles* of Honoré Bouvet,[17] and *Le livre des faits d'armes et de chevalerie* of Christine de Pizan,[18] which reproduces almost entirely the words of the first.[19] The latter two works, dating respectively from the years 1387 and 1410, also develop the idea of different qualities as between the different ways of acquiring a coat of arms. Honoré Bouvet telescopes the different themes of Bartolus's discourse and, for instance, affirms with regard to the arms taken at will by a complainant's father: 'It seems that anyone who take for himself the arms that my father first took for himself does so in shame and contempt of him, with a view to enmity and strife, so that it is the sovereign's duty to find a remedy.'[20] The prior of Salon then repeats the examples of the German fortuitously wearing the same arms[21] and that of the coat of arms usurped by the man of

---

[15] *Ibid.*, pp. 110, 145–6 (English translation).

[16] Évrard de Trémaugon, *Somnium viridarii*, ed. Marion Schnerb-Lièvre, 2 vols (Paris: Centre national de la recherche scientifique, 1993–5); French translation of 1378, in British Library, Royal MS 19 C. IV, printed as *Le songe du vergier*, ed. M. Schnerb-Lièvre, 2 vols (Paris, 1982).

[17] Honoré Bonet, *L'arbre des batailles*, ed. Ernest Nys (Brussels and Leipzig, 1883); printed in English as *The Tree of Battles of Honoré Bonet*, intro. and transl. G.W. Coopland (Liverpool, 1949). On Bouvet's book see also N.A.R. Wright, 'The *Tree of Battles* of Honoré Bouvet and the Laws of War', in *War, Literature, and Politics in the Late Middle Ages*, ed. C.T. Allmand (Liverpool, 1976), p. 12–32.

[18] There is no recent French edition of this book, extant in nearly twenty manuscripts, but there is an English translation: Christine de Pizan, *The Book of Deeds of Arms and of Chivalry*, transl. Sumner Willard, ed. Charity Cannon Willard (Pennsylvania, Pa., 1999).

[19] I. Villela-Petit, 'La dame à la biche: Christine de Pizan et le droit d'armes', text online (http://www.i-villela-petit.fr/i-villela-petit fr/5/Entrees/2016/7/2_La_ dame_a_la_biche....html).

[20] *Tree of Battles*, pt IV, ch. cxxvi; transl. Coopland, p. 204. 'Il semble que cestuy cy qui prent pour luy ces nouvelles armes que mon pere a premier prinses pour luy, qu'il le face en despit et en desplaisance de luy, pour avoir mieulx occasion de mouvoir contens, riotes et debatz contre luy, pourquoy le souverain du lieu y devroit remedier par raison, car ce ne seroit pas chose raisonnable ne licite...'

[21] *Ibid.*, pt IV, ch. cxxvii; transl. Coopland, pp. 204-5. 'Ung alemant vient a Paris pour veoir la court du roy et congnoître la seigneurie de France. Si treuve d'aventure ung chevalier ou ung escuyer portant les armes de son lignaige, auquel il dit que mal porta oncques les armes de son lignaige et que ainsi ne demourera il pas. Le françoys lui dit courtoisement : sire, pourquoy vous courroucez vous ainsi encontre

bad reputation.[22] The first case is settled amicably, since the two men with the same arms 'are not of one and the same kingdom under a single lord'. The latter, on the other hand, presents 'good and just cause for proof by trial by battle', even though Bouvet expresses reservations about the applicability of this honourable solution if the other party is a criminal or of proven evil and unjust life, while he also discusses intervention by the Crown: 'I dare not to speak of the gibbet or of beheading, for I am a man of the Church. But if he (the king) did good and strict justice, I should not be astonished thereat.'[23] The author extends his discussion to the case of those mercenaries who put on the arms of their captain, so as to receive more honour and more credit, or to have better wages,[24] insisting on the fact that 'The king at the instance of a complainant may very well punish him.'[25]

In Honoré Bouvet's writings, there are three ways, broadly speaking, in which conflicts of homonymy may be settled: the amicable solution; the wager of battle (*jugement d'armes* or trial by battle); and justice administered by the ruler of the place, or the judgment of the king in Parlement.

What about the practice as documented in the French sources of this period? Among many relevant records, more or less well known, different sources from late medieval Poitou recount the conflict between Jacques de Surgères, lord of La Flocelière, and Louis de Granges, each apparently from the same family and therefore bearing identical coats of arms.[26] This instance of homonymy, at first without any dire results, became problematical in 1378 when Thibaut de Granges set up his arms in the Jacobins' church at Fontenay-le-Comte, prompting Jacques de Surgères to go and destroy with

miy, ne puis ie pas bien porter les armes que mon pere et mes predecesseurs ont tousiours portées au temps passé…'

[22] *Ibid.*, pt IV, ch. cxxvii; transl. Coopland, p. 205. 'Sinon qu'il congneust que le chevalier françoys ou ung aultre qui les porteroit les portast par maulvaise vie, coureur de pays, pillart et larron qui se tinedroit sur les marches de Lorraine ou de Bourgongne, pillant et portant les armes d'ung vray preud'homme d'Alemaigne en faisant telles mauvaisetez et tels outraiges, san faulte ce bon preud'homme d'Alemaigne, considerant que le peuple auroit cause et occasion de cuyder et croyre auqqi que ce fust il qui feist toutes ces maulvaistiez, pource que l'autre seroyt vestu de pareilles armes comme les siennes, adoncques auroit il bonne et juste cause de l'en appeler de gaige de bataille…'

[23] *Tree of Battles*, pt IV, ch. cxxvii; transl. Coopland, p. 205. 'Je n'ose pas bonnement parler du gibet ne de trencher la teste pource que je suis homme d'Eglise. Mais s'il (le roi) en faisoit bonne et dilligente justice, je n'en appelleroye pas.'

[24] *Ibid.*, pt IV, ch. cxxviii; transl. Coopland, p. 205: 'How those who wear the arms of another in order to commit a fraud must be punished.' ('Comment doivent estre pugnis ceulx qui portent les armes d'autrui pour commettre mauvaiseté.')

[25] 'Le roy a l'instance de partie l'en debveroit tresbien pugnir.'

[26] D. Massiou, *Histoire politique, civile et religieuse de la Saintonge et de l'Aunis*, 2nd edn, 6 vols (Saintes, 1846), I, p. 170.

the tip of his lance the shield in question. Told of the affair by the Jacobins, Jean, duc de Berry, who was also count of Poitiers, then directed the lord of Surgères to re-set up the shield, which he refused, obliging the friars to do it for him. Learning of this deed of reinstatement, Jacques de Surgères attacked the restored shield once again. Summoned to the duke's court of justice in Poitiers, he refused to appear and simply let the matter lie. The two parties were then summoned by the duke of Berry to a court at Niort in August 1379, which imposed judgment on the offender and obliged him to restore the injured coat of arms.

As may be seen in such narratives, many of the heraldic conflicts that are documented in medieval France were really disputes about social superiority, perhaps exemplified in the right to affix one's arms to a religious edifice over which one party claimed a right, most often as a matter of honour but also sometimes for a legal or financial reason. It was, indeed, public and widely known displays of authority of this sort that tended to reveal problematic homonymies or competing claims.

In January 1457, a prominent citizen of Poitiers and La Rochelle, Jean Mérichon,[27] complained to the Augustinian friars of Poitiers about the state of repair of the heraldic insignia set up by his maternal ancestor, founder of their monastery, alleging that they had 'destroyed the tomb which had been erected over the burial place of their founder, and had razed it to the ground'. To which they replied 'that they had in no way razed it or taken it down, but that it had been broken in the course of building the choir of the said church' and that Jean Mérichon or others for him could 're-erect the said tomb of the founder, in stone or brass, in the same position and in the same form and design, or otherwise as they preferred, as was the right of the founder of the same church, and to paint on this the arms of the said founder ...'[28]

Dom Fonteneau's book also mentions the dispute between the monks of the Abbaye des Châtelliers and the local lords of the Chourses family, whose black mourning cloths and armorial stained-glass windows were destroyed

---

[27] L. Hablot, 'Poitiers à la fin du Moyen Age: Une capitale artistique? Le mécénat des frères du Fou, de Jean Mérichon et de quelques amateurs éclairés du XVe siècle', *Revue historique du Centre Ouest*, 12: *Les mécènes, leurs demeures et leurs jardins (XVe–XXe siècle)* (2015, for 2013), pp. 227–42.

[28] ('... qu'ilz ne l'avoient aucunement razée ne abatue mais avoit esté rompue en faisant le cuer de ladite église ... faire enlever de pierre ou de cuyvre ladite sépulture desdits Berlans ondit lieu où elle est assise en la forme et manière qu'elle souloit estre ou autrement ainsi que bon leur semblera et comme il appartient au fondateur de ladite église et en icelle faire empaindre les armes dudit fondateur et au plus honnorable lieu qu'il sera par icelluy Mérichon ou les siens advisé ') René Crozet, *Textes et documents relatifs à l'histoire des arts en Poitou (Moyen Âge–début de la Renaissance)* (Poitiers, 1942), pp. 139–40, no. 554.

in the years 1468–9 before the dispute brought them all up before King Louis XI, who imposed upon them all a mourning cloth with the arms of his mother Marie d'Anjou, whose entrails were buried on the spot.[29]

Not much later in date, in about the year 1500, the lord of Bressuire had the arms of Hilaire des Loges removed from the walls of a chapel built on his land. His prosecutor brought him to order and told him that he was in the wrong because he had given his consent to his vassal to build this chapel and by so doing allowed him as of right (*de jure*) to set up his arms there.[30]

Heraldic conflicts of this sort often developed into very real and tangible attacks on all sorts of rights, even extending to those of the king. In France, attacks on the royal coat of arms greatly increased in the course of the thirteenth to the fifteenth centuries, in reaction to the Capetian and Valois dynasties' strengthening of their authority. These attacks targeted everything that bore the royal lilies (*fleurs-de-lis*) – banners, boundary stones, escutcheons, seals, officers – and at the least aimed at the rights of the king, and at worst at the person of the sovereign himself. Thus, in 1265, in order to challenge the king's rights, the people of the Vicomtesse de Limoges tore down royal banners that had been affixed to the monastery of Saint-Yrieix as a sign of protection; they were immediately summoned to Parlement.[31] The Crown, on the other hand, was prepared to recognise when its claims were excessive. In the *Historia episcorum Autissiodorensium*, the tale is recounted of how, in the 1260s, officials whom Louis IX had sent to clear the river Yonne exceeded their powers and set in the river-bed, in the narrows below the bridge at Auxerre, which was part of the domain and property of the bishopric, two posts, on top of which they fixed iron lilies (*fleurs-de-lis*) to denote the king's sovereignty. When the bishop, the fearless Guy de Mello II (1247–69), heard of this he at once ordered the posts to be taken down and brought to the episcopal palace. His enemies at Court had him summoned to the king's presence, but once there he argued successfully that the officials had exceeded their authority:

[29] Poitiers, Médiathèque François Mitterrand, MS 459, Collections of Dom Léonard Fonteneau, vol. V, pp. 271, 277 and 279.

[30] The procurator himself took advice from Jacques Beaussé, mayor of Poitiers (Niort, Archives Départementales des Deux-Sèvres, E. 1751). The case is analysed in detail in *Inventaire sommaire des archives départementales antérieures à 1790*: Deux-Sèvres, Série E, articles 1219–2119: Chartrier de Saint-Loup; Médiathèque, côte BP 2481. I am grateful to Robert Favreau for these precious references.

[31] This is a fascinating case, and well documented. A banner was offered by Guy VI de Limoges to Saint Yrieix Monastery in 1256, then in around 1265 someone removed these arms, substituting for them the French lilies. The Vicomtesse Marguerite de Bourgogne ordered the royal banners to be taken down, and was thereupon summoned to the Parlement. Henri de Courances – a prominent knight (Henri Stein, *Henri de Courances, maréchal de France (1255–1268)* (Paris, 1892)) and at the time the royal seneschal for this area – was then ordered to investigate the case. See Bayonne, Archives des Pyrénées Atlantiques, E. 880.

his adversaries were confounded and he left the king free and victorious.[32] In 1377, Jean Lucas, the provost of La Rochelle, ordered a wooden cross bearing the royal arms to be erected in a certain part of the *châtellenie*, near La Rochelle, on the way to Tasdon and the court of Chayenne, without the knowledge or consent of the lord of Châtelaillon, Guillaume Larchevêque, and his officials. Jean Morisset, sergeant of the lord of Châtelaillon, knocked down the cross at night. The governor of La Rochelle had him put in prison, but royal letters of pardon were subsequently granted to him on the strength of the fact that the cross had in fact been lawfully taken down for the upholding of the rights of the lord of Châtelaillon.[33]

Even these few and well-known examples do not always clearly show which bodies were responsible for settling such cases, but we can nonetheless see their frequency as well as how they were resolved: by direct intervention on the part of the king, count or their lieutenant, or judgment of the Parlement, or settlement out of court, or the formal opinions of local experts.

Heraldic jurisdiction in medieval France

In the light of this handful of documented events, it is also possible to review the observations made by Rémi Mathieu in the middle of the last century in his chapter on 'Jurisdictions with competence in matters of heraldic law'. The author of the celebrated and invaluable *Le système héraldique français* enumerated the situations where conflicts might arise and the authorities that dealt with their resolution. He argued, in particular, that heraldic judgments were the usual solution in the settlement of heraldic disputes until the fourteenth century, when these cases were first brought before the law-courts.[34] As we have seen, this idea of the chivalric solution was still being presented by Honoré Bouvet (d. *c.* 1410), although so far as I am aware there is no documented source that illustrates the actual practice.

From the moment that this sort of contention first prompted recourse to the law-courts, in the course of the fourteenth century the question would arise as to which courts had the required competence. Cases of this sort involved principally – although not exclusively – the nobility, and so the first jurisdiction to turn to was that of the *baillis* and seneschals, who were still being used for such disputes in the sixteenth century,[35] even though, from

---

[32] *Les gestes des évêques d'Auxerre*, ed. Michel Sot, Guy Lobrichon et al., 2 vols, Les Classiques de l'histoire de France au Moyen Âge, 42–3 (Paris, 2002–6), II, pp. 314–17 (ch. 63).

[33] Paris, Archives nationales, JJ 110, n° 276 (14 Feb. 1377). I am grateful to Robert Favreau for this valuable reference.

[34] Mathieu, *Le système héraldique* (Paris, 1946), pp. 136–7.

[35] See examples quoted by Rémi Mathieu for Britanny, Lyonnais and Burgundy.

the fifteenth century, they habitually delegated their authority to deputies or ordinary judges. This was the case, for example, in Poitiers in 1378, where it was the deputy or lieutenant representing the Count's seneschal who received 'Letters of John, count of Poitou, bearing commission to his seneschal or his lieutenant to have postponed to Poitiers Jacques de Surgères, knight, lord of La Floceliere, against whom the count had declared to be in default for non-appearance, and forbidding him (Jacques de Surgères) from troubling Louis de Granges in the matter of his coat of arms.' In 1449 again, the bailiff of Alençon heard an appeal against a sentence given by his lieutenant at Exmes, in a dispute over the use of full arms.[36] Ordinarily, however, appeals against such judgments were brought directly before the Parlement. Medieval instances of summons or appeals to the Parlement of Paris or to provincial parliaments in heraldic disputes are relatively numerous, and almost all concern the sort of conflict discussed above, which were matters of public law: disputes about the right to coats of arms[37] or disputes about the use of full arms,[38] and conflicts about heraldic boundary marks or about precedence, etc.; or, from the sixteenth century onwards, matters of private law: the capacity to bear arms and physical external displays of arms. The most virulent conflicts, culminating in insults, blows and fisticuffs, and even broken bones, sometimes even meant that these cases came under the criminal justice system, in this case the Tournelle of the Parlement of Paris.

As has been pointed out, the crime of *lèse-majesté* against the royal arms was also a matter for the Parlement. Thus in 1412, the duke of Lorraine was found guilty of *lèse-majesté*, summoned and then condemned by the Parlement of Paris for storming Neufchâteau and dragging escutcheons bearing the royal lilies at the tail of his horse.[39] Some other cases equally clearly fell within the remit of the justice system, such as the condemnation of the Constable, Charles III de Bourbon, for the crime of '*lèse-majesté*, rebellion and felony' by a judgment of the Paris Parlement, pronounced in a *lit de justice* (that is,

[36] Paris, Bibliothèque nationale de France, Carrés d'Hozier, vol. 320, f. 25, cited by Mathieu, *Le système héraldique*, p. 56 and n. 5, and p. 106.
[37] E.g., Gaucher de Châtillon in 1403 asked for the annulment of the sale made by his elder brother Jean of his estates and arms to Charles de Châtillon, their uncle (brother of their father), on the pretext that the sale was made without the consent of his relatives. In his defence, Charles insisted, *inter alia*, that it was not a matter of whole arms (borne, in any case, by the counts of Blois) but of differenced arms (those of the lords of Châtillon, lords of La-Ferté-en-Ponthieu, or Châtillon with a mark of cadency. (André du Chesne, *Histoire de la Maison de Chastillon sur Marne* (Paris, 1621), pp. 446 et seq.) A judgment of the Parlement of Paris, 1407, finally annulled the sale (Paris, Archives Nationales, X1A 54, no. 210, ff. 399v–402). Cited in Mathieu, *Le système héraldique*, p. 161 and note.
[38] See examples in Mathieu, *Le système héraldique*, p. 104. A dispute about the arms of Salvaing was presented to the Parlement of Grenoble.
[39] Quoted by C. Beaune, *Jeanne d'Arc* (Paris, 2004), pp. 32–3.

pronounced from the king's throne in the Parlement) on 27 July 1527, with the consequent destruction of his arms in all places where they were affixed.[40]

But, as Rémi Mathieu points out, heraldic lawsuits could still be judged by special courts and, later, by certain jurisdictions. Thus, the King's Council could be approached on heraldic questions, in particular those involving the coats of arms of the king and the royal family, crimes of heraldic *lèse-majesté*, decisions of common interest on heraldic practice and cases of treason. Medieval instances are not numerous but one might mention the documented case of the creation of the arms of Gian-Galeazzo Visconti, who in 1394 sought a grant of the lilies of France and the debates that this request aroused within the Council which resolved the question.[41] In 1507, again it was the *Grand Conseil* meeting at Bourges which condemned the lords of Rosny and Tibivillers, gentlemen of the royal palace accused of having 'abandoned the place and (heraldic) insignia with which they were entrusted, in favour of the duchy of Milan': they were ordered to be degraded of their nobility and, in Rosny's case, to be deprived of his coat of arms.[42]

The heraldic decisions of the Marshals' Court, examined in this volume by Bertrand Schnerb (chapter 7), are known above all for the sixteenth century. For this period, armorists and scholars have written at length about the ignominious penalties applied to the coats of arms of noblemen convicted of treachery or breach of duty. Modern treatises on coats of arms and chivalry tell us that conviction of the crime of *lèse-majesté* involves, in the first instance, the degradation of the nobility, during an elaborate ceremony. This ritual is associated with public defamation of the name, fief and coat of arms; and any descendants may also be deprived of heraldic capacity.[43]

The heraldic actions of the tribunal in the Middle Ages seem less dramatic. One might have imagined that the case presented by the three treatises quoted above, of the employee usurping the coat of arms of someone else to commit misdeeds or to claim undue reward, was within the limits of its jurisdiction, but, so far as I am aware, no medieval source provides such an example. The same applies to defamations linked to the practice of *subversio armorum*, which was gradually brought into the range of penalties provided

---

[40] On this political trial see *Recueil de copies d'arrêts, lettres d'abolition et autres pièces relatives aux procès de lèse-majesté ou procès analogues*, Paris, Bibliothèque nationale de France, MS Dupuy 38, ff. 149–88, 208–13. It is specifically recorded that the palace of Petit Bourbon, which the duke had just restored in Paris, was the object of this heraldic condemnation, the coats of arms being destroyed and the doors and windows smeared with yellow by the royal hangman. Cf. Mathieu, *Le système héraldique*, pp. 58, 234.

[41] Eugène Jarry, *La vie politique de Louis de France, duc d'Orléans, 1372–1407* (Paris, 1889), pp. 419 et seq.

[42] Paris, Bibliothèque nationale de France, MS Fr. 18429, f. 15.

[43] Mathieu, *Le système héraldique*, pp. 232–9.

for by the *jus armorum*[44] and became in effect a guarantee of words of honour given in the particular contexts of war and the practice of ransoms.[45] But even here, conflicts of jurisdiction are very evident. Thus, in 1368, the capture by an English squire of a knight from the region of Brie, Jean de Melun, gave rise to a complex set of proceedings. Although he had undertaken to pay his ransom in letters obligatory which he had sealed, Jean de Melun was unable to settle this debt within the prescribed time, and accordingly suffered a *subversio armorum*; this he considered abusive, however. The Marshals' tribunal, applied to as a court of first instance, was in the event divested of the case; instead, it was the Parlement that ruled that the application of the *subversio* cancelled Melun's debt. Profiting from these terms, Melun then demanded a full apology and the *erectio armorum* in all the places where his arms had been defamed.[46] In most cases of defamation of coats of arms, however, this jurisdictional competition did not take place, the customary mode of settlement being accepted by the opposing parties by force of arms and without recourse to any higher

---

[44] Évrart de Trémaugon said, in his *Songe du vergier*, in 1378, 'que nul chevalier ou escuier ne se puet obligier de faire aucune chose, sur poyne que sez armes soient ranversées ... Car c'est honte à toute une noble lygnie quant lez armes de leur hostel sont ranversées.' Évrart de Tremaugon, *Le songe du vergier*, ed. Schnerb-Lièvre (cit. in n. 16), I, p. 293 (book I, chap. cxlviii, art. 22). In the early years of the French campaigns of the fifteenth century, English kings seem to have revised the *jus armorum*. A book of the *laws of war* was attributed to Henry of Lancaster (*c.* 1310–61), duke of Lancaster: see Philippe Contamine, *Guerre, état et société à la fin du Moyen Age* (Paris and the Hague, 1972), p. 187 and n. 24. In these treatises is specified the penalty incurred by perjured hostages who do not pay their ransom: the public display of their coat of arms, reversed. See also M.H. Keen, *The Laws of War in the Late Middle Ages* (London and Toronto, 1965), p. 20, and his 'The Jurisdiction and Origins of the Constable's Court', in *War and Government in the Middle Ages*, ed. J. Gillingham and J.C. Holt (London, 1984), pp. 159–69. On the Court of Chivalry, see G. D. Squibb, *The High Court of Chivalry* (London, 1959), pp. 1–28; *English Suits before the Parlement of Paris, 1420–1436*, ed. C.T. Allmand and C.A.J. Armstrong, Camden Fourth Ser., 26 (Royal Historical Soc., 1982); and A. Rogers, 'Hoton v. Shakell : A Ransom Case in the Court of Chivalry, 1390–5', *Nottingham Mediaeval Studies*, 6 (1962), pp. 74–108, and 7 (1963), pp. 53–78.

[45] In 1358, Raoul de Renneval pledged to pay the redemption to the English of the castle of Poix, in association with three knights and a squire, under penalty of being reputed 'perjurors, traitors and infidels by all Christendom', in addition to having their shields of arms exposed upside down and being fined. P.-C. Timbal, *La Guerre de Cent Ans vue à travers les registres du Parlement (1337–1369)* (Paris, 1961), pp. 297–8. In 1364, after the battle of Cocherel where he was captured, Jean de Grailly, the famous Captal de Buch, promised by a sealed deed that he would always remain a 'true and loyal prisoner of Charles V and not try to have any secret dealings with the King of Navarre', failing which: 'je vueil et consens que je soie tenuz pour faux, mauvais et desloial chevalier et pour parjure et foy mentie et que, en signe de ce, mes armes soient tournées et mises ce dessus dessoubz'. Paris, Archives Nationales, JJ. 616, n° 6.

[46] Timbal, *La Guerre de Cent Ans*, pp. 307–13.

authority, or else being directly adjudged by the king. This was the case with Bertrand du Guesclin's defamation in 1371, for instance.[47]

Not to be overlooked, too, is the role played by the assemblies of the chivalric orders in passing heraldic sentences, their modalities of operation illustrating the general practice of the law in this field. The ranges of heraldic sanctions that were applicable are most often recorded in the orders' statutes and in the registers of the orders' annual assemblies. Different levels of degradation were available to punish traitors, apart from expulsion,[48] through some temporary modification of arms,[49] to the inversion and public defamation of the traitor's name and arms, which were often displayed, painted above the members' stalls in the chapel of the order. Thus, the statutes of the Order of the Star, made on 6 November 1351, stipulate, for example, that in the case of flight from the battlefield the guilty member: 'will be suspended from membership of the Order, and will not be able to wear its robes; and in the [chapel (*presumably*) of the] Order, his arms and his crest will be turned upside down, without defacing them, until such time as he may be reinstated by the prince and his council, as having been restored by his good conduct'.[50] A few decades later, members of the Order of the Golden Fleece who had supported Louis XI underwent a similar fate. On the occasion of the order's feast at Bois-le-duc in 1481, the Burgundian chronicler Jean Molinet records the sanctions imposed on the traitors: 'for the demerits of these lords [brethren of the order], their paintings [of their arms] were removed and set apart from

---

[47] *La chronique de Bertrand du Guesclin* reports that on the occasion of the siege of Moncontour, in 1371, he was engaged on his property and land to pay the ransom of one of his followers, hostage of the English captain of the city. The Breton having forgotten to settle this debt, the Englishman, a certain Jannequin Lovet, had his arms painted on a shield, which he dragged from the tail of a horse, and then hung upside down for perjury: 'Oy dist l'escuyer, regardés la douleur | les armes de Bertrand, ou tant a de vigeur, | Ont penduë laidement, ainsi comme trahiteur, | et traisnée aussi au long d'un quarrefort, | et les ont enversées, en montrant par frenour [à grand bruit], | que Bertrand de Glaequin a cuer de boiseour [traître, fourbe].' (Du Cange, *Glossarium mediae et infimae Latinitatis*, ed. G. Henschel, 7 vols (Paris, 1840–50), I, art. *arma reversata*.) The town having been taken, du Guesclin seized the culprit, dragged him off and hanged him in the very place where his arms had been humiliated (Cuvelier, *Chronique de Bertrand du Guesclin*, ed. E. Charrière (Paris, 1839), pp. 216–17, vv. 19672–90). Note, however, that Bertrand du Guesclin was the superior authority in question, in his capacity as Constable.

[48] D'A.J.D. Boulton, *The Knights of the Crown: The Monarchical Orders of Knighthood in Later Medieval Europe, 1325–1520*, 2nd edn (Woodbridge, 2000), pp. 468–9.

[49] For example, by the statutes of the Order of the Knot: *ibid.*, pp. 211 et seq.

[50] *Ordonnances des rois de France de la troisième race*, ed. E.J. de Laurière et al., 21 vols (Paris, 1723–1849), II, p. 466; L. Pannier, *La noble-maison de Saint-Ouen* (Paris, 1872), p. 90: 'il sera souspendu de la compaignie, et ne pourra porter tel habit, et li tournera l'en en la Noble-Maison ses armes et son timbre sanz dessus dessous, sans deffacier, jusques a tant qu'il soit restituez par le prince et son conseil et tenu pour relevez par son bien fait.'

the others; and even the painting and arms of the lord of Esquerdes (Philippe de Crèvecoeur) were brought to the doorway of the church and reversed, top to bottom'. To this public defaming of arms may be added that those of Philippe Pot, less seriously guilty, were also turned upside down, but only in the chapel of the order.[51]

The great omissions from the story seem here to be the heralds. However, even if some modern authors believe that heralds had any legal capacity in the field of armorial law,[52] their remarks need to be substantially revised for the period that concerns us. It is in fact extremely rare to find any evidence for direct intervention by heralds in any heraldic conflict of the sort that has been discussed above, before the end of the fifteenth century and the creation of the office of marshal of arms by Charles VIII.[53] At best, the heralds might act as counsel or as sentencing officials. One such rare instance is the celebrated case of the dispute about the arms of the family of Brimeu, reported in the Chronicle of Jean Le Fèvre de Saint-Rémy, Toison d'Or King of Arms.[54] The case – about the right to the arms of Brimeu, undifferentiated, brought by Florimond de Brimeu against his uncle – was examined on 13 August 1435 in Arras by an 'heraldic court' composed of members of the Burgundian nobility, in the presence of the ducal Office of Arms, and enlightened by opinions collected from lawyers in Paris and Amiens. But Toison d'Or was only acting as the spokesman of the Office of Arms: in no way can he be described as the judge of this matter.[55]

A few decades later, in the intervention by Louis XII about the misuse of the undifferentiated arms, and the name, of Brittany, the heralds were merely responsible for seeing to the application of the Crown's sanctions. Rémi Mathieu has set out the chain of events: how the de Brosse family had presumptuously and improperly asserted their right to the Breton *ermine plain* arms and the family name 'de Bretagne' (then held by Queen Anne), and how a commission was given to Normandy King of Arms to go to each member of the de Brosse family and inform them of the King's prohibition of this. Normandy was directed to tell them that they must abandon and straightway leave off using the Queen's arms, and have them removed from all churches,

---

[51] Jean Molinet, *Chroniques*, ed. G. Doutrepont and O. Jodogne, 2 vols (Brussels, 1935), I, pp. 362–3.

[52] See Rémi Mathieu's chapter IV, section C (1): 'Les juridictions spécialisées en matière de droit héraldique. Les rois, hérauts et poursuivants d'armes.'

[53] The office of marshal of arms of the French was given to Gilbert Chauveau, Bourbon Herald, who was tasked with establishing a general armorial of the kingdom and correcting errors so that 'leurs dicts successeurs en puissent jouir et user sans aucun different, debat ou contrarieté', as quoted by Mathieu, *Le système héraldique*, p. 64, from Paris, Bibliothèque nationale de France, MS Nouv. acq. fr. 7243, f. 176.

[54] *Chronique de Jean Le Févre, Seigneur de Saint-Remy*, ed. F. Morand, 2 vols (Paris, 1876–81), II, pp. 323–4.

[55] Mathieu, *Le système héraldique*, p. 66.

dwelling-places, stained glass, tapestries and all other places and locations. A month later the herald reported back on how he had been to Boussac, Clisson, Rochefort-en-Terre and Pont-L'abbé, to the sons and daughters of the de Brosse family: most had responded in the same way as Jean de Rieux, husband of a de Brosse daughter, 'that within ten days there would be not one ermine left in his house and that he would not let his wife wear them any longer'.[56]

Conclusion

If we sum up these different sets of events, it is quite clear that, behind the apparent confusion of competing jurisdictions, it was indeed the prince who became the sole judge in all legal matters concerning coats of arms in the Middle Ages. This principle was gradually built up as a side-effect of the authority – at first feudal and then sovereign – of the monarch and then was enlarged as the Early Modern state began to be constructed. It was based on such practices as the granting of arms, first orally and then in an official way by letters patent; the ever tighter control over the use of the Crown's heraldic emblem of sovereignty (the lily, eagle or leopard); and the setting up of the royal arms as a sign of reassurance, headship of the social hierarchy, feudal overlordship or direct ownership throughout the kingdom. Heraldry was thus a means of social control. The authors of treatises on nobility and of 'mirrors for princes' at the turn of the fifteenth and sixteenth centuries expressed this principle of the sovereign's control over the emblems of his authority, in language that then was still largely theoretical; but the idea had already taken concrete shape in the interventions made by the king in all aspects of the law relating to heraldry, even before legislation of a more general sort was enacted throughout Early Modern Europe.[57]

---

[56] *Ibid.*, pp. 266, text 5, and 266–7, text 6, printing Paris, Archives nationales, J 246, no. 121.

[57] See further my article 'Le roi fontaine de justice héraldique' (cit. in n. 7).

CHAPTER 3

Art, Objects and Ideas in the Records of the Medieval Court of Chivalry*

Julian Luxford

'Whoever in discussion adduces authority uses not intellect but rather memory.'

(Leonardo da Vinci)[1]

Maurice Keen has given such an accessible introduction to the business of the medieval Court of Chivalry that it is unnecessary to explain the institution to anyone who may pursue this book for the current chapter alone.[2] It will suffice to say that material objects were variously and extensively brought to bear as evidence in just one branch of the court's work: that is, cases in which rights to bear given coats of arms were tried. Of these cases, substantial records survive for just three: Scrope v. Grosvenor, Lovell v. Morley (both initiated in 1385) and Grey v. Hastings (initiated in 1400). Currently, only the first of these is available in print.[3] Keen called the references to objects in the surviving documents 'iconographical evidence', which he distinguished from 'autobiographical evidence' about people, their actions, situations and so on.[4] In art history, the word 'iconography' has technical meanings relating to subject-matter in representational imagery and formal and symbolic paradigms in architecture, so Keen's usage, while perfectly reasonable, will be set aside here. However, his appreciation of the value of material evidence was clear-sighted, and he has written more about it than practically anyone else to date.[5]

* Acknowledgements: I thank Jeremy Goldberg, David King, Philip Morgan, and particularly Nigel Ramsay for advice.
[1] *The Notebooks of Leonardo da Vinci*, ed. and transl. E. MacCurdy (New York, 1955), p. 88.
[2] M.H. Keen, *Origins of the English Gentleman: Heraldry, Chivalry and Gentility in Medieval England, c.1300–c.1500* (Stroud, 2002), pp. 25–42.
[3] Nicolas, *Scrope and Grosvenor Controversy*. Nigel Ramsay is currently editing the records of all three cases for publication by the Selden Society.
[4] Keen, *English Gentleman*, p. 47.
[5] *Ibid.*, pp. 47–58. See also, though much more briefly, A.C. Ayton, 'Knights, Esquires

Notwithstanding Keen's publications, the surviving documentation from the Court of Chivalry's cases is valuable to art historians and others directly engaged with material objects, for reasons which until now have mainly been noticed only incidentally: in order to support arguments about the socio-political functions of heraldry. Although this value is manifold, and ultimately depends on the individual scholar's aims, it has two dominant aspects. The first is that the documents record many objects, in various media, which no longer exist. Moreover, they record them *in situ* in interiors and landscapes which have themselves vanished.[6] For anyone not acquainted with it, this data is bound to enrich knowledge of both specific classes of object and the contexts of these objects' use. As such, its worth is basically inventorial: it supplies grist to the scholarly mill. The second, arguably more important aspect is evidence for how people thought about material objects. There is rather a lot of this, because the documentation consists largely of statements by individual witnesses who were officially directed to say if they had seen contested coats of arms in particular places and on specific types of object, what the dates of these objects were and why they were associated with a given protagonist. As in canonisation proceedings, *de visu* evidence was actively pursued and considered to have real forensic validity, and consequently, all six protagonists in the three lawsuits discussed here summoned it. While this eyewitnessing (to use Peter Burke's term) was to some extent conditioned by the questions that the court officials put to deponents, and its character as transmitted to posterity was presumably influenced by the formulae adopted for the written record, the historian can still extract a great deal of information from it about attitudes to buildings, furnishings and moveable things.[7] Anyone normally obliged to spin hypotheses about the purpose and function of objects out of the objects themselves will recognise such testimony for the gold-dust that it is.

The main purpose of the following investigation is to enlarge upon these points using examples recorded in the trial documents. This chapter is therefore more a hermeneutic exercise than an attempt to prove a specific historical point. After an overview of the range of objects mentioned in the documents, I will

---

and Military Service: The Evidence of the Armorial Cases before the Court of Chivalry', in *The Medieval Military Revolution: State, Society and Military Change in Medieval and Early Modern Europe*, ed. A.C. Ayton and J.L. Price (London, 1995), pp. 81–104, at 87; R.W. Barrett, *Against All England: Regional Identity and Cheshire Writing, 1195–1656* (Notre Dame, Ind., 2009), pp. 140–2. I have also considered this material, in J. Luxford, 'Medieval Tombs as Forensic Evidence', *Church Monuments*, 24 (2009), pp. 7–25, at 13–17, and 'The Hastings Brass at Elsing: A Contextual Analysis', *Trans. Monumental Brass Society*, 18 (2011), pp. 193–211.

[6] 'Landscape' evidence includes the churchyard monuments mentioned below, and such things as the Bradley cross in Appleton (Ches.), which stood on a public highway and had heraldry painted on it: Nicolas, *Scrope and Grosvenor Controversy*, I, p. 287.

[7] P. Burke, *Eyewitnessing: The Uses of Images as Historical Evidence* (Ithaca, NY, 2001).

consider the historical significance and descriptive language of the evidence. I also want to consider what this evidence reveals of knowledge, attitudes, and beliefs about material display in given contexts. At the end, and with the scruples of the art historian particularly in mind, I will question the ontological and forensic relationship between heraldry and the things it was physically applied to, although what is said about this will necessarily be concise.

At the outset, it should be said that by using the terms 'things', 'objects' and 'artefacts', I do not mean to extend the conversation about historical materiality found in recent (and recent-ish) work by Alfred Gell, Caroline Walker Bynum, Hans Belting and others.[8] The fundamental goal here is to promote the values of the documentation for anyone interested in the share that objects have in historical processes, and particularly for what may be called broad-minded art historians. As it happens, the evidence is inherently hospitable to this. Of course, the conventional interests of art history in style, iconography and influence are hardly served by lost objects, but the discipline's overarching concern with the relationship of art and architecture to ideas is particularly well catered for. In fact, the perennial art historical concern with dating the production of things is occasionally met, a matter that may as well be instanced now. This happens either directly, as where a precise date is given by a man named Thomas Codlyng for the installation of stained glass in the chancel at Elsing parish church in Norfolk (some of this glass survives, and more was drawn by eighteenth-century antiquaries), or indirectly, as with the build-date of *c.* 1360 that can be estimated for the abbot's hall at St Benet's Holm, north-east of Norwich, on the basis of multiple depositions by local monks.[9] The hall is lost, but the chronology of any such building remains important, as St Benet's was one of the oldest, wealthiest monasteries in Norfolk. Arguably, however, the depositions are more interesting for what they suggest about ignorance of proper dates, a point to which I will return.

Buildings, works of art, books and other types of thing were mentioned in cases tried by various medieval courts. Sometimes, the evidence gives a tantalising glimpse of beauty and quality, as with the 'golden table painted

---

[8] E.g. A. Gell, *Art and Agency: An Anthropological Theory* (Oxford, 1998); C.W. Bynum, *Christian Materiality: An Essay on Religion in Late Medieval Europe* (New York, 2011); H. Belting, *An Anthropology of Images: Picture, Medium, Body* (Princeton, 2011). Personally, I am averse to the flirtation with the pathetic fallacy encouraged by such work.

[9] For the Elsing glass see College of Arms, London, MS Processus in Curia Marescalli (hereafter PCM), 2 vols, I, p. 512; Luxford, 'Hastings Brass', p. 195. In 1386–7, four monks of St Benet's abbey testified that a certain shield of Morley arms had been in a window in their abbot's hall for around 25 to 27 years (Kew TNA, C 47/6/1, witnesses 144–7). In the context, the dates are simultaneously variable and specific enough to show that the witnesses were remembering the erection of the hall or, much less probably, one of its windows. (They will not have been remembering the installation of a single panel of heraldic glass.)

with images of the Trinity and covered with precious stones' cited in an inquisition held to prove the majority of Thomas Montagu, earl of Salisbury, in 1409.[10] The reader learns that this object was a christening gift, given in 1388, in the parish church of St Botolph at Shenley (Hertfordshire). Unquestionably, this is interesting, potentially useful information, but it is both isolated and fundamentally inert. The advantages of the Court of Chivalry records are the copiousness of the evidence, what it demonstrates about the social economy of objects, and, crucially, the suggestion arising from it that due to their heraldry, these objects were considered to have a sort of agency that transcended the passive status which the golden table just mentioned has in the context of its description. The evidential value, and with it the vitality, of medieval artefacts is rarely clearer in English sources.[11] Before all else, perhaps, these documents are useful for the challenge they pose to the reductive assumption – pervasive in the literature on late medieval art – that objects personalised through heraldry or inscriptions and kept in religious houses, churches and chapels were always designed to elicit intercessory prayers. While any one of the artefacts cited in court may have performed that function, their valency was evidently broader and more sophisticated. They served the interests of individuals, families and their causes in the present and future, over and perhaps above the souls of the dead.

The object domain

This is not the place to attempt a full inventory of the artefacts mentioned in these cases. However, an impression of the object domain and its interest can easily be given by ranging across the depositions. Before diving in, it is important to note that what is recorded and how it is described are

---

[10] 'Morley vs. Montagu (1399): A Case in the Court of Chivalry', ed. M.H. Keen and M. Warner, in *Camden Miscellany, XXXIV: Chronology, Conquest and Conflict in Medieval England* (Royal Historical Soc.: Camden Fifth Ser., x, 1997), pp. 146–97, at 163–4.

[11] Church historians as well as historians of material culture have overlooked this material. For instance, one can make seven additions concerning the dates and status of Norwich monks to Joan Greatrex's magisterial *Biographical Register of the English Cathedral Priories of the Province of Canterbury c.1066–1540* (Oxford, 1997) on the basis of the Lovell *v.* Morley depositions alone: compare TNA, C 47/6/1, membrs 24–5, witnesses 113 (two amendments), 114, 115, 116 (two amendments), 117 with (in witness order) Greatrex, *Biographical Register*, pp. 539 (Joseph de Martham), 483 (Richard de Bylney), 555 (Bartholomew de Scrowteby), 491 (John de Carleton), 530 (John de Kirkeby). Again, compare the agnosticism about the identity of the thirteenth-century Abbot Thomas of Jervaulx in *The Heads of Religious Houses: England and Wales, II: 1216–1377*, ed. D. Smith and V.C.M. London (Cambridge, 2001), p. 286, with Nicolas, *Scrope and Grosvenor Controversy*, I, p. 95, where he is identified as a Scrope. The larger point here is to indicate how document sets that lie in given disciplinary channels can flood profitably into other domains.

conditioned to a significant extent by officially set parameters. For example, in the Scrope *v.* Grosvenor proceedings, it is stated in the general brief that witnesses should consider muniments, chronicles, tombs, paintings, glass, vestments and 'other evidences' ('autres evidences') as relevant contexts of display.[12] Such things were also mentioned in the context of the Lovell *v.* Morley trial.[13] Banners and flags ('baneres et penons') were identified in the Grey *v.* Hastings trial two decades later.[14] As well as this, the questions which the plaintiffs and defendants required to be asked of opposing witnesses also specify objects. For example, Reginald Grey wanted deponents for Edward Hastings to mention certain sorts of object, 'especially muniments [...] and how they are sealed, and the description of the seal or seals', with names, dates and places of writing and sealing.[15] How such requirements were met can be traced in detail in the depositions: for example, one Thomas Lucas of East Dereham produced a banner and flag in court in support of Hastings, while Hastings himself submitted a letter patent 'sealed with green wax'.[16]

The object domain may be said to begin with architecture, which looms up largely and variously whenever the reader tries to imagine how the cases actually proceeded. In each trial, the court heard evidence in a range of halls and chambers, secular and ecclesiastical, and visited parish churches and monasteries to view objects *in situ*. Buildings were normally the overarching contexts of heraldic display, of course, and often a field for the representation of arms in their own right. Geoffrey Chaucer's evidence in the Scrope *v.* Grosvenor trial is a familiar example: he cited a sign with the arms *azure a bend or* hanging on a hostel, one of hundreds of painted signs that hung 'on the hoop' outside London buildings in the period.[17] Chaucer had wrongly thought that the arms signified Richard Scrope, for whom he testified, but the mistake is understandable, for, as another witness stated, Scrope hung his arms in plain sight outside all his residences.[18] Others favouring Scrope reported arms on the walls of castles and manor houses.[19] The roofs or canopies ('celure' is the common term) of various choirs and chapels also had arms on them, and they were painted on the walls of the Lady chapels of Osney abbey in Oxford and Wymondham priory in Norfolk.[20] Architecture

---

[12] Nicolas, *Scrope and Grosvenor Controversy*, I, p. 40; Keen, *English Gentleman*, p. 54.

[13] PCM, II, p. 43.

[14] PCM, II, pp. 1, 2.

[15] PCM, I, p. 390: 'munimentz en especial [...] et coment ils fuerent enseales, et de le description de le seal ou sealx'.

[16] PCM, I, pp. 446 (Lucas), 120 ('enseele ove verte cere').

[17] On Chaucer's evidence see Nicolas, *Scrope and Grosvenor Controversy*, I, pp. 178–9; II, pp. 404–12; *Chaucer Life-Records*, ed. M.M. Crow and C.C. Olson (Oxford, 1966), pp. 370–4.

[18] Nicolas, *Scrope and Grosvenor Controversy*, I, pp. 52–3; II, p. 174.

[19] E.g. *ibid.*, I, pp. 98, 118; II, pp. 278, 313.

[20] E.g. TNA, C 47/6/1, membrs 24 (Norwich cathedral, St Olave's priory), 25

is sometimes offered as evidence of age and entitlement independently of armorial display, particularly where a given individual was invoked as a builder or patron of a church or other structure. Thus, for example, the court officials in the case of Grey *v.* Hastings thought it worthwhile to record testimony that Hugh Hastings (d. 1347) and his wife Margery Foliot had built the nave of Elsing parish church.[21]

Monumental furnishings crop up frequently. Tombs and stained glass windows, in particular, were mentioned for their images as well as their heraldry. With the possible exception of banners, glazed shields are the most numerous of all items cited in the depositions, and appear in ecclesiastical and secular contexts alike. They were popular both for their visibility and (crucially) their resilience; their colours did not deteriorate like paint, nor did moth or rust corrupt them. A protagonist might be heavily invested in a single example: Thomas Morley produced three witnesses to testify about one glass shield in Aylsham parish church and four to vouch for another at Haddiscoe (both in Norfolk).[22] These two shields were the only objects that the seven deponents mentioned between them. In some instances, it is clear from the description that a tomb and a window formed a sort of commemorative unit, a phenomenon increasingly recognised in art historical scholarship.[23] Tombs were considered especially important. The Scrope *v.* Grosvenor trial records include a summary list of sixty-three locations in which the contested arms were displayed, compiled for Scrope by an assiduous researcher named William of Irby, in which tombs, where extant, are cited first.[24] Tombs are sometimes described as being of a given type. The obvious example is the brass of Sir Hugh Hastings (d. 1347) at Elsing, specified by the court officials as a work of gilded latten ('de laton dore') **(see Fig. 3.1)**.[25] A distinction was made by the abbot of Easby abbey, near Richmond, between 'un haut toumbe' and 'plate peers' (flat stones).[26] Six miles away, at Wensley parish church, there were flat stones carved with inscriptions in the cemetery, along with a burial arranged 'in the old way, in a stone coffin with a stone on top' ('en la veille manere en un cooffre de pere et un pere amont').[27] At Nether Peover (Cheshire), a cross in the cemetery was painted with the arms *azure a bend or*: variously referred to as 'un crois' and 'la crois', this may have been

(Buckenham priory), 26 (Wymondham); Kew, TNA, PRO 30/26/69, membr. 17 (preamble to depositions taken at Osney) (also at PCM, II, p. 275).
[21] PCM, I, 512; Luxford, 'Hastings Brass', p. 197.
[22] TNA, C 47/6/1, membr. 33 (witnesses 167–73).
[23] E.g. at Elsing, and in the Carmelite church at Doncaster (Luxford, 'Hastings Brass', pp. 200–1, 208). A forthcoming volume of the Corpus Vitrearum Medii Aevi by Richard Marks will examine tomb-window combinations in depth.
[24] Nicolas, *Scrope and Grosvenor Controversy*, I, pp. 222–6; II, pp. 330–1.
[25] PCM, I, pp. 349–50; Luxford, 'Hastings Brass', p. 203.
[26] Nicolas, *Scrope and Grosvenor Controversy*, I, p. 95.
[27] *Ibid.*, I, p. 129; II, 329–30.

3.1 Brass of Sir Hugh Hastings (d.1347) at Elsing (Norfolk).

a communal, 'village' cross rather than an individual grave-marker.[28] In the Lady chapel of Roydon parish church, near Diss (Norfolk), two knightly effigies of Morleys were specified, one a 'chivalerot' lying on a tomb-chest with arms on it, the other a 'petite chivalerot moevable' marking a heart-burial. The adjective suggests that the latter was not fixed to a chest or niche, or perhaps that it incorporated moving parts.[29]

'Tables' are often mentioned in churches, chapels and ancillary buildings: for example, heraldry on a table in the refectory at Osney abbey is recorded.[30] It is unlikely that all of these objects were altarpieces, or for that matter smaller devotional images, although some of them certainly were. The Franciscans at Chester, for example, had a 'table du autre' with the arms *azure a bend or* on it, as did the Cistercians of Combermere abbey in Cheshire (both cited in evidence for Robert Grosvenor).[31] And a painted 'table' produced before the court in the church of Stratfield Mortimer (Berkshire) by John Lovell's proctor is described in a way that implies devotional purpose. At the centre of this panel painting was the Virgin Mary, flanked by the kneeling figures of Philip Burnell (d. 1294) and his wife, each of whom held up a heraldic shield.[32] The art historian, at least, will find it interesting that similar votive figures – also kneeling and holding shields – were part of Phillip Burnell's tomb (the comparison will become clearer below). Occasionally, such articles as screens appear in the records: an 'old parclose of a tomb' in Swanton Morley church (Norfolk), was said to incorporate a shield with the arms whose ownership was contested in the Lovell *v.* Morley trial, that is, *argent a lion rampant crowned and armed or*.[33] The arms contested by Scrope and Grosvenor were on the organ-loft ('pareis des orgons') in York Minster.[34]

---

[28] *Ibid.,* I, pp. 266, 267, 270, 273.

[29] TNA, C 47/6/1, membrs 29–31 (witnesses 148–57); Luxford, 'Forensic Evidence', p. 16. For the small effigy, something like the late thirteenth-century Purbeck memorial of William of Albini at Bottesford (Leics.) is probably to be envisaged: see F.H. Crossley, *English Church Monuments A.D. 1150–1550* (London, 1921), p. 179. Another possibility is suggested by the seventeenth-century tomb illustrated in N. Llewellyn, *Funeral Monuments in Post-Reformation England* (Cambridge, 2000).

[30] TNA, PRO 30/26/69, membr. 17 (preamble) (also at PCM, II, p. 276).

[31] Nicolas, *Scrope and Grosvenor Controversy,* I, 256 (simply 'en un altre'), 268, 318 (Franciscan church); 317 (Combermere). Most of the objects mentioned in testimony for Grosvenor are listed in R. Stewart-Brown, 'The Scrope and Grosvenor Controversy 1385–1391', *Trans. Historic Soc. of Lancs. & Ches.,* 89 (1937), pp. 1–22, at 17–19. The evidence for glass in particular is noted in P. Hebgin-Barnes, *The Medieval Stained Glass of Cheshire*, Corpus Vitrearum Medii Aevi, Great Britain: Summary Catalogue 9 (Oxford, 2010).

[32] TNA, PRO 30/26/69, membr. 18, preamble to depositions taken at Stratfield Mortimer (also at PCM, II, pp. 280–5). The procurator did not know the name of Philip's wife (i.e. Maud Fitzalan).

[33] TNA, C 47/6/1, membr. 33.

[34] Nicolas, *Scrope and Grosvenor Controversy,* I, p. 141; II, p. 347.

Textiles are very frequently mentioned, reflecting their proportionately large representation among the chattels of wealthy late medieval people. Many banners and flags were evidently preserved in churches. The reader gets a vivid impression of the practice – otherwise largely invisible – of the distribution and display in naves and chancels of both funerary banners and redundant campaign banners which were entitled to respect but for which there was no other obvious home. Surcoats, armour, arms and horse-trappings crop up too.[35] Where found in a church, such things must usually have belonged to the mortuaries offered when a knight died.[36] Armour shown to the court in the Carmelite church at Doncaster was said to have been given when Hugh II de Hastings died in 1369, and a surcoat in Hallingbury church (Essex) with *argent a lion rampant* on it was surely deposited when William Morley died at Hallingbury in 1379.[37] Ecclesiastical vestments with heraldry are well represented. Most of the priests called to witness could cite at least one example, and they used the specialist terms one would expect of them: besides chasubles and albs, amices, stoles, apparels, fanons and in one case a morse are specified as bearers of arms.[38] There are other textile objects. Curtains, bench-covers and beds 'painted' with the arms *argent a lion rampant* were cited for Lovell, while the same arms on a lenten veil in the nave of Norwich cathedral were claimed for Morley.[39] The arms *or a manche gules*, contested in the Grey *v.* Hastings case, adorned a cloth that covered a seat in the chancel of the Franciscan church at Doncaster, and also a black pall lying on a tomb in the Carmelite church in the same town.[40] At Swanton Morley there was embroidered heraldry all around the high altar, on flags ('pennons') apparently hanging from the horns of the altar, on an altar-cloth, an embroidered reredos and a corporas case.[41] The hospital of St

---

[35] E.g. TNA, C 47/6/1, membr. 32 (surcoat); PCM, I, pp. 361, 368 (swords, trappings).

[36] For example, at Peterborough abbey in the fourteenth century, the mortuary payable to the sacrist included a haketon, gambeson, hauberk, helmet, bascinet, gauntlets (plated or protected with whalebone), greaves, shield, lance, sword, saddle and bridle: W.T. Mellows, *Mediæval Monuments in Peterborough Cathedral* (Peterborough, 1937), p. 21. Many examples are cited in the register compiled in July 1404 by the Peterborough sacrist George Fraunceys (see pp. 280–336), a manuscript owned by the Duke of Buccleuch and Queensberry, and deposited at the Northamptonshire Record Office. (I thank Crispin Powell for access to it.)

[37] PCM, I, p. 361; TNA, C 47/6/1, membrs 32–3 (witnesses 165–6).

[38] E.g. TNA, C 47/6/1, membr. 28 (vestments at Walsingham priory); Nicolas, *Scrope and Grosvenor Controversy*, I, pp. 100; II, 279–80.

[39] TNA, PRO 30/26/69, membr. 23, witness 223 (also at PCM, II, p. 324: compare Nicolas, *Scrope and Grosvenor Controversy*, I, pp. 142, 169; II, pp. 349, 385); TNA, C 47/6/1, membr. 24 (Norwich).

[40] PCM, I, pp. 525 (Franciscans), 360–1 (Carmelites).

[41] TNA, C 47/6/1, membr. 33.

Nicholas, near Richmond, had a silk altar-frontal embroidered with the arms *azure a bend or.*[42]

Books are mentioned, although not as often as one might expect, or certainly like. Their forensic value usually seems to have resided not in any heraldry they contained, but rather in what they could show about a connection between a given protagonist or his ancestors and a place or event where the arms that he claimed were represented. Two canons of Bridlington displayed a volume of chronicles to this end, while a canon from the Gilbertine priory of Watton mentioned another chronicle 'from the time of the Conquest' at his own house, but evidently did not exhibit it.[43] The prior and a fellow monk of Bardney (Lincolnshire) mentioned an old book of chronicles in their abbey 'made and written out in an old hand' ('de antiqua manu scriptum et factum'), but, again, did not bring it to court.[44] A 'cronyke' in Skirpenbeck parish church near York was said to prove the date of an ancient burial.[45] (All this testimony was for Richard Scrope.) In the Lovell *v.* Morley trial, 'deux livres appellez policronica' were produced to prove the date of the battle of Bannockburn.[46] The *Polychronicon* was very commonly cited as evidence in late medieval England, and use of two copies here must represent an instance of collation in order to confirm the point at issue.[47] Martyrologies were also cited for evidence of patronage and burial. Perhaps the volume at Skirpenbeck was in fact one of these. When a session of the Lovell *v.* Morley proceedings was held at the house of the Austin friars at Oxford, in order to view material evidence, an 'old martyrology' ('veaux martiloge') was produced, with entries 'in ancient writing' ('danciene lettre'). This book contained a prayer that supported claims about the ancestry of the plaintif, John Lovell.[48] In the Grey *v.* Hastings trial, extracts from another martyrology were put on record, this time from the Franciscan house at Doncaster. Again, the evidence consisted of the text of a prayer rather than anything with heraldry on it.[49] Similar evidence was also offered from the 'collectorie' of the Doncaster Carmelites.[50] Five Augustinian friars of Norwich said that they had often seen the heraldry on vestments in their house described as that of Morley

---

[42] Nicolas, *Scrope and Grosvenor Controversy*, I, pp. 130–1; II, p. 331.

[43] *Ibid.*, I, pp. 102, 103; II, pp. 282, 283. Compare *ibid.*, I, p. 278 (a claim that Grosvenor's Conquest-era pedigree existed in chronicles).

[44] *Ibid.*, I, pp. 229–30.

[45] *Ibid.*, I, p. 113; II, p. 305.

[46] PCM, II, p. 61.

[47] The record is very unlikely to indicate a single copy in two volumes. No surviving copy of the *Polychronicon* has this format: J. Freeman, 'The Manuscript Dissemination and Readership of the *Polychronicon* of Ranulph Higden, c. 1330 – c. 1500', Ph.D. thesis, University of Cambridge, 2013, pp. 207–339.

[48] TNA, PRO 30/26/69, membrs 16–17, witnesses 211, 212 (also at PCM, II, pp. 265–7).

[49] PCM, I, pp. 525–9; Luxford, 'Hastings Brass', p. 207.

[50] PCM, I, p. 521; see also p. 248 (Coventry Franciscans).

in a certain register of the ornaments of their church ('la comune registre faite sur les ornamentz del esglise du dice couvent').[51] One unambiguously illuminated book, again called 'old', is mentioned in the Scrope *v.* Grosvenor proceedings, in the form (as Keen noted) of a roll of arms. Produced by the abbot of Selby, this had coloured shields of kings, princes, nobles, knights and esquires, with the appropriate name written over each.[52]

As well as books, pedigrees and muniments were either produced in court or cited by witnesses. Thomas Morley tabled 'various pedigrees in old handwriting' ('diverses pees de gree de ancien escripture') in support of Edward Hastings, whose contents he seems to have been able to rattle off *ad libitum*.[53] The muniments were usually charters concerned with land transfer, although 'Chaunterie Rolles' are also specified, and the Augustinian canons of Buckenham (Norfolk) produced a papal bull which was read in court.[54] Again, there are many examples, and here, too, the modern scholar gets an insight into the documentary culture of the period. It is interesting, for example, that cartularies were not brought to bear (with the possible exception of a 'livere de terres' mentioned in the Grey *v.* Hastings contest).[55] Understandably, and in line with the sorts of parameters mentioned above, the court wanted to see original documents where possible. For their part, the protagonists in the trials knew where documents could be found and how to maximise their impact as visible, tangible evidence. These observations extend to the seals on documents, whose colour and iconography are sometimes mentioned. It certainly mattered that some seals showed the arms contested in a given trial, and numerous witnesses produced examples in support of their allies.[56] The abbot of Vale Royal, a Cistercian monastery in Cheshire, thus brought seven charters into court, all sealed with the arms claimed by Robert Grosvenor.[57] Sometimes it was thought relevant to record the colour of the sealing wax (green or white).[58] The most striking testimony of this sort came from the canons of Bridlington, who exhibited two charters with 'solemn' seals representing mounted knights holding swords, 'like those

---

[51] TNA, C 47/6/1, membrs 23–4 (witnesses 107–11).

[52] Nicolas, *Scrope and Grosvenor Controversy*, I, pp. 92–3; II. p. 271; Keen, *English Gentleman*, p. 55.

[53] For pedigrees, see e.g. PCM, I, pp. 56–7, 257, 411–12, 436–7 (quotation); II, pp. 5–8, 113.

[54] PCM, II, pp. 47–8; Nicolas, *Scrope and Grosvenor Controversy*, I, p. 130; II, p. 331; TNA, C 47/6/1, membr. 25 (witness 121).

[55] PCM, I, pp. 312–13.

[56] Nicolas, *Scrope and Grosvenor Controversy*, I, pp. 93–5, 100–1, 130, 132, 137, 139, 141, 266, 267, 268, 270 etc.; II, pp. 272, 273–4, 280, 331, 333, 342, 344, 346. See also PCM, I, pp. 220, 330; II, pp. 46–7; Stewart-Brown, 'Scrope and Grosvenor Controversy' (cit. in n. 31), pp. 13–15.

[57] Nicolas, *Scrope and Grosvenor Controversy*, I, p. 254.

[58] *Ibid.*, I, pp. 93, 132, 141; II, pp. 272, 333, 346; PCM, I, p. 120.

used at the time of the Conquest' ('come ceux de Conquest userent').[59] This claim about the antiquity, and by extension the symbolic heft, of a certain sort of imagery was not these canons' invention. They had, after all, no charters of their own dating from the time of the Conquest: Bridlington priory was not founded until the twelfth century. Rather, it expressed a received idea arising from actual eleventh-century evidence (including William of Normandy's own seal), and undoubtedly familiar to Richard Scrope himself, who supposedly 'came from a line of grand *gentils hommes* from the time of the Conquest'.[60] Another Yorkshire manuscript that expresses the same concept, unrelated to the Court of Chivalry but nicely illustrative of the point, is the secular cartulary made *c.* 1450 by one Thomas of Anlaby (Cambridge, Fitzwilliam Museum, MS 329). One of the charter transcripts in it has a drawing in red ink of a seal with a mounted rider brandishing a sword, encircled by an inscription (folio 43). At the top, Anlaby wrote: 'Here makys mencion how Sir Robert of Meus [Meaux] come into yngland at the conquest ac wyttnes hys sell of this dede, qwher he ryddis on hys hors wyth hys swerd in hys hand.'[61] The idea here is that the iconography self-evidently signifies involvement in the Conquest, and as such supports the other, commonplace assumption that such involvement vouchsafes legal and historical integrity. This integrity is obviously what the canons of Bridlington meant to suggest, because the charters they showed were datable by other means.

The description and 'biography' of individual objects

Categorisation of the object domain in this way embodies a modern view of material culture, although not one wholly divorced from the understanding or language of the trial documents. It would be possible to specify further categories of object (e.g. heraldic plate, which is sometimes mentioned collectively), or to subdivide others more searchingly than has been done above with reference to tombs and vestments.[62] However, there are alternatives to this approach which bring out the value of the material differently. One of these is through prosopography, and specifically by considering what given individuals knew and assumed about the objects they mentioned. This has been done elsewhere with reference to Chaucer, and its potential arises

[59] Nicolas, *Scrope and Grosvenor Controversy*, I, p. 101; II, pp. 281–2.

[60] *Ibid.*, I, p. 134 (quotation); II, pp. 336–7. On the class of seal attached to the Bridlington documents see C.H. Hunter Blair, 'Armorials upon English Seals from the Twelfth to the Sixteenth Centuries', *Archaeologia*, lxxxix (1943), pp. 1–26, at 1–7 and pls I–III.

[61] Anlaby drew the seal at the bottom of the page to suggest the position of an actual seal on a single-sheet charter.

[62] For plate, see e.g. TNA, PRO 30/26/69, membr. 23, witness 223 (also at PCM, II, p. 324); Nicolas, *Scrope and Grosvenor Controversy*, I, p. 191; II, p. 453.

wherever individuals are mentioned in relation to objects they knew about.[63] Another way in is by recognising the relative cultural importance of places or institutions. While all of the information in the documents is potentially important, it is not all of equal scholarly interest. Some of it stands out because it has to do with major institutions. For instance, one revelation of these records, that a shield with the arms *argent a lion rampant sable* was painted 'within and above' the north entrance to the chapel of the Virgin at Walsingham priory, and also appeared at least fourteen times on vestments at the same monastery, will be more interesting to more people than the fact that the same arms appeared in (say) Aylsham parish church.[64] This is also true of another epiphany, contained in testimony about Norwich cathedral. Here, monks of the house pointed to depictions of the arms on and in various objects, including 'on a screen beneath the great cross', evidently the rood-screen.[65] These are tantalising words, as this major screen, which stood in the nave four bays west of the crossing, is otherwise known only through excavation of its footings. Moreover, from as early as *c.* 1300, the altar against it was called St William's altar, after the putative child martyr St William of Norwich.[66] It thus seems possible that the existence of the heraldry on the screen indicates the Morley family's interest in a cult which now attracts much scholarly and popular attention.[67] The Norwich evidence is also poignant for its inclusion of what is very probably a surviving coat of the arms contested in Lovell *v.* Morley, now in a window in the north ambulatory (see **Plate I**).[68]

The fact that the court visited places to view monumental evidence *in situ* seems to have contributed to a willingness to describe some objects at greater length than one normally expects of a medieval source. Not all such visits generated equally detailed accounts, which is interesting in itself for what it suggests about the attitudes of the court officials to what they saw, or heard about, given that most of the material evidence viewed was of similar potential value to the ultimate business of making a decision. Thus, while it is possible to be disappointed that things like the interiors of the Carmelite church at

---

[63] E.g. L. Patterson, *Chaucer and the Subject of History* (Madison, WI, 1991), pp. 179–98.

[64] TNA, C 47/6/1, membr. 28: '1 escuchon dez dictes armes entiers peyntez dedeinz et desuis le north huis de la chapelle notre dame.'

[65] TNA, C 47/6/1, membr. 24: 'sur une perche desuis la grande croice esteant en la corps du dicte esglise'. For 'perche', compare Middle English 'perke', the common term for rood-screen in late medieval East Anglia.

[66] W.H. St J. Hope, 'Quire Screens in English Churches, with Special Reference to the Twelfth-Century Quire Screen formerly in the Cathedral Church of Ely', *Archaeologia*, lxviii (1917), pp. 43–110, at 99–101.

[67] See most recently E.M. Rose, *The Murder of William of Norwich: The Origins of the Blood Libel in Medieval Europe* (Oxford, 2015).

[68] The shield is listed in D.J. King, 'The Panel Paintings and Stained Glass', in *Norwich Cathedral: Church, City and Diocese, 1096–1996*, ed. Ian Atherton et al. (London, 1996), pp. 410–30, at 420.

Doncaster and the Franciscan church at Coventry are not described in more detail, there are compensations in the descriptions and object-biographies (for want of a better term) offered elsewhere. These suggest a further possible approach to the evidence, through case studies which could be developed with the help of other sources. The example of the Hastings brass at Elsing, visited by the court in 1408 during the Grey *v.* Hastings hearings, makes the point with exceptional clarity **(see Fig. 3.1)**. It is exceptional because the brass and its setting largely survive, and also because the description of the brass is so detailed: more so, in fact, than that of any other object in the court records. Along with its heraldry, the iconography and epitaph are rehearsed, the material noted, and the psychological impact of the object evoked by the use of language like 'belle et bien oeuvre', 'une ymage grand et de belle estature', 'une ymage honorablement du Roy Dengleterre' and so on.[69] The latter phrase suggests that the brass received so much attention because it incorporated an image of a king, Edward III. Edward Hastings, who had requested the court to visit it, also seems to have considered it especially valuable evidence, although this impression may be in part an effect of the description. To some degree, William Leche and Richard Vaus, the court officials, seem to have been interested in it as an object, which suggests the brass's ability to do the jobs it was made for as well as any other written evidence concerning a medieval English tomb.

Another tomb viewed by the court was also described in detail, although without quite the same enthusiasm for its appearance. But its appearance certainly mattered, and left its mark in the record. This was the tomb of Philip Burnell in the Austin friars' church at Oxford, in a wall on the north side of the choir, adjacent to both the high altar and Philip's grave. It was presented in April 1386 by Thomas Hyne, John Lovell's procurator, who also pointed out a shield and two very old funerary banners, the latter described as 'graundes et bien vieulx baneres'.[70] The tomb itself is called a painting on a wall ('un ymage en un mure depeinte'), but its overall form as described, plus the fact that two figures belonging to it held stone shields (see below), shows that it was actually a work of sculpture painted in colours. This, indeed, is what one would expect of the monument of a late-thirteenth-century knight from the west of England.[71] It had a recumbent knightly effigy ('chivalret jesaunt') wearing a hauberk painted with the contested arms. There was a belt around the waist of the effigy, and spurs on its heels. At its feet were two other effigies,

---

[69] PCM, I, pp. 349–50; A.R. Wagner and J.G. Mann, 'A Fifteenth-Century Description of the Brass of Sir Hugh Hastings at Elsing, Norfolk', *Antiquaries Jnl*, xix (1939), pp. 421–8, at 423; Luxford, 'Hastings Brass', pp. 202–3.

[70] TNA, PRO 30/26/69, membr. 7 (preamble to the depositions) (also at PCM, II, pp. 160–4).

[71] A two-dimensional painting with the imagery described, including a recumbent effigy, would in any case be practically or actually unique in the period in England.

both kneeling and surely – though no indication of this is given – of smaller size.[72] One represented a lady – evidently, Philip's wife, Maud Fitzalan (d. 1316) – dressed in a mantle painted with the same arms. Facing her was a knight, wearing a hauberk with a haketon over it, together with a shield of the said arms on a cord around its neck. It had a sword hanging between its legs and spurs on its heels. Each kneeling figure held a shield of freestone ('ffraunche piere') with the contested arms on it, although the heraldry was largely consumed by age.[73] An inscription bordering the recumbent effigy was also pointed out, but this, too, was very damaged. Indeed, the damage seems to have been pretty general, and extended to the funerary shield, which 'due to its great age is eaten up by worms'.[74] Time was evidently getting the better of one of its trophies here, although there is no indication that anyone thought the decay shameful. Friars who were called to witness echoed the proctor's claims, and added that Philip Burnell was considered one of the founders of their house. They also said that the shield and banners had been given at his funeral in perpetual memory of him, that the shield was made of wood ('de boys'; as its worm-ridden state implies), and that the heraldic paintwork had existed for a long time and had once been gay with colour.[75]

---

[72] Figures in size and orientation like the kneeling, book-holding figures in albs at the feet of the (considerably later) effigy of Henry Chichele at Canterbury, complete by 1426, are perhaps to be imagined.

[73] Readers will find the description useful: 'Auxint exhibua a nous un ymage en un mure depeinte en la north partie del quer de mesme lesglise jouste le haut autier desur et pres le lieu ou monsieur Philippe nageirs seigneur de Burnell come il afferma [i.e., Thomas Hyne] estoit encevyle; la quele ymage come il afferma de dit monsieur Philippe fuist une ymage come un chivalret esaunt vestu dun haberk et desur un cotearmure des armes dez queux est fait action en lavauntdicte cause, seintee du sceinture, eiant lez mayns joynez et enhaucez et en sez pees paunche-prikles; et monstra a nous as pees de mesme la ymage une aultre ymage dune dame come lez genuz flecchez, vestu dun mantell dez armes queux est fait action, la quele ymage est en la sue greindre partie degastee. Auxint monstra a nous mesme le procuratour un chivalret come flecche sur lun genu al encountre la dicte dame, vestu de hauberk et dun akton desur, eiant entour son colle un escu dez ditz armes, sceinte dune sceinture, ove un esplie eiant ensyt en ses pees paunceprikles; lez queux ymages teignont parentre lour maynz un escu de ffraunche piere sur le quel estoient depeintez come mesme le procuratour afferma lez armes dez queux est fait mencion, la peinture adecertes de lyon en mesme lescu est en tant degastee pur launcientee de sa picture' etc. (TNA, PRO 30/26/69, membr. 7). Note that in this case, 'ffraunche piere' cannot possibly mean 'stone from France', as it relates only to two small shields whose material origins would have been invisible. Compare C. Wilson, 'The Neville Screen', in *Medieval Art and Architecture at Durham Cathedral*, British Archaeological Association Conference Trans., 3 (Leeds, 1980), pp. 90–104, at 90–1.

[74] 'pur la sue vetustee fuist corose des vermes'.

[75] TNA, PRO 30/26/69, membrs 16–17, witnesses 211–13 (testimony of the Oxford Austin friars Alexander Kingham, William Everley and John Cerne) (also at PCM, II, pp. 263–74).

This description has a fundamental art historical value. It records in detail a sophisticated monument that is otherwise undocumented, and opens a small but valuable window onto the appearance of a practically unknown church that was once significant in relation to Oxford university.[76] More technically, it provides access to the uses to which a work of commemorative sculpture might be put. It also demonstrates and implies attitudes to this work, along with a sense of the tomb's significance to its caretakers (notwithstanding the condition of its paint). The monument's position by the high altar would be sufficient to imply that the friars took notice of it, but the depositions also show that they discussed it among themselves independently of the trial. Opinions about its age and paintwork were cited on behalf of one Nicholas of Abingdon, who had died six years previously (so, in 1380) at the age of eighty, before the trial was initiated.[77] As in the case of Elsing, the vitality of these topics is quickened by other evidence in the depositions. Thus, there was also a shield of the contested arms on the choir roof at Candich, and another, purportedly old ('vieulx'), in the west window of a guesthouse next to the refectory. This had a helmet above it with a garland and crest of a black lion with gold crown and claws.[78] There is also the evidence cited earlier of the prayers from the friars' martyrology.

As mentioned above, aspects of the Burnell tomb were paralleled in the painting exhibited at Stratfield Mortimer (Berkshire). Here is an object-biography which plots the circulation of a work of art as well as its patronage, form and iconography. The latter was evidently complex, consisting of various figures, with the Virgin in a separate space at the centre. She was flanked by the shield-holding figures mentioned above, with the knight on her left side (i.e. at the Virgin's right hand) and the lady on her right.[79] This object was evidently once given by the wife of Philip Burnell to Aline (d. 1363), wife of Edward Burnell, and then by her to a friend, Margaret, wife of Thomas de la Mare, lord of Aldermaston in Berkshire. Margaret had put it in the chapel of

---

[76] For its relationship to the university see *The Victoria History of the County of Oxford*, II, ed. William Page (London, 1907), pp. 143–8.

[77] TNA, PRO 30/26/69, membrs 16–17, witnesses 211, 212. William Everley noted other friars who had affirmed the authenticity of the paintwork.

[78] TNA, PRO 30/26/69, membr. 7, preamble (PCM, II, p. 163): 'un vieulx escu des ditz armes, et desur ycelle escu un healme, ove une chapelle, et desur ycelle chapelle un creste, et en ycelle creast un leon de sable corone et enarme dore'.

[79] TNA, PRO 30/26/69, membr. 18 (again, the salient section is worth reproducing): 'exhibua devaunt nous une table en quele estoient depeintz plusours ymages et entour le mylieu dycell table en une pane fuist et est depeint une ymage de nostre dame et en lune partie de dicte ymage est depeint une ymage dun seigneur come lez genuz flecchez vestu desur dun lunge vesture en le manere dune surcot ovec eiant lez maynz joynez et eshaucez et entre mesmes lez maynz un escu des armes des queux est fait action en sa dicte cause; et en lautre partie dicelle ymage de notre dame est depeint une ymage dune dame ensemblement genuflecthant eiant auxint les mayns joynes et eshaucez et entre lez dictes maynz un aultre escu dycell armes'.

Aldermaston manor house, which explains why it was produced at nearby Stratfield Mortimer. In 1386, it had been in this household chapel for at least twenty-six years. The painting seems formerly to have been at the Franciscan house at Bridgnorth in Shropshire, where Aline had stayed for an unspecified period after her husband's death. The fact that it was portable and evidently suitable as a gift suggests it was a personal devotional image rather than a more substantial object originally intended for an altar at the Austin friars of Oxford or elsewhere.[80] Its loss means that nothing can be said of the style of its painting, although the high status of its patron supports an expectation of high quality. However, its movement by stages over a fairly wide area is still interesting evidence for the circulation of an identifiable type of artwork. There is precious little written testimony to the circulation of such things at this time and in these parts of England.

Another object-biography containing evidence for women's patronage is valuable for what it reveals about the Benedictine nunnery of Blackborough (west Norfolk).[81] It also crops up in testimony for John Lovell. The visual culture of Blackborough is highly obscure, and in light of the nuns' poverty it was probably never very impressive.[82] A red chasuble and amice powdered with silver scallop shells (for Scales), with an orphrey with the Burnell arms, must have been an aesthetic highlight.[83] According to the deponents, who were secular priests formerly employed at Blackborough, it was given by Isabel, wife of Robert de Scales. This Isabel was a daughter of one of the lords Burnell, although the priests did not know his name. Each year, they testified, the vestment was placed on Isabel's tomb on the anniversary of her death. It also emerged that an apparel from a vestment with the Burnell arms, along with another amice, were given by Isabel to Middleton parish church when she was purified after childbirth.[84] Middleton was impropriate to Blackborough, and the testimony illustrates the value of vestments in ritual contexts other than the mass, along with the normal intrusion of heraldry into even local networks of gift-giving where armigerous families were involved.

---

[80] TNA, PRO 30/26/69, membr. 19 (witnesses 216, 217) (also at PCM, II, pp. 280–5); compare Ayton, 'Knights, Esquires' (cit. in n. 5), p. 100 n. 39.

[81] TNA, PRO 30/26/69, membr. 19 (preamble to the depositions about the vestments from Blackborough and Middleton) (also at PCM, II, pp. 286–95).

[82] In 1291, it had a net income of around £36 and forty-four inhabitants (including servants). The 1530s valuation was just £42. For a painting of John the Evangelist there see F. Blomefield and C. Parkin, *An Essay Towards a Topographical History of the County of Norfolk*, 11 vols (London, 1805–10), IX, p. 33.

[83] What this looked like can be envisaged with reference to a chasuble with heraldic orphreys of mid-fourteenth-century English make now in the church of St Sebastian at Ponta Delgada in the Azores: see *The Age of Opus Anglicanum*, ed. M.A. Michael (Turnhout, 2016), pp. 82–3.

[84] TNA, PRO 30/26/69, membr. 19, witnesses 218–20: 'et donast ladite parure en une amyce a ladite esglise de Middelton au temps qele estoit purifie illeosces dun enfant'. (Also at PCM, II, p. 291.)

Particularly, it suggests that vestments were used as sepulchral palls, a function to which heraldic examples were clearly suited.[85]

Thinking and feeling about objects

Testimony of this sort, based on personal experience, inevitably embodies various indications of how people thought and felt about material culture. This fact has already been instanced with reference to such things as the Bridlington canons' production of documents with equestrian seals, the official description of the Hastings brass, and the evidence that the Austin friars of Oxford discussed the tomb of Philip Burnell among themselves independently of the trial. Such information can often be reliably gauged in spite of the formulaic nature of the testimony, and a thorough examination of all the evidence, contextualised with reference to related written and material sources, would be a considerable service to scholarship. As with the other subjects addressed in this chapter, the intention here is to indicate the potential value and use of the documents without any pretension to completeness.

To begin with, it is worth noting the resolutely non-religious tenor of the evidence, which contrasts so conspicuously with what the art historian, at least, is used to dealing with. While much of the richest information emerges from priestly testimony, and many of the objects discussed existed in secular churches or religious houses, the tone of the evidence is rarely, if ever, pietistic. The validity of claims is never buttressed with reference to the spirituality of the protagonists, or to the ritual contexts or use of objects bearing coats of arms. A given coat of arms is not, for example, represented as being more forensically powerful just because it was worn by a priest when celebrating mass. That such information seems to have been thought irrelevant in the course of trials which dealt routinely in emotive and impressionistic testimony is striking and cannot simply be dismissed by identifying the court as 'secular'. Perhaps the atmosphere of the institutions visited and the solemn aura of objects implicated in religion (whether they were produced in court or just mentioned) was silently pervasive and influential enough in the context of testimony sworn on the gospels. Spiritual significance might have gone without saying, just as great deeds might not be chronicled if the evidence for them was plain enough in material terms. But the tenor of the depositions and summaries does not indicate this.

As Keen, Ian Jack, Andrew Ayton and others have suggested, the strongest affective impressions arising from these three Court of Chivalry trials have

---

[85] For an example of a chasuble being used as a pall for an Easter sepulchre see *Lateinische Schriftquellen zur Kunst in England, Wales und Schotland vom Jahre 901 bis zum Jahre 1307*, ed. O. Lehmann-Brockhaus, 5 vols (Munich, 1955–60), II, p. 135, no 2743.

to do with peer relationships between knights as well as patron–client relationships between the protagonists and churchmen or social inferiors. The evidence of material objects is implicated at all points in these relationships as they arise from the documents, commonly in the non-specific claim that a given party, or some ancestor thereof, had displayed the disputed arms in military settings, including those of the tournament. It was also normal for witnesses to say that a protagonist's entitlement to a particular coat of arms was a local and enduring tradition, with the implication that many people were acquainted with the arms by sight. Some distinctive evidence is also forthcoming. The fact that the coat of arms of one knight was displayed in the residence of another represents an attitude to self-fashioning which is basically familiar, but amenable in certain cases to more nuanced interpretation. Thus, John and Hugh Hastings, brothers, testified that their grandfather (the knight who lay at Elsing) had put a shield of the Scrope arms *azure a bend or* in a window in his chapel – presumably in his manor-house – some sixty years before 'because of the companionship' he had shared with Sir Geoffrey Scrope in various voyages and battles ('par cause de compaignie entre lour deux').[86] This represents an extension of the sentimental construction of chivalrous companionship found on the Elsing brass, which does not include Geoffrey Scrope among the eight brothers-in-arms flanking the main effigy. Evidence of a similar stripe emerged from another pro-Scrope deponent, the Augustinian prior of Marton in North Yorkshire. He stated that Alexander Neville had given his house an object that had been worn in battle against the Scots: an embroidered coat of arms whose quarterings were filled up with smaller shields of the arms of his friends ('lez armez de cez amys'). He also recalled a window with the arms of Scrope and Quenby in it, made, he said, at the foundation of the priory in the late twelfth century. The window was a gift of Robert Hackett, lord of Quenby, to mark the special friendship of two knights who had loved one another very much. ('Robert Haket [...] amast tant un de lez Escropes et celuy dez Escropes amast tant le sire de Quenby que por amor le un fist fair un fenestere' etc.)[87] This may indicate a close, affectionate bond between two knights, of the sort that Alan Bray has discussed with reference to the heraldic tomb of William Neville and John Clanvowe (both d. 1391) from the Dominican house at Galata (Istanbul).[88]

---

[86] Nicolas, *Scrope and Grosvenor Controversy*, I, p. 51; II, pp. 168–9.

[87] *Ibid.*, I, p. 140; II, pp. 344–5. See also M.H. Keen, 'Chivalrous Culture in Fourteenth-Century England', *Historical Studies*, 10 (1976), pp. 1–24, at 22. The fact that the prior identified no precise location for the window at Marton suggests that it no longer existed, as such identification was usual. If so, then his knowledge of it is an interesting matter in its own right, suggesting a written record or conventual tradition.

[88] A. Bray, *The Friend* (Chicago, 2003), pp. 13–19; see also S. Düll, A. Luttrell and M. Keen, 'Faithful unto Death: The Tomb Slab of Sir William Neville and Sir John Clanvowe, Constantinople 1391', *Antiquaries Jnl*, lxxi (1991), pp. 174–90.

Presumably, evidence of such intimacy is often swamped in surviving sources by more exigent considerations, and indeed, it appears here only fugitively. As evanescent strands in the cobweb of personal and social inter-action, the aspects of this evidence can be impossible to distinguish from a distance, although they were probably recognisable enough in the living voices and gesticulation of the courtroom. Other matters are more plainly visible, including the local knowledge that people had about objects with heraldry on them and the etiquette of heraldic display, particularly in ecclesi-astical settings. The point about personal knowledge of material culture needs little emphasis, because it lies on the surface of most of the depositions. It goes without saying that, whether at some remove or none, everything claimed of the status of arms in the depositions relies on personal eyewitnessing of material examples. From the status of the witnesses who were called and the nature of the questions they were asked, it is clear that professional religious men (and, through men, female religious like the nuns of Blackborough and also of Marrick priory near Richmond) were considered to have the most reliable knowledge of objects such as tombs and vestments. It is equally clear that laymen often shared this knowledge, whether the objects in question were in churches or out of them. For example, one Adam Neusom, a layman aged fifty-four, was able to state on oath that the Grosvenor tombs in Chester abbey did not have coloured heraldry on them (perhaps because they were brasses or unpainted incised slabs), but that various windows throughout the church did.[89] This suggests personal acquaintance, whereas the identical testimony given by two laymen in the Lovell *v.* Morley case about a tomb at Buildwas abbey (Salop) with heraldry 'painted, sculpted and drawn' ('depeintez, sculpt[e]z et designez') savours of hearsay, implying as it does that the witnesses did not really know how the arms were executed.[90]

Interestingly, priests and laypeople alike appear to have been innocent of the fact that heraldry is highly unlikely to have been displayed in such contexts as stained glass windows in the twelfth century. The mistakes relate to a pervasive concern with the oldness of evidence, which itself stemmed from a perception that the older something was, the greater its forensic value. Witnesses for Scrope swore on the gospels that glass in the conventual churches of Marrick, Lanercost and Marton had been installed when those churches were founded or first built; 'since the time of King Henry II', as the prior of Lanercost insisted.[91] Canons of Buckenham priory (Norfolk) were adamant that the arms they attributed to Morley had been in their refectory

---

[89] Nicolas, *Scrope and Grosvenor Controversy*, I, pp. 68–9; II, pp. 222–3.

[90] TNA, PRO 30/26/69, membrs 24–5, witnesses 225, 226 (also at PCM, II, pp. 331, 334). Of course, a sculpted shield was usually also painted. For a possible fragment from the tomb in question see M. Downing, *The Medieval Military Effigies Remaining in Shropshire* (Shrewsbury, 1999), pp. 12–13, 40–1.

[91] Nicolas, *Scrope and Grosvenor Controversy*, I, pp. 99 ('lez ditz fenestres depuis le

since the foundation of their priory in 1179, and they produced the aforementioned papal bull to demonstrate the date, as if this proved the date of the arms.[92] There is no indication that the quality of this evidence was tested by the court officials, and the suggestion which arises, perhaps unsurprisingly, is that while men of the period may sometimes have been able to estimate the age of handwriting, they had few if any grounds for dating architecture and art unless they personally remembered its construction or installation – as Thomas Codlyng did of the glass at Elsing.

Ideas and apprehensions about heraldic objects are differently visible in the programmes of research that went into marshalling material evidence in the periods leading up to the courtroom proceedings. Although not mentioned as such in the documents, this research is manifest in the social profile of the witnesses assembled, the fact that these men always had their stories straight when testifying about the same objects, the things that were available for showing in court, and the places that were visited so that evidence could be viewed *in situ*. It is unclear how much knowledge any of the protagonists had of the sum total of available material evidence when the cases first arose: perhaps their personal acquaintance with tombs, windows and so on did not extend much beyond their manor houses and ancestral *Grabkirchen*. However, it is easy to see how they would have obtained the information they needed, by applying to priests and local laymen for information in regions where their forebears had exercised influence, and also, perhaps, by trawling their ancestors' wills. Occasionally, the reader gets an insight into this process. William of Irby, the 'official de Richemond' who went around gathering evidence for Richard Scrope, has already been mentioned.[93] Edward Hastings sent a man to King's Lynn to fetch a single banner from the Carmelites there; he is unlikely to have known of it without information gained through research. In another case, he despatched a servant to ask the Franciscans at Doncaster whether their church contained Hastings family burials and tombs with the arms he claimed 'painted, portrayed or sculpted' on them.[94] At other points in the lawsuit, both he and Reginald Grey produced images of tombs and heraldry in windows, along with copies of epitaphs, which were done on pieces of parchment and were perhaps incorporated into the court registers.[95] All of this suggests both a good idea of where to start looking for evidence and a crash-course, drawing on the efforts of numerous people, in where precisely the evidence was. Many coats of arms will have been overlooked: the records can represent only a partial repertory

fesance de lour esglise le quele esglise fuist fait en le temps du Roy Henr[y] le second'), 132, 140, 186; II, pp. 279, 333, 345, 442.
[92] TNA C 47/6/1, membrs 25–6 (witnesses 121–5).
[93] For Irby's vocations see Nicolas, *Scrope and Grosvenor Controversy*, I, p. 220.
[94] PCM, I, pp. 355–7, 524–8; Luxford, 'Hastings Brass', pp. 206–7.
[95] PCM, I, pp. 180–1, 364, 368; Luxford, 'Hastings Brass', pp. 208–10.

of the potentially relevant objects. John Smyth of Nibley, the chronicler of the Berkeley family, stated that he had seen that family's arms in over 100 churches and chapels in Bristol, Somerset and Gloucestershire alone.[96] There seems no reason to think that the Scrope, Morley or Hastings families were much (if at all) less well represented than this, but the pieces of evidence brought to bear, though more widely dispersed, were not so numerous. On the other hand, the almost obsessive zeal with which some of the protagonists submitted single, modest objects suggests that they pulled in everything that was known to them.

Various indications are given of the etiquette of heraldic display in churches and their environs. The topic naturally relates to the standards and expectations of both the individuals who bore the arms and the churchmen who displayed them. It should not automatically be assumed that the former were responsible for arranging and paying for a given shield, although where heraldry was found on a tomb, banner or armour, lay patronage is at least probable. The fact is that medieval churchmen often erected coats of arms to advertise their social capital (an important consideration for any scholar who uses heraldry as evidence of art and architectural patronage). One need only look at the heraldry in the choir of Westminster Abbey and the nave of York Minster, or on the gatehouse façades at Kirkham priory (near York) and Butley priory (Suffolk), to get a sense of this. In any case, the interests of both parties interpenetrated to the extent that the testimony is always relatable to each. Thus, for example, the erection of armour, banners and other such evidence in churches simultaneously proved the social and spiritual reach of armigerous people and the constancy of the clergy who displayed them, even if, as with a Morley banner in the tiny Augustinian priory of Thremhall (Essex), much of the evidence was consumed by age.[97] The same is also true of heraldry on and around tombs, and in the windows of churches. After churches, much the most common locations of display at religious houses were refectories and guesthalls. Arms are reported in refectories at Easby, Byland, Lanercost, Newburgh, Watton, Osney and Buckenham, in the abbot's hall at St Benet's Holm, the 'hall' at York Minster and the guest-house 'near the refectory' at the Austin friary at Oxford.[98] The main reason for this was almost certainly because important laymen were routinely entertained in these buildings, where they would notice the arms and respect the influence

---

[96] J. Smyth, *The Berkeley Manuscripts: The Lives of the Berkeleys*, ed. J. Maclean, 2 vols (Gloucester, 1883), II, p. 37. Admittedly, Smyth's heraldry must have included post-medieval examples (his history ends in 1618).

[97] TNA C 47/6/1, membrs 31–2 (witnesses 158–60).

[98] Nicolas, *Scrope and Grosvenor Controversy*, I, pp. 95, 96, 99, 100, 102–3, 142; II, pp. 275, 276, 279, 280, 282–3, 347; TNA C47/6/1, membrs 25, 29; TNA, PRO 30/26/69, membr. 7 (preamble): 'une meason pres de le refreture dez dites ffreres appelle le hosterye'. (Also at PCM, II, p. 163.)

of those who bore and displayed them. The abbot of Byland gave spirited testimony to this in the Scrope *v*. Grosvenor case, stating that he had often heard local knights visiting his refectory say '*Regardez*, there are the arms of Sir Richard Scrope!'[99] The expectation that refectories and halls were suitable to secular as well as religious purposes is suggested by the use that the Court of Chivalry itself made of them, as for example at Abbotsbury in Dorset and mendicant houses at Doncaster (Carmelites and Franciscans), Coventry and Dunstable.[100]

The display of arms on ecclesiastical vestments is another aspect of etiquette that deserves some attention, not least because it seems by ideal standards to have contravened decorum. For all its normalness, there was a recognised *bobance* about the display of arms: this must be why the Carthusian order banned it from charterhouses in 1424.[101] In Florence in 1496, Savonarola was of the same mind, angrily denouncing the presence of arms 'on the back of vestments, so that when the priest stands at the altar, the [coats of] arms can be seen well by all the people'.[102] As suggested in the case of Blackborough, vestments were variously used in medieval churches, but their essential function was as honorific, moving components of ritual. Here, it is tempting for the ideas-driven scholar to compare mass vestments with armour, as the latter also identified, dignified and protected its wearer. However, such parallels will only bear so much weight, notwithstanding Durandus's interest in them.[103] The primary purpose of putting heraldry onto vestments was not to extend the authority of the knight through the person of the priest by suggesting quasi-sacerdotal status for him, or to imply that clerics were a cadre of spiritual liveryman (although this notion seems to have occurred to Savonarola). Instead, and more mundanely, it was to increase the number of examples of a given coat in the public domain, particularly where a legal right like advowson existed. The complexity of baronial portfolios of such rights in the period of the trials can hardly be overstated.[104] Perhaps, as well, there was an intention to acquire some sort of spiritual advantage through

---

[99] Nicolas, *Scrope and Grosvenor Controversy*, I, p. 96 ('et sovent fois quant lez chivalers du paiis ount este en labbey ils ount dit regardez la sount lez armes de monsire Richard Lescrope'); II, p. 276.

[100] *Ibid.*, I, p. 76; PCM, I, pp. 359, 362, 363, 366.

[101] For an abstract of the Carthusian statute in an English source see Kew, TNA, E 315/490, f. 22v.

[102] *Italian Art 1400–1500: Sources and Documents*, ed. C.E. Gilbert (Englewood Cliffs, NJ, 1980), p. 158.

[103] *William Durand, On the Clergy and Their Vestments: A New Translation of Books 2–3 of the Rationale divinorum officiorum*, transl. T.M. Thibodeau (Chicago, 2010), pp. 132–6 (i.e. book 3, part 1, 4–6).

[104] For a sense of this, referring to the affairs of Reginald Grey, see I. Jack, 'The Ecclesiastical Patronage Exercised by a Baronial Family in the Late Middle Ages', *Jnl of Religious History*, 3 (1964), pp. 275–95.

what M.A. Michael has called 'the privilege of proximity'.[105] Obviously, it is difficult to make a crisp distinction between secular and spiritual prudence here, and it would be pointless to deny that arms were displayed by knights *ex devocione*. The manuscript called the *Beauchamp Pageant* gives a whole page to a pen drawing of Richard Beauchamp (d. 1439), earl of Warwick, garbed as a pilgrim, piously setting up a shield over the tomb of Christ in Jerusalem.[106] However, the language of the law-court supports the idea that displaying arms on vestments and other objects used in churches was chiefly a proprietary matter. In general, churches were good places to display arms because a great many people visited them and their contents were relatively stable.

The value of material evidence and the stake of objects in this value

As all of this evidence shows, much can be gleaned from the case histories about the distribution and knowledge of arms in late medieval England. However, a conceptual tension exists between the heraldry on which the lawsuits centred and the objects to which that heraldry was applied. The art historian, who is used to interrogating the material and social ontology of physical objects, is perhaps more likely to perceive this tension than is the historian, for whom objects have only the ancillary status of illustrative colouring. The issue can be encapsulated by asking why the court bothered with the different sorts of object discussed here, why it troubled to visit churches and examine evidence *in situ* given the time and expense this took, and why it was prepared to listen to so much testimony about an object or objects whose heraldry was often only a few decades old. In the final analysis, the plaintiffs Scrope and Grey and the defendant Morley appear to have won their cases through pedigree evidence and political leverage which existed independently of any heraldic banner, tomb or vestment. There is nothing to show that the presence of heraldry on material objects influenced the final judgments. It is true that Scrope and Morley produced more witnesses who mentioned more objects, but Reginald Grey, confident of his family tree, did not subject the court to nearly as much travel and object-inspection as Edward Hastings insisted upon. The glories of Elsing parish church, the stained glass and tombs in the mendicant houses at Coventry and Doncaster, the transcripts and drawings produced for Hastings in court: none of these made any difference. Ultimately, legal recognition of rights transferred by marriage was what counted.[107]

---

[105] M.A. Michael, 'The Privilege of "Proximity": Towards a Re-definition of the Function of Armorials', *Jnl of Medieval History*, 23 (1997), pp. 55–74.

[106] *The Beauchamp Pageant*, ed. A. Sinclair (Donington, 2003), pp. 84–5.

[107] See I. Jack, 'Entail and Descent: The Hastings Inheritance, 1370 to 1436', *Bull., Institute of Historical Research*, 38 (1965), pp. 1–19; M.H. Keen, 'English Military

Perhaps material objects were only produced by the protagonists because court practice expected it. If so, then this begs the question why the court made demands on what looks from a distance like epiphenomenal, impotent evidence. This question requires deeper investigation than it can receive here; but presumably the officials assumed *a priori* that interrogation of such material might conceivably throw up influential data, and that given this important possibility, the exercise was worth the candle. At the very least, some amount of urban and rural sampling of the distribution and knowledge of arms confirmed the basic legitimacy of a claim. If there had turned out to be very little material evidence to link a given coat of arms to a given protagonist then this would presumably have told against his case; although a single piece of older evidence in a heraldic roll or other source would in theory have trumped any number of more recent instances produced by an opposing party. (This consideration may help to clarify the interest of witnesses in affirming the oldness of the evidence they cited.) In all this, one must keep in mind the fact that medieval standards of proof in a juridical context were often different from the modern ones that are apt to influence casual scholarly assumptions, and conversely, that modern legal praxis also admits impressionistic, epiphenomenal testimony, particularly obviously in the context of jury trials. Here, the expectation, or hope, is that such testimony will appeal to the heart rather than the head. Court of Chivalry cases were not jury trials, but the power of an object like the Hastings brass at Elsing to move such sober, objective men as William Leche and Richard Vaus is still clear enough.

The question of the relationship between material object and heraldry is of a different order. It can be expressed by asking whether the court was really interested in the object *per se* or only in the fact and nature of the heraldry on it. At stake is the medieval understanding of the agency of different sorts of objects as bearers of meaning. It is naturally tempting for the modern scholar with a taxonomist's approach to evidence to anticipate that an object's typology influenced the way that any heraldry displayed on it was understood. Thus, heraldry on a tomb, which stood near or on top of the actual body of its bearer and would witness his or her resurrection at the Last Judgement, might seem to provide relatively strong support for a given claim. Heraldry on objects associated with relics or liturgy appears to draw increased forensic value from spiritual associations – which also discouraged any temptation to dissemble.[108] The same may be said of a shield over the

Experience and the Court of Chivalry: The Case of Grey *v.* Hastings', in *Guerre et société en France, en Angleterre et en Bourgogne, XIVe–XVe siècle*, ed. P. Contamine, C. Giry-Deloison and M.H. Keen (Lille, 1991), pp. 123–42, at 126.

[108] Lying about material evidence for heraldry and pedigree was not obviously an issue in these cases, as it was in other circumstances (see e.g. S.A.C. Dudok van Heel, 'Amsterdamse Burgemeesters zonder Stamboom: Die Dichter Vondel en de Schilder Colijns Vervalsen Geschiedenis', *De Zeventiende Eeuw*, 6 (1990), pp.

door of the Holy House at Walsingham, or one shadowed by the great rood at Norwich cathedral. In such cases, the artefactual settings of heraldry suggest an intention to act in good faith. A panel of glass skied in a nave window or painted on a wall in a refectory may by comparison seem less potent as evidence.

There are two things to say about this. The first is simply that the heraldry displayed on any object had a constituent stake in that object, and vice versa. For practical purposes, it is impossible to distinguish where one ended and another began: the two components were essentially conflated as long as the relationship existed. Thus, whatever general associations a tomb or a chasuble or a seal was imbued with, were shared and presumably influenced by its heraldry in ways that depended on the mental equipment of the viewer. The implications of this conflation can even be stated more emphatically than this, according to scholarly taste. For example, if the point about insepa-rable conflation is acceptable, then objects shared in whatever symbolic and legal status their heraldry possessed. In a rather forbidding article on how medieval heraldry signified, Walter Seitter has made a case for understanding the coat of arms as a 'secondary body' ('Zweitkörper'), with the status of a 'legal entity' ('juristische Person') that can exist independently of its owner by signifying him, or her, in ways that were tantamount to actual presence.[109] The claim is supported by the fact that the heraldic view of a coat of arms is that of the bearer (whether present in effigy or notional) rather than the viewer.[110] Through objects, owners of coats of arms could thus be multiply present in places where they were physically absent in body. Ultimately, the secondary body might transcend the primary one:

> [E]scutcheons and [heraldic] symbols are in many ways stronger than bodies of flesh and blood: at most, they are immortal, and can give a shape to mortal remains in the form of a tomb or reliquary or document; give a permanence to mortal life which can otherwise only be dreamed of, i.e. believed in.[111]

144–51; M.J. Bok, 'Laying Claims to Nobility in the Dutch Republic: Epitaphs, True and False', *Simiolus*, 24 (1996), pp. 209–26). The main implication of the denial of the value of material evidence by a given protagonist (see e.g. Luxford, 'Hastings Brass', p. 206) is that the opposing party was simply mistaken to think a given object or objects relevant.

[109] W. Seitter, 'Das Wappen als Zweitkörper und Körperzeichen', in *Die Wiederkehr des Körpers*, ed. D. Kamper and C. Wulf (Frankfurt am Main, 1982), pp. 299–312. Seitter's ideas are sampled but only partially represented in Belting, *Anthropology of Images*, pp. 62–83 (ch. 3, 'The Coat of Arms and the Portrait: Two Media of the Body').

[110] Seitter, 'Wappen als Zweitkörper', p. 303.

[111] *Ibid.*, p. 304: 'daß Schilde und Zeichen in vieler Hinsicht stärker sind als die Körper aus Fleisch und Blut: im Grenzfall sind sie unsterblich und vermögen als Grabmal oder Reliquienschrein oder Urkunde sterblichen Überresten eine Fassung,

While the force of Seitter's argument depends on one's willingness to accept the ability of arms wherever they were displayed to exert influence over viewers, and also, fundamentally, on how one understands his terminology, the quoted passage undoubtedly resonates with the depositions and summaries of evidence contained in the trial documents. This is not of itself saying very much, because the immortality of heraldry was taken for granted by the protagonists and the court. What matters for present purposes is the idea that this immortality was also expressed through the medium of the individual objects with which the heraldry was conflated. Once attached to something, the blazon could not signify by itself.

However – and this is the second point – there is no support in the court documents for anatomising the simple, indissoluble relationship between heraldry and its support with reference to different sorts of object. If anything, differing social and spatial contexts of heraldic display were more significant than object typology. As noted previously, different types of objects were specified in the court briefs, and tombs and banners, in particular, tend to have been asked after first in the questioning of witnesses. But this is not sound evidence that such things were thought intrinsically more reliable for what they were. It is rather that they were more likely to be situationally reliable, because associated with particular places and historical circumstances: again, this is why the oldness of things with heraldry on them mattered.

Conclusion

It is instructive to observe just how large and varied a body of evidence about material culture spills out of the documentation of just three court cases. Although the testimony was curated, and thus cannot really be taken to represent 'typical' or even widespread knowledge of material heraldry, it is revealing of heraldry's distribution, and also the range of attitudes to it, at least among adult males. One gets a glimpse of the material and heraldic apparatus at the disposal of legally challenged knights which could otherwise be built up only partially, and very laboriously, through surviving fragments and antiquarian sources. The Court of Chivalry documents also show this apparatus – or parts of it – mobilised and exploited to its ultimate ends. They encourage the reflection that widespread distribution of arms not only was normal (see also the Berkeley evidence reported by Smyth of Nibley), but also was calculated to demonstrate mundane entitlements which were essentially unrelated to spiritual commemoration.[112] This is not to imply

sterblichen Leben eine Dauer zu geben – von der ansonsten nur zu träumen, d. h. zu glauben ist'. (My translation.)

[112] Compare what the Florentine banker Francesco Sassetti told his sons coats of arms were for (in 1488): '[family] honour and a sign of our antiquity'. He did not mention

that all coats of arms, or even many of them, were set up with the express intention of supplying legally admissible evidence. However, as is indicated by the documents considered here, they were forensic in the broad sense of being suitable for pleadings in court, and it would probably be misguided to consider those who commissioned them blind to the fact. This conclusion tends to emphasise how close matters of honour, pedigree and status were to the operation of law in a society where litigation was a powerful, anxiety-inducing constant in the changeable course of affairs. While there is, perhaps, nothing very surprising in this, it is worth stressing that the operation of artefacts in relation to any aspect of medieval law is normally hard to grasp. One advantage of the Court of Chivalry records is that they bring the subject to the surface, albeit in a context unusually invested in objects and their display. If the context is unusual, the attitudes and beliefs are not obviously so, and on this basis the three cases of contested arms stand as some of the best available evidence for the social life of things in late medieval England.[113]

commemoration. See F.W. Kent, *Household and Lineage in Renaissance Florence: The Family Life of the Capponi, Ginori, and Rucellai* (Princeton, NJ, 1977), p. 257.

[113] One might also say 'chivalrous life of things': see Keen, 'Chivalrous Culture', p. 22 and *passim*.

CHAPTER 4

Sir Robert Grosvenor and the Scrope–Grosvenor Controversy

Philip Morgan

The Grosvenors of Hulme

Perhaps, like any sensitive parent, Robert Grosvenor had hung on to life until the Christmas season was over. Two days after Epiphany, on 8 January 1465 he made his will. [1] He died on the following day leaving six daughters as his heirs, the estate ultimately divided amongst them, though not explicitly mentioned in the will. Grosvenor's career was by this time lengthy and respectable. He had sat on final concord panels as an esquire, been a collector for the Cheshire tax, the mise, in Northwich hundred, and in 1433 had been granted custody of the lands of Sir Hugh Calveley, son of the great Cheshire soldier; in 1441 he was amongst a select group of Cheshire gentry retained by Humphrey, duke of Buckingham, as men who could broker the duke's influence in the county.[2] Grosvenor's rank and standing in East Cheshire were thus well-established and, as a man in his late fifties, he ought perhaps to have paid more attention to that all too common but always unwelcome prospect for the late-medieval gentry, failure in the male line. The evidence is, however, somewhat equivocal. Aware of the demise of his name and memory at Hulme, and, reacting like many gentry facing similar problems, he had been investing heavily in the building of a new family chapel at nearby Nether Peover.[3] His testament asked for burial in the cemetery there, but its terms were later expanded to include an endowment for a perpetual chaplain to sing for the souls of himself and his wife, Joan, and his heirs in the chapel newly 'being built'. The church of St Oswald at Nether Peover is

---

[1] Chester, Cheshire Archives and Local Studies, DLT/A31/1b. Writs of *diem clausit extremum* were issued on 14 January, and letters of administration were granted by the Dean of Frodsham on 16 January 1465.

[2] Dorothy J. Clayton, *The Administration of the County Palatine of Chester, 1442–1485* (Chetham Soc., 3rd ser., xxxv, 1990), pp. 72, 193, 198.

[3] Nigel Saul, *Lordship and Faith: The English Gentry and the Parish Church in the Middle Ages* (Oxford, 2017), p. 169.

one of the county's surviving timber-framed churches, the body of the church and its aisles all originally under a single timber roof. Grosvenor's chapel was probably the aisle to the south side of the chancel; but the scale of the new building work is not clear from this document, however. Presumably he anticipated that his tomb would be translated there at completion. The remainder of the testament, witnessed by two chaplains and his 'whole household' (*cum tota familia*), not yet dispersed after the Christmas festival, contained cash bequests to his brother, chaplain and servants, with 3*s*. 4*d*. to 'each varlet in his service'. It has about it a palpable sense of urgency.

Certainly there was no mention of the disposition of his lands; his wife Joan, appointed as executrix, was given authority only to dispose of the remainder of his goods. The Grosvenors of Hulme had fallen into oblivion, and Robert Grosvenor's memory now entered into the realm of later legal cases and the antiquarian musings of gentlemen – 'Robert Grosvenor that had the six daughters and coheiresses was no knight', as a later member of the Leycester family would note.[4] Several centuries later it would be revived by the collateral heirs to his name, the dukes of Westminster. The succession of the estate was not a happy one and Robert's brother Ralph, of Eaton near Chester, opposed the partition, arguing that in 1416 Robert's estates had been entailed in the male line by their father, Thomas Grosvenor, with a remainder in the first instance to Ralph himself. Robert the son ought perhaps to have made some provision, since his six daughters were all safely married. In the light of the testament it does indeed seem odd that he appears to have made no preparation for the descent of his lands – though even lawyers were often caught out. The bitterness of the dispute may be judged by the enrolment of ten recognisances of 500 marks to keep the peace between 1466 and 1469. In that year a negotiated settlement was achieved and an award made which upheld the rights of the daughters. Ralph Grosvenor of Eaton received an annual payment for life, although, as the award noted, this was 'by reason of the greate unkindness that hath beene betweene the sayd parties, for the establishment of faithfull love and alliance betweene them, and for no right that the said Raufe yet shews'.[5] That terse phrase, 'no right', consigned to the past, no doubt in the interests of restoring some kind of amity, an elaborate scheme by Ralph to manufacture the necessary evidence of his right, all of which had been revealed in hearings at the episcopal palace in Eccleshall (Staffordshire) and at the collegiate church of St John in Chester in February 1466.

The confession of Nicholas Bothe pointed to an elaborate conspiracy which had produced the forged deed of May 1416 entailing the Grosvenor estates in Cheshire and Staffordshire to the heirs male of Sir Thomas Grosvenor of Hulme (d. 1430), the father of both Robert and Ralph. Bothe was to have been

---

[4] Chester, Cheshire Archives and Local Studies, DLT/A30/26.
[5] George Ormerod, *The History of the County Palatine and City of Chester*, 2nd edn, ed. T. Helsby, 3 vols (London, 1882), III, pp. 149–50.

paid eight marks a year for life, underwritten by a letter of obligation for forty marks for 'the copy and the dede I enforget'. He had met Grosvenor himself at the church at Eccles (Lancashire), purportedly responding to a public assembly where Ralph had denounced those who might be withholding evidence concerning his inheritance. Bothe had volunteered that he had a deed of Grosvenor's father in his possession. Thereafter, mostly using Grosvenor's servant, Jenkyn Robynson, and the vicar of Eccleston as intermediaries, Bothe had attended meetings at a Grosvenor house in Shropshire, at Chester and at Ralph's manor at Eaton, before finally delivering the forgery to him at the house of Henry Bucley in Manchester. The process itself required carefully chosen contacts, and the indenture, blank on one side, had been forged by one Edward Lees of Burnley, and the seal added by an 'old man' named Ralph Walker, both suggested by Bothe. Later, when summoned to appear before the mayor in Chester, Bothe had sworn 'on the book' that Robert Grosvenor had delivered the deed into his hands, 'which was trew because Robert son of Raulyn Grosvenor had given it to me that morning at Eton'. That it was Robert the grandson rather than Robert the grandfather has about it all the glib plausibility of the petty criminal.[6] And, what makes the case of even greater interest is that the Grosvenors had form for forgery.

A generation earlier, in a ceremonial settlement at Macclesfield church in April 1412 the father of Ralph and Robert, Sir Thomas Grosvenor, had been obliged to celebrate mass amongst an assembly of the county's gentry and then affirm on the host that he believed in the veracity of charters by which he claimed estates at Pulford near Chester which were part of a property dispute with Robert Legh of Adlington. Fifty-eight of his gentle neighbours added their own affirmation of his claims in a show of hands, Legh having agreed to a public adjuration as a means of settlement. Michael Bennett has argued that the occasion expressed the solidarity and cohesion of the Cheshire gentry community, some two-thirds of the county's leading men taking part in the occasion.[7] Such large gatherings were not routine but they did depend upon a common culture and experience of regional gentility. And, it was a culture to which Thomas's own father, Sir Robert Grosvenor, had once appealed during a case in the Court of Chivalry between 1385 and 1390. In the summer of 1385 the Yorkshire knight Sir Richard Scrope had challenged Grosvenor during the king's expedition to Scotland for the right to bear the arms *Azure a bend or*, the case later heard by the Constable and the Earl Marshal. Such armorial disputes seem to have been common in the later fourteenth century, although detailed records of proceedings survive for only two further examples, that

---

[6] Chester, Cheshire Archives and Local Studies, DSS 3991/367, DSS 3991/462.

[7] Michael J. Bennett, 'A County Community: Social Cohesion amongst the Cheshire Gentry, 1400–1425', *Northern History*, 8 (1973), pp. 24–44; *idem, Community, Class and Careerism: Cheshire and Lancashire Society in the Age of Sir Gawain and the Green Knight* (Cambridge, 1983), pp. 22–6.

between Reginald, Lord Grey of Ruthyn, and Sir Edward Hastings, following Henry IV's campaign in Scotland in 1400, and that between John, Lord Lovel and Thomas, Lord Morley, like the Scrope–Grosvenor dispute, also as a result of Richard II's expedition to Scotland in 1385.[8]

The Scrope–Grosvenor Case, 1385

The evidence of the Scrope–Grosvenor hearings was published as early as 1832 in an excellent edition by Sir Nicholas Harris Nicolas, but more recent scholarship has been slow to exploit the interest of the three cases. Michael Prestwich was disparaging about the estimates of ages which knights and esquires gave in their testimony, characterised the evidence as 'often tedious depositions', and whilst accepting the importance of heraldry in military service, pointed out that knights at war often discarded arms or wore someone else's.[9] Other historians have been kinder. Andrew Ayton has used the Lovel–Morley evidence to discern the varying patterns of military experience by social rank, especially amongst esquires, whilst Maurice Keen felt that he detected a move away from chivalric values and bellicosity amongst the Grey–Hastings witnesses, dependent as they often were on the experiences of 'old soldiers'.[10] Contrariwise, two studies of the Scrope–Grosvenor materials have dealt with the testimonies more as literary texts indicative of the construction of social memory – memories of the military workplace in Joel Rosenthal's neat phrase, although he adds the observation that Scrope's witnesses bore a close relationship to the Lancastrian affinity.[11] More ambitiously, and also less comfortably for most empirical historians, Robert Barrett has seen the testimonies as a chivalric 'topographic inscription', regional writing shouting its distinctive part in the Trojan diaspora, the legal speech of the Court of Chivalry being rooted in the same soil and culture as texts like the poem

---

[8] Andrew Ayton, 'Knights, Esquires and Military Service: The Evidence of the Armorial Cases before the Court of Chivalry,' in *The Medieval Military Revolution: State, Society and Military Change in Medieval and Early Modern Europe*, ed. A. Ayton and J.L. Price (London, 1995), pp. 81–104, at 84–5.

[9] Michael Prestwich, *Armies and Warfare in the Middle Ages: The English Experience* (New Haven, Conn., and London, 1986), pp. 54, 113, 223.

[10] Ayton, 'Knights, Esquires and Military Service', pp. 96–7; Maurice Keen, 'English Military Experience and the Court of Chivalry: The Case of Grey v. Hastings', in *Guerre et société en France, en Angleterre et en Bourgogne, XIVe–XVe siècle*, ed. P. Contamine, Charles Giry-Deloison, and Maurice Keen (Villeneuve d'Ascq, dépt. Nord, 1991), pp. 123–42, at 134–6; reprinted in M.H. Keen, *Nobles, Knights and Men-at-Arms in the Middle Ages* (London and Rio Grande, OH, 1996), pp. 167–85, at 177–8.

[11] Joel Rosenthal, *Telling Tales: Sources and Narration in Late Medieval England* (University Park, Pa., 2003), pp. 88–91.

Gawain and the Green Knight.[12] My own more modest question here is to say a little about the biography of the Cheshire deponent, Sir Robert Grosvenor, and to ask what the evidence has to show about his family's relationship to its own past and lineage. We must needs start with the meeting between two knights outside both of their countries on England's northern border.

Richard II's first military campaign to Scotland as an eighteen-year-old is sometimes seen as the king's assertion of a manly authority in the face of a political opposition which deployed his youth and effeminate looks in an effort permanently to infantilise him.[13] The result was one of the largest English armies raised in the fourteenth century, of at least 13,000 men, some veterans of the lean years of the Hundred Years War but many, like the king, bearing arms for the first time. In July 1385, as Michael Bennett has shrewdly observed, 'it must have seemed that all England was heading north'.[14] Although serving for pay the army was summoned by feudal levy, the last summons of this kind in the Middle Ages, but from which Cheshire was traditionally exempt. The veteran Cheshire knight and professional soldier, Sir David Hulgreve, led ten men-at-arms and ten archers, whilst ten other men led a combined retinue of some 439 men-at-arms and archers, all in the mainguard of the army, the costs of six of the retinues borne by the chamberlain of Chester. Other Cheshiremen served in the retinues of other lords, including Peter and John Legh of Lyme who were in the following of the king's half-brother Sir John Holland.[15] Neither Sir Richard Scrope nor Sir Robert Grosvenor seem to have been listed as leaders of retinues in Scotland in their own right, nor even to have taken out letters of protection and attorney.[16] The campaign of 1385 is famous for its brevity; the Scottish border was crossed on 6 August but the army had returned to England by 20 August. Although Richard II is credited with putting his enemies to flight, and responded to his success with a group of noble promotions, it had been an unhappy campaign in other ways. Camped outside York on 16 July whilst the royal army was en route to Scotland, Sir Ralph Stafford, heir of Hugh, earl of Stafford, was killed in a brawl at Bustardthorpe on the outskirts of the city by the king's cousin, Sir John Holland. The two Legh brothers, members of Holland's retinue, were indicted alongside him, though it is not clear whether

---

[12] Robert W. Barrett, *Against All England: Regional Identity and Cheshire Writing, 1195–1656* (Notre Dame, Ind., 2009), pp. 140–52.

[13] Christopher Fletcher, *Richard II: Manhood, Youth and Politics, 1377–99* (Oxford, 2008), p. 137.

[14] M.J. Bennett, 'William Called Long Will', *The Yearbook of Langland Studies*, 26 (2012), pp. 1–25, at 10–11.

[15] Gary Paul Baker, 'The English Way of War, 1360–1399'. Ph.D. thesis, University of Hull, 2011, pp. 321–7; Kew, TNA, Special Collections, Ministers' & Receivers' Accounts, SC 6/772/20; Bennett, 'William Called Long Will', p. 13.

[16] Baker, 'The English Way of War', pp. 321–7.

other Cheshire retinues were camped here as well. We cannot be sure then exactly when or where Sir Richard Scrope and Sir Robert Grosvenor first confronted each other on the matter of their shared arms. A general proclamation summoning the parties to a preliminary hearing in Newcastle on 20 August was made throughout the king's host in Scotland on the 17 August, so perhaps the challenge had been made when the army itself was assembled in Scotland.[17] Whilst Stafford's murder attracted the attention of many chroniclers, none mentioned the two heraldic disputes which arose thereafter, not even the short set of annals composed in Chester covering the years 1385 to 1388 which do mention the expedition.[18]

The first hearings in Newcastle had adjourned the case to be heard before the Constable and the Marshal in the White Chamber in the palace of Westminster on 20 October 1385, although postponements and delays meant that it was not until 28 May 1386 that the final form of the process of enquiry was established: parallel sets of regional commissioners nominated by the parties, who would invite the production of ancient charters and authentic proofs alongside the testimony of 'men of honour'. The two parties named their commissioners at this stage, and by 21 January 1387 they were to have made their proofs 'by view of charters, chronicles, tombs, and the testimony of abbots, priors and other men of the Holy Church', as well as by 'lords, knights and esquires of honour, and gentlemen having knowledge of arms and by no other men of the commons or of other estate'.[19] The calculation of social rank already weighed heavily in favour of Sir Richard Scrope; amongst his nominees was the archbishop of York and the bishops of Durham and Lincoln. The list of Scrope's secular commissioners included Grosvenor's regional neighbours in north Wales, Lancashire and Staffordshire, as well as some Cheshiremen such as Sir John Mascy of Puddington in Wirral. Grosvenor's more modest list contained the abbot of Dieulacres and the chamberlain of Chester but signally omitted his own diocesan, Richard Scrope, who was appointed to the see at Lichfield on 18 August 1386. He had received his first rectory from his uncle, Richard Scrope of Bolton, Grosvenor's rival claimant.[20]

The surviving evidence for the Grosvenor examinations is in three sources. The original roll, stitched Chancery style, is incomplete, although three membranes were recovered from the unsorted miscellanea of the Chancery as recently as 1927.[21] Sir Nicholas Harris Nicolas's edition of 1832 prints all but

---

[17] Alastair J. MacDonald, *Border Bloodshed: Scotland and England at War, 1369–1403* (East Linton, East Lothian, 2000), pp. 87–95.

[18] Philip Morgan, 'Historical Writing in the North-West Midlands and the Chester Annals of 1385–88', *Fourteenth Century England*, IX, ed. J. Bothwell and G. Dodd (2016), pp. 109–29, at 127–9.

[19] Nicolas, *Scrope and Grosvenor Controversy*, I, pp. 40–1.

[20] Peter McNiven, 'Scrope, Richard (c. 1350–1405)', in *ODNB*, 49, pp. 562–4.

[21] Kew, TNA, Chancery Miscellanea, C 47/6/3. Membranes 25–7 were returned

these last three membranes of the roll, but in 1832 he reported that much of the roll was 'disarranged, imperfect, and occasionally much defaced ... Traces exist of the membranes having been fastened together; but there is no figure or mark to show the order.'[22] His edition follows the order of an abstract of the original roll made by the Cheshire archivist and merchant, Ralph Starkey (d. 1628), which listed the names of the witnesses and the places at which they had been examined.[23] In another 'booke of coppies of euidence' Starkey recorded the mandate of 11 December 1390 for the deposit into Chancery of the records in the case of Scrope and Grosvenor.[24] Soon thereafter the Cheshire knight, Sir Richard Grosvenor of Eaton, commissioned a copy of the proceedings with an illuminated frontispiece showing Richard II, each of the witness testimonies being prefaced by an illuminated copy of the arms *Azure a bend or,* and three half-page portraits, one of Sir Richard Scrope and another of Sir Robert Grosvenor, each bearing a banner with the arms and standing by a pennon of the same, and a final portrait of the two knights standing together holding shields, Scrope with the original arms and Grosvenor with the arms differenced by a *bordure argent.*[25] By contrast, the evidence for the Scrope case is in excellent condition.[26]

The examinations of witnesses which took place between September 1386 and January 1387 followed an irregular itinerary in Cheshire, Lancashire and at Coventry. The commissioners were local men, and included ones with substantial clerical experience. John Rossendale had probably acted as town clerk in Macclesfield.[27] Although the Grosvenor evidence is on the whole more formulaic than that on behalf of the Scropes, the loss of nearly sixty of the testimonies on behalf of Grosvenor is problematic, not least since it included some important figures such as Sir John Mascy of Tatton. Those who did appear on his behalf are a fair sample of Cheshire society, representative but not comprehensive. None of the Venables, one of the Cheshire families which maintained the antique title of 'baron', gave evidence, and nor did Sir Nicholas Audley of Helegh, at whose castle Richard II was to stay on his visit to Cheshire in 1387. And in the current literature it is difficult to escape

---

in 1927 by Charles Johnson and add some of Scrope's objections to Grosvenor witnesses.

[22] Nicolas, *Scrope and Grosvenor Controversy,* I, p. 359.

[23] London, BL, MS Harley 293, pp. 183–93. There are abstracts, made *c.* 1597, in BL, MS Lansdowne 85, art. 75.

[24] London, BL, MS Add. 39851, p.56.

[25] Chester, Eaton Hall, Grosvenor Estate Archives, Adds 1264. The references given in *The Papers of Sir Richard Grosvenor, 1st Bart. (1585–1645),* ed. Richard Cust (Record Soc. of Lancs. & Ches., cxxxiv, 1996), pp. xii and xxix n. 15 have been superseded. The order of the transcript is closer to that of the current sequence in Kew, TNA, Chancery Miscellanea, C 47/6/3.

[26] Kew, TNA, Chancery Miscellanea, C 47/6/2.

[27] Bennett, *Community, Class and Careerism* (cit. in n. 7), p. 149.

from the prejudice that the Grosvenors were somehow unworthy opponents, knights from the periphery, and not fluent in French. Who then was Sir Robert Grosvenor?

Sir Robert Grosvenor and Hulme (Cheshire)

Sir Robert Grosvenor's estates were listed in his inquisition *post mortem* in 1396, and extended across a modest territory in east Cheshire.[28] According to the jurors he held two manors, both by socage tenure: at Hulme from John Holford, one of his witnesses, and at Allostock from the abbot of Vale Royal, who had also given evidence for him. Other lands in Nether Peover, Henbury and Pexall, Over Alderley, Kettleshulme and Dunham Mascy were valued at little more than £40 annually; the sheriff had ordered seizure of his goods to meet arrears in the office of sheriff of some £210. It is for that reason that the inquisition *post mortem* also includes an inventory of the manor house at Hulme. It is a revealing document which values Grosvenor's possessions at little more than £200, with a further £50 for the value of crops and livestock at Allostock. Grosvenor's annual income, if one uses the calculations applied to the gentry of Nottinghamshire, would have placed him at the lower margin of the second rank of gentle families, only a small group of about ten Nottinghamshire families having an annual income of above £100, with a further fifteen in the range of £40 to £100.[29] More significant was the fact that the Grosvenor estates were tightly focused within a few neighbouring parishes, a feature of many Cheshire gentry estates.[30]

The Cheshire Lostocks, two townships in an unprepossessing and watery landscape on the edge of Rudheath, 'pig sty hamlet', probably named from the pasturage of swine on Rudheath, had been divided in the late eleventh century. One portion was named Nether or Lower Lostock to distinguish it from Allostock, possibly Hall or Old Lostock. Lostock was also referred to as Lostock Gralam from the late twelfth century, a manorial suffix derived from the grandson of the original grantee, whilst Allostock acquired a manorial affix much later in the thirteenth century, although the name 'Grosvenoreslostock' is not attested until 1329.[31] Although the philological detail seems complex, the outline of the development of landscape and lordship is clear enough

[28] Kew, TNA, Palatinate of Chester: Exchequer of Chester: Inquisitions Various, CHES 3/15(9).

[29] S.J. Payling, *Political Society in Lancastrian England: The Greater Gentry of Nottinghamshire* (Oxford, 1991), p. 14.

[30] *A New Historical Atlas of Cheshire*, ed. A.D.M. Phillips and C.B. Phillips (Chester, 2002), pp. 32–5.

[31] Chester, Cheshire Archives and Local Studies, DSS 3991/181/37; John McN. Dodgson, *The Place-Names of Cheshire*, Pt II (English Place-Name Soc., xlv, 1970), pp. 189–90, 216–18.

Table 4.1 Scrope *v.* Grosvenor: The Grosvenor witness hearings, 1386–7

Date of hearing	Place of hearing	Names of commissioners	Number of witnesses; Source
4 September 1386	Chester, St John	Sir John Woodhouse, the chamberlain William Bromburgh, parson of Aldford	34 + 1 (lost) Kew, TNA, C 47/6/3, mm. 1, 2, 9, 10, 11, 15,
8 September 1386	Stockport	Sir Nicholas Vernon William Bromburgh, parson of Aldford John Rossendale	43 (14 lost) Kew, TNA, C 47/6/3, mm. 2, 3
11 September 1386	Knutsford	Sir Nicholas Vernon William Bromburgh, parson of Aldford	Lost
12–13 September 1386	Warrington Friary	Sir John Butler, baron of Warrington Sir Nicholas Vernon Sir Thomas Gerard William Bromburgh, parson of Aldford	35 Kew, TNA, C 47/6/3, mm. 3, 7, 13
19 September 1386	Lancaster Castle	Sir John Butler, baron of Warrington Sir Thomas Gerard	28 Kew, TNA, C 47/6/3, mm. 4, 6
1 October 1386	Nantwich	William Bromburgh, parson of Aldford John Rossendale	13 Kew, TNA, C 47/6/3, mm. 5, 12
26 November 1386	Coventry Priory	Thomas Stretton, canon of Lichfield John Grendon Esq.	13 (lost)
8 January 1387	Sandbach	William Bromburgh, parson of Aldford John Rossendale	5 (lost)
9–12 January 1387	Chester: St Mary on the Hill	William Bromburgh, parson of Aldford John Rossendale	12 + 25 (lost)

for it was at Allostock that a branch of the Grosvenor family had sought to establish its territorial authority in the thirteenth century. This is a process especially characteristic of the lesser and even the parochial gentry, confined by a narrow landscape but entirely visible and often the dominant authority within that same local territory. The building of halls and chapels, and the exploitation of the agrarian landscape, perhaps by new nucleated settlement or the construction of mills, are hallmarks of the process, and the acquisition of a manorial affix indicative of a place-name revolution which greatly expanded the repertoire of English place-names in the thirteenth and fourteenth centuries and connected it firmly to the rise of the English gentry.[32] The Grosvenor enterprise, however, was only partially successful.

The family's two principal estates, at Hulme and Allostock, formed part of a single township within the chapelry of Nether Peover in one of Cheshire's great parishes, that at Great Budworth, and the rise of a spiritual authority in the creation of a lordly parish was of paramount importance. The church at Great Budworth had formed part of the original endowment in *c.* 1115 of Runcorn priory, later the Augustinian house at Norton, founded by William fitz Nigel, the constable of Chester, and the connection would be important, not least because Norton was amongst Cheshire's older houses, possessed of its own significant historical traditions.[33] The loss of the prior of Norton's testimony to the Scrope–Grosvenor hearings is thus especially to be regretted. But in 1269 Robert Grosvenor was the leading man amongst a group of 'parishioners' who reached an agreement with the prior of Norton for the provision of a parochial chapel with rights of baptism subject to the mother church at Great Budworth at Nether Peover.[34] To a lordly chapel the family soon added a lordly residence, and a late-thirteenth-century deed speaks of a 'new hall' of the Grosvenors in an outlying site to the west of Allostock.[35] But a mill, that final symbol of lordly rule, may have been a late acquisition. Grosvenor's acquisition of Hulme in the mid-thirteenth century had explicitly been made subject to a prohibition of the construction of a mill, and he seems only to have acquired Allostock mill in the 1270s, from Adam Marston.[36]

---

[32] Richard Jones, 'Thinking Through the Manorial Affix: People and Place in Medieval England', in *Life in Medieval Landscapes: People and Places in the Middle Ages. Papers in Memory of H.S.A. Fox*, ed. Sam Turner and Bob Silvester (Oxford, 2012), pp. 251–67.

[33] Patrick Greene, *Norton Priory* (Cambridge, 1989), pp. 1–18.

[34] Chester, Cheshire Archives and Local Studies, DSS 3991/182/1.

[35] H. Farnham Burke, 'Some Cheshire Deeds', *The Ancestor*, no. 2 (July 1902), pp. 129–47, at 132. The Grosvenor of Hulme deeds seem not to have been greatly used by antiquaries and historians, and long remained in private hands but now form part of the Shakerley of Hulme and Somerford collection at the Cheshire archives office. The latter's catalogue is a terse one; however, a large number of the early deeds were calendared by Burke in *The Ancestor*, while still in private hands.

[36] Chester, Cheshire Archives and Local Studies, DSS 3991/566; Burke, 'Some Cheshire Deeds', p. 141.

We know a good deal, however, about the Grosvenors' lordly hall at Hulme thanks to the inventory included with the inquisition *post mortem* of Sir Robert Grosvenor in 1396.

Hulme Hall stands within a characteristic moated site, an island *c.* 60m × 54m, surrounded by a waterlogged moat *c.* 10m–30m wide and 1.5m deep with a 10m-square projection at the southern corner. It is much the same size as the moated site at Lea Newbold, which was acquired by the Calveleys in the fourteenth century, such sites being generally designed to proclaim the authority and prestige of their holders.[37] The moat was crossed by a stone-built bridge and the platform contains the undated footprint of an H-plan house; in 1396 'Grosvenour Hulme' contained a hall, knight's chamber, chapel, buttery, and wine cellar, with an associated granary, cattle shed, and stable.[38] The knight's chamber was perhaps the solar. A later inventory, of 1429, lists the lesser chamber, pantry, buttery, larder, dayhouse, malthouse, and haybarn, as well as the nightingale arbour, the little arbour, and the bridge.[39] In 1590 the Chester herald, Randle Holme, noted that 'in the roofe round the hall are painted these coats of arms [eighteen shields, including *Azure a bend or*] but some are worne out'.[40] The hall's furnishings are those appropriate to a knightly residence, the knight's chamber containing a hauberk, plate armour, daggers and a sword called 'le conquestshor' valued at 26s., together with furred cloaks, jewellery and other silver work, and a hart in the king's livery worth 26s. 8d. The chapel contained vestments, a chalice, dossals (embroidered wall cloths) and a breviary. At the time of the Scottish expedition Grosvenor sat on commissions of the peace, and in early 1389, in the midst of the case before the Court of Chivalry, he was also appointed sheriff of the county and deputy constable of Chester castle.[41] Here then was a man whose current social rank and standing in Cheshire were unimpeachable, a leading man of knightly status in a distinctive regional society. But what would be at issue in the case before the Court of Chivalry was rather ancient lineage, the veracity of the claim of both families that their status was not newly made but inherited, and also that it conformed to the expectations of a chivalric culture, and that their ancestors had fought in war. As the orders to the commissioners in 1386 had suggested, witnesses were to be asked 'whether Robert and his predecessors had borne arms and in what lands, reigns, wars and campaigns, under which kings, princes, earls and captains'.[42]

---

[37] Chester, Cheshire Historic Environment Record, 744/1/1, 1800/1.

[38] Kew, TNA, Palatinate of Chester: Exchequer of Chester: Inquisitions Various, CHES 3/15/9.

[39] *Ibid.*, CHES 3/34/4.

[40] London, BL, MS Harley 2151, p. 169.

[41] Kew, TNA, Palatinate of Chester: Exchequer of Chester Enrolments, CHES 2/61, mm.1d, 3d.

[42] Nicolas, *Scrope and Grosvenor Controversy*, I, pp. 252–3.

The calibration of gentility: Warfare, honour and arms

The contemporary standing of the Scrope family was of a qualitatively different order. The mere count of witnesses, 246 appearing for Scrope and 151 for Grosvenor, taken alongside the imbalance between the two groups – Scrope mustering a duke, earls and bishops in his favour – must have seemed intimidating to Grosvenor's counsel. Brigette Vale further argues that Scrope's witnesses reflected a wider network of influence and connection in the country, whilst Grosvenor's were more closely tied to his affinity and family in the north west.[43] But whilst the Scropes were undoubtedly better connected, their recent history was not altogether different. Both families, as Lionel Stones long ago pointed out, were newly made, the Scropes descending from the lawyerly careers of two brothers (Sir Geoffrey Scrope, d. 1340, and Sir Henry Scrope, d. 1336) which had transformed initially modest family estates, and the Grosvenors from lesser gentry slowly moving ahead in a relatively closed county community.[44] The very recent construction of Bolton castle, with building commencing only in 1378 and not being completed until 1399, may have been a much grander symbol of the Scropes' family authority in Yorkshire, but the vocabulary was no different to that of the Grosvenors at the start of the century.[45] And even a lordly castle could house a lawyer. Sir John Mascy of Tatton, who gave evidence both for Scrope and for his Cheshire neighbour and cousin, Sir Robert Grosvenor, coldly observed that, 'he had heard that two of his (Scrope's) ancestors had borne the said arms, that Sir Richard Scrope had a man of law for his father, and that another man of law was father of Sir Henry Scrope, the which were the first men of the Scropes who had used the said arms'.[46] The slur was echoed elsewhere and may have been deployed on the advice of Grosvenor's counsel. It was well enough known for at least one of Scrope's witnesses to offer a rebuttal. John Thirlwall, who recalled the demise of Scrope's father, Sir Henry Scrope (d.1336), when the old knight 'could not walk for some time before his decease', and noted that the old man had addressed his sons from his death-bed, warning that 'I hear that some say that Sir Henry Scrope is no great gentleman because he is a man of the law.'[47] It was indeed the law which had advanced the Scropes, and E.L.G. Stones felt that their witnesses in the Court of Chivalry were at pains to stress their prowess in war and at the tournament lest their descent from a

---

[43] Brigette Vale, 'The Scropes of Bolton and of Masham, *c.* 1300–*c.* 1450: A Study of a Northern Noble Family, with a Calendar of the Scrope of Bolton Cartulary', Ph.D. thesis, University of York, 1987, 2 vols, I, pp. 95–105.

[44] Brigette Vale, 'Scrope, Sir Geoffrey (*d.* 1340)', in *ODNB*, 49, pp. 550–1.

[45] Vale, 'The Scropes of Bolton', I, pp. 89–90.

[46] Nicolas, *Scrope and Grosvenor Controversy*, I, p. 79.

[47] *Ibid.*, I, pp. 181–3, and II, pp. 425–7.

family of lawyers, however eminent, be thought unwarlike.[48] Henry Scrope's death-bed homily reminded everyone that his father had been knighted at Falkirk in the disputed arms. In such ways the memories of the dead could be remembered by the living. Once the full impact of this worry is acknowledged, much of the significance of the evidence from witnesses on both sides can be properly grasped.

Neither knight doubted the other's honour, or indeed his right to bear arms, but merely his right of precedence. One of Scrope's witnesses, Thomas Marshal, agreed that Grosvenor 'was a gentleman from a good family'.[49] Indeed the witnesses on both sides seem to have been bound by a kind of chivalric *omertà* when it came to knowledge of the occasions on which they might have seen the other claimant in the disputed arms. This is especially the case for the eleven Cheshire witnesses who gave evidence for Sir Richard Scrope at Chester, most of whom seem to have known nothing. Sir Hugh Calveley of Cheshire, examined only on behalf of Scrope, had agreed that he had seen Scrope in the arms, and had not seen Grosvenor before the Scottish expedition, but had also heard that Grosvenor had the greater right.[50] The exception elsewhere, of course, is the well-known testimony of Geoffrey Chaucer (Fig. 4.1), examined in the refectory at Westminster abbey on 15 October 1386, and who seems to have been the only witness to have challenged Grosvenor over the bearing of the arms *Azure a bend or*, seen by him hanging outside an inn in Friday Street in London as he was walking down the road.[51] But though literary scholars have squeezed the testimony for a secure date of the poet's birth, none seem to have worried precisely when Chaucer might have been walking down Friday Street. It is a question of some moment, to which we need later to return, although here we must consider the broader discourse of the witnesses. They were invited to report upon the evidence of material culture, charters, chronicles, glass, tombs and buildings, to record their own memories of these things and of actual campaigns, and to affirm the lengths of their own careers in arms. Some commentators have mistrusted the reports, have questioned the veracity of particular memories, and have looked to undermine certain witnesses whom they have caught out in inconsistencies, seeing the returns as being as fictive as inquisitions for *probatio aetatis*.[52] Certainly the process itself must have encouraged a certain homogeneity to the reports, prescribed questions producing standard answers; the recent rise in military participation, especially in England or

---

[48] E.L.G Stones, 'Sir Geoffrey Le Scrope (*c.* 1285–1340)', Ph.D. thesis, Glasgow University, 1950, p. 16.

[49] Nicolas, *Scrope and Grosvenor Controversy*, I, p. 64.

[50] *Ibid.*, I, pp. 69, 79–83.

[51] *Ibid.*, I, p. 178.

[52] Philip Morgan, 'Making the English Gentry', in *Thirteenth Century England*, V (1995), 24–7; Rosenthal, *Telling Tales* (cit. in n. 11), p. 63.

4.1 Geoffrey Chaucer's witness-statement in the case Scrope *v.* Grosvenor. TNA, Chancery Miscellanea, C 47/6/2.

Scotland, must have encouraged a greater awareness of arms. Many of the hearings which collected evidence for Sir Richard Scrope were held in the south-west of England, close to the ports used for the embarkation of John of Gaunt's army to Castile in 1386; twenty-one were life retainers of the duke, with another twenty-five retained just for this campaign.[53] Real military experience, both very recent and from the youths of older soldiers, lay at the heart of their evidence and formed the bonds of bands of brothers. In the case of Sir Robert Grosvenor it extended beyond the Scottish campaign of the summer of 1385, for in the late summer and autumn of 1386 a French invasion was felt to be imminent. Richard II intended to lead the defence of his kingdom in person and musters were ordered for Michaelmas, troops to be kept within a sixty-mile radius of London. From Cheshire, 18 retinues comprising some 43 men-at-arms and 818 mounted archers were dispatched to the sea coast in preparation for the invasion.[54] Grosvenor is not listed as a captain in the account of the Cheshire chamberlain, but he had taken out letters of protection on 26 September, and later received a reward from the Crown for coming to the aid of the king.[55] Of 38 Cheshire captains, half acted as witnesses for Grosvenor during his case before the Court of Chivalry, including Sir William Brereton of Brereton who was fined £20 for his refusal to give testimony to the proctor of Sir Richard Scrope. He was, as he later admitted, Grosvenor's cousin in the third and fourth degrees.[56] That such a proportion of evidence on both sides was taken from men actually going to war is, I think, of some significance.

And so to Friday Street. On what possible occasion might Geoffrey Chaucer have seen arms borne by Robert Grosvenor in London? According to the evidence of witnesses, Grosvenor's military career had been revived in 1385; he had not served abroad since the collapse of the Principality of Aquitaine in 1369, being then cited for desertion.[57] If, as seems entirely plausible, it was the routine issue of letters of protection and attorney which brought Grosvenor to London, then the only likely occasion for the meeting was the autumn of 1386; the Cheshire knight had, of course, continued to bear the disputed arms, and had displayed them outside his temporary town house. Within the space of a month Chaucer had challenged a household servant there. The poet's evidence has generally been taken as a sign of his

---

[53] Vale, 'The Scropes of Bolton', I, p. 103.

[54] Fletcher, *Richard II*, 143–6; Kew, TNA, Special Collections Ministers' and Receivers' Accounts, SC 6/772/20.

[55] Kew, TNA, Palatinate of Chester: Exchequer of Chester: Enrolments, CHES 2/57, m. 6d; Vale, 'The Scropes of Bolton', I, p. 116.

[56] Nicolas, *Scrope and Grosvenor Controversy*, I, p. 83.

[57] Philip Morgan, *War and Society in Medieval Cheshire, 1277–1403* (Chetham Soc., 3rd ser., xxxiv, 1987), pp. 132, 147.

own accepted social status in London; he might also have been just a stooge, sent to question Grosvenor's standing in the capital.[58]

A certain reticence amongst soldiers to challenge each other's arms was understandable. The adoption of arms still embodied a variety of practices, including grants by lords to their followers. In 1404 James Tuchet, Lord Audley, holder of estates which straddled the Cheshire–Staffordshire border, had granted arms derived from his own to two brothers,[59] and a number of Cheshire families already bore arms related to those of the Audleys, whether by grant of the family or in allusion to their authority in the region. In 1417 Henry V sought to regulate the process, complaining that on recent campaigns too many men had adopted *cotearmures* for which they had had no grant by a person of sufficient authority.[60] That there might have been a scramble for arms at the end of the fourteenth century is perhaps not altogether a fanciful suggestion. Two of the witnesses in the Scrope and Grosvenor hearings, Sir John Mascy of Tatton and Sir John Mascy of Puddington, had themselves been involved in a case before the Court of Chivalry at Gloucester in November 1378 concerning the arms *Quarterly, or and gules, in the first a lion passant argent*, which the lieutenants of the Constable and Marshal wearily observed neither had actually carried. The award granted both parties the arms *Quarterly or and gules* differenced from each other, but prohibited recourse by either family to the arms under debate.[61] It is difficult not to see the dispute as a speculative bid for a simpler form of the arms which both families already carried. It was in this fashion that the evidence of real and recent experience, as well as national politics, gave way to history and lineage.

The lordship of time

Both the Scrope and Grosvenor families had created foundation myths for their lines, and both have been dismissed as nugatory. At two religious houses, Watton and Bardney, ecclesiastical supporters of the Scropes were involved in identifying the autochthonous founder of the family, but produced two

[58] Derek Pearsall, *The Life of Geoffrey Chaucer* (Oxford, 1992), pp. 9–10.

[59] W. Paley Baildon, 'Heralds' College and Prescription', Pt IV, *The Ancestor*, no. 9 (April 1904), pp. 214–24, at 219.

[60] Oxford, Queen's College, MS 139, no. 3; Anthony R. Wagner, *Heralds and Heraldry in the Middle Ages: An Enquiry into the Growth of the Armorial Function of Heralds*, 2nd edn (London, 1956), pp. 56–64. I am grateful to John Titterton for discussion on this issue and for advance sight of his edition of two original grants of arms of 1415 and 1442 from Staffordshire.

[61] The original case does not survive but the award is noted in a number of later antiquarian manuscripts and in the visitation record of William Flower in 1580, London, BL, MS Harley 1178, f. 44; Chester, Cheshire Archives and Local Studies, DDX 364/1, ff. 56–7.

candidates. The cellarer at Watton had asserted that the first Scrope was noted in a list of the companions of the Conqueror, but that he could not recall his proper name; whilst the prior of Bardney abbey pointed to the family of Richard Scrob, a favourite of Edward the Confessor who had settled in England before the Conquest, and was later involved in the suppression of the rising of Eadric the Wild from 1067 to 1069. The former may perhaps allude to a source somewhat similar to the Battle Abbey Roll, the latter to a version of the chronicle of John of Worcester, though it seems unlikely that the connection can have formed part of the Scrope family history until 1386. Grosvenor's objections drew attention to the apparent contradictions between the two founding fathers.[62] From the outset Sir Robert Grosvenor had likewise asserted that his right to the arms *Azure a bend or* rested on the fact that a Sir Gilbert Grosvenor had entered England bearing the same arms with William the Conqueror, and was a cousin of the first earl of Chester, Hugh of Avranches. The appropriate genealogy was rehearsed by the abbot of Vale Royal as of 'common fame and opinion in Cheshire and neighbouring counties'; his testimony was likewise rebutted by Scrope as a forgery composed without recourse to chronicles or authentic evidence in a religious house of recent foundation.[63] But Grosvenor did in fact proffer a second aboriginal founder to explain the family's presence at Allostock. In the testimony of Sir John Holford, Grosvenor's superior lord at Hulme and Allostock, the knight presents a complex justification for the family's ancient status. He accepts that Grosvenor's ancestor had arrived in the company of Earl Hugh of Chester at the time of the Conquest, but then recounts how the earl had recovered the lordship of Lostock from a man killed at the 'battle of Nampwiche' and had passed it to Hugh de Rowechamp, an ancestor of Holford himself who had granted it to Robert the son of the founding Gilbert.[64] There is here an inventive attempt to explain by misdirection the existence of two branches of Grosvenors, one at Great Budworth and a second at Hulme and Allostock, as well as a certain truncation of the necessary chronology. The battle of 'Nantwich' – perhaps properly speaking Wych Brook on the county boundary – took place in 1146 when Robert Montalt defeated Madog ap Maredudd.[65] In both cases, however, it is important to recognise that both accounts of family origins functioned as origin myths. Whether either, or even both, had circulated within the two families and amongst their neighbours as part of the creation and upholding of esteem and self-validation over any length of time, or whether both were essentially *pièces*

---

[62] Nicolas, *Scrope and Grosvenor Controversy*, I, pp. 229–30, 323.

[63] *Ibid.*, I, pp. 253–4.

[64] *Ibid.*, I, pp. 269–70.

[65] Philip Morgan, 'Cheshire and Wales', in *Power and Identity in the Middle Ages. Essays in Memory of Rees Davies*, ed. Huw Pryce and John Watts (Oxford, 2007), pp. 195–210, at 200.

d'occasion, essentially proclamatory and educative in the context of the events of 1385, is perhaps a moot point, though the evidence is that Grosvenor had done so in collaboration with the abbot of St Werburgh in Chester. William Hulme, examined in Stockport, said that after the start of the case the abbot, Thomas Newport, had told him that he had established from the abbey's chronicles and muniments that the Grosvenors had arrived in the company of Earl Hugh of Chester. Newport died in March 1386 and his successor, Abbot William Merston (who survived only until January 1387), supplied what can only be described as a terse statement of support, omitting the detail of the eponymous founder, but noting that he had seen the name in the abbey's *sanctorum prisca*, the foundation charter of the abbey.[66]

More concrete evidence was that of material culture. Both parties here could point to tombs, seals, glass and manuscripts, though the survival of such things has been kinder to the Scropes. The evidence of Sir Andrew Luttrell does not cite the well-known psalter in which the arms of his mother, Beatrice Scrope, appear twice. And, despite the chapel breviary there is no Grosvenor manuscript to compare with the copy of the *Speculum Devotorum* that bears the arms of John Scrope, fourth Baron Masham.[67] Occasional finds of medieval horse furniture are generally attributed to the Scrope family on no better grounds than the family's success in the Court of Chivalry.[68] The Grosvenor witnesses pointed to the appearance of the family's arms in thirteen Cheshire churches but none now survives, and only one is known from the record of Early Modern church notes.[69] Burials too were problematic since the large size of Cheshire parishes created great competition for burials in mother churches, and Nether Peover acquired burial rights only in the fourteenth century, although Hamo Ashley did mention a cross in the cemetery there with the Grosvenor arms, close to the spot where another witness had seen the burial of Robert's father. Thomas Buddenhale, the rector of Rostherne, remembered the burial of Sir Robert's grandfather at Great Budworth and the

---

[66] Nicolas, *Scrope and Grosvenor Controversy*, I, p. 272. A Radulfus Venator, Ralph the Huntsman, appears in the charter, for which see *The Charters of the Anglo-Norman Earls of Chester, c. 1071–1237*, ed. Geoffrey Barraclough (Record Soc. of Lancs & Ches., 126, 1988), nos 3, 28.

[67] Michael Camille, *Mirror in Parchment: The Luttrell Psalter and the Making of Medieval England* (London, 1998), p. 65; Paul J. Patterson, 'Myrror to devout people (*Speculum devotorum*): An Edition with Commentary', Ph.D. thesis, University of Notre Dame, In. 2006, p. 1.

[68] Lot 2312 sold by TimeLine Auctions Limited, sale of Antiquities, Harwich, 23–4 February 2017, was listed as '13th–14th century AD. A gilt-bronze heater-shaped pendant with hinge and attachment stud, blue enamelled field with a single gilt bend, possibly lost by a member of the Scrope family'.

[69] R. Stewart-Brown, 'The Scrope and Grosvenor Controversy, 1385–1391', *Trans. Historic Soc. of Lancs & Ches.*, 89 (1938, for 1937), pp. 1–22, at 17–19; Penny Hebgin-Barnes, *The Medieval Stained Glass of Cheshire* (Oxford, 2010), pp. lxxix, lxxxviii, cx, 56, 165.

hanging of his arms in the church, but he pointedly did not say that they were still there, though many witnesses recalled the shield hanging in the church.[70] Sir Robert's great-grandfather, the founder of the chapel at Nether Peover, was buried in Chester in the Franciscan church, and ten witnesses reported his tomb there.[71] The distribution of the arms in the churches, chapels and houses of the county is entirely consistent with a knight of Grosvenor's standing, as is also the frequent mention of charters bearing either the family's name or its arms. To the witnesses, charters were always ancient, and they bore the name and the arms of the Grosvenors, though no witness described the seals which were affixed to them, and indeed no surviving charter has yet been identified bearing the heraldic seal [*Azure*] *a bend* [*or*]. The issue perhaps was that just as the Scropes had a less chivalrous background as lawyers, so too did the Grosvenors as office holders. The late-thirteenth-century seal (Plate II) of Sir Robert Grosvenor's kinsman, Warin Grosvenor of Budworth, shows him standing with a bow, hunting dog and horn, the epitome of his office as master forester of Delamere, a role to which an ancestor had been appointed between 1153 and 1160 and in which they continued until deprived in 1348 for misuse of office.[72] Grosvenor's *cognomen*, the name adopted by the founder of his line and later transformed into a surname, was that of an office holder, *grossus venator*, 'the chief huntsman'. Of that lineage there is only a profound silence in the evidence before the Court of Chivalry.

And there was silence too at the conclusion of the hearings since no judgment was returned until 12 May 1389 when the Constable found against Grosvenor, who was condemned with costs, and assigned to him the same arms *'with a plain bordure, argent'*. Grosvenor at once appealed against this decision, also later alleging that Scrope had obtained commissioners in the appeal by fraud. Even now there was further delay, Scrope petitioning the Council that Grosvenor was procrastinating, and the king's decision was not finally delivered until May 1390, when the judgment of the Constable was confirmed but the award of differenced arms annulled.[73] The king complained about the duration of the case. On 28 November 1390 letters patent were issued directing that Grosvenor was to be held liable for the costs, which amounted to £466 13s. 4d., and on 3 October 1391 a further fine of 50 marks was imposed for his contumacy. Amity was only restored in November 1391, when Grosvenor was challenged in parliament by Scrope and pleaded poverty. In return for remission of the costs he was compelled to withdraw all

---

[70] Nicolas, *Scrope and Grosvenor Controversy*, I, pp. 266–7, 285.

[71] J.H.E. Bennett, 'The Grey Friars of Chester', *Jnl, Chester & N. Wales Archaeological Soc.*, New Ser., 24 (1921–2), pp. 5–85, at 73–4.

[72] Kew, TNA, Exchequer: Treasury of Receipt: Ancient Deeds, Series AS, E 42/112; J.A. Green, 'Forests', in Victoria County History, *Cheshire*, II (1979), pp. 167–87, at 174.

[73] Kew, TNA, Special Collections: Ancient Petitions, SC 8/185/9218–9219; P. Morgan, 'Grosvenor, Sir Robert (*d.* 1396)', in *ODNB*, 24, pp. 98–9.

charges of falsehood, which, he said, had only been spoken on the advice of his lawyers, and he agreed to the enrolment of a final memorandum which, since he had little French, was read to him in English by John of Gaunt, duke of Lancaster.[74]

Grosvenor's reluctance to avoid recognition of the judgment, and to have done so over several years, is perplexing, though at one level his poverty can certainly be accepted as a sufficient explanation. Nevertheless, it can also be argued that the case had had the contingent effect of promoting the knight from a local to a national figure. In 1391 the final confrontation in the case commenced at the opening of the November parliament when Lord Scrope 'found Sir Robert Grosvenor in the parliament chamber at Westminster', and the final settlement was held nearly two weeks later before the whole parliament. Since Cheshire sent no MPs to medieval parliaments, Grosvenor's presence in London is difficult to explain on this occasion. But the county had also played a central part in national politics in the previous few years, as the site of a royal visit in 1387, and had seen the establishment of a comital court by the king's favourite, Robert de Vere, earl of Oxford. In 1387 Cheshire had contributed heavily to the army which confronted the Appellant lords at the battle of Radcot Bridge. Is it possible that Grosvenor had hoped ultimately to challenge the court's decision? Certainly his part in the case before the Court of Chivalry had affirmed his own part and power in a regional society, and it had brought him to the notice of a wider chivalric society. Robert Barrett describes his appearance at the parliament as a 'chivalric performance'.[75] His son, Sir Thomas Grosvenor (he of the forged document of 1416) would serve with Richard II in Ireland in 1399, in campaigns against Owain Glyn Dŵr, and with Sir Henry Percy at Shrewsbury in 1403. His arms, *Azure a garb or*, the garb or sheaf of corn being in allusion to the arms of Ranulf III, earl of Chester, explicitly referenced the claims of ancient status and connection to the first earl of Chester which his father and his witnesses had so boldly asserted.[76]

---

[74] *Cal. Close R., 1389–92*, pp. 517–19, reproducing Kew, TNA, Chancery & Exchequer: King's Remembrancer: Parliamentary & Council Proceedings, C 49/12/6.

[75] Barrett, *Against All England* (cit. in n. 12), pp. 146–8.

[76] David Crouch, *The Image of Aristocracy in Britain, 1000–1300* (London, 1992), p. 237.

CHAPTER 5

From Brittany to the Black Sea: Nicholas Sabraham and English Military Experience in the Fourteenth Century

Andrew Ayton

It has long been recognised that the recorded testimony of witnesses in the armorial cases before the Court of Chivalry provides an abundance of information about the military careers of both the witnesses themselves and the families whose armorial claims they were supporting.[1] These recollections of campaigns, well-known and obscure, are in themselves invaluable and they are made all the more so when they can be corroborated and supplemented by data found in governmental military–administrative records: muster rolls, retinue lists and the documentation generated by the issue of letters of protection and grants of pardon. Enriched in this way, Court of Chivalry testimony can add a precise and structured martial dimension to an all-too-often shadowy life story. For some witnesses, it was the predominant dimension of their lives, at least in the 'public' sphere. And while recapturing the essence of individual military careers is worthwhile and interesting, research of this kind is elevated to an altogether higher level when men are studied in groups as well: when biographical work becomes prosopography and when the architecture and dynamics of social networks are investigated. As a contribution to this broader research agenda, this chapter seeks to show how the careers of individual witnesses, as revealed by their enriched Court of Chivalry testimony, can be further illuminated when they are viewed alongside those of their (often more fully documented) associates and located within the wider military–prosopographical landscape. Within the compass

---

[1] Most recently and with different emphases: Maurice Keen, *Origins of the English Gentleman: Heraldry, Chivalry and Gentility in Medieval England, c. 1300 – c. 1500* (Stroud, 2002), Chapters 2–4; A. Ayton, 'Military Service and the Dynamics of Recruitment in Fourteenth-Century England', in *The Soldier Experience in the Fourteenth Century*, ed. Adrian R. Bell, Anne Curry et al. (Woodbridge, 2011), pp. 9–59, at 45–59; Philip Caudrey, 'War, Chivalry and Regional Society: East Anglia's Warrior Gentry before the Court of Chivalry', in *Fourteenth Century England*, VIII, ed. J.S. Hamilton (Woodbridge, 2014), pp. 119–45.

of one chapter, this task is necessarily approached through a case study focusing on the career of one Court of Chivalry witness. There are, however, advantages in such an approach, not least that richness of detail can be combined with an elaborated context, yielding a methodological model that may commend itself for wider application.

A soldier's testimony before the Court of Chivalry

On 17 September 1386, in the chapter house of York Minster, Nicholas Sabraham, esquire, provided testimony in support of Richard, Lord Scrope of Bolton's right to the arms *Azure a bend or*, which was being asserted against the claims of Sir Robert Grosvenor of Cheshire.[2] (See Plates IV and V for illustrations of the arms.) Aged sixty years and more, and drawing on a career with the sword that had begun in the 1340s, Sabraham is one of the most celebrated of all Court of Chivalry witnesses. His remarkably wide-ranging career, taking in crusading as well as the king's wars, has been summarised or mentioned a good many times in both specialist studies and textbooks. Time and again he has been held up as the quintessential fourteenth-century English professional soldier, a man whose life experience showed what was possible, a trend that has culminated with his inclusion in the *Oxford Dictionary of National Biography*.[3] Yet in elevating Sabraham to the podium of noteworthy English soldiers we run the risk of isolating him from the social and military circumstances that shaped his career in arms. Contextualising Sabraham's career is essential if we are to understand it, and in this respect we should start with how, as an esquire in his sixties, he compares with the 220 other secular witnesses who were called in support of Scrope's case.

The testimony was gathered in several large regional sessions, supplemented by a number of smaller meetings and home visits. The largest sessions were held in Westminster and Plymouth, the latter being a matter of convenience, since that was the port of embarkation for the army that John of Gaunt was about to take to Spain.[4] That Sabraham was one of forty secular witnesses to provide testimony in York Minster suggests membership of the military community of northern England, while not actively being of Gaunt's martial affinity; and it also suggests some proximity to the Scropes' sphere of influence. Given the nature of the exercise, it is only to be expected

---

[2] Nicolas, *Scrope and Grosvenor Controversy*, I, pp. 124–5.

[3] Timothy Guard, 'Sabraham, Nicholas (*b. c.*1325, *d.* in or after 1399)', in the online *ODNB*: http://www.oxforddnb.com/view/article/92452

[4] Nicolas, *Scrope and Grosvenor Controversy*, I, pp. 47–243. Numbers of secular witnesses: Plymouth (70), Devon and Dorset (10), Chester (10), Yorkshire (43), Nottingham and Leicester (7), Westminster (71) and Lincolnshire (10). The witnesses at the Chester session were actually aligned with Grosvenor.

that men of mature or advanced years whose military recollections stretched back over decades would predominate among Scrope's supporters.[5] But if, in terms of age and length of career, Sabraham was not exceptional, his social and military rank did assign him to a minority group. For what is immediately striking about Scrope's secular witnesses, when viewed collectively, is that three-quarters of them were of at least knightly rank. By contrast, only a third of Thomas, Lord Morley's secular supporters in his contemporaneous armorial dispute were knights:[6] a proportion that is more in keeping with the reality of the military scene of the time, in which markedly fewer knights were militarily active than had been the case in the early to mid-fourteenth century.[7] That Richard, Lord Scrope was able to mobilise the cream of English chivalry can be attributed to the backing that he received from John of Gaunt's extended military affinity, as well as to his high status among the political elite of the realm.[8] Clearly, he could be choosy when it came to selecting subknightly men-at-arms, mostly esquires, to speak on his behalf. What he needed were men who could provide distinctive testimony concerning the Scropes' military past, and the further back – and afield – their recollections reached, the better. Thus, of the esquires who gave evidence in Yorkshire, the Scropes' home territory, William Heselrigg's memories stretched back to the battle of Halidon Hill (1333); Amand Mounceaux recalled Richard Scrope 'en Escoce a un jour de Marche devant la bataille de Duresme' (Neville's Cross, 1346) in the company of Sir Henry Percy; and John Rithre, able to expound at length when interviewed at his home in Scarborough, provided a richly detailed account of the Scropes' adventures at war and on the tournament field.[9] As a North Country esquire of long and varied military experience who had encountered the Scropes in unusual places, Sabraham more than adequately fitted the required profile.

The testimony that Sabraham gave in York Minster is preserved, in the French of England, in a single, contemporary copy from the now lost original

---

[5] Over 80 per cent of those who stated their age were at least forty years old.

[6] A. Ayton, 'Knights, Esquires and Military Service: The Evidence of the Armorial Cases before the Court of Chivalry', in *The Medieval Military Revolution: State, Society and Military Change in Medieval and Early Modern Europe*, ed. Andrew Ayton and J.L. Price (London and New York, 1995), pp. 81–104, at 95.

[7] In the armies raised during the 1370s and 1380s, from 5 to 15 per cent of serving men-at-arms were knights, as compared with the 25 per cent that had been usual earlier in the century. James Sherborne, 'Indentured Retinues and English Expeditions to France, 1369–80', in *War, Politics and Culture in Fourteenth-Century England*, ed. Anthony Tuck (London and Rio Grande, 1994), pp. 12–15, 27–8; Adrian R. Bell et al., *The Soldier in Later Medieval England* (Oxford, 2013), p. 56; Andrew Ayton, *Knights and Warhorses: Military Service and the English Aristocracy under Edward III* (Woodbridge, 1994), pp. 228–9.

[8] Ayton, 'Knights, Esquires and Military Service', p. 85; Keen, *Origins of the English Gentleman*, pp. 56, 65.

[9] Nicolas, *Scrope and Grosvenor Controversy*, I, pp. 126, 134, 144–6.

Court transcripts.[10] As required by the Court, Sabraham focused primarily on campaigns in which members of the Scrope family had served bearing the disputed arms, and in the process he revealed a good deal about his own career with the sword. As it stands, the deposition does not provide a chronologically ordered list of expeditions; indeed, it is imprecise about the date, purpose and location of much of his campaigning. But, taken as a whole, what the testimony indicates is a military odyssey that had carried Sabraham to practically every corner of Christendom and, indeed, beyond. As we might expect, the king's wars in Scotland and France figure prominently, but what really stand out are the references to more scattered and exotic theatres of war in Iberia, Prussia, Hungary, the eastern Mediterranean and the Black Sea region. Two of the events that are readily datable – the battle of Crécy in 1346 and the amphibious assault on Alexandria in 1365 – provide some indication of the length of Sabraham's campaigning career, though we must strongly suspect that his odyssey continued for some years after the Egyptian expedition. If the career profile that can be reconstructed from this testimony lacks the chronological shape and the precision that are to be found in a good many Court of Chivalry depositions, what Sabraham does provide is an evocation of the world of a fourteenth-century warrior that intrigues, perplexes and invites further inquiry.

The strengths and weaknesses of Court of Chivalry depositions as a body of evidence for the study of military careers are nicely illustrated by Sabraham's recorded testimony. He is typical of many warriors, otherwise obscure and ill-served by conventional records, whose appearance before the Court has brought them briefly but vividly into the documentary limelight. And because so much of what is known of his career in arms derives from his own testimony, it follows that the core features of his reconstructed martial life are unaffected by the military service prosopographer's most familiar methodological problem: 'namely, how, using sources of varied provenance, character and reliability, to identify and isolate individuals and to apply consistent criteria to the task of piecing together their lives'.[11] On the other hand, in its mixture of clarity and imprecision, Sabraham's testimony is also illustrative of the interpretative difficulties that attend many Court of Chivalry depositions. Because he was responding to questions designed to yield evidence germane to the Scrope *v.* Grosvenor armorial dispute, Sabraham was more specific about those occasions when members of the Scrope family were serving than about the remainder of his martial life. Given the passage of time since the beginning of his career, it is possible that his recollections had been influenced by those of others, or by the collective memory of his social

---

[10] Kew, TNA, Chancery Miscellanea, C 47/6/2. Nicolas, *Scrope and Grosvenor Controversy*, I, pp. 124–5. For an English translation of Sabraham's testimony, see the Appendix to this chapter.

[11] Ayton, 'Military Service and the Dynamics of Recruitment', p. 45.

circle. More generally, Sabraham gives no indication that his memory was failing, as do certain other witnesses; but for this inference, as with others, we are reliant on the written record that has come down to us. While, here and there, the deposition preserves what look like distinctive turns of phrase, overall it has the appearance of a summary of what was said rather than a verbatim record. And for a clear indication of the role played by the Court's clerk in determining the substance of depositions we need only compare the spare, formulaic records of the Plymouth hearings with the altogether more detailed and individually shaped ones emanating from the sessions held in York Minster. Add to that the possibility that textual changes were inadvertently made by copyists and it can be seen that the imprecision and ambiguity displayed by these depositions are as likely to have been introduced during the creation of the written record as by the character of the original verbal testimony.

However they originated, the interpretative problems that we encounter when seeking to understand Sabraham's testimony are of three kinds. First, amidst the anecdotal recollections and unspecific references to places, few events or spells of service are immediately identifiable; only three, in fact. Second, the vantage point from which Sabraham viewed events, and specifically the Scropes' activities in the field, is not always clear. At times he implies that he was serving alongside them, in the same retinue; elsewhere we are left wondering how well acquainted with them he really was. Third, in places the text prompts doubts as to whether Sabraham was an eyewitness to the events described or merely passing on hearsay evidence, a distinction that has obvious implications for understanding his career in arms. As a consequence of these problems, while Sabraham's testimony yields a rich, if enigmatic, core of evidence that is suggestive of a distinctive and varied career, which hints at underlying recruitment dynamics and to which data from other sources might be linked, it cannot in itself provide an unambiguous, chronologically precise profile of his life with the sword.

Who was Nicholas Sabraham?

Clearly, if we are truly to understand Sabraham's military career, much depends on the extent to which his Court testimony can be corroborated and supplemented by other sources. Although voluminous, the military–administrative records that preserve the names of men who served in royal armies and garrisons are far from complete, especially prior to the 1370s. Many men-at-arms of obscure or parish gentry origins – and a large proportion of the archers – slip through the documentary net, leaving no trace. Service as a freelance soldier or crusader is still more patchily documented. Earlier studies, while demonstrating how Court of Chivalry witnesses from all levels of the military hierarchy can indeed be traced in the military–administrative records, suggest that it is often easier to supplement information than to corroborate it. That is certainly the case with Sabraham. Nothing has yet been found to corroborate any part of Sabraham's testimony concerning when and where he served. As for supplementation: two promising leads have thus far been found in the records, and if they do relate to our man, they would stretch Sabraham's career into the 1370s. The first concerns a spell of duty in the garrison of Roxburgh castle, for which a 'Nicholas Sabrame' secured a letter of protection in April 1371.[12] The second takes us into the shadowy freelance sphere. In July–August 1378, a man called simply 'Sabraam' can be glimpsed in the company of none other than Sir John Hawkwood, who at that time was leading a brigade in the service of the Milanese tyrant Bernabò Visconti.[13] The likelihood that these two soldiers and the Court of Chivalry witness were one and the same man will be considered further as we explore the dynamics driving Nicholas Sabraham's career. But it is worth noting here that his combination of less common forename with unusual surname makes him a particularly suitable subject for an investigation dependent on nominal record linkage.

The apparent scarcity of men bearing Nicholas Sabraham's name in mid- to late-fourteenth-century England and their consistent association with Northumberland has been of undoubted assistance to those seeking to identify our soldier and flesh out his life in the non-military sphere.[14] He has been convincingly linked to the Nicholas Sabraham who, around 1364–5, had married a well-to-do widow and heiress: Alice Orde, née Graper, whose inheritance in Northumberland included land in Burradon and Jesmond, and 'divers tenements and rents' in Newcastle upon Tyne.[15] This linkage

[12] Kew, TNA, Chancery: Scotch Rolls, C 71/50, m. 4; *Calendar of Documents Relating to Scotland*, V, ed. Grant G. Simpson and James D. Galbraith (Edinburgh, 1986), p. 524, no. 3971.

[13] William Caferro, *John Hawkwood: An English Mercenary in Fourteenth-Century Italy* (Baltimore, 2006), pp. 200–1, 390, nn. 52, 59. I am indebted to Professor Caferro for sending me a copy of the relevant document: Archivio di Stato di Mantova, Archivio Gonzaga, busta 2388, no. 284. For an abbreviated translation, see *Calendar of State Papers Relating to English Affairs in the Archives of Venice*, I: 1202–1509, ed. Rawdon Brown (London, 1864), no. 72.

[14] E.g. a Gilbert Sabraham held a messuage in Newcastle in 1342: *Cal. Close R., 1341–3*, pp. 483–4. While N.H. Nicolas thought Sabraham might have been from Yorkshire (Nicolas, *Scrope and Grosvenor Controversy*, II, p. 323), Timothy Guard is surely right to conclude that he was 'a native of Northumberland': Guard, 'Sabraham, Nicholas', in *ODNB*.

[15] Alice (b. about 1326) was co-heiress of her father, Adam Graper, and her mother, Agnes, co-heiress of Richard Emeldon and his widow Christiana. Alice had married Robert Orde by 1349, with whom she had a son and heir, John, who was 30 years and more in 1399. She married Sabraham some time after the death of Christiana in December 1363, and had given birth to a child by mid-June 1366. *Cal. Close R., 1364–8*, pp. 234, 331–2; *Cal. Fine R., 1356–68*, p. 334; *A History of Northumberland*, 15 vols (Newcastle, 1893–1940), IX, p. 45; *Cal. I.P.M.*, VII, no. 536 (Richard Emeldon);

further suggests that our much travelled warrior was one and the same as the 'Nicholas Sabram' who was returned as a parliamentary burgess for Newcastle upon Tyne in the parliaments of 1373, 1376 and 1380.[16] Soon after his appearance at York Minster in September 1386, Sabraham and his wife entailed their half of the manor of Burradon on their daughter, Alice, and her husband, Walter Lewyn.[17] After that we hear nothing more of him before his wife's death in November 1398; and the record of her inquisition *post mortem* implies that Nicholas was still alive in late July 1399.[18] The availability of concrete details about Sabraham's domestic and public life in England from the mid-1360s onwards is of great value since, for at least the second half of his military career, we are able to assess how his life with the sword was combined with private and public responsibilities. That his roots can be traced to Northumberland is also of particular importance, since we can reasonably infer that the beginning, and perhaps much of, his martial life would have been shaped by that regional military community. If we look closely at the company that Sabraham was keeping in York Minster on 17 September 1386, and specifically at the four esquires who gave testimony immediately after him, we find that two – William Heselrigg and John Cressewelle – were certainly from Northumberland, and that a third, William Biset (and perhaps also the fourth, William Spenser) had fought under the same magnate's banner as Sabraham.[19]

Looking for further documentary references to corroborate or supplement Sabraham's Court of Chivalry testimony can get us only so far. A different approach to recapturing the life of this elusive man would be to examine Sabraham's career not simply as an exercise in individual biography, but rather as one of many, contributing to a wider collective biographical – or prosopographical – portrait: as a single thread in a complex tapestry. Sabraham did not serve in isolation, and one way in which we may be able to imagine the dynamics of recruitment that shaped his martial career is to locate what we know of that career within the collective experience of English soldiers at this time, and notably that of the comrades in arms with whom he served at retinue level. In their personal circumstances and connections, and in their career paths, both as individuals and collectively, we can begin to recapture something of the world in which Sabraham moved, with which he interacted and upon which he would have left an imprint. The circumstances

---

ibid., IX, no. 211 (Agnes Graper); *ibid.*, XI, no. 598 (Christiana, widow of Richard Emeldon); *ibid.*, XVII, nos 1249–51; Kew, TNA, Chancery: Inquisitions Post Mortem, Series I, Richard II, C 136/106/5 (Alice, wife of Nicholas Sabraham).

[16] *Return of the Name of Every Member of the Lower House of the Parliaments of England, Scotland and Ireland, 1213–1874*, Parl. Papers, 1878, vol. LXII, parts I–III, 3 vols (London, 1878), I, pp. 191, 194, 204.

[17] *History of Northumberland*, IX, p. 45.

[18] *Cal. I.P.M.*, XVII, nos 1249–51.

[19] Nicolas, *Scrope and Grosvenor Controversy*, I, pp. 125–9, II, pp. 324–9.

of a shadowy individual are thereby illuminated by the collective experience of the group with which he had been associated. And in acquiring a surer grasp of so distinctive a life as Sabraham's, we add nuance to our understanding of that collective experience.

Sabraham's early career

The first interpretative problem that we encounter with Sabraham's Court of Chivalry testimony concerns when he first took up the sword. According to the Court record, by September 1386 he had been armed for thirty-nine years. This would tie in quite well with the Crécy campaign of 1346, which happens to be the first easily datable spell of service in his deposition. If his age declaration is reliable, he was in his early twenties at this time. We might wonder how it was that a Northumbrian, like Sabraham, found himself at Crécy, given the preoccupation of the northern military communities with the defence of the Scottish March. The answer lies in Sabraham's evident connection with William Bohun, earl of Northampton, which is twice mentioned in his testimony. Northampton, one of Edward III's front-rank captains at Crécy, had an extensive recruiting reach that included the far north of England: a fact rooted in his landed interests in the Western Scots March (the lordship of Annandale and Lochmaben castle)[20] and cultivated by his active participation in the Scottish campaigns of the 1330s. When, from the last years of that decade, Northampton was called upon to contribute a retinue to the king's war in France, some of his Northumberland-based comrades in arms accompanied him: men like Walter Selby and the Widdrington brothers, Gerard and Roger.[21] Sabraham himself is not visible in this process, but men close to him are, most notably William Heselrigg, another esquire from Northumberland, who was the next but one witness to give testimony at York Minster on 17 September. Heselrigg was an older man from a martial family; he had fought at Halidon Hill in 1333, and had been accompanying Northampton to France since the campaign in Brittany in 1342.[22] When he served with Northampton at Crécy he did so as part of a contingent of north-country soldiers that also included Sir Gerard Widdrington and Sir William Lengleys.[23] Association with this group, and Heselrigg in particular, is the most likely explanation

[20] G.A. Holmes, *The Estates of the Higher Nobility in Fourteenth-Century England* (Cambridge, 1957), pp. 20, 22.

[21] For the service of these men and others in Northampton's retinue in Scotland and France, see A. Ayton, 'The English Army at Crécy', in *The Battle of Crécy, 1346*, ed. Andrew Ayton and Sir Philip Preston (Woodbridge, 2005), pp. 205–10.

[22] Nicolas, *Scrope and Grosvenor Controversy*, I, pp. 126–7, II, pp. 325–7.

[23] Kew, TNA, Chancery: Warrants for the Great Seal, Series I, C 81/1734, no. 28; Chancery: Treaty Rolls, C 76/22, m. 2. For Lengleys' land in Cumberland and Westmorland: *Cal. I.P.M.*, VIII, no. 527.

for Sabraham's presence under Northampton's banner at Crécy. Indeed, it is possible that Sabraham had already accompanied these northerners to war the previous year when a cluster of them, including Heselrigg, Lengleys and Widdrington, enlisted in Northampton's retinue for the campaign in Brittany.[24] It might have been this expedition that Sabraham was thinking of when, in his deposition, he referred in passing to service in Brittany.

Sabraham's early career, as tentatively reconstructed here, is nicely illustrative of the circumstances and experience of many young, would-be soldiers at this time, and of the problems that historians have in imagining their lives. Two aspects of this merit further comment. The first concerns Sabraham's socio-economic background and invisibility in the records. Nothing is known about his family, but when he refers, in his Court testimony, to his ancestors' knowledge of heraldic heritage, thereby associating them with the gentry of 'his country', he seems to be suggesting gentility or at least aspiration to such status. His invisibility in the available military–administrative documentation of the 1340s is simply the consequence of the paucity, at that time, of systematic muster records, without which we are necessarily reliant on sources related to the issue of letters of protection and grants of pardon. A landless scion of a 'parish gentry' family – our best guess regarding Sabraham's status – is unlikely to have had need of a protection at this stage of his career; and, as yet, there is no evidence of criminality that might have prompted him to serve in return for a 'military' pardon. While it is most likely that he rode to war as a man-at-arms from the start of his career, the possibility that he began as a mounted archer cannot be discounted. It was not unusual for families on the margins of gentility to furnish mounted archers;[25] and it was not unknown for men who had spent much of their careers wielding the longbow to give evidence before the Court of Chivalry.[26]

The renown as a warrior that Nicholas Sabraham had attained by 1386 can be gauged from the fact that he was the first of the esquires to provide testimony at York Minster, and we can be sure that his testimony did not disappoint. And yet there are aspects of his journey to the podium of high repute that are not altogether clear. Perhaps he achieved fame and/or fortune with the sword, which in turn enabled him to make an advantageous marriage and, later, to represent Newcastle upon Tyne in parliament. Without adequate documentation, such explanatory forays can only be speculative. Fortunately, more light is cast on another aspect of Sabraham's early career, namely how it was shaped by the dynamics of recruitment. The records documenting his recruiting relationships, while not perfect, do demonstrate a proximity to identifiable individuals at specific stages of his life, and from this inferences

---

[24] Kew, TNA, Chancery: Warrants for the Great Seal, Series I, C 81/1735, nc. 21; C 81/1752, no. 36; Chancery: Treaty Rolls, C 76/20, m. 21.

[25] Bell et al., *The Soldier in Later Medieval England* (cit. in n. 7), pp. 162–4.

[26] *Ibid.*, pp. 167–70.

can be made. We have seen how 'horizontal' social ties based on locality had brought Sabraham into the world of a leading magnate. The consequences that this might have are of direct relevance to his contribution to the Scrope *v.* Grosvenor armorial dispute. Admission to the earl of Northampton's military affinity meant not only expanded service opportunities but also contact with men from different regions within the earl's extensive recruiting network. And so it was probably in Brittany in 1345, or during the Crécy campaign the following year, that Sabraham first encountered the Scropes at close quarters as fellow members of one of the great war retinues of the age. In 1342, Northampton had needed to expand his retinue for the campaign in Brittany, and it was at this point that Henry Scrope of Masham, together with his cousin William, of Bolton, joined the earl's team.[27] William was seriously wounded at the battle of Morlaix,[28] but Henry returned to the earl's banner for his next campaign, in Brittany in 1345.[29] Henry's brothers, William and Stephen, were with Northampton at Crécy. That our Northumbrians were not particularly close to the Scropes is suggested by the faulty evidence that both Sabraham and Heselrigg gave as to precisely which members of the Scrope family fought at Crécy (for example, they confused William Scrope of Bolton, who was already dead, with his namesake cousin, of Masham). In this respect, by contrast, John Rithre, a Yorkshireman, was spot-on in his testimony.[30]

To return to our chronological survey of Sabraham's early career: after participating in the triumph at Crécy, and having experienced the early stages of the siege of Calais, he was back in northern England by the spring of 1347. Some Crécy veterans returned straight away and managed to fight at the battle of Neville's Cross, outside Durham, on 17 October 1346; but had Sabraham done so he would surely have mentioned it, since Richard Scrope was knighted on the battlefield. What he does mention, right at the start of his deposition, is a chevauchée led by Edward Balliol, upon which at least one of the Scropes served. This has been assigned to 1339,[31] but that would mean that Sabraham had been armed for over forty-five years, rather than thirty-nine. It is more likely to have been the chevauchée that Balliol mounted during the summer of 1347, which was a large scale, if ineffectual, follow-up to the victory at Neville's Cross.[32] There is documentary evidence that the

[27] Kew, TNA, Chancery: Warrants for the Great Seal, Series I, C 81/1735, no. 22; Chancery: Treaty Rolls, C 76/17, mm. 36, 41.

[28] Morlaix: Nicolas, *Scrope and Grosvenor Controversy*, I, p. 145. William Scrope died in 1344; the wardship of Richard, his brother and heir's lands, was entrusted to the earl of Northampton: *Cal. I.P.M.*, VIII, nos 546, 606.

[29] Kew, TNA, C 81/1735, no. 21; C 76/20, m. 21.

[30] Nicolas, *Scrope and Grosvenor Controversy*, I, pp. 125, 127, 145.

[31] Guard, 'Sabraham, Nicholas', in *ODNB*.

[32] A period of paid service that began in mid-May and lasted, for some contingents, until early September: Kew, TNA, King's Remembrancer: Accounts Various, E 101/25/10, mm. 5–6. A second, much shorter chevauchée into Scotland was

cousins, Henry Scrope of Masham and Richard Scrope of Bolton, took part in this expedition.[33] Whom Sabraham served with is not clear. Northampton was not involved, but all the prominent northern captains were, including Gilbert Umfraville, earl of Angus, for whom Sabraham acted as feoffee in 1375.[34]

A firm date can also be suggested for the second item in Sabraham's deposition: the evocatively described torch-lit chevauchée that the earl of Northampton made from Lochmaben to Peebles. This is unlikely to have taken place as early as 1343, as has been suggested recently,[35] for although Northampton intended, in the autumn of that year, to ride to Lochmaben to re-victual his besieged castle, the task was accomplished peacefully, by licence of the Scots, without the earl needing to proceed further than Carlisle.[36] A better case can be made for the autumn of 1350, after 18 October, when Northampton was appointed captain of the English Marches towards Scotland, with full military responsibility for the region.[37] At the same time, a cluster of men intending to serve in the earl's retinue at Lochmaben castle were securing letters of protection. Significantly, these included Sir Henry Scrope of Masham, whose banner Sabraham tells us he saw.[38] And, as we would expect, among those who probably accompanied the earl on his torch-lit chevauchée were others who had ridden with him before,[39]

mounted in October 1347, but Balliol does not appear on the payroll for this army: E 101/25/10, m. 11. Michael Brown, *The Wars of Scotland, 1214–1371* (Edinburgh, 2004), p. 248; A. King, 'A Good Chance for the Scots? The Recruitment of English Armies for Scotland and the Marches, 1337–1347', in *England and Scotland at War, c. 1296–c. 1513*, ed. Andy King and David Simpkin (Leiden and Boston, 2012), pp. 119–56 (145–8).

[33] Henry secured a letter of protection for service in Sir Ralph Neville's retinue, as did Richard Scrope for service under Sir Henry Percy. Kew, TNA, Chancery: Scotch Rolls, C 71/27, mm. 7, 13.

[34] *Cal. Pat. R., 1374–7*, p. 126; *Cal. I.P.M.*, XV, no. 434.

[35] Guard, 'Sabraham, Nicholas', in *ODNB*.

[36] *Cal. Close R., 1343–6*, p. 233; A.A.M. Duncan, 'A Siege of Lochmaben Castle in 1343', *Trans. Dumfriesshire & Galloway Natural History & Antiquarian Soc.*, 3rd ser., 31 (1952–3), 74–7, which discusses the related but variant accounts of the Anonimalle and Lanercost chronicles.

[37] *Rotuli Scotiae*, ed. D. Macpherson et al., 2 vols (London, 1814–19), I, p. 737. According to Geoffrey le Baker, Northampton mounted an expedition against the Scots, based on Lochmaben, in 1353; but as E.M. Thompson notes, the 'incursion does not appear to be noticed elsewhere'. It has probably been misdated by the chronicler, for whom chronology was not always a strong suit. *Chronicon Galfridi le Baker de Swynebroke*, ed. E.M. Thompson (Oxford, 1889), pp. 123, 289.

[38] Kew, TNA, Chancery: Scotch Rolls, C 71/30, m. 1.

[39] E.g. Thomas Warde: Kew, TNA, C 71/30, m. 2. *Treaty Rolls*, II: *1337–9*, ed. J. Ferguson (London, 1972), no. 291 (1338). Chancery: Warrants for the Great Seal, Series I, C 81/1735, no. 17; Chancery: Treaty Rolls, C 76/17, m. 38 (1342); C 81/1735, no. 21; C 76/20, m. 21 (1345).

notably Sir William Lengleys, who had been with the earl in Brittany in 1345 and at Crécy.[40] Indeed, the records suggest that Lengleys had been serving in the Lochmaben garrison for some time, from late 1348 and throughout 1349.[41] Given the connection that we have already noticed, it may well be that Sabraham was there with him, for a spell of garrison duty offered steady remuneration as well as occasional bursts of excitement – like the torch-lit chevauchée in Annandale and Tweeddale.

Sabraham's later career

After the relative precision of the mid- to late-1340s, little is known about Sabraham's career for much of the 1350s and we can but speculate about what he was doing. One possibility is that he participated in the campaigns of the mid-1350s. Continued service under Northampton would have taken him briefly into Picardy, where the King campaigned in November 1355, and then to Scotland during the early weeks of 1356.[42] However, the fact that Sabraham omitted to mention that Richard Scrope had served with Northampton in both Picardy and at the relief of Berwick may indicate that he was elsewhere at this time.[43] It is likely that Sabraham fell back on the careerist soldier's staple diet: garrison service, perhaps at Lochmaben or Roxburgh, or – as so many other Englishmen did – in a freelance capacity in France, which would have all but ensured his invisibility in the records. We would not expect Court witnesses to mention freelance service, unless – like John Neuland, esquire – to explain why they had missed 'lez graundez batailles & journez'.[44] The vivid recollection of another esquire, John Charnels, that Sir William Scrope, brother of Sir Henry, had shared his adventures riding forth from a castle called 'Quarranteau' is exceptional.[45] It is tempting to suggest that it was during these years that Sabraham bore arms in Gascony and Spain – two unspecific locational references in his deposition that are otherwise difficult to interpret.[46] Fortunately we return to an identifiable event at the very end

---

[40] Kew, TNA, C 76/20, m. 21 (1345); C 76/22, mm. 2, 3 (1346); C 76/26, m. 3 (1348).

[41] Kew, TNA, C 71/28, m. 4; C 71/29, m. 1; C 71/30, mm. 2, 5.

[42] According to Sir Gerard Lound (a York Minster witness of 17 September), after serving in Picardy, Northampton was appointed the king's lieutenant on the 'marche de Escoce': Nicolas, *Scrope and Grosvenor Controversy*, I, pp. 108–9.

[43] Nicholas Reymes, esquire, recalled that Scrope was in Northampton's retinue in Picardy, and with Sir Gerard Widdrington and Sir Edward Letham (who would have been with the earl) at the relief of Berwick. *Ibid.*, I, p. 216.

[44] John Neuland, esquire, spent time in garrisons in Normandy, Brittany and Burgundy and with 'lez grauntez compaignies': *ibid.*, I, p. 138.

[45] *Ibid.*, I, pp. 211–12.

[46] For example, to locate Sabraham with John of Gaunt in Iberia in 1367 would appear to conflict with our warrior's movements in the Mediterranean region.

of Sabraham's deposition. Here Sabraham refers to the Reims campaign of 1359–60, noting that, during the siege of Paris (April 1360), the Scropes' arms had been challenged by a certain Carminow, whom other witnesses identify more precisely as an esquire, forenamed Thomas, from Cornwall.[47] Sabraham does not state explicitly that he was an eyewitness to these events, and it is possible that he was passing on hearsay evidence (as was the case with Sir Thomas Fychet);[48] but the most likely explanation is that he was indeed there, serving as before under the earl of Northampton's banner (though by this time Richard Scrope had switched allegiance to John of Gaunt).[49] That a Northumbrian contingent was recruited by Northampton for the climactic campaign of 1359–60 is evident from the letters of protection that were issued to Sabraham's comrades from the 1340s, William Heselrigg and Gerard Widdrington, for service in the earl's retinue.[50] As Constable, Northampton would have played a central role in resolving an armorial dispute within the royal host, and that events would have been closely watched by members of his retinue can easily be imagined.

After 1360 Sabraham's career became more varied and exotic. For the historian it becomes interpretatively more complex. The 1360s, the years of the peace of Brétigny, were a time when soldiers who had been engaged in the war in France were free for alternative employment, whether in the Italian or Iberian peninsulas, or in crusading adventures, notably in *Pruce* (Lithuania) or the eastern Mediterranean. Appropriately enough, Sabraham recalls the amphibious assault on Mamluk Alexandria that was masterminded by King Peter of Cyprus in 1365. Sabraham's testimony is vivid and precise, and he is the only witness to mention that Stephen Scrope was elevated to knighthood on the landing beach by the King of Cyprus. But this is the single immediately identifiable event from the 1360s in Sabraham's deposition. Should we assume that it was also during these years that he bore arms in Prussia, Hungary, Constantinople and the 'bras de St Jorge' and Messembria? It is sometimes suggested that Sabraham took part in Count Amadeus of Savoy's remarkable expedition of 1366–7, which captured Gallipoli from the Ottomans and then, in support of the Byzantine emperor, sailed into the Black Sea, taking the Bulgarian port of Messembria (modern Nessebar) and unsuccessfully besieging Varna.[51] Although an English contingent certainly did participate

---

[47] *Ibid.*, I, pp. 50, 62, 146, 214. Sir Laurence Dutton reported that Carminow had been challenged by Sir John Daniell, on behalf of Robert Grosvenor, who was 'juyn et de petit age': *ibid.*, I, p. 256.

[48] *Ibid.*, I, p. 62.

[49] Simon Walker, *The Lancastrian Affinity 1361–1399* (Oxford, 1990), p. 281.

[50] Kew, TNA, Chancery: Treaty Rolls, C 76/38, m. 17.

[51] Timothy Guard, *Chivalry, Kingship and Crusade: The English Experience in the Fourteenth Century* (Woodbridge, 2013), pp. 78, 108, 236. On the expedition, see E. Cox, *The Green Count of Savoy: Amadeus VI and Transalpine Savoy in the Fourteenth Century* (Princeton, 1967), Chapter 7.

in this expedition,[52] there are good reasons to doubt Sabraham's involvement. Admittedly, given the paramount focus of Sabraham's testimony on the Scropes, neither his failure explicitly to mention the Count of Savoy, nor his unspecific reference to Constantinople and the 'bras de St Jorge' (the Bosphorus) can be taken as clear indications one way or the other.[53] However, there is separate documentary evidence that Sabraham was in England, preoccupied with his own affairs in June 1366, just as Count Amadeus was preparing to leave Venice.[54] Moreover, Sabraham's vivid (and unique) testimony concerning the Scrope tomb in a church in Nessebar suggests a visit made *after* the capture of the town, rather than that he participated in the attack.[55]

As before, Sabraham's testimony is best approached through an understanding of military lordship and locality-rooted comradeship. The contours of our subject's early career in arms had been shaped by his association with the earl of Northampton. After the latter's death in 1360, his military responsibilities and territorial interests were taken over by his son, Humphrey. Indeed, they grew because, on the death of his uncle in 1361, Humphrey became earl of Hereford and Essex as well as Northampton. In these circumstances we might expect the old earl's followers, men like Sabraham, to transfer their allegiance to his son; and some certainly did so,[56] perhaps the most notable being Sir Richard Waldegrave, who was later to be elected Commons Speaker.[57] That Sabraham's deposition does not mention Hereford should not concern us unduly, any more than should the absence of his name from the records that document that earl's retinue for campaigns in France and at sea in 1369, 1371 and 1372. For we have become accustomed to the selectivity of Sabraham's recorded testimony and his invisibility in the records, just as we have to a research method that seeks to recapture the martial opportunities that were open to him by examining the more fully documented careers of his close associates. On this occasion it is William Biset, esquire, the very next witness after Sabraham to give testimony at York Minster, who is our

---

[52] Guard, *Chivalry, Kingship and Crusade*, pp. 102–8.

[53] Cf. Sir Maurice Bruyn: his paid participation in the expedition is documented, and yet his Court testimony referred only to service 'outre le grande mere'; *Illustrazioni della spedizione in oriente di Amedeo VI*, ed. F. Bollati di Saint-Pierre (Turin, 1900), p. 60; Nicolas, *Scrope and Grosvenor Controversy*, I, p. 161.

[54] *Cal. Close R., 1364–8*, pp. 331–2; *Cal. Fine R., 1356–68*, p. 334. Cox, *Green Count*, pp. 210–13.

[55] For a suggested identification of the church in Nessebar, see Peter Schreiner, 'Zwei englische Soldaten in Mesembria', *Études Balkaniques*, 43 (2007), pp. 153–6.

[56] For Hereford's permanent retainers and military following, see Holmes, *Estates*, pp. 56, 70, 80; Guard, *Chivalry, Kingship and Crusade*, pp. 141–3.

[57] Nicolas, *Scrope and Grosvenor Controversy*, I, pp. 165–6; *The History of Parliament: The House of Commons, 1386–1421*, ed. J.S. Roskell et al., 4 vols (Stroud, 1992), IV, pp. 735–9.

guide. First armed at the battle of Sluys (1340), Biset was several years older than Sabraham. He tells us that he fought with Northampton at the naval battle of 'Les Espagnols sur Mer' in 1350 and the military–administrative records show that he served with Hereford on every available occasion after the French war resumed in 1369.[58] Comparison of Biset's career with what can be inferred about Sabraham's serves to highlight the range of opportunities presented to those who associated themselves with a magnate's varied interests and responsibilities. Owing to the usual patchiness of the records, we cannot be certain that Sabraham missed the 1369 campaign, which is most often remembered for the stand-off at 'Balyngham Hill',[59] but the complete rolls that survive for Hereford's retinue in 1371 and 1372 leave us in no doubt.[60] In fact, Sabraham was absent from Hereford's naval expedition of 1371 because, having secured a letter of protection on 29 April, he was now based at Roxburgh castle, serving in the company of the long-time keeper, and pillar of the Northumberland gentry, Alan Strother.[61] Sabraham may not have shared Biset's evident penchant for maritime operations, or he may simply have decided to return to his home 'country'. But we should not forget the Bohuns' interests in the Scottish March. Like his father before him, Hereford needed to deploy part of his military affinity in defence of his estates there, centring on Lochmaben. This was not a royal castle, and the garrison is patchily documented. But in the skeletal career profile that can be pieced together for William Stapelton, esquire, we have another pertinent model from which the practical possibilities of Sabraham's career may be imagined. Stapelton accompanied Hereford to France in 1369 and was retained by him for life, with a £20 annuity, the following year.[62] We then glimpse him as keeper of Lochmaben castle in 1374.[63]

Despite his evident military connection with Hereford, it is noteworthy that William Biset's testimony in support of Scrope's armorial claim makes no reference to service in Prussia or around the Mediterranean. For it was mainly through supporting crusading ventures in these theatres of war that Hereford was able to pursue his martial ambitions during the 1360s. And it is precisely these aspects of Sabraham's testimony that are most easily explained if we

---

[58] Nicolas, *Scrope and Grosvenor Controversy*, I, pp. 125–6; Bell et al., *The Soldier in Later Medieval England* (cit. in n. 7), p. 119.

[59] E.g. Nicolas, *Scrope and Grosvenor Controversy*, I, p. 128.

[60] Kew, TNA, King's Remembrancer: Accounts Various, E 101/31/15; E 101/32/20.

[61] Kew, TNA, Chancery: Scotch Rolls, C 71/50, m. 4. For Strother, see Simon Walker, 'Profit and Loss in the Hundred Years War: The Subcontracts of Sir John Strother, 1374', *Bull., Institute of Historical Research*, 58 (1985), pp. 100–6, at 101 and n. 8.

[62] Kew, TNA, Chancery: Treaty Rolls, C 76/52, m. 9; 'Private Indentures for Life Service in Peace and War, 1278–1476', ed. Michael Jones and Simon Walker, in *Camden Miscellany XXXII*, Camden 5th ser., 3 (Royal Historical Soc., 1994), pp. 83–4, no. 53.

[63] Kew, TNA, Chancery: Scotch Rolls, C 71/53, m. 5.

assume service under Hereford's banner, or at least service sponsored by
him. Thus, Sabraham's tour of duty in Prussia was most likely undertaken
with the young earl during the winter of 1362–3.[64] And an association with
Hereford also probably explains Sabraham's presence at Alexandria in 1365,
since, on balance, the evidence suggests that the earl was there with King
Peter of Cyprus.[65] After a diplomatic and military interlude in Italy, Hereford
returned to the Eastern Mediterranean to assist the king of Cyprus in the late
summer of 1367,[66] fighting at Tripoli in September.[67] Sabraham may have
been with him. He was at that time preoccupied with his wife's inheritance;[68]
but after June 1366, when Edward III took his homage, he could have joined
Hereford's retinue prior to its departure for Italy.[69] Thanks to the recollections
of others among Hereford's retainers who, in 1386, gave testimony in support
of Richard Scrope's claim, Sabraham can be imagined fighting 'al pris de
Nofe' in 'Lumbardy', and witnessing the renewal of a treaty with the Emir of
Tekke 'en Turkye a Satillie'.[70] If it was indeed the maritime expedition to the
Syrian port of Tripoli that Sabraham had in mind when referring to service
'outre le graund meer',[71] what of his reference to Constantinople and the
Bosphorus? This could plausibly relate to John, Lord Mowbray's expedition
of 1368, which was part-financed by Hereford.[72] If so, having survived the
stiff fight that led to Mowbray's death outside Constantinople, Sabraham
would have been well placed to offer his services to the Byzantine state.[73]

---

[64] Guard, *Chivalry, Kingship and Crusade*, pp. 76–7, 89–92, 94. Note that Sabraham
did not mention Geoffrey Scrope of Masham's death at the siege of Pillen in 1363,
nor his burial in Königsberg cathedral, as reported by others: Nicolas, *Scrope and
Grosvenor Controversy*, I, pp. 146, 188; Guard, *Chivalry, Kingship and Crusade*, p. 88.

[65] Hereford's presence is doubted by Anthony Luttrell, 'English Levantine Crusaders,
1363–1367', *Renaissance Studies*, 2 (1988), pp. 143–53, at 150–1, but see *The Anonimalle
Chronicle, 1333–1381*, ed. V.H. Galbraith (Manchester, 1927), p. 51, and Guard, *Chivalry,
Kingship and Crusade*, pp. 41–2, 46.

[66] Luttrell, 'English Levantine Crusaders', pp. 151–2; Guard, *Chivalry, Kingship and
Crusade*, pp. 47–8.

[67] Guillaume de Machaut, *La Prise d'Alixandre*, ed. R. Barton Palmer (New York and
London, 2002), p. 325.

[68] Specifically matters arising from the death in December 1363 of his wife's grand-
mother, Christiana, widow of Richard Emeldon: *Cal. I.P.M.*, VII, no. 638; *ibid.*, XI, no.
598; *Cal. Fine R., 1356–68*, pp. 296, 334; *Cal. Close R., 1364–8*, pp. 234, 331–2.

[69] Hereford and some of his men appointed attorneys in July 1366: *Cal. Pat. R., 1364–7*,
pp. 303–4.

[70] Nicolas, *Scrope and Grosvenor Controversy*, I, pp. 70 (Sir Alexander Goldingham), 166
(Sir Richard Waldegrave).

[71] Another Hereford retainer, Sir William Lucy, used the same phrase and was
certainly involved: *ibid.*, I, p. 78; *Cal. Pat. R., 1364–7*, p. 304; Holmes, *Estates*, pp. 70,
80.

[72] Guard, *Chivalry, Kingship and Crusade*, pp. 100–1.

[73] Cf. the case of a Picard petty nobleman from around 1380: Mark C. Bartusis, *The Late
Byzantine Army: Arms and Society, 1204–1453* (Philadelphia, 1992), pp. 209–10.

It was perhaps through such employment that we can most convincingly explain his presence in Byzantium's recently acquired Black Sea outpost at Nessebar, where he encountered the tomb that – apparently to his surprise – was identified by the churchwardens as being that of a fellow Englishman, a member of the Scrope family.

If much of Sabraham's military odyssey was shaped by military lordship and locally rooted comradeship, how are we to explain what is perhaps the most enigmatic aspect of his testimony: his service in *Hungarye*? The implication appears to be that Sabraham spent time in the realm of St Stephen during the long reign of that most warlike of kings, Louis the Great (1342–82). The Ottoman expansion into south-eastern Europe was under way, but Louis's frequent campaigns were mostly focused on his immediate southern neighbours, the Serbs, the Wallachians and the Bulgarians;[74] and given 'the vast resources of the treasury', fuelled by the Hungarian gold mines,[75] these were well-financed and, therefore, potentially attractive enterprises. What makes Sabraham's passing reference to Hungary so striking is that, despite the opportunities for freelance soldiering that existed there, it is hard to find evidence of English participation in Hungarian service prior to the Nicopolis expedition of 1396.[76] The destruction of the Hungarian royal archive during the Ottoman period is no doubt the principal problem here. Without the kind of systematic records that document, for example, the service of English mercenaries in the Italian peninsula at this time, we must perforce rely on fragments of evidence wherever we can find them. Perhaps the most useful fragment is the Hungarian chronicler János Thuróczy's reference to the service of English men-at-arms and archers at the recently constructed Törcsvár in Transylvania, on the border with Wallachia.[77] This would have been late in Louis the Great's reign: about 1380.

How would an Englishman seeking military employment have reached Hungary? From England, the usual route, taken by diplomatic missions, involved travelling up the Rhine until Mainz, then south east to Nuremberg, joining the Danube at Regensburg. But it would be a costly journey, requiring an outlay of several shillings per day.[78] On balance, it is more likely that

---

[74] Norman Housley, 'King Louis the Great of Hungary and the Crusades, 1342–1382', *Slavonic & East European Review*, 72 (1984), pp. 192–208; Pál Engel, *The Realm of St Stephen: A History of Medieval Hungary*, ed. A. Ayton (London and New York, 2001), pp. 163–7.

[75] Engel, *Realm of St Stephen*, pp. 155–6, 185–7.

[76] For the English at Nicopolis, see Guard, *Chivalry, Kingship and Crusade*, pp. 112–13.

[77] Now Bran castle, Romania. Johannes de Thurocz, *Chronica Hungarorum*, vol. I: *Textus*, ed. E. Galántai and J. Kristó, Bibliotheca Scriptorum Medii Recentisque Aevorum, series nova, vol. 7 (Budapest, 1985), p. 182.

[78] Having submitted an exhaustively detailed schedule of his expenses for his mission to Hungary in 1346, Walter atte More (with a companion, two servants and two horses) was allowed 5s. per day, not including the cost of crossing the Channel.

Sabraham moved on to Hungary from another Continental campaigning theatre of war. Prussia or the Balkans might be considered candidates, but the best case can be made for the Italian peninsula, which was a crossroads and skills exchange for the international military community at that time. It had become a stamping ground for English freelance soldiers in the 1360s, during the Peace of Brétigny, and also for Hungarians since Louis the Great's military intervention in the Kingdom of Naples in 1347: that was to be the start of decades of Hungarian royal expeditions and private enterprise activity in the Italian peninsula. Well-documented, mixed companies of English and Hungarian mercenaries are evident in the 1360s, a notable example being a force of 5,000 men formed in 1365 when the White Company, commanded by Hugh Mortimer, joined forces with Nicholas Toldi's Hungarian company.[79] When Sir John Godard, another Scrope supporter in 1386, mentioned service 'en la compaignie del duk' de Duras outre Venize', he seems to be indicating the involvement of Englishmen in one of the Hungarian Charles of Durazzo's campaigns.[80] Elsewhere, the records show Englishmen and Hungarians standing surety for each other.[81] An entirely plausible next step would be for English freelances to seek paid employment in Louis of Hungary's wars in the Balkans, perhaps in the company of men with whom they had been serving in Italy.[82] Of course, Sabraham made no reference to the Italian peninsula in his Court of Chivalry deposition; but, as with his failure to mention the earl of Hereford, this should not be considered significant since we know that he spent time there on several occasions, whether passing through on his way to the eastern Mediterranean or for tours of duty, as (probably) in 1366 and, with Hawkwood, in 1378.

Sabraham in England

An understanding of the second half of Sabraham's military career, during the 1360s and 1370s, must perforce take account of what we know of his life and

---

Kew, TNA, King's Remembrancer: Accounts Various, E 101/312/22. Fritz Trautz, 'Die Reise eines englischen Gesandten nach Ungarn im Jahre 1346', *Mitteilungen des Instituts für Österreichische Geschichtsforschung*, 60 (1952), 359–68.

[79] *Codex Diplomaticus Dominii Temporalis S. Sedis*, ed. Augustin Theiner, 3 vols (Rome, 1861–2), II, pp. 419–26; Attila Bárány, 'The Communion of English and Hungarian Mercenaries in Italy', in *The First Millennium of Hungary in Europe*, ed. Klára Papp and János Barta (Debrecen, 2002), pp. 126–40, at 126.

[80] Nicolas, *Scrope and Grosvenor Controversy*, I, p. 172; Bárány, 'Communion', pp. 136–7. This is unlikely to have been in 1367, as Godard fought at Nájera in April of that year: cf. Luttrell, 'English Levantine Crusaders', p. 151 n. 77.

[81] For this insight I am grateful to Professor William Caferro: personal communication, 2 September 2009.

[82] Bárány, 'Communion', p. 133.

commitments in England. Assuming, as we should, that our soldier was one and the same as the now married Newcastle burgess who was thrice returned to parliament, how did his military career dovetail with his domestic responsibilities? Marriage to an heiress was surely important to Sabraham, enabling him to rise (as the schedule of charges for the 1379 poll tax expressed it) from the status of esquire without land, who 'est en service ou ad este armez', to that of 'esquier de meindre estat'.[83] His new-found landed status would explain why, apparently for the first time while in the king's pay, he secured a letter of protection for his tour of duty at Roxburgh in 1371. It would also have made it easier to finance a career with the sword that became particularly adventurous during the 1360s, and which clearly involved much time away from hearth and home. Sabraham's wife, Alice, will have become accustomed to lengthy absences during these years; for, in contrast with the settled conditions of occupation and settlement in Lancastrian Normandy, the peripatetic life of the fourteenth-century careerist soldier was not one that a wife could easily share.[84]

The inherited landed wealth that Alice brought to their marriage gave Sabraham a substantial propertied stake in the borough of Newcastle upon Tyne,[85] and it was this that effectively qualified him for election to parliament. He was first returned to represent the borough in 1373, and again in 1376, the second occasion being an experience that he shared with his old comrade, William Heselrigg, who was elected (for the first time) as knight of the shire for Northumberland.[86] And quite an experience it proved to be, for this was the Good Parliament, from which emerged the process of parliamentary impeachment and the office of Speaker.[87] The majority of parliamentary burgesses at this time were drawn from the merchant community, whether 'great capitalist or small trader',[88] but Sabraham was more akin to a second group of the borough's representatives: those who were 'primarily landowners whose interest in commerce was almost exclusively official rather than personal'.[89] Even more typical of that second group was

---

[83] Given-Wilson, *PROME*, VI: *Richard II, 1377–1384*, ed. G.H. Martin and C. Given-Wilson, p. 115.

[84] Anne Curry, 'Soldiers' Wives in the Hundred Years War', in *Soldiers, Nobles and Gentlemen: Essays in Honour of Maurice Keen*, ed. Peter Coss and Christopher Tyerman (Woodbridge, 2009), pp. 198–214.

[85] *Cal. Close R., 1364–8*, pp. 331–2; *Cal. I.P.M.*, XVII, nos 1279–51; *Cal. Pat. R., 1335–9*, p. 283. However, the Gilbert Sabraham who held at least a messuage in Newcastle in 1342 was probably related to Nicholas: *Cal. Close R., 1341–3*, pp. 483–4.

[86] *Return of the Name of Every Member* (cit. in n. 16), p. 194.

[87] Galbraith, *Anonimalle Chronicle*, pp. 79–92; W. Mark Ormrod, *Edward III* (New Haven and London, 2012), pp. 550–62.

[88] May McKisack, *The Parliamentary Representation of the English Boroughs during the Middle Ages* (Oxford, 1932), p. 106.

[89] Roskell, *Commons, 1386–1421*, I, p. 548.

Laurence Acton (d. 1386/7), who accompanied Sabraham to parliament in both 1373 and 1376.[90] Acton owned 'extensive property' in Newcastle and holdings elsewhere in Northumberland. Like his father, William, before him, he was a long-serving bailiff of Newcastle. When, also like his father, he represented Newcastle in parliament, in 1371, 1372, 1373 and 1376, he would therefore have brought a wealth of pertinent knowledge to the task. What he seems to have lacked, however, was what Sabraham possessed in abundance: military experience.[91] To what extent Sabraham's martial credentials set him apart from other elected burgesses is as yet unclear. While William Heselrigg's campaigning experience was typical of knights of the shire at this time,[92] it has been suggested that burgesses were 'much less martially inclined'.[93] Port boroughs may have been different, however. Coastal raids, the predation of commerce on the high-seas and the mounting of sea-keeping patrols, whether financed by the Crown or of the self-help variety, thrust such communities into the front line of the war. It is easy to see why the electors of Newcastle might choose a military veteran to represent their interests, especially one who was known personally to some of the peers and knights of the shire in parliament.[94] Of Sabraham's role in these parliaments, we know nothing. His more experienced colleague Laurence Acton no doubt took the lead in sponsoring a petition on behalf of the town of Newcastle concerning a long-running dispute with Tynemouth Priory.[95] But Sabraham was well qualified to comment on matters relating to war, whether, at the Good Parliament, seeking the king's assistance for English knights and esquires who, having been taken prisoner, had to find 'great and outrageous' ransoms,[96] or – more obviously related to Newcastle's predicament – at the parliaments of 1373 and 1380, requesting appropriate remuneration to ship-owners and masters whose vessels had been commandeered for royal service.[97]

If there was a certain logic in Sabraham's transition from soldier and local landowner to parliamentary burgess, he clearly had no intention of following a prescribed *cursus honorum*. Having represented Newcastle in successive parliaments, Sabraham resumed his life of adventure with the sword. For some men, election to parliament formalised the end of an active military

---

[90] *Ibid.*, II, p. 9.

[91] Acton's son, also Laurence, served in the Berwick castle garrison, 1382–4: Kew, TNA, Chancery: Scotch Rolls, C 71/61, m. 1; C 71/63, m. 9.

[92] Andy King, 'What werre amounteth': The Military Experience of Knights of the Shire, 1369–1389', *History*, 95 (2010), pp. 418–36.

[93] *Ibid.*, p. 433.

[94] For example, Sir Richard Waldegrave represented the county of Suffolk in 1376: *Return of the Name of Every Member*, p. 194.

[95] Petition 90: Given-Wilson, *PROME*, V, pp. 357–8, 386; cf. *Ancient Petitions Relating to Northumberland*, ed. C.M. Fraser (Surtees Soc., 176, 1961), pp. 82–4, no. 64.

[96] Petition 70: Given-Wilson, *PROME*, V, pp. 344–5.

[97] 1373: petitions 16 and 17: *ibid.*, V, pp. 284–5; 1380: *ibid.*, VI, pp. 179–80.

I Stained glass window showing the arms *Argent a lion rampant sable crowned and armed or* in a north ambulatory window at Norwich cathedral. These are the arms that were contested in the Lovell *v.* Morley lawsuit, and this window may be the 'armes peyntez […] en verrure dune fenestre del north partie du dicte esglise' mentioned in the record of the case in TNA, C 47/6/1, m. 24.

II Seal of Warin Grosvenor, of Budworth (Cheshire), showing him with symbols of his office as Chief Forester of Delamere Forest: bow, hunting-dog and horn. Datable to 1274×7. TNA, E 42/112.

III The opening folio of a manuscript with the Middle English texts known as *Speculum Devotorum* and *The Craft of Dying*, written in the early fifteenth century. University of Notre Dame (South Bend, Indiana), MS Eng. d. 1.

IV Detail from Plate III, showing the arms of John Scrope (d. 1455), Fourth Baron Scrope (of Masham) (differenced by the addition of a label of three points, for a son and heir), impaling those of his wife Elizabeth, daughter of Sir Thomas Chaworth. The presence of the label on Lord Scrope's arms shows that he was still only the heir to the barony and had not yet received the writ that first summoned him to parliament (1426).

V Piece of horse harness, gilt-bronze, with hinge and attachment stud, with the enamelled arms, *Azure a bend or*, that were disputed between Sir Richard le Scrope and Sir Robert Grosvenor, 1385–90.

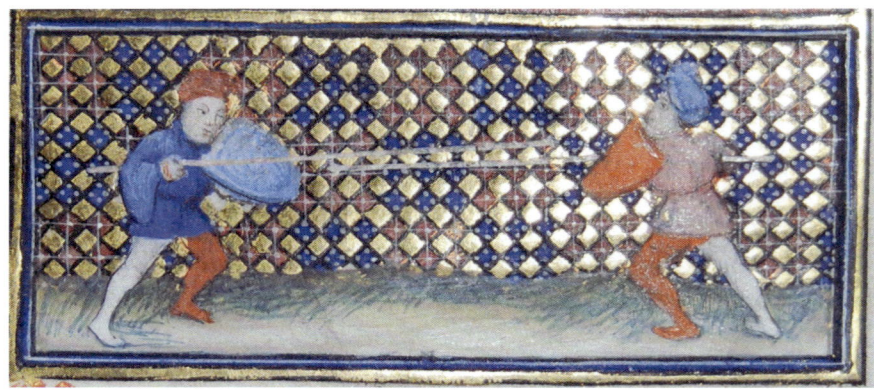

VI Young men train to be soldiers. Detail from a fifteenth-century French manuscript of Vegetius, *De re militari*. Glasgow Museums, RL Scott Library, MS E.1939.65.1621, f. 45.

VII Mail provides a flexible defence, being formed of interlocking riveted rings of steel; it would be lined with fine leather. Detail from a pair of sixteenth-century European mail sleeves, now Glasgow Museums, accession no. 2.135.

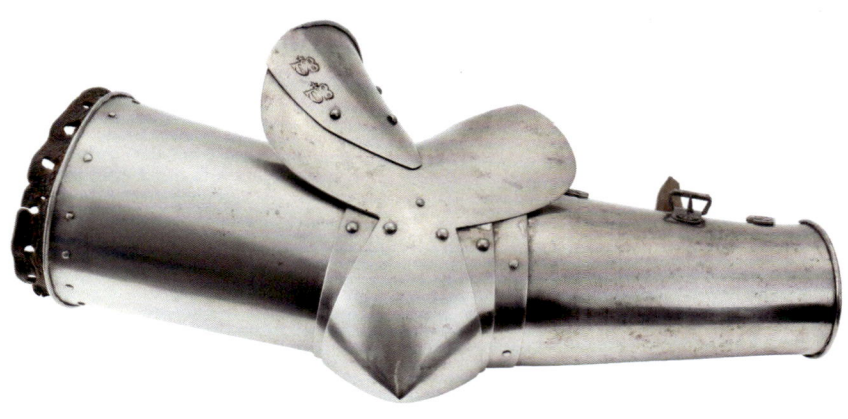

VIII (a) and (b) Arm defences (vambraces) are constructed of articulated steel plates to offer protection and manoeuvrability. These are part of the 'Avant' armour illustrated in Plates IX and X.

IX, X Field harness (war armour) made in Milan between 1438 and 1440; it is the oldest near-complete plate armour in existence. Known as the 'Avant' armour, it formed part of R.L. Scott's bequest to the city of Glasgow, 1939. It was designed for use in war and not for single combat, and thus differs from the equipment described in John Hill's treatise. Glasgow Museums, accession no. E.1939.65.e.

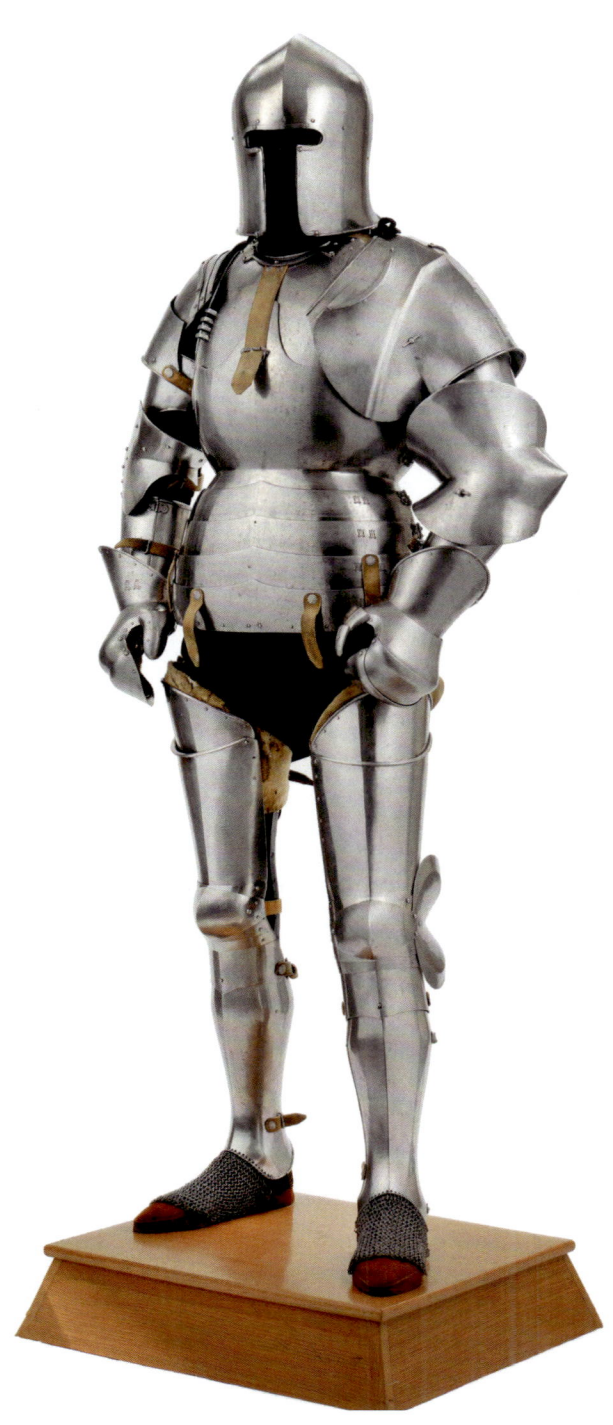

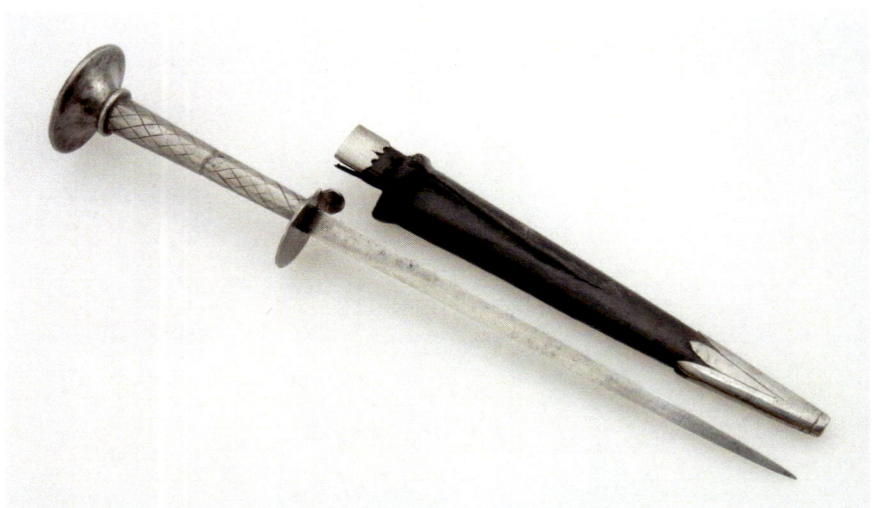

XI Rondel dagger, German *c.* 1500: a vicious weapon, used to thrust into the gaps of an opponent's harness. Glasgow Museums, accession no. 2.119.

XII Common seal of the Marshalcy of France (appended to a document dated 1410). Diameter: about 33 mm. This was the official seal of the two marshals of France, whose arms are shown impaled: Jean II Le Maingre, otherwise Boucicaut (at left), and Jean de Rieux (right). Boucicaut was marshal between 1391 and 1415 (when he was captured at Agincourt) while Jean de Rieux held office 1397–1411 and 1413–17; the seal must therefore have been made between 1397 and 1410. The full inscription was: 's. COMMUN DE LA MARESCHAUCEE DE FRANCE'. Dijon, Archives Départementales de la Côte-d'Or, B 11776

career.[98] This was certainly the case for William Heselrigg, but Sabraham was perhaps ten years younger than his comrade in arms and, as an investigation of the careers of MPs during this phase of the Anglo-French war makes clear, alternated military and parliamentary experience was not unusual.[99] What was perhaps exceptional was Sabraham's deviation from the king's war into the freelance sphere in Italy. We can only speculate about his motivation. He would have known that the profitability of soldiering in Italy was by no means guaranteed. Perhaps we are seeing the wanderlust of a man of action reluctant to accept the implications of his advancing years; a man, moreover, who was disconcerted by the nature and pace of change at home. The untimely death of Hereford without male heir in early 1373, which may have prompted Sabraham's foray into parliamentary politics, deprived him of a natural outlet for his martial skills. That an era had indeed come to an end was signalled even more forcefully by the death of the old king in June 1377. The subsequent French coastal raids may not have reached Northumberland, but there are indications that Newcastle suffered a serious demographic and economic crisis at this time. A claim, made around 1380, that the town, which had 2,647 taxpayers in 1377, had recently lost over 6,000 souls to the plague can be taken with the pinch of salt;[100] but the deleterious consequences of disease, taxation and war are persistent themes of the documents at this time, and the suggestion that a third of the town had been 'degaste et deshabite par pestilence' during the 1370s is not necessarily to be dismissed.[101]

It is easy to see why Sabraham might wish to escape from the north-east of England – and, indeed, the Anglo-French war – and resume soldiering elsewhere. The Italian peninsula was the obvious place to go, offering plentiful employment opportunities, not least with 'English' companies. Moreover, Sabraham must have had some familiarity with the necessary travel routes. When precisely he joined Sir John Hawkwood is not known. We have only a single documentary snapshot, which reveals that by July–August 1378 'Sabraam' was, in Hawkwood's words, one of the senior figures in the English company.[102] It is likely that these men had long been acquainted. Hawkwood's early career is even less well documented than Sabraham's,

---

[98] For example, the mercenary captain Sir John Thornbury, having returned to England from Italy, acquired land in Hertfordshire and was elected knight of the shire in 1382, the first of five occasions. Roskell, *Commons, 1386–1421*, IV, pp. 591–3.

[99] King, 'What were amounteth', pp. 423–4.

[100] J. Kermode, 'The Greater Towns, 1300–1540', in *The Cambridge Urban History of Britain*, I: *600–1540*, ed. D.M. Palliser (Cambridge, 2000), pp. 441–65, at 442–3; *Cal. Pat. R., 1377–81*, p. 510.

[101] Fraser, *Ancient Petitions*, pp. 34–7, nos 29–30.

[102] 'Cuidam ex maioribus …': Archivio di Stato di Mantova, Archivio Gonzaga. busta 2388, no. 284; Brown, *Calendar of State Papers Venice*, I (cit. in n. 13), no. 72. For the operations of Hawkwood and his army during this period, see Caferro, *John Hawkwood*, pp. 196–208.

but our best guess would be that he followed the natural recruitment path for a young man from Essex and, via a local subcontractor, joined the earl of Northampton's campaign retinue, doing so at very much the same time as Sabraham did from his home in Northumberland.[103] At this stage they were surely men of similar social and military status. What they were doing throughout much of the 1350s is unclear, but during the 1360s their careers certainly diverged, Hawkwood building his reputation exclusively in Italy, while Sabraham ranged widely across Christendom and beyond. That said, their paths may well have crossed during the years 1366–8: either initially, while Hereford negotiated the marriage of Lionel, duke of Clarence, to Violante, daughter of Galeazzo Visconti, lord of Pavia, or later when a contingent of English mercenaries, doubtless including Hawkwood, escorted Clarence from Pavia to the wedding venue in Milan.[104] That Sabraham was one of Hawkwood's lieutenants in 1378 suggests respect for his expertise, if not prior experience of working together. It may also suggest that Sabraham joined the English company as a sub-contractor leading a contingent of troops.

What we know of Sabraham's service with Hawkwood serves as a reminder that, in their relations with the civilian population, soldiers did not always have it their own way. Sabraham was waylaid while travelling in Mantuan territory and robbed of two horses, his swords and travelling bags. Although Ludovico Gonzaga, Lord of Mantua, ordered restitution of the property, one of the bags was empty when it was returned. Hawkwood wrote to Gonzaga on 6 August seeking recovery of what had been withheld – presumably valuables or money – concluding that he hoped Sabraham and the company would not have cause 'to do something mutually disagreeable'.[105] Unfortunately, nothing more is known of this episode, nor is it clear how long Sabraham spent in Italy. He had certainly returned to England in time to be elected as one of Newcastle's two parliamentary burgesses for the parliament of January 1380, but the circumstances of his return are unclear. What we do know is that Hawkwood's army had 'devolved into chaos and disorder' to an unprecedented degree during the summer of 1378.[106] Distracted commanders lost their grip at a time of pay arrears, supply shortages and poor morale. Men turned to pillaging and the local population retaliated, as Sabraham found to his cost. Dismayed by personal humiliation and loss, as well as by his comrades' indiscipline, he may have decided to take his leave of the Italian scene sooner than originally intended. Perhaps, indeed, it was at this time that he travelled to Hungary, attracted by the prospect of paid service in Louis the Great's wars. There had been contact with Hungarians, some of whom had been taken prisoner by Hawkwood's company during the aborted campaign

---

[103] Caferro, *John Hawkwood*, pp. 31–42.

[104] Ormrod, *Edward III*, p. 443; Caferro, *John Hawkwood*, p. 134.

[105] Brown, *Calendar of State Papers Venice*, I, no. 72.

[106] Caferro, *John Hawkwood*, pp. 198–9, 201–4.

against Verona,[107] and the timing of such a spell of duty would fit well with Thuróczy's report of Englishmen serving at Törcsvár.

Conclusions

Providing testimony before the Court of Chivalry at York Minster in September 1386 was one of Sabraham's last public acts for which documentary evidence has been found. (We know that he outlived his wife, who died in 1398, but how he spent the remainder of his life is unknown.) For him, it was fitting – and, no doubt, a proud moment – that he should be offered an opportunity, late in life, to report on his eventful career with the sword before an assembly of his peers. For us, the record of that occasion, while in some respects elusive, has ensured that a remarkable life can be both instructive and thought provoking: indicative of how a man might pursue a military career, while suggesting further avenues for inquiry. Our investigation of Sabraham's martial life through close, contextualised scrutiny of his testimony prompts a number of conclusions. The first is something of a commonplace that Sabraham's career illustrates what was possible for an English soldier in the fourteenth century. Our man's real life in arms makes the fictional one assigned by Geoffrey Chaucer to his Knight seem a little less fantastic.[108] Indeed, Sabraham might even have been a model of sorts for Chaucer's Knight. Having discovered the 'Sabraam document' in the Mantuan archives, William Caferro went on to argue that Geoffrey Chaucer and this Sabraham were actually in the same place at the same time, and probably met.[109] Sabraham's career has also been seen as emblematic of how crusading in its various forms was still an important, indeed vibrant, part of the English military community's varied diet of soldiering. Indeed, Timothy Guard has argued that, during the fourteenth century, Englishmen enjoyed 'probably their greatest degree of crusade involvement' since Richard I's reign, the 'pattern of traffic' no doubt related to the 'variety of war-frontiers and briefer terms of service' [110] We cannot be sure what proportion of all militarily active Englishmen (or even knights and esquires) were involved, but it may be instructive to note that only 10 out of the 221 lay deponents who supported Scrope's claim admitted to some experience of the crusade. Even if we exclude those who gave their testimony in the Plymouth session of the Court, where the witnesses' words appear to have been heavily summarised for the record, only 6 per cent of Scrope supporters mentioned crusading expeditions. And, in terms of variety

---

[107] *Ibid.*, pp. 205–6.
[108] S.H. Rigby, 'The Knight', in *Historians on Chaucer: The 'General Prologue' to the Canterbury Tales*, ed. S.H. Rigby and A.J. Minnis (Oxford, 2014), pp. 42–62.
[109] Caferro, *John Hawkwood*, pp. 200, 203.
[110] Guard, *Chivalry, Kingship and Crusade*, p. 4.

of experience, none of them comes close to Sabraham. If his testimony was in a number of respects distinctive, so too his military career, in terms of its geographical and political range, was certainly not the norm and may have been exceptional.

Sabraham's life is particularly instructive as a guide to the recruitment dynamics underpinning the service of the careerist – or 'proto-professional' – soldier. However, it is important to recognise that his experience of military careerism was altogether different from that of the defining age of the medieval English professional soldier: the three decades from the late 1410s to 1450, when a large garrison establishment was maintained by the English Crown on a permanent footing in Normandy and the *pays de conquête*. Long-term service by careerist soldiers within a single institutional context appears properly 'professional' in the modern sense; and this was the predominant form of military service accessible to Englishmen at that time.[111] Conditions were not at all like this is in Sabraham's day. While the careerist became a prominent and ubiquitous feature of the English military scene during the mid- to late-fourteenth century, it is far less easy to characterise him and his circumstances precisely.[112] This was a period that, apart from garrison establishments like Calais, lacked defining institutional structures; a period in which employment opportunities, paid or parasitical, might arise in every corner of Christendom, often owing to economic and political instability. In a world of diverse opportunities and identities, we might expect to find the typical careerist's service to have been socially 'unembedded' (as Stephen Morillo has termed it), indeed politically detached.[113] These were certainly the classic characteristics of the mercenary: men like Hawkwood, who belonged to a mobile, self-interested transnational pool of soldiery. Sabraham spent time with such men, but what his career illustrates so well is how the service of proto-professionals could also be socially embedded, shaped by military lordship and by comradeship groups that were rooted in the social networks of regional military communities. Indeed, as we have seen, it was entirely natural for an aspiring soldier to begin his career in this way. And military lordship fostered careerism further by transporting men to potential employers and war zones that would otherwise have been inaccessible; by providing opportunities for new connections to be made, both within the social organism of the magnate's campaign retinue and, beyond that, across international recruitment networks, thereby encouraging the emergence of true freelance careerism.

---

[111] Bell et al., *The Soldier in Later Medieval England* (cit. in n. 7), pp. 266–70.

[112] Andrew Ayton, 'The Military Careerist in Fourteenth-Century England', *Jnl of Medieval History*, 43 (2017), pp. 4–23.

[113] Stephen Morillo, 'Mercenaries, Mamluks and Militia: Towards a Cross-Cultural Typology of Military Service', in *Mercenaries and Paid Men: The Mercenary Identity in the Middle Ages*, ed. John France (Leiden and Boston, Mass., 2008), pp. 243–60.

If military lordship offered foundational experience upon which careerists could build personal career paths, the individuality of those paths, which is so striking a feature of the fourteenth-century proto-professional, arose from the particularity of circumstances and of men's responses to them. In Sabraham's case, the onset of official peace in the Anglo-French war in 1360 coincided with the coming of age of Humphrey Bchun, earl of Hereford: a young man keen to emulate his father's exploits, who would have to do so in the crusading sphere, at least until the French war recommenced in 1369. Whereas Sabraham's comrade, William Heselrigg, probably considered himself too old to begin a new chapter of military life, Sabraham was in his prime in the early 1360s and was no doubt valued by Hereford as a reliable veteran. These circumstances, and Sabraham's willingness and capacity to take advantage of opportunities when they presented themselves, were the motors that shaped the second, notably colourful phase of his career: the phase that has really captured the imagination of historians. That 'capacity' was no doubt assisted by an advantageous marriage, which also, in due course, paved the way to public office. Thus, while Sabraham's career demonstrated what it was possible for a careerist soldier to achieve, this was one man's distinctive response to the opportunities with which he had been presented. Given that he left so few traces in the conventional military–administrative records, we have reason to be grateful that the Court of Chivalry provided a podium for men who were destined to slip into the shadows of history. And the benefit for us lies not simply in having a source that yields facts about an obscure man's life. It is also in the glimpse of an occasion in which is revealed how Sabraham's peers regarded him: their respect for the knowledge and experience of a much-travelled warrior, irrespective of his relatively obscure social origins.

Appendix: Deposition of Nicholas Sabraham, York, 17 September 1386.[114]

Nicholas Sabraham, esquire, aged sixty years and more, armed thirty-nine years, brought forward by Sir Richard Le Scrope's party, [was] sworn in and examined. Asked if the arms *Azure a bend or* belong, or should belong, by right and by inheritance to Sir Richard Scrope: [Nicholas] said yes, for he had seen the arms of Scrope on banner and coat-armour during the *chevauchée* of Sir Edward Balliol in Scotland. And also he saw the arms of Scrope, *Azure a bend or*, on a banner in the company of the earl of Northampton, when he rode by torchlight out of Lochmaben as far as Peebles, and in his company was Sir Henry Scrope with his banner. Likewise, concerning the muster from

---

[114] Translated from Nicolas, *Scrope and Grosvenor Controversy*, I. pp. 124–5.

all parts of Christendom, assembled at the instigation of the King of Cyprus for his planned expedition to Alexandria in ships and galleys: Nicholas said that immediately upon landing, one Sir Stephen Le Scrope, armed in the arms of Scrope, *Azure a bend or with a label argent* for difference, received the order of knighthood from the king of Cyprus. Likewise, Nicholas said that he had been armed in *Pruce*, in Hungary, at Constantinople, *a la bras de Seint Jorge* [the Bosphorus] and at *Messembre* [Nessebar, on the Black Sea coast of Bulgaria]. And in a church in the said *Messembre* one of the Scropes lies buried and above him on the wall are painted the arms of Scrope, *Azure a bend or with a label, and on the label three bezants gules.* Asked how he knew that they were the arms of Scrope and the name [of the deceased], [Nicholas] said that the wardens of the said church had told him. Also the said Nicholas had seen Sir Henry Scrope armed in France with a banner in the company of the earl of Northampton, [and] Sir William Scrope, elder brother of the said Sir Richard, in the same company, armed in the arms entire or with differences, at the battle of Crécy, at the siege of Calais, in Normandy, in Brittany, in Gascony and in Spain, and beyond the great sea [the Mediterranean], in many places where many deeds of chivalry have been performed. And in all the places he had been, he had never heard Sir Robert Grosvenor spoken of, nor any of his ancestors. Asked how he knew that these are the Scrope arms, he said that he had often heard his ancestors say that they are the Scrope arms, and that the ancestors of Sir Richard Scrope have used and possessed the said arms, and have been in continual and peaceable possession [of them] from time immemorial; and [because] he heard from his ancestors and from old men, lords, knights and esquires in his country, now deceased, that they have been passed down by rightful lineal descent from the time of the Conquest. Asked if he had ever heard that [possession of] the said arms was at any time challenged or interrupted by the said Sir Robert Grosvenor, or by his ancestors, or by anyone on his behalf, [Nicholas] said that he had never heard Sir Robert Grosvenor spoken of, nor any of his ancestors. There was the challenge that Carminow [*Carmynau*] made to Sir Richard Scrope before Paris, concerning which the king and the late duke of Lancaster concluded that both [parties] had always been entitled to bear the arms entire and thus the matter was closed. The said Nicholas had heard of no other challenges.

CHAPTER 6

'Armed and redy to come to the felde': Arming for the Judicial Duel in Fifteenth-Century England

Ralph Moffat

This chapter provides a short investigation into a treatise describing the arming process for trial by combat or, as it is so couched, for a 'bataille of Treason sworne withinne Listes before his Souverain Lorde' (MS, p. 376). Described by its author, John Hill, as a 'Traytese […] of the poyntes of worship in Armes that Longeth to a Gentilman in Armes. And how he shall be diversly Armed' (p. 376), it provides a great amount of detail on the arming process and was written by a man with hands-on experience of the production and care of armour.

The text of the treatise, as Anglo has helpfully pointed out, survives only in two seventeenth-century copies.[1] They are housed in the library of Lincoln's Inn, London (Hale MS 11, ff. 70-4) and the Bodleian Library, Oxford (MS Ashmole 856, pp. 376–83).[2] There is negligible difference between the two, so this author has selected the Bodleian Library's copy for the purposes of this work. The treatise's author invites the 'reders to correcte adde and amenuse where need is' (p. 376), and so this reader has taken the liberty of rendering into modern English the relevant sections and endeavouring to provide an explanation thereof. The full original transcribed text is provided at the end of the chapter.[3]

---

[1] S. Anglo, *The Martial Arts of Renaissance Europe* (New Haven, Conn., and London, 2000), pp. 206 and 349, n. 17. Little is known about the circulation of Hill's text in the fifteenth century, but it may have been used as one basis for another short treatise on the armour and equipment needed for foot combat, extant in British Library, MS Lansdowne 285, f. 9r–v, and at least two other MSS: see G.A. Lester, *Sir John Paston's 'Grete Boke': A Descriptive Catalogue … of British Library MS Lansdowne 285* (Cambridge, 1984), pp. 84–5.

[2] I am grateful to Drs Robin Darwall-Smith and Robert Athol for their kind assistance.

[3] It has not previously been published with any accuracy, although it was printed in *Illustrations of Ancient State and Chivalry, From Manuscripts Preserved in the Ashmolean Museum*, ed. W.H. Black (Roxburghe Club, 56, 1840), pp. 3–11, and, with errors, by C. ffoulkes, *The Armourer & His Craft* (London, 1912), pp. 173–6, Appx.C. A summary was given by L.O. Pike, *A History of Crime in England*, 2 vols (London, 1873–6), I, pp. 389–92.

Background of the author

According to his treatise, the author, John Hill, was an 'Armorier and Sergeant in thoffice of Armorye with Kynges Henry the 4[the] and Henry the 5[the]' (p. 376). An account made by him for armour in the Tower of London survives from 1416–18.[4] Previous to this post, Hill was undoubtedly what was known as a linen armourer, that is, a craftsman who produced and affixed the fabric linings and coverings such as the helmet linings to steel armour. This is evidenced by the appearance of a John Hill in an account of payments from 29 September 1410 to 1 April 1412: 'Armatura. John Hill stuffing bacinetts, paletts, vantbraces, rerebraces, and other harness for a voyage to Calais'.[5] That 'stuffing' means equipping steel armour with fabric is demonstrated in the household accounts of the Earl of Derby of 1393–4. In these, there are payments to a Richard Stuffer for lining a plate collar, stuffing a helm, and lining a mail neck defence ('Ricardo Stuffer pro linura unu' coler' de plate […] pro stuffura unu' helm' […] pro linura unu' pysen').[6] Hill was also, we are told, one of the 'Wardeins of the Fraternite of Taillours and lynge armurers of Seint John Baptiste in the Citee of London' on 23 July 1451.[7] This contradicts the statement in the treatise that 'Johan Hyll dyed at London in Novembre the xiij[the] yeer of Kyng Henry the Sixt' [1434] (p. 382). There is always the possibility that the roman numerals have here been mis-transcribed.

Hill appears fleetingly in the contemporary record. As mentioned above, he appears in a list of payments from 1410 to 1412 and in his account at the Tower of 1413–18. We find him acting as mainpernor (one who stands surety that another will appear in court) along with seven other armourers for a fellow armourer in 1420.[8] This suggests that he was a senior and respected member of the civic community by this time. He was a benefactor towards the Armourers' Hall, included in a list of men who provided for its windows in 1428.[9] He sat on an assize for a property complaint in the parish of St Martin

---

[4] Kew, TNA, Exchequer Pipe Office, Wardrobe Accounts, E 361/6, rot. 11d; this is an account from March 1413 of John Hill, King's armourer.

[5] J.H. Wylie, *History of England under Henry the Fourth*, 4 vols (London, 1884–98), IV, pp. 226–7.

[6] Kew, TNA, Duchy of Lancaster: Various Accounts, DL 28/1. I am grateful to Dr Adrian Ailes for all his kind assistance in locating relevant documents in the National Archives.

[7] *Calendar of Letter-Books … of the City of London … Letter-Book K*, ed. R.R. Sharpe (London, 1911), p. 337. For further discussion of linen-armourers, see M. Davies and A. Saunders, *The History of the Merchant Taylors' Company* (Leeds, 2004), pp. 11–13, 49–52.

[8] *Calendar of the Plea and Memoranda Rolls … of the City of London, 5: 1413–1437*, ed. P.E. Jones (Cambridge, 1943), p. 81.

[9] London, London Metropolitan Archives: City of London, CLC/L/AB/G/002/MS 12105: Armourers & Brasiers' Company Benefactions Book, f. 28.

without Ludgate in 1433.[10] His healthy appetite is attested by the fact that a certain Walter Mangeard, cook, of London and Sussex, in his will of 1433 tells us that I 'bequethe and ȝeue alle the dettes thet Iohn Hille, Armerer, owyth me, to the chirche werkes of seynt Brides [Fleet Street]'.[11]

The treatise and interpretation

Our Sergeant Armourer begins his treatise with the fabric undergarments and footwear:

> First, he (the appellant) needs to have a pair of red hose without vamps (feet and ankles) and the said hose cut at the knees and lined within with grey linen cloth as the hose are.
>
> A pair of shoes of thin red leather fretted underneath with whipcord and pierced and lined within with grey linen cloth three fingers in breadth from the toe to an inch above the ankle. And so behind the heel from the sole half a quarter-yard up: this is to firmly fasten [the shoes] to his sabatons (foot defences) and the same sabatons fastened to the sole of the foot in two places.

That the hose need be red is explained by the author later on in the treatise. The whipcord on the sole of the shoe is to prevent slipping during combat. (Plate VI is a contemporary depiction of fifteenth-century doublet and hose worn by warriors in training.)

> He also needs a petticoat and the outer layer of a doublet. His petticoat should be without sleeves three quarters in size around without collar. And the other part (i.e. the doublet) be no further than the waist with straight sleeves and collar and certain eyelets in the sleeves for the vambraces and rerebraces (arm defences).

This slightly confusing section is most likely a description of the arming doublet. This foundation garment was designed especially for the attachment of mail and plate armour. No examples survive from the medieval period but they do appear in illustrations and documents. One of the earliest instances is

---

[10] H.M. Chew, *London Possessory Assizes: A Calendar* (London Record Soc., 1, 1965), no. 246.

[11] F.J. Furnivall, *The Fifty Earliest English Wills in the Court of Probate, London, AD 1387–1439*, Early English Text Soc., Orig. Ser., 78 (1882), p. 94. Note, however, that there was a John Hille, citizen and armourer, of St Bride's parish, London, who made his testament and last will on 4 October 1444 and died very soon afterwards, since it was proved in the court of the Bishop of London's Commissary on 10 October 1444: London, London Metropolitan Archives: Diocese of London archives, DL/CL/C/B/004/9171/4, f. 148v.

a mention of a doublet of black worsted (woollen cloth) for armour ('doublet de worstede noir p[u]r armo[u]r') in an inventory of the possessions of an English knight in 1387.[12] By 1414 the garment was known in English as an 'armyngdoublet'.[13] Hill's insight into the thickness of the material (i.e. three fingers) reinforces the earlier assertion of his profession as a linen armourer. The 'certain eyelets' are small holes in the arming doublet reinforced with metal rings to take the arming points (laces to attach the armour). We know this because an inventory of the Tower of London in 1455 lists eight haubergeons (mail shirts) three of which were 'broken to make slewys [...] and yes'.[14]

> First it behoves him to have sabatons, greaves, and closed cuisses with voiders of plate or mail and a closed breech of mail with five buckles of steel the tissues straps of fine leather. And, after all the arming points have been knotted and fastened on his armour, that their points be cut off.

The process of arming from the feet up is ubiquitous in scenes from medieval romance. Thus the legharness follows with the foot, lower-leg defences, and thigh defences: sabatons, greaves and cuisses. All of these are comprised of steel plates articulated with rivets and leather straps simply known as 'leathers'. 'Closed' here refers to the piece of armour fully encompassing the part of the body it is designed to protect. Next come the voiders. These are pieces of mail to protect the parts of the body not defended by the steel plates: the voids such as the armpits and the inside of the elbows. Further documentary evidence corroborates this. An inventory of 1397 lists 'thirty pieces of mail in the shape of voiders' ('xxx petitz peces de maile a guyse de voiders').[15] Long and short voiders along with a pair specifically for cuisses (thigh defences) and vambraces (arm defences) ('j par' voiders long' and j par' voiders parum pro Cusscheux and j par' voiders pro les vantbrace') were purchased in an account of 1414–15.[16]

The breech of mail is for the protection of the lower torso and groin. This had to be carefully shaped by the mail maker to ensure freedom of movement and suitable protection for this vulnerable area. A Scottish earl had the misfortune to lose one testicle in battle.[17] The item is also referred to

---

[12] Oxford, Bodleian Library, MS Eng. hist. b. 229, f. 4. I am grateful to Dr Robin Darwall-Smith for his assistance in locating this document.

[13] Receiver-general's account of John Mowbray, second duke of Norfolk, March 1414 – March 1415. Berkeley Castle (Glos), Berkeley Castle Archives and Library, Muniment D1/1/30 [GAR 428]. Transcribed with the kind permission of the Berkeley Will Trustees. I extend my thanks to Dr Tobias Capwell for sharing with me this fascinating document.

[14] Kew, TNA, Chancery: Patent Rolls, C 66/480, membr. 7.

[15] Kew, TNA, Exchequer: King's Remembrancer, Miscellanea of the Exchequer, E 163/6/13.

[16] Berkeley Castle Archives, Muniment D1/1/30 [GAR 428].

[17] Walter Bower, *Scotichronicon*, gen. ed. D.E.R. Watt, 9 vols (Aberdeen and Edinburgh, 1987–98), VIII, p. 58.

as a brayer or brayette. The 'fine leather' is for the lining of these mail pieces. The lining of mail in this manner is alluded to in many documents. (See Plate VII, which shows a detail of sixteenth-century mail, from a pair of European mail sleeves.)

The arming points, as aforementioned, are laces for the attachment of the steel plates of the armour to the arming doublet. It is interesting here that the excess material is to be cut off after tying. This is perhaps to ensure that no weapon catches on them or causes them to be severed, leading to undue injury during combat.

That gussets and voiders are not synonymous is attested in the documentary record. For example, in an account of 1416–18 are 'j breeke de maile j pair gusset iij pair voiders' (one breech of mail, one pair of gussets, three pairs of voiders) and in an account of 1397 are one pair of gussets, one little brayer, and three pairs of voiders ('j peir' gussets j petit braieux et iij peir voidours').[18]

> And then a pair of closed gussets strong 'sclave not draw' and that the gussets be three fingers within his [pair of] plates (torso defence) at both sides.

This section is unclear, as the word 'sclave' has not been identified. There are two possible interpretations. The first is that this may refer to the cross section of the wire of the mail links or rings, the preference here being for flat section rather than the wire drawn through a metal plate, whence 'not draw'. There are, however, clear references in the fifteenth century to round and flat mail. For example, a Southwark armourer in 1454 had one 'habergeon de [...] Ronde maile' and one 'jaket de Flat maile'.[19] The second possible interpretation is that there should be a sleeve of mail; but this is uncertain. That these mail defences for the armpit are to be three fingers within the torso defence is most likely in order to ensure that no blade can easily pass through to this vulnerable part of the body.

> And then a pair of plates weighing twenty pounds – his breech and his plates attached together with wire or [arming] points

Next comes the torso defence. A pair of plates is a defence of multiple steel plates riveted to a fabric foundation and then covered – often by a luxurious covering of velvet or leather. Its use was starting to wane by the opening of the fifteenth century; the cuirass (solid back- and breastplate) was starting to take over. It is of note that the writer's defence of choice is the more old-fashioned pair of plates rather than the cuirass. This may give some indication of the

---

[18] London, Westminster Abbey Muniments, WAM 12163, f. 12r–v; Kew, TNA, Exchequer: King's Remembrancer: Escheators' Particulars of Account, E 136/77/4.

[19] London, London Metropolitan Archives, Corporation of London Records Office collections, CLA/024/01/02, Plea & Memoranda Roll A 80, membr. 4.

advanced age of our writer, as his preference is for the more antiquated of the two types of defence for the torso.

> A pair of rerebraces shut within the [pair of] plates at the front with two forlocks (clasps) and behind with three forlocks.
> A pair of closed vambraces with mail voiders fretted thereunto.

Plate arm defences: vambraces (from the French *avant bras*) for the forearms and rerebraces for the upper arm (*arrière bras*) are secured to the pair of plates. There is no mention of the elbow defence (couter) but, as curtly explained by Mann, '"couter" and "poleyn" [knee defence], are comparatively rare in medieval texts, because their presence was understood as being included in the larger compound'.[20] (See Plate VIII (a) and (b).)

> A pair of gauntlets of advantage which may be devised.

The plate hand defences are described as 'of advantage'. The meaning of this is not entirely clear.

> A bascinet of advantage for the lists which is of no use for any combats but man-to-man save that necessity have no law. The bascinet locked, bevor and visor locked or charnelled (hinged), [the bascinet] also [affixed] to the breast and back with two forlocks.

This type of helmet is what is now termed a 'great bascinet' to differentiate it from its diminutive originator. The bevor is a chin and throat defence. It is worth dwelling on Hill's point here that this equipment is not for use in war. It has been developed exclusively for the field of single combat: 'man for man' (p. 377). Texts such as Hill's should thus be employed with caution when used to describe arming for war. This bascinet is securely affixed to the pair of plates by clasps (forlocks) before and behind. (See Plates IX and X for images of war armour made in Milan between 1438 and 1440. Unfortunately, no medieval helmets designed solely for single combat survive.)

> And, when this aforesaid gentleman appellant is thus armed and ready to come to the field, place on him his coat armour of single beaten (i.e. decorated) tartarin[21] for advantage in fighting. And his legharness should be completely covered with red tartarin – which is called little tunics – for the covering of his legharness is done because his adversary should not easily espy his blood. And therefore his hose should also be red for, if they are of

---

[20] J.G. Mann, 'The Nomenclature of Armour', *Trans. Monumental Brass Soc.*, ix (1952–62), pp. 414–28, at 422–3.

[21] 'A fabric, most likely a tabby-woven silk, made in (or originally made in, or imported via) Tartary', *Encyclopaedia of Medieval Dress and Textiles of the British Isles, c. 450–1450*, ed. G. Owen-Crocker et al. (Leiden, 2012), p. 579.

another colour, blood will easily be seen. For in old times in such a combat nothing would have been seen uncovered save his bascinet and gauntlets. And then tie a pair of besagews on him.

In this section Hill reveals his deep understanding of the psychology of the trial by combat. Red, we are told, prevents the appellant and defendant from perceiving the amount of blood lost and therefore the likelihood of imminent victory or defeat. The allusion to 'old times' may shed some more light on the age of our author as he recalls judicial combats from years past. The fourteenth century was one in which covered armour was ubiquitous. Numerous examples are to be found in documents of the period.

The besagews are steel pieces designed to offer extra protection to the vulnerable armpit; usually circular in shape. They are frequently depicted on contemporary tomb brasses and effigies.

A coffer or a pair of bags, also therein charcoal and bellows.

This is essential equipment for an armourer in the field.

A spear, longsword, a short-sword, and a dagger fastened upon himself. His swords fretted and with besagews before the hilt and before the hand at the pommel and near their hilts.

(See Plate XI.) Fretting denotes the leather cord covering the grip of the sword. The besagews here are what are currently known as rondels: disk-shaped defences for the hand.

If the present author has not fully explained all the technical terms he should be forgiven. As Beard pointed out in an article of 1928, 'the men who best knew the meanings of these technical words were the Store Keepers at Greenwich and the Tower, soldiers like Sir John Smyth, Markham and Barret, and armourers like John Hyll'.[22] When John Hill died he took this advanced knowledge with him and thus 'he accomplisshed noo more of the complyng of this Trayties; on whos soulle God have mercy for his endles passion. Amen' (MS, at pp. 382–3).

The treatise[23]

Traytese compyled by Johan Hill Armorier and Sergeant in thoffice of Armorye with Kynges Henry the 4^{the} and Henry the 5^{the} of the poyntes of

---

[22] C.R. Beard, 'Armour, and the "New English Dictionary"', *Connoisseur*, 81 (May–Aug. 1928), pp. 235–7, at 235.

[23] Oxford, Bodleian Library, MS Ashmole 856, pp. 376–83. See above, p. xii, for the editorial conventions applied in the presentation of this text.

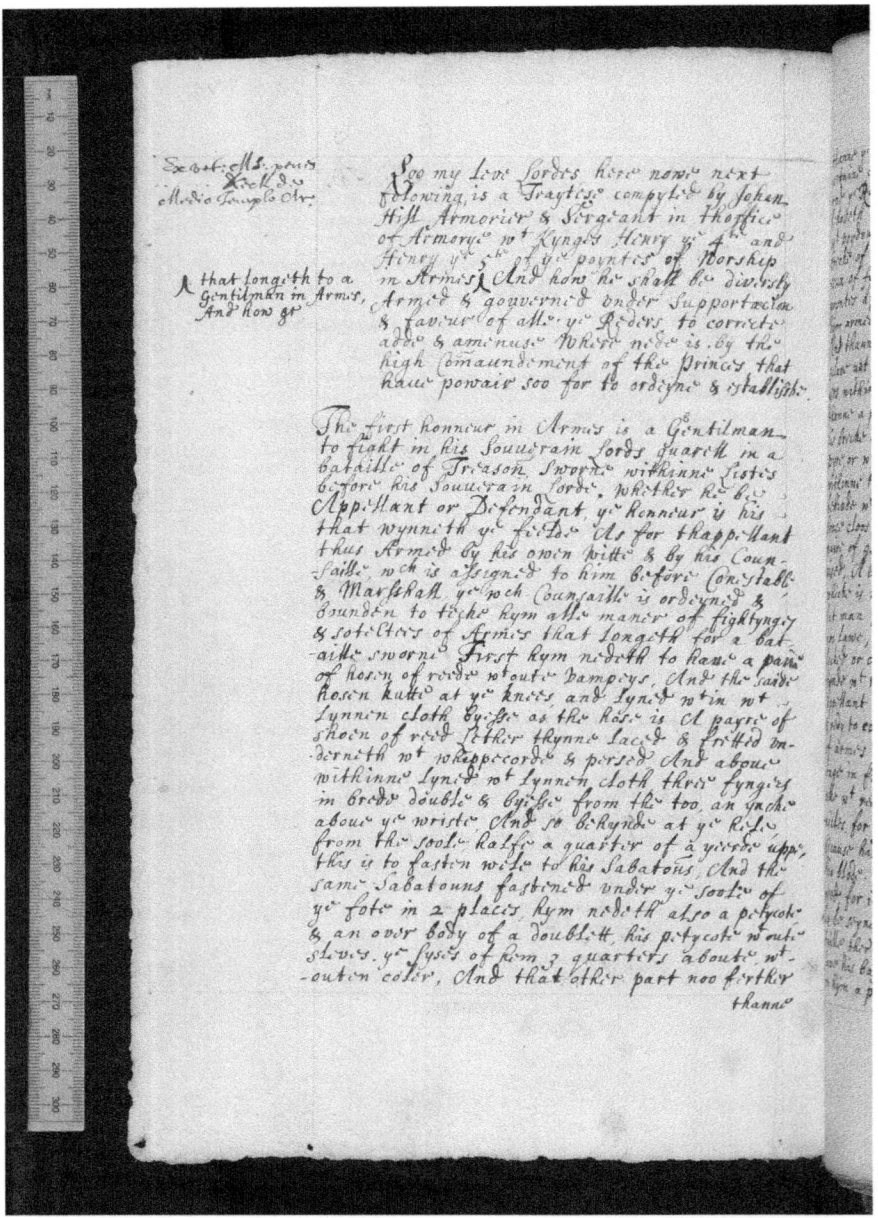

6.1 Opening page of the treatise of John Hill. Bodleian Library, MS Ashmole 856, p. 376.

Worship in Armes that longeth to a Gentilman in Armes. And how he shall be diversly Armed.

[*marginal note*: Ex vet: MS: penes . . . Keck de Medio Templo.[24]] Loo my leve Lordes, here nowe next folowing is a Traytese compyled by Johan Hill Armorier and Sergeant in thoffice of Armorye with Kynges Henry the 4[the] and Henry the 5[the] of the poyntes of Worship in Armes [*marginal insert:* that Longeth to a Gentilman in Armes] And how he shall be diversly Armed and gouverned under Supportacion and faveur of alle the Reders to correcte adde and amenuse where need is, by the high Commaundement of the Princes that have powair soo for to ordeyne and establishe.

The first honneur in Armes is a Gentilman to fight in his Souverain Lords quarell in a bataille of Treasoun, sworne withinne Listes before his Souverain Lorde, whether he be Appellant or Defendant, the honneur is his that wynneth the feelde As for thappellant thus Armed by his owen witte and by his Counsaille, which is assigned to him before Conestable and Marsshall, the which Counsaille is ordeyned and bounden to teche hym alle maner of fightynges and soeteltees of Armes that longeth for a bataille sworne.

First hym nedeth to have a paire of hosen of reece withoute vampeys. And the saide hosen kutte at the knees, and lyned within with Lynnen cloth byesse as the hose is. A payre of shoen of reec Lether thynne laced and fretted underneth with whippecorde and persed And above withinne lyned with Lynnen cloth, three fyngers in brede double and byesse from the too, an ynche above the wriste.[25] And so behynde at the hele, from the sole, halfe a quarter of a yeerde uppe, this is to fasten wele to his Sabatouns. And the same Sabatouns fastened under the soole of the fote in 2 places, hym nedeth also a petycote and an over body of a doublet, his petycote withoute sleves, the Syses of hem 3 quarters aboute, withouten coler. And that other part noo ferther /p. 377/ thanne the waste, with streyte sleves and coler and certaine oylettes in the sleves for the vauntbras and the Rerebrase.

Armed in this wise. First behoveth Sabatouns greevis and cloos qwysseux with voydours of plate, or of mayle, and a cloos breche of mayle, with 5 bokles of stele, the tisseux of fyne lether. And alle the armyng poyntes after they ben knytte and fastened on hym armed. that the poyntes of hem be kutte of. And thanne a paire of cloos gussetts, stronge sclave not drawe, and that the gussetts be thre fyngers withinne, his plats at both assises. And thanne a paire of plates of xx[ti] lib' weight, his breche and his plat[es] enarmed to gider with wyre, or with poyntes. A pair of Rerebrace shitte withinne the plates, before with two forlockes and behinde with thre

---

[24] Keck is doubtless identifiable as Thomas Keck, who was admitted to the Middle Temple in 1651 and rose to be a Master of the Bench. Cf. H.A.C. Sturgess, *Register of Admissions to the Honourable Society of the Middle Temple: From the Fifteenth Century to the Year 1944* (London Middle Temple, 1949). The next three items in Ashmole 857 (artt. 23–5 in W.H. Black's catalogue of the Ashmole MSS) were all transcribed from the same manuscript. I am grateful to Dr Nigel Ramsay for this information.

[25] I.e., ankle.

forlocks. A paire of vauntbrace cloos, with voydours of mayle y fretted. A paire of gloves of avauntage, whiche may be devised. A basnet of avauntage for the listes whiche is not goode for noon other batailles, but man for man, save that necessitee hath noo lawe, the basnet locked baver and vysour locked or charnelled also to the brest and behynde with two forlockes.

And this Gentilman appellant aforesaide whanne he is thus armed and redy to come to the feelde, do on hym his cote of armes of sengle tartren y beten for avauntage in fighting. And his leg herneys covered all with reed taretryn, the whiche ben called tunicles, for the coveryng of his leg herneys is doen, bicause his adversarie shal not lightly espye his blode. And therefore also ben his hosen reed, for in alle other coleurs, blode wil lightly be seyne, for by the oolde tyme, in such a bataille ther shulde noo thing have be seyn bare save his basnette and his gloves. And thanne tye on hym a paire of besgewes

Also it sitteth[26] /p. 378/ the forsaide counsaille, to goo to the Kyng the day before the bataille and aske his logging nigh the listes. Also the forsaide counsaille muste ordeyne hym the day of his bataille, thre preests to synge hym thre masses: the first masse of the Trinite, the seconde of the Holy goste, and the thirde of oure Lady, or elles of what other sainte or saintes, that he hath devocion unto. And that he be watched alle that night unweting hym, that he is watched, and light in his Chambre alle that night that his counsaille may wite how that he slepeth. And in the morning whanne he goeth to his Masses, that his herneys be leyde at the North end of the Auter, and covered with a cloth, that the gospell may be radde over it, and at the laste masse for to be blessed with the preest; and whanne he hath herde his Masses, thanne to goo to his dyner. And soo to his Armyng in the fourme aforesaide.

And whanne he is armed and alle redy, thanne to comme to the feelde in forme tofore reherced, thanne is his counsaille bounden to counsaille hym and to teche hym, how he shal gouverne hym of his requests to the Kyng or he come into the feelde, and of his entree into the felde, and of his gouvernance in the feelde, for the saide Counsaille hath charge of hym before Conestable and Mareschal, til that Lesses les aller be cryed. The whiche requestes ben thees, that the saide Appellant sende oon of his counsaille to the Kyng for to requere hym that whanne he commeth to the barrers to haue free entree with his counsaille, Confessour and Armorers with alle maner of Instruments, with brede and wyne, hymself bringing in, in [*sic*] an Instrument, that is to saye a cofre or a pair of bouges. Also therein fyre cole and belyes, and that his chayer /p. 379/ with certaine of his servants may be brought into the feelde and sette up there, the houre of his Commyng, that it may cover hym and his counsaille whanne he is commen into the feelde, this forsaide gentilman appellant commyng to the listes, whether he wol on horsebak or on fote with his Counsaille, Confessour and other servaunts aforesaide, havyng borne by fore hym by his counsaille, a spere a long swerde a short swerde and a dagger fastened upon hymself, his Swerds fretted and beasgewed [*sic*] a fore the hiltes, and afore the hande,

---

[26] Mistranscribed as 'fitteth'.

her pomelles nere her hiltes havyng noo maner of poynts, for and ther be founden that day un [*sic*] hym moo [*sic*] poyntes of wepons thanne foure, it shal tourne hym to greet reproof.

And this gentilman appellant shal come to the barrers at the Southeest Sonne, his visier downe.[27] And he shal aske entree; Where shal mete hym Conestable and Mareschal, and aske hym what art thou. And he shal saye, I am suche a man, and telle his name to make goode this day by the grace of God, that I have saide of suche a man, and telle his name before my Souverain Lord, and they shal bidde hym putte up his visier, and whanne he hath putte up his visier, they shal open the barrers and latte hym inne and his counsaille before hym, and with hym his Armoriers, and his Servaunts shall goo streight to his chayer with his breed, his wyne and alle his instruments that longe unto hym, save his wepons. And whanne he entreth into the felde, that he blesse hym sobrely and so twys or he come before his Souverain Lord. And his counsaille shal do thair obeissaunce before thair souverain Lord twyes or they come to the degrees of his Scaffolde, and he to obeye him with his heed at both tymes, thus whanne they to fore thair souverain Lord, they shal knele adown and he also, they shal aryse or he aryse, he shal obeye hym with his heed to his Souverain Lord, and thanne aryse, and whanne he is up opon his feete, he shal blesse hym and turne hym to his chayer, and at the entryng of his /p. 380/ chayer sobrely torne hym, his visage to his Souverain Lord wards, and blesse hym, and thanne tourne hym agayne, and soo go into his chayer, and there he may sitte hym downe and take of his gloves and his basnet, and so refressh hym til the houre of his Adversarie approche with breed and wyne, or with eny other thing that he hath brought in with hym. And whanne the defendant his Adversarie commeth in to the feelde, that he be redy armed againe or that he come into the felde standing withoute his chayer, taking hede of his Adversaries commyng in, and of his countenance that he may take counfort of. And whanne the defendant his Adversarie is come into the felde, and is in his chayer, thanne shal the Kyng sende for her wepons and se hem, and the Conestable and the Mareschal also, and if they be leefull they shal be accepted, and if they be not leeful they shal be kept in the feelde, and kutte the same day by the commaundement of the Kyng, and the Conestable and Mareschal in the Kynges behalve. And thanne fitteth it to the foresaide counsaille to arme hym, and to make hym redy against that he be called to his first ooth, and whanne he is called to his first ooth, thanne sitteth it to alle his forsaide counsaille to goo with hym to his first ooth for to here what the Conestable and Mareschal seyen unto hym, and how he swereth, and what countenaunce he maketh in his sweryng. And whanne he hath sworne, they shal ryse up by the commandement of the Conestable and Mareschal. And whanne he is on his feete he shal obey hym to his Souverain Lord and blesse hym and thanne torne hym to his chayer, his visage to his

---

[27] As W.H. Black pointed out, the sun is in the south-east at about 9 a.m. – although in the ordinances for single combat reportedly made by Thomas, duke of Gloucester, the appellant or challenger is required to appear by the hour of prime or 6 o'clock.

Souverain Lord wards, and in his going blesse hym twyes by the weye, or he come to his chayer. And at /p. 381/ the entryng to his chayer, sobrely tourne hym his visage to his Souverain Lord wards, and blesse hym, and soo go into his chayer.

Thanne sitteth it to his forsaide counsaille to awayte whan the defendant shal come to his first ooth, and that they be there as sone as he for to here how he swereth, for he must neds swere that al that ever thappellant hath sworne is false substance, and alle. And if he wol not swere that every worde and euery sillable of every worde substance and alle is false, the Counsaille of the said Appellant may right wisly aske Jugement upon him. And the Kyng shal of right yeve hym Jugement by Lawe of Civile and raison of Armes, for after the Juge is sette ther shulde noo plee be made afore hym that day. And if soo be that the defendant swere duely, thanne the Counsaille of the forsaide Appellant shal goo to his Chayer agayne and abide there, til they be sent for. And thanne shul [*sic*] they bringe hym to his seconde Ooth, and here how he swereth and whanne he hath sworne, they shal goo with hym to his chayer agayne in the fourme aforesaide. And whanne he is in \his/ chayer the saide Counsaille shal awayte whanne the Defendant commeth to his seconde ooth, and here howe he swereth, and if he swere under eny subtil teerme cautele or cavellacion, the forsaide Counsaille of thappellant may requere the Jugement. And if he swere duely, thanne shall the Counsaille of the forsaide Appellant goo to his chayer agayne, and abide there til they be sent for. And thanne shall they brynge hym to his thirde ooth and assurance. And whanne they be sworne and assured, the saide Appellant with his Counsaille shal goo agayne to his chayer, in the fourme aforesaide and there /p. 382/ make hym al redy, and fastene upon hym his wepons, and so refresshe hym, til the Consetable and Mareschall bid hym come to the feelde.

Thanne shal his Armoriers and his servants voyde the Listes with his chayer and alle his Instruments at the Commandement of the Conestable and Mareschal, thanne fitteth it to the Counsaille of the saide Appellant to aske a place of the Kyng afore hym withinne the barre upon his right hande, that the saide Counsaille of thappellant may come and stande there, whanne they ben discharged of the saide Appellant. The cause is this, that suche pyte may be yeuen to the Kyng of God, that noon of hem shal dye that day, for he may by his powair royal in suche a cas take it into his hande; the forsaide Counsaille of thappellant to abyde in the saide place til the King have yeven his Jugement upon hem. And thanne the Conestable and Mareschal shal deliver the forsaide Appellant by the Commandement of the Kyng to his forsaide Counsaille to governe hym of his going oute of the feelde as wele as they did of his comyng in, his worship to be saved in al that lyeth in hem. And soo to brynge hym to his Logging agayne to unarme hym, counforte hym, and counsaille hym. And sum of his Counsaille may goo to the Kyng and common with hym, and wite of the Kyng how he shal be demeaned.

This enarmyng here aforesaide is best for a bataille of arreste with a swerde, a dagger, an Ax, and a pavoys til he come to thassemblee his sabatouns and his tunycles evoyded.

132

And thanne the Auctor Johan Hyll dyed at London in Novembre the xiij^the yeer of Kyng Henry the Sixt,[28] so that he accomplisshed noo more of the compylyng of /p. 383/ this Trayties; on whos soul̄e God have mercy for his endles passion. Amen.

[28] 1434.

CHAPTER 7

The Jurisdiction of the Constable and Marshals of France in the Later Middle Ages

Bertrand Schnerb

The legal power of the highest French military offices at the end of the Middle Ages is a topic which formed part of Gabriel Le Barrois d'Orgeval's monograph, *Le tribunal de la connétablie en France du XIVe siècle à 1790*, published in 1918.[1] This study was the first specific one to be published on the subject. Since its publication, a few authors have made important contributions, especially M.H. Keen[2] and, more recently, L. Cazaux.[3] However, a major problem for scholars is that of documentary sources. We have to observe, indeed, that there is a distinct lack of legal records. Before the sixteenth century, French legal records – and especially those in the archive of the Parlement de Paris – contain no specific archive relating to military jurisdiction. The activities of the *cour de la Connétablie* and of the *cour des maréchaux* (the courts of the Constable and the Marshals of France) are not completely unknown, however. There exist some clear traces of both courts' work, but these traces are widely scattered and have to be sought in a variety of categories of documents, especially in the letters and judgments of ordinary courts in which the judicial power of military office-holders is mentioned.[4]

Moreover, there are a few ordinances and other normative texts which are particularly useful and of which the best known is entitled *Les droiz du connétable*. This document was registered by the king's Chambre des comptes in Paris. A copy was produced in January 1382 at the request of Olivier de

---

[1] G. Le Barrois d'Orgeval, *Le tribunal de la connétablie de France du XIVe siècle à 1790* (Paris, 1918). See also *idem*, *Le maréchalat de France des origines à nos jours*, 2 vols (Paris, 1932).

[2] M.H. Keen, *The Laws of War in the Late Middle Ages* (London and Toronto, 1965), *passim*, but especially pp. 26 ff.

[3] L. Cazaux, 'Le connétable de France et le Parlement: la justice de guerre du royaume de France dans la première moitié du XVe siècle', in *Justice et guerre de l'Antiquité à la Première Guerre mondiale*, ed. M. Houllemare and P. Nivet (Amiens, 2011), pp. 53–62.

[4] See for example *English Suits before the Parlement of Paris, 1420–1436*, ed. C.T. Allmand and C.A.J. Armstrong, Camden Fourth Ser., 26 (Royal Historical Soc., 1982).

Clisson, who was appointed Constable of France after the death of Bertrand du Guesclin in 1380. Unfortunately, the text does not describe the judicial powers of the Constable – not even briefly. It mentions only what interested Clisson: that is to say the Constable's authority, his military power and above all his financial rights.[5] Another text, more complete, once existed in the registers of the Chambre des comptes and was published in Anselme de Sainte-Marie's *Histoire généalogique*. It was entitled *Ce sont les droits que le connestable doit avoir pour cause de sa connestablie* ('These are the rights the constable must have in respect of his constableship').[6] Both of these normative texts are undated, but they are probably of the mid-fourteenth century.

Certain royal ordinances set out the military and administrative duties of the Constable and the Marshals: during the reign of Charles VI, for example, in April 1411, a royal ordinance settled a dispute between the Marshals of France and the Master of the Crossbowmen about their respective judicial powers.[7] Two years later, through ordinances of January and May 1413, the royal government declared that the Constable and the Marshals (or their lieutenants) were the only competent officers to receive the musters and reviews of soldiers serving in the royal army (which was not without consequences for their judicial authority, as will be seen).[8]

There is no specific royal ordinance setting out the judicial power of the Marshals of France and of their provosts before that of January 1537,[9] but there is an undated Burgundian ducal ordinance entitled *Ordonnance de prevost des marissaulx* (ordinance of the provost marshals).[10] This ordinance, which is probably from the end of the fifteenth century, contains a substantial amount of information. In addition, it is worth referring to the articles concerning the Marshal in the *Decreta Sabaudiae Ducalia* of 1430[11] because a comparison with the practices in great lordships outside the kingdom of France – in the duchy of Savoy, for example – is richly illuminating.

---

[5] Anselme de Sainte-Marie et al., *Histoire généalogique et chronologique de la Maison royale de France*, 9 vols (Paris, 1726–33), VI, pp. 234–5; E. Cosneau, *Le connétable de Richemont (Arthur de Bretagne) (1399–1458)* (Paris, 1886), pp. 504–5.

[6] Anselme de Sainte-Marie et al., *Histoire généalogique et chronologique*, VI, p. 233.

[7] *Ordonnances des rois de France de la troisième race*, ed. E.J. de Laurière et al., 21 vols (Paris, 1723–1849), IX, pp. 589–90.

[8] *Ibid.*, X, pp. 57–8 (May 1413), and Paris, Archives nationales, JJ 168, no. 99, and B. Schnerb, *L'honneur de la maréchaussée: Maréchalat et maréchaux en Bourgogne des origines à la fin du XVe siècle* (Turnhout, 2000), pp. 110–12 (Jan. 1413).

[9] 'Ordonnance conférant aux prévôts des maréchaux une juridiction d'exception en dernier ressort sur les excès des gens de guerre vagabonds, ceux-ci fussent-ils rentrés à leur domicile', in *Ordonnances des rois de France: Règne de François Ier*, VIII (Paris, 1963–72), pt 2, pp. 242–5, no. 768.

[10] Lille, Archives départementales du Nord, B 1288, no. 16526; published in Schnerb, *L'honneur de la maréchaussée*, pp. 212–21.

[11] *Decreta Sabaudiae Ducalia* (Glashütten-Taunus, 1973; reprint of the edn of Turin, 1477), ff. 111v–112v.

The *coutumiers* (or collections of customs) – like *La somme rurale* (the *Rural Summary*), the last great French *coutumier*, which was set down by the lawyer Jehan Boutillier in about 1395 – also contain useful information. This particular collection includes two short chapters, one of which is entitled 'Des droits du connestable de France', and the other 'Du droit des mareschaulx de France'; each includes remarks about the judicial powers of these office-holders.[12]

Some French didactic treatises, especially Honoré Bouvet's *L'arbre des batailles*[13] and Christine de Pizan's *Livre des faits d'armes et de chevalerie*[14] (the latter closely related to Bouvet's treatise), are also sources of information about what these judicial powers comprised, and it is not surprising to find that Arthur de Bretagne, count of Richemont, who was Constable of France between 1425 and 1458, owned a copy of Honoré Bouvet's book.[15]

Some other, more miscellaneous documents, like the royal letters of appointment and the text of the Constable's oath, are also valuable for the topic.

The origins of the military jurisdiction

We have no precise information about the origins of the two offices' juris-dictional powers. The first tangible evidence of their existence dates from the beginning of the fourteenth century (there is nothing before that time, although the offices of the Constable and Marshals existed as great military offices from at least the end of the twelfth century). A letter from King Philip V dated 9 February 1317 was sent to the bailiff of Amiens, ordering him to arrest a squire named Thomas Banot. This man-at-arms belonged to a royal garrison on the borders of Flanders. He was involved in a quarrel with another French man-at-arms, and the letter mentions the fact that he was previously 'ex certis causis ad duelli vadium provocatus et appelatus [...] in curia marescallorum Francie'. He did not dare to fight and escaped, and so his arrest was ordered.[16]

Four years later, in December 1321, in a judgment of the royal court (Parlement), it was noted that the Constable of France (at this time Gaucher

---

[12] Paris, Bibliothèque nationale de France, MS français 202, ff. 48–51.

[13] Paris, Bibliothèque nationale de France, MS français 1263; P. Contamine, 'Penser la guerre et la paix à la fin du XIVe siècle: Honoré Bouvet (v. 1345–v. 1410)', *Quaestiones medii aevi novae*, 4 (1999), pp. 3–19.

[14] *Une femme et la guerre à la fin du Moyen Âge: Le Livre des faits d'armes et de chevalerie de Christine de Pizan*, ed. D. Martini, C. Le Ninan, A. Paupert and M. Szkilnik (Paris, 2016).

[15] P. Contamine, *Guerre, état et société à la fin du Moyen Âge: Études sur les armées des rois de France, 1337–1494* (Paris – La Haye, 1972), p. 203.

[16] Paris, Archives nationales, X1a 1, f. 118v (Feb. 1317); Le Barrois d'Orgeval, *Le tribunal de la connétablie*, pp. 323–4, no. 1.

de Châtillon) argued that he had 'racione officii dicte constabularie in saisina habendi et exercendi omnimodam jurisdictionem in familiares suos'. Consequently the Constable declared that he had the power to judge any of his own *famuli* who committed murder.[17]

These early texts are valuable because they show two cases of judicial intervention by the Crown's military officers. In the first place, it is clear that the two Marshals of France presided in the *curia marescallorum* and were competent to judge cases in which soldiers serving in the royal army were involved. And secondly, the legal proceedings of the *curia marescallorum* included, as means of proof, the *duelli vadium* (in French, *gage de bataille*) – that is, judicial duel or judicial combat.

In the second text it is also made clear that *ratione personae*, the Constable of France had judicial power over his *famuli*, that is to say, members of his *familia* or household. In fact, an investigation was carried out at this time by the Chambre des comptes to determine the validity of this claim, and subsequently this special competency was included in one of the normative texts registered by the Chambre des comptes. The text states as follows: 'Item, nuls n'a connoissance, justice, seigneurie ne jugement sur les gens de l'hostel le connestable, fors li et li maistre de son hostel' ('nobody has the right to judge members of the Constable's household, except he himself and the master of his household').

From the middle of the fourteenth century onwards, legal documents refer to the military jurisdiction of the Constable and Marshals with increasing frequency. And from this time, too, the *prévôts des maréchaux* (provost marshals) start to appear in accounts and records. They acted as lieutenants of the two Marshals of France: they were their delegates, with local or regional power. The judicial records of the Parlement show that the *prévôts des maréchaux* were closely linked to the Marshals and hierarchically subordinated to them. It was possible to appeal against a provost's judgment before the *curia marescallorum*, or even before the Constable himself, because he was hierarchically superior to the Marshals (*superior marescallorum*). And, of course, it was possible to appeal against a judgment of the Constable's or Marshals' courts before the Parlement.[18]

In a lawsuit in 1456, however, one of the parties contested the fact that the other had appealed to the Constable's court against a judgment of the *curia marescallorum*, arguing that 'les mareschaulx ne ressortissent devant le connestable, ains s'en vont de plain vent en la court de parlement' (the Marshals are not in the Constable's jurisdiction, but their causes come directly before the Parlement). The other party answered: 'y a encore plus

---

[17] Paris, Archives nationales, X1a 5, f. 150 (Dec. 1321); Le Barrois d'Orgeval, *Le tribunal de la connétablie*, pp. 324–5, no. 2.

[18] Paris, Archives nationales, X1a 16, ff. 101v–102v (Jan. 1354); Le Barrois d'Orgeval, *Le tribunal de la connétablie*, pp. 325–8, no. 3.

de C causes venant des mareschaulx devant le connestable' ('there are at present more than a hundred cases coming from the Marshals' court before the Constable').[19]

The proceedings of military courts: in the field and at the
Siège de la Table de Marbre

Both military courts (the *curia marescallorum* and the Constable's court) held hearings in the field when the Constable and the Marshals were campaigning. But, in the second half of the fourteenth century, both also held hearings in Paris at the *Table de Marbre* (*apud Tabulam marmoream* – at the Marble Table) which was one of the most important places in the Great Hall of the Palais de la Cité in Paris. The earliest clear reference to a hearing held by the *curia marescallorum* at the Marble Table is to be found in a judgment of the Parlement dated 12 August 1370. During the next year, 1371, an appeal is mentioned for the first time as being heard in the Constable's court at the *Table de Marbre*. In the same year, the existence of the *sceau aux causes de la connétablie de France* – that is, a seal that was used only for legal matters – is also documented for the first time).[20]

It is not known precisely how the Constable's and Marshals' field sessions were held, but the proceedings are mentioned in Burgundian sources: we know that in the fifteenth century the Marshal of Burgundy (who regarded himself as a third Marshal of France) held hearings twice a week (on Mondays and Thursdays, which were *jours de plaid*); he judged the cases with the help of some captains and even a few lawyers, acting as his judicial counsellors.[21] Philippe de Clèves, in his military treatise, *Instruction sur toutes manières de guerroyer* (published in 1516), suggested that the Marshal should always have a copy of Honoré Bouvet's *Arbre des batailles* ('car c'est un livre qui déclaire beaucoup de choses selon la justice militaire': it is a book in which many things are declared about military justice). Philippe de Clèves commented that nobody could criticise the Marshal if he judged the cases according to Bouvet's book. Without question, this affirmation, although contained in a sixteenth-century treatise, reflected the opinion of military judges of the fifteenth century.[22]

Hearings in the field settled ordinary cases (and the most urgent). Otherwise, the most important and the most complicated cases were judged

---

[19] Paris, Archives nationales, X1a 9211, f. 2 (Sept. 1456); Le Barrois d'Orgeval, *Le tribunal de la connétablie*, pp. 362–3, no. 32.

[20] Paris, Archives nationales, X1a 22, f. 36 (Aug. 1370); Le Barrois d'Orgeval, *Le tribunal de la connétablie*, pp. 335–6, no. 9.

[21] Schnerb, *L'honneur de la maréchaussée*, p. 166.

[22] *Ibid.*

at the *Table de Marbre*. There the Constable and the Marshals could themselves sit and adjudicate. More commonly, however, they were not present and the sessions of both courts were heard by lieutenants who were professional lawyers. For example, Maître Ponce Quartier was the Constable's lieutenant at the Marble Table from 1371 to 1380, in the time of Bertrand du Guesclin; and Maître Jehan de Troissy held the same position in the 1440s, in the time of Arthur de Richemont. By this date the lieutenant, whose function was becoming increasingly prestigious, bore the title of *lieutenant général*.[23]

We find exactly the same state of affairs in the court of the *amiral de France*, according to a royal ordinance dated 7 December 1373. By this ordinance, King Charles V intended to reform the authority, the competences and the judicial power of the French Admiral. In article 14, it is noted:

> Item, s'il advenoit matieres de grant prix en aucuns lieux ou les lieuxtenans particuliers de nostredit amiral veissent qu'ilz ne peussent pas bien estre obeys ou recouvrer du conseil pour faire seur jugement, pourront renvoier icelles matieres, s'ilz veoient que bon soit, avec les parties adjournees devant nostredit amiral ou son lieutenant, en son siege de la Table de marbre.[24]

In other words, it was confirmed that major cases must be judged by the Admiral's lieutenant sitting at the *Table de Marbre*.

Judicial competence

As we have seen, at the beginning of the fourteenth century it emerged that the Marshals of France were competent to judge cases involving soldiers serving in the royal army. At the same date, the Constable claimed the right to judge members of his own household, and this right was upheld by royal decision. (It is noteworthy, too, that at the end of the fourteenth century, Jehan Boutillier in his *Somme rurale* stated that 'Item encoires, le connestable a congnoissance de tous les officiers de son domicile et de son hostel'.[25]) Hence, for example, in 1367, Robert de Fiennes, Constable of France, claimed that a man named Henri Maugier, his *varlet de chamber, tailleur et officier*, who

---

[23] Le Barrois d'Orgeval, *Le tribunal de la connétablie*, pp. 43–6 and 51–2; *Letters, Orders and Musters of Bertrand du Guesclin, 1357–1380*, ed. M. Jones (Woodbridge, 2004), nos 406, 430, 699; E. Cosneau, *Le connétable de Richemont*, p. 157, 292, 461, 465, 551, 570, 574–9.

[24] *Construire l'armée française: Textes fondateurs des institutions militaires*, I: *De la France des premiers Valois à la fin du règne de François Ier*, ed. V. Bessey (Turnhout, 2006), pp. 68–74.

[25] Paris, Bibliothèque nationale de France, MS français 202, f. 48v.

had been arrested by the bailiff of the bishop of Paris, should be released and delivered to him.[26]

Thereafter, the range of judicial competence of the Constable and Marshals was much more firmly established, as is evident from royal legislation and the records of the Parlement.

The Constable's jurisdiction

Besides the right to judge his own *famuli*, the Constable had a special jurisdiction over cases involving the king's *sergents d'armes* (*servientes armorum*, sergeants-at-arms). From at least the beginning of the fourteenth century, these royal officers belonged to the royal household and formed a standing troop, along with the king's knights, the king's squires and the *huissiers d'armes*. Moreover they were in charge of various missions and could be considered as the *hommes à tout faire* ('odd job men') in the royal household and army.[27]

The Constable's jurisdiction over the *sergents d'armes* is mentioned in judgments dated August and September 1371;[28] in the latter, it is stated that the *sergents d'armes* considered the privilege of adjudication by the Constable's court as a part of their *libertéz, franchises et usages* (that is to say one of their privileges). Twenty years later, this privilege is also mentioned in Jehan Boutillier's *Somme rurale*.

> Sy sachés que au connestable, a cause de son noble office, compete et appartient la congnoissance de tous sergans d'armes du roy et a lui ou a son lieutenant, et doit estre retourné, ventillé et demené en tous cas que en defendant ilz auroient affaire et dont ilz seroient poursieuvis et approchiees de quelque aultre juge, ne doivent ne ne sont tenus de proceder s'il ne leur plaist, car par la nature de leur office de serganterie, ilz en sont exempts et francs ne n'ay point veu que se [= si] quelque sergant d'armes ait esté approchié par devant autre juge, soit que ce ait esté en cas de delit ou autrement, qu'il n'ait convenu que la chose soit retournee par devant ledit connestable ou son lieutenant a la Table de marbre a Paris, reservé causes et actions reelles, car de celles convient il estre demené par devant les juges dont les heritages contemptieux soient tenus; et ainsi a il esté fait par tant de cas et exemples que sans nombre et qu'il ne le fault ramener en doubte

---

[26] Paris, Archives nationales, X1a 1469 (Jun. 1367), f. 215; Le Barrois d'Orgeval, *Le tribunal de la connétablie*, p. 331, no. 6.

[27] M. Ornato, *Dictionnaire des charges, emplois et métiers relevant des institutions monarchiques en France aux XIVe et XVe siècles* (Paris, 1975), pp. 185–6.

[28] Paris, Archives nationales, X1a 22, ff. 204v and 237, and X1a 1469, f. 468; Le Barrois d'Orgeval, *Le tribunal de la connétablie*, pp. 338–41, nos 11 and 12.

ne difficulté aucune, meismement puisque ce a regard en riens en leur office de sergantise.[29]

For Jean Boutillier, that is to say, this authority was exclusive, except when a *sergent d'armes* expressly chose some judge other than the Constable, or when he was involved in a case concerning real estate or inheritance, not as a royal officer but as a private person – which, as will be seen, would provoke some conflicts of jurisdiction.

Of course, one of the most important judicial competences of the Constable's court was that of trying cases involving soldiers. In a letter dated 31 December 1370, King Charles V stated that his Constable (at this time Bertrand du Guesclin) claimed he had to judge all the crimes of 'quelconques gens d'armes chevauchant soubz lui ou nos mareschaux', that is, all soldiers campaigning under the authority or command of either the Constable or the Marshals.[30]

In the second half of the fourteenth century this part of the Constable's authority was so important that it was included in the text of the oath that the Constable took after his appointment. In 1392, when Philippe d'Artois, count of Eu, made his oath, he said 'avec ce, le fait de justice qui appartient a mon office, je feray et feray faire bien et loyaument, aussi bien au pauvre comme au riche, sans faveur ou acception de personne' ('I will do fair and good justice, according to my office, and I will be as fair to the poor as to the rich, without showing favour to anyone').[31]

The Marshals' jurisdiction

The Constable's competence was closely matched by that of the Marshals. In the *Somme rurale*, Jehan Boutillier wrote:

> Item, a cause de leur office ont la court et congnoissance de tous faiz de criesmes et malefices quelz qui soient qui adviennent en l'ost et chevaulcié du roy, soit en bonne ville ou dehors, et de tous les poursieuvans de l'ost ou chevaulcié puisqu'ilz sont yssus de leurs maisons pour venir en l'ost ou chevaulcee jusques a tant qu'ilz y sont retournez.
>
> Item, ont la congnoissance de tous les gaings et pillages faiz en l'ost ou chevaulcee puisque que contens en seroit.[32]

The Marshals had cognizance of all cases of crimes and other illegalities committed by soldiers and other people following the army in wartime,

[29] Paris, Bibliothèque nationale de France, MS français 202, f. 48r–v.

[30] Paris, Archives nationales, Y2, f. 49v (Dec. 1370); Le Barrois d'Orgeval, *Le tribunal de la connétablie*, pp. 336–7, no. 10.

[31] Le Barrois d'Orgeval, *Le tribunal de la connétablie*, p. 23.

[32] Paris, Bibliothèque nationale de France, MS français 202, f. 49v.

whether within a town or outside it. They also had to settle disputes concerning plunder and loot. Men-at-arms and other soldiers were subject to the Marshals' court from the moment they left their home to join the army until they had returned home.

In the royal ordinance of January 1413, concerning the power and authority of the Marshals of France and of the Master of Crossbowmen, it is stated that:

> Compete et appartiengne aux mareschaulx et maistre des arbalestriers de France, seulz et pour le tout, a cause de leurs diz offices, de veoir ou fere veoir, par leurs lieuxtenans ou aucuns de leurs lieuxtenans et commis, en monstres et reveues, toutes manieres de gens d'armes et de trait et autres gens de guerre servans a noz gaiges, de recevoir et passer ceulx d'icelles gens qui sont a ce convenable et souffisamment ordonnéz ...; et avecques ce leur compete et appartiengne la court, congnoissance, juridiction et correction en tous cas de toutes les dictes gens ainsi passez a monstres et reveues et autres surveneus pour occasion de la guerre.[33]

To summarise this, all men-at-arms, bowmen and crossbowmen and all the other people serving in the royal army in wartime were subject to the Marshals' court (and it seems that the fact that the Marshals had mustered the soldiers was the reason of their judicial competence over them – on this point, it should be noted that in April 1411, a royal ordinance stated that the Marshals had authority not only over men-at-arms but also over bowmen and crossbowmen, despite the claims of the Master of Crossbowmen – as had been ruled following a dispute between Marshal Boucicaut and Jehan de Hangest, the Master of Crossbowmen).[34] (See Plate XII for Boucicaut's seal as Marshal.)

The same principle is stated in the great ordinance entitled *Decreta Sabaudiae Ducalia*, dated 1430, in the time of Amadeus VIII, duke of Savoy. In an article of these *Decreta* concerning the Marshal of Savoy, we read:

> Ipsos autem marescallos nostros judices et cognitores omnium et singularum causarum et controversiarum casuum et negociorum militarium inter militares equites et pedites quoscunque tempore guerre occurrencium. Necnon dispositores omnium et singulorum ad guerram et bellum incumbencium et jus militare concernencium juxta regulas ipsius officii marescallie cum deliberacione nostra si presentes fuerimus [...].[35]

In Burgundy, the Marshal and his *prévôt des maréchaux* had to judge and punish all acts of indiscipline committed by soldiers of the ducal army.[36] In 1465, letters of appointment of a Burgundian *prévôt des maréchaux* stated

---

[33] Paris, Archives nationales, JJ 168, no. 99. Schnerb, *L'honneur de la maréchaussée*, pp. 110–12.

[34] *Ordonnances des rois de France de la troisième race*, ed. de Laurière et al., IX, pp. 589–90.

[35] *Decreta Sabaudiae Ducalia*, f. 112v.

[36] Keen, *Laws of War* (cit. in n. 2), pp. 27 and 81.

that this officer had to 'prendre, saisir, emprisonner [...] toutes manieres de malfaicteur de nostre dite armee, iceulx punir et faire punir et corriger a l'exemple de tous autres, selon leur demerites et l'exigence des cas' ('to arrest all the criminals of the army and to punish them exemplarily, according to their crimes and the circumstances of the case'). In the same text, we read that the *prévôt* acting as delegate of the Marshals had to settle the disputes that occurred between members of the army.[37] It seems clear that the jurisdictional competences of the Marshal of Burgundy were similar to those of the Constable and the Marshals of France.

A French royal ordinance of 1537 stated that the Marshals' provosts and lieutenants had the special authority to arrest, judge and condemn all the

> 'gens de guerre, de cheval et de pied, de noz ordonnances et autres, vaccabons et domicilliés [qui] oppriment grandement notre pauvre peuple en leurs personnes et biens en mainctes manieres, tenans les champs, pillant, robbant leurs hostes, forceant et viollant femmes et filles, destroussant et meurtrissant les passans allans et venans' ('men-of-war, horsemen or infantrymen, belonging to the compagnies d'ordonnance or not, roaming or belonging to a garrison, who sorely oppress our poor subjects in many ways, occupying the country, pillaging, stealing, looting, raping women and girls, attacking and murdering the travellers').[38]

In criminal cases, the Constable of France, as the king's lieutenant, could deliver *lettres de remission* or *lettres de grâce*, and a few such letters given by Bertrand du Guesclin are still extant today.[39] However, pardons for capital offences could only be given by the king. In the Burgundian *Ordonnance de prevost des mareschaulx*, it is stated that 'boute feus, forceurs de fame, traittres, mordriers et tous ceulx qui sont chargiés de criesmes de leesmajesté' ('arsonists, rapists, traitors, murderers and all who are guilty of *lèse-majesté*' cannot be pardoned, save by the prince himself).[40]

The cases

The Constable and the Marshals had to judge crimes and acts of disobedience or indiscipline committed by soldiers in wartime. The Marshals' court had specifically to judge cases concerning the military administration: for example,

---

[37] B. Schnerb, 'Un thème de recherche: l'exercice de la justice dans les armées des ducs de Bourgogne (fin XIVe – fin XVe s.)', *Publications du Centre européen d'études bourguignonnes*, 30 (1990), pp. 99–115, at 113–14.

[38] *Ordonnances des rois de France: Règne de François Ier*, VIII (cit. in n. 9), pt 2, pp. 242–5, no. 768.

[39] *Letters, Orders and Musters of du Guesclin*, ed. Jones (cit. in n. 23), *passim*.

[40] Lille, Archives départementales du Nord, B 1288, no. 16526; Schnerb, *L'honneur de la maréchaussée*, p. 213.

disputes about the payment of wages or about musters and reviews. Moreover, the Constable and the Marshals also determined cases governed by the *jus armorum*, especially questions about prisoners of war and ransom and all related issues.[41] In 1367, for example, the Constable had to adjudicate in a case between two French knights, Gaudry de Ballore and Le Galois d'Achy, who both claimed the English knight Robert Chesnel (Cheyney) as their prisoner.[42] In December 1396, the Marshal's court judged a case involving Hugues, lord of Saint-Vidal, former captain of the bailiwicks of Velay, Vivarais and Valentinois, who had been captured by the English in June 1384 and had agreed to pay a heavy ransom to be released. The amount of the ransom was so high that Hugues had to ask three noblemen of the region (Armand IX, viscount of Polignac, Guy de Montlaut and Louis de Joyeuse) to help him. They promised him 100 francs, and gave him letters of obligation. But twelve years later the sum was still unpaid. So the Marshals' court ordered the debtors (or their heirs) to pay their debt.

The preceding examples have been taken from the records of the Parlement. Unfortunately, the loss of all the records of both the Constable's and the Marshals' courts deprives us of detailed knowledge of the cases ruled by the *jus armorum* in which they presided. However, thanks to Honoré Bouvet's *L'arbre des batailles*, we can at least hypothesise some of the various questions which may have been raised in these courts. For example: if a man-at-arms lost in battle either armour or a horse which he had borrowed or rented, must he pay recompense for these? How should the spoils be divided after a battle? Did a prisoner of war have the right to escape? What categories of people could enjoy a privilege of immunity in war? How should a judicial combat be organised? etc. There were also some specific questions that concerned heraldry: could a man wear the coat of arms of another, as he pleased? What punishment should there be for a man-at-arms who wore the coat of arms of someone else to commit offences or crimes?[43] Of course, it is hard to know if such questions were purely theoretical or if they corresponded to real cases.

Conflicts of jurisdiction

In the article of the *Decreta Sabaudiae Ducalia* concerning the Marshal of Savoy, it is declared that this officer is to judge solely those cases that concern military matters and military law (*jus militare*).[44] So the Marshals' compe-

---

[41] Keen, *Laws of War*, passim; and see also R. Ambühl, *Prisoners of War in the Hundred Years War: Ransom Culture in the Late Middle Ages* (Cambridge, 2013).

[42] *La Guerre de Cent Ans vue à travers les registres du Parlement (1337–1369)*, ed. P.-C. Timbal (Paris, 1961), pp. 315–22. For the next case, see Le Barrois d'Orgeval, *Le tribunal de la connétablie*, pp. 357–9.

[43] Paris, Bibliothèque nationale de France, MS français 1263, ff. 1–6v.

[44] *Decreta Sabaudiae Ducalia*, ff. 111v–112v.

tence was not only *ratione personae*, but also *ratione materiae*. Was the situation similar in France? Could the Constable and the Marshals judge criminal and civil cases involving soldiers even when the cases had nothing to do with the *jus militare*, and could they judge cases involving soldiers in peacetime?

In point of fact, legal records show that the Constable and Marshals could only judge in wartime and in matters related to war. For example, in July 1367, a judgment of the Parlement cancelled all the proceedings of a civil case adjudicated by the lieutenant of the Marshals of France.[45] A few years later, in September 1371, a ruling of the Parlement stated that the Constable could not judge a civil case involving a *sergent d'armes du roi* as private person.[46] It should be noted that this kind of action went directly against royal legislation and, for example, in an ordinance dated 5 December 1363, King John II had previously declared '[nous] voulons que nos connestable, mareschaux, maistre de nos arbalestriers ... et tous autres telz officiers soient seulement contens de ce qui regarde leurs offices senz entreprendre autre chose' ('we order that our Constable, Marshals, Master of Crossbowmen and other such officers deal only with what concerns their respective offices').[47]

A more significant problem was that created by the frequent conflicts between the courts of the Constable and Marshals and ordinary jurisdictions. Many of the cases judged by the military jurisdiction could equally well be dealt with by the ordinary courts, especially by the royal bailiffs. When such conflicts occurred, the judges of the Parlement frequently referred the matter to them rather than to the extraordinary jurisdictions.

A good example is given by a case that was heard in 1368. Twelve years earlier (in 1356) a knight from Picardy, Raoul, lord of Gandicourt, was retained along with three squires of his company by Raoul de Clermont, to serve under his command in the king's war. Raoul de Clermont promised to pay daily wages, at the rate of one crown for the knight and a half crown for each squire. The lord of Gandicourt served for sixty-five days and took part in the siege of Breteuil-sur-Iton; unfortunately, after the campaign, Raoul de Clermont died before paying his men their wages. So the lord of Gandicourt had Clermont's widow, Isabelle, Lady of Tartigny, brought before the Marshals' court at the *Table de Marbre*. Lady Isabelle asked the Parlement to refer the case back to the court of the bailiff where she was justiciable. She won the case.[48]

Sometimes, however, for political reasons, the king himself preferred to favour the military jurisdictions. There is a clear example from the beginning

---

[45] Paris, Archives nationales, X1a 21, f. 182r–v (Dec. 1366); Le Barrois d'Orgeval, *Le tribunal de la connétablie*, pp. 332–3, no. 7.

[46] Paris, Archives nationales, X1a 1469, f. 468, and X1a 22, f. 237 (Sept. 1371); Le Barrois d'Orgeval, *Le tribunal de la connétablie*, pp. 339–41, no. 12.

[47] *Ordonnances des rois de France de la troisième race*, ed. de Laurière et al., III, p. 647.

[48] Paris, Archives nationales, X1a 21, f. 259v (March 1368); Le Barrois d'Orgeval, *Le tribunal de la connétablie*, pp. 334–5, no. 8.

of December 1370. Probably just a few weeks before, a French knight, Gilles de Mailly, along with three men-at-arms – all four serving under the banner of Mouton de Blainville, Marshal of France – were in Paris. One night they broke down the door of a house where Agnès de La Tramblaye and a young girl lived. They attempted to rape the lady and the girl and when the *sergents du guet* came and tried to arrest them, they resisted with sword in hand. So, the next day, the provost of Paris gave the order to arrest them and they were put in prison at the Châtelet. At this moment, Bertrand du Guesclin, recently appointed Constable of France, claimed that these men-at-arms serving under the Marshals were subject to his own jurisdiction. King Charles V knew that the case had nothing to do with the *jus militare*, but nevertheless 'pour consideration de nostre dit connestable' ('out of respect for his Constable's authority') he ordered the provost to release the prisoners and deliver them to the Constable's justice. But at the same time, he gave a *lettre de non prejudice*, stating that his decision would not be prejudicial in the future to the authority, power and jurisdiction of the provost of Paris. This royal decision was thus a clear royal exception.[49]

In conclusion: the fourteenth century was a crucial time for military jurisdiction in France. We have no evidence of its existence before the beginning of the fourteenth century. But from 1317 until the end of the fifteenth century, this jurisdiction became more and more firmly established: its proceedings and its competence were defined, albeit more through customs, usages and jurisprudence than by means of royal legislation.

The hierarchy of institutions appeared clearly through the hierarchy of appeals: the provost marshals were under the direct authority of the Marshals; the Marshals were subject to the authority of the Constable; and the Constable himself was under the judicial authority of the Parlement.

Despite many attempts to the contrary, the legal powers and competence of high military officers were over time reduced to just military matters and cases related to wartime – with the single exception of the Constable's special competence concerning his own household and the king's *sergents d'armes*.

---

[49] Paris, Archives nationales, Y2, f. 49v (Dec. 1370); Le Barrois d'Orgeval, *Le tribunal de la connétablie*, pp. 336–7, no. 10.

CHAPTER 8

The Origins and Jurisdiction of the English Court of Admiralty in the Fourteenth Century

Thomas K. Heebøll-Holm

In the seminal article 'The Sovereign and the Pirates, 1332', published in 1970, Frederic Cheyette demonstrated how the adjudication of piracy disputes was essential to the formulation both of sovereignty and of the jurisdiction of the French and English admirals in the fourteenth century. Cheyette used as an illustrative example a court case from Agde, in 1332, where the king of France contested the right of the local lord, the bishop of Narbonne, to jurisdiction over some recently captured Genoese pirates. The bishop argued that justice over the coast in that area was his legal prerogative, but the French king countered that he had sovereignty over the waters of his kingdom and hence also to try piracy. This claim to sovereignty over the sea was a novel political manoeuvre, and it specifically entailed the 'sovereign legitimation of the violence of war and sovereign limitation of the violence of justice'.[1] The officer directed to exercise this sovereign right over the sea was the French admiral, yet before 1332 no French admiral ever exercised justice. Indeed, complaints over piracy normally went to ordinary royal officers, or to local lords or to Paris. This led Cheyette to conclude that the 'office of admiral may [...] be the rarest bird in the mediaeval administrative bestiary: one that was created in theory before it was instituted in practice'.[2]

That conclusion is equally applicable for England in the fourteenth century. In 1875 Stubbs had remarked that

> The history of the jurisdiction of these officers [admirals] is as yet obscure, both from the apocryphal character of all the early records of the Admiralty and from the nature of their authority, which was the result of a tacit compromise between the king as sovereign and lord of the sea, entitled to demand for office or defence the services of all his subjects, the privileged corporations of the sea-port towns with their peculiar customs and great

---

[1] Frederic L. Cheyette, 'The Sovereign and the Pirates, 1332', *Speculum*, 45 (1970), pp. 40–68, at 42.

[2] Cheyette, 'The Sovereign and the Pirates', p. 50.

local independence, and the private adventure of individuals, merchants, and mariners, whose proceedings seem to be scarcely one degree removed from piracy.[3]

Though much research has been conducted into the maritime history of England since 1875, the origin and history of the admirals' jurisdiction still remain obscure.

In this chapter, I shall provide an argument for the date when the English admirals can first be said to have enjoyed a specified jurisdiction embodied in an institutionalised court of law, the Court of Admiralty, where they passed judgment according to a law code wholly different from that followed by the traditional English courts of law. The beginnings of the Court of Admiralty can broadly be placed between the 1290s and the 1360s. Certainly by the latter date an institutionalised Court of Admiralty was very much a reality, as the judgments of the admirals were increasingly the subject of complaints and frustrations expressed by other courts of law and by parliaments. Consequently in the last decades of the fourteenth century numerous measures were implemented to limit and define the jurisdictional competence of this court.[4] It is, however, much more difficult to determine when the admirals can first be said to have possessed enough legal authority and jurisdictional rights to constitute a court of law of their own. To a certain extent the answer to this question depends on one's own definition of jurisdiction. Essentially, the question hinges on when the Admiralty went from having an ad hoc jurisdiction with no specific legal prerogative beyond being an officer of the Crown to being a distinct and specialised legal institution applying a specified set of laws and with specific legal prerogatives.

Overall, there are three possible dates for the origin of the Court of Admiralty: these depend to a large extent on whether one thinks practice is enough to constitute a legal institution or if one prefers to emphasise the need for a formal establishment of such a court with specific legal powers. The first dating is around 1300, for by that time admirals sometimes passed judgment and thus *de facto* had some sort of jurisdiction. If that is unsatisfactory, one may argue – as most historians do – for an origin between 1340 and 1357. By then the admirals' jurisdiction was seemingly backed up and confirmed by Edward III's claim to sovereignty at sea. However, this is the only thing that separates it from the practice of *c.* 1300, since the jurisdiction

---

[3] William Stubbs, *The Constitutional History of England in its Origin and Development*, 1st edn, 3 vols, (Oxford, 1875), II, p. 289.

[4] David Simpkin, 'Keeping the Seas: England's Admirals, 1369–89', in *Roles of the Sea in Medieval England*, ed. Richard Gorski (Woodbridge, 2012), pp. 79–102, at 90; *Select Pleas in the Court of Admiralty*, ed. Reginald G. Marsden, 2 vols (Selden Soc., vi and xi, 1894–7), I, pp. xliii–l; Robin Ward, *The World of the Medieval Shipmaster* (Woodbridge, 2009), pp. 37–43.

was still neither mandated nor certified in principle by the king. This brings me to the third possible dating, namely 1361, when Admiral Robert Herle both in practice and by royal order was presiding over a physically fixed and permanent court of admiralty with specific legal prerogatives. What separates the first two dates from the last is that they focus on the *practice of jurisdiction*, whereas the latter necessitates a specified and statutory royal decree of the *right to jurisdiction* in order for the admiralty jurisdiction – and thus the Court of Admiralty – to be a legal institution separate and distinct from the other courts of law of the realm.

In this chapter I emphasise sovereignty over the sea as the necessary prerequisite for the existence of a Court of Admiralty. My approach to the subject is thus somewhat conservative. Accordingly I think that the establishment of the Court of Admiralty should be dated to 1361. I do recognise however that the admirals' right to jurisdiction was certainly a case of gradual evolution, rather than a sudden imposition by the Crown at a specific date. Accordingly, therefore, I shall trace the development of the jurisdictional powers of the admirals in the years leading up to the formal and final institutionalisation of the Court of Admiralty in 1361.

The origins of the admiralty

In all likelihood the word 'admiral' is derived from the Arabic *amir*, originally meaning commander of an army and later meaning governor or ruler. It presumably entered Western usage in about 1072 with the Norman conquest of Palermo on Sicily. According to Hiroshi Takayama, as the population of Sicily was predominantly Muslim the Norman rulers chose a Latinised Arab term, *amiratus*, for their Norman ruler of the city, in order to reassure the Muslim population of the duke's intention to continue ruling in accordance with the island's traditional, Muslim customs. During the twelfth century the *amirati* grew in power to become some of the highest officers of the Norman kings of Sicily, and by the time of William II (1166–89) the title could either denote the commander of the royal navy or simply be an honorary title given to a senior member of the royal bureaucracy. Interestingly, this senior officer often had previously – or sometimes concurrently with his tenure of the office of admiral – served as chief justiciar of the king's great court.[5]

The German Emperor Henry VI's employment of Genoese naval commanders and his successors' conquest of the Kingdom of Sicily meant that from the end of the 1190s until at least the end of the reign of Frederick

---

[5] Hiroshi Takayama, '*Amiratus* in the Norman Kingdom of Sicily – A Leading Office of Arabic Origin in the Royal Administration', in *Forschungen zur Reichs-, Papst- und Landesgeschichte*, ed. Karl Borchardt and Enno Bünz (Stuttgart, 1998), pp. 133–44. See also Léon-Robert Ménager, *Amiratus – Ἀμηρᾶς* (Paris, 1960).

II, Genoese were appointed as admirals (in the sense of fleet commanders) by the German rulers of southern Italy. In 1208 there is mention of a Venetian admiral, and in 1210 of a Pisan, but not until 1226 did the city-state of Genoa officially employ an admiral. Of further interest is that in 1239 the admiral of Sicily, the Genoese Nicolas Spinola, was given not only jurisdiction over the crews in the royal fleets, but also the exclusive right to grant reprisals, to license privateers and to hear civil and criminal cases.[6] In 1245 Aragon adopted the title of admiral with the conquest of Valencia, and in the following decades the responsibilities and legal prerogatives of the admirals grew as the title became permanent. However, by the 1290s, due in part to economic difficulties, the Aragonese admiral's power was reduced to merely controlling the ships and arsenal of Barcelona; control of the royal fleets went back to the Crown's bailiffs.[7] In neighbouring Castile the admiralty had by 1254 become a royal office, and by the reign of Alfonso XI (1312–50) the *almirante mayor* (high admiral) was the overall naval commander charged with preparing the royal fleets, with the duty of gathering ships and outfitting them, recruiting crewmen, and keeping a written record of the state of the navy. In addition he was responsible for the royal shipyards in Castro Urdiales and Seville, and in peace-time he was charged with securing the legal, efficient and safe operation of the kingdom's ports. In the fourteenth century he received a tax on merchandise that was transported through Castilian ports and a fee for anchorage in these ports.[8] The Castilian admiral thus had quite extensive legal powers, making him possibly the most powerful admiral in the fourteenth century.

At an early date, the French adopted the title of admiral for their commander of naval operations in the Mediterranean. In 1247, Louis IX of France used the title for the first time for the two French officers who were in charge of the fleet carrying his crusade to Egypt.[9] However until 1336 all French admirals seem to have served on an ad hoc basis: most were experienced professional mariners from the Mediterranean and are to be regarded

---

[6] Enrico Basso, 'Pirateria, politica, ceti dirigenti: Alcuni esempi genovesi del Tardo Medioevo', in *Seeraub im Mittelmeerraum*, ed. Nikolas Jaspert and Sebastian Kolditz (Paderborn, 2013), pp. 209–50, at 211–20; Steven A. Epstein, *Genoa and the Genoese* (Chapel Hill, NC, 1996), pp. 88, 103; Cheyette, 'The Sovereign and the Pirates', pp. 47, 50-1.

[7] Lawrence V. Mott, 'Export Control and the Rise of the Office of the Admiral in the Crown of Aragon 1245–1282', in *Ricchezza del mare, ricchezza dal mare: secc. XIII–XVIII: Atti della trentasettesima Settimana di studi, 11–15 aprile 2005* (Prato, 2005), pp. 1179–86.

[8] Nicolas Agrait, 'The Castilian Navy in the Reign of Alfonso XI', in *The Emergence of Léon-Castile, c. 1065–1500: Essays Presented to J.F. O'Callaghan*, ed. James Todesca (Farnham, 2015), pp. 114–16; Susan Rose, *Medieval Naval Warfare, 1000–1500* (London, 2002), pp. 51–2.

[9] Eric Barré, 'Notes sur l'amirauté de France en Normandie au Moyen Âge', *Revue d'histoire maritime*, 19 (2014), pp. 21–31, at 21.

as maritime *condottierri*. They had little or no jurisdictional authority beyond the fleet, nor were they intended to have such.[10] Justice in maritime cases was until the Hundred Years' War handled by royal bailiffs or local lords and it was they who enforced the judgments of the *Parlement de Paris*, the supreme court in France, in cases of prize litigation. In 1342 the Admiral of France was made independent from the command of the Constable of France.[11] Nine years later, in 1351, the admiral's legal prerogatives were confirmed by royal ordinance, but it was stressed that the bailiffs, viscounts and provosts of Normandy were not to tolerate any encroachment or usurpation of their jurisdiction by the admirals. The exact and specific legal nature of the French admiral's jurisdiction in 1351 remains unclear however. Not until 1373 did Charles V issue a more detailed ordinance setting out the legal powers of the admiral, namely to repress piracy, protect passengers on merchant ships, arm ships to attack the enemy, and validate prizes taken by French privateers. His jurisdiction was to take place at the Marble Table in the Palais de la Cité in Paris, but it is uncertain how often this court sat. It is possible, however, to make some remarks on the nature of this jurisdiction before 1373. In 1356–7 the États Généraux granted the admiral rights to part of the spoil taken by French privateers – from 1359 a tenth of the prize – and the admiral was also given the authority to judge the lawfulness of the prizes taken. According to Auguste Dumas, it was this right to a tenth of the prize, together with the right to command and discipline both the sailors in royal service and privateers, that constituted the origin and backbone of the French admirals' jurisdiction. It was from these rights that the admirals' civil jurisdiction stemmed, which effectively came to be the admirals' legal competence in all matters relating to felonies committed at sea or on the coasts. Nevertheless, throughout the next two centuries the admirals remained in legal matters inferior to the royal bailiffs, and their legal authority was continually subjected to challenge by local lords.[12]

In sum, the development of the admiralty in these kingdoms roughly progressed as follows. While the office had from the start a certain jurisdictional authority, the admiral was first and foremost charged with commanding the royal fleets in wartime. From this grew by necessity certain administrative functions such as the raising and provisioning of the fleet, along with the jurisdictional powers necessary in order to maintain discipline in the fleets.

---

[10] Auguste Dumas, *Étude sur le jugement des prises maritimes en France jusqu'à la suppression de l'office d'amiral* (Paris, 1908), pp. 44–7.

[11] Barré, 'Notes sur l'amirauté de France', pp. 21–3; *Ordonnances des rois de France de la troisième race*, ed. E.J. de Laurière et al., 21 vols (Paris, 1723–1849), II, p. 408; Dumas, *Étude sur le Jugement*, pp. 33–5, 38–9.

[12] Twiss, *Black Book of the Admiralty*, I, pp. 430–42. For a preliminary comparison of the French and English admirals, see Thomas K. Heebøll-Holm, 'Law, Order and Plunder at Sea: A Comparison of England and France in the Fourteenth Century', *Continuity and Change*, 32 (2017), pp. 37–58.

The final stage in making the admiralty a jurisdictional authority was to make it permanent and charge it with fighting the enemy, validating prizes, guarding the waters of the kingdom and protecting merchants and mariners from piracy. The foundation of maritime law and admiralty jurisdiction was indeed, as Elisabeth Murray remarked, prize law, and the adjudication of claims to wrecks and to captures made at sea in legitimate warfare.[13]

However, there were also important differences between the countries. While the French admirals remained primarily concerned with naval matters and prize regulation, the Mediterranean admirals had wider powers which also entailed jurisdiction over commerce. As we shall see, the English seem to have struck a middle ground between these two approaches.

The earliest English admirals and maritime law

All historians who have looked into the origins of the Court of Admiralty agree that it developed in the fourteenth century as a result of the increasing inadequacies of the common law and the increasingly complex and international nature of maritime disputes. Most historians emphasise prize jurisdiction as the core of the problem and hence of the admiralty jurisdiction, but as I will show here, the English jurisdiction went beyond naval matters and touched upon problems that were much more fundamental than merely prize regulation.

The commanders of English fleets in the thirteenth century were termed captains and there was no clear difference between the titles of admiral and captain until the beginning of the fourteenth century when the English started organising the impressed fleet of the kingdom into two, namely the Northern Fleet, which included ships from the ports north of the Thames to Berwick-upon-Tweed, and the Western Fleet, which comprised ships from the ports south and west of the Thames all the way round to Bristol.[14] In 1295 the Gascon knight Barrau de Sescars was appointed the first English admiral, with that title, to lead the Bayonne fleet against the French in the Gascon War of 1294–7.[15] In 1296 two Englishmen, William Leyburne and John

---

[13] K.M.E. Murray, *The Constitutional History of the Cinque Ports* (Manchester, 1935), p. 120.

[14] N.A.M. Rodger, *The Safeguard of the Sea* (London, 1997), p. 134.

[15] R.G. Marsden, 'The Vice-Admirals of the Coast', *Eng. Hist. Rev.*, 22 (1907), pp. 468–77, at 468. While historians traditionally assume that the title 'admiral' was passed from France to England (e.g. Rodger, *Safeguard of the Sea*, p. 131), Marcel Gouron and Eugène Goyheneche have argued that the title entered English governmental usage through Castile thanks to the familial and amical relations between the Castilian and the English royal families: M. Gouron, *L'amirauté de Guienne* (Paris, 1938), p. 89; E. Goyheneche, *Bayonne et la région bayonnaise du XIIe au XVe siècle* (Bilbao, 1990), p. 322.

de Botetourt, were appointed admirals and captains (*admirallos et capitaneos flote, amiraus a cheventains*), and in 1300 Gervase Alard was named admiral of the Cinque Ports fleet.[16] From this time onwards the English kings employed admirals for all their wars, but until 1360 the post remained temporary and at times, for instance in the years from 1328 to 1333, there was no English admiral. These early admirals were primarily charged with commanding royal fleets in military operations (though not necessarily in combat), with patrolling the coasts, and in wartime with escorting the convoys of wine fleets to Gascony.[17] They had some administrative powers and some severely limited legal roles. In fact, the Crown had for years employed commanders of the fleet in times of war under the title 'captain', and at first it seems that nothing changed but the name.[18] Indeed, uncertainty about the title persisted. For instance in 1324 and 1325 Edward II termed both John Crombwell and Nicholas Kyriel 'admiral and captain', interchangeably. The terminology seems to have remained uncertain far into the reign of Edward III.[19]

An institutionalised system for administering the wartime fleets of England was far older, dating back to the reign of King John. F.W. Brooks argued that the naval institutions or systems that were created by King John and modified by Henry III were 'the germ' of the admiralty, and that the keepers of the coast – royal officers in charge of the coastal areas in some parts of England – were the direct precursors of the titular admiral. However, although these officers were concerned with naval administration, they were not naval commanders and they had no legal jurisdiction. Rather, they were concerned with gathering together the mariners and fleets of England for royal war service and making sure that the ships and men were fit for duty. As for justice for maritime offences such as piracy or wreck, these were judged by bailiffs, sheriffs, keepers of the coast, the Warden of the Cinque Ports and ultimately by the King's Council or Chancery, applying the common law or the law merchant. The admirals were indeed sometimes appointed as commissioners to inquire into cases, apprehend suspects and arrest their goods, but they did not act with any clear jurisdictional authority stemming from their office.[20] Thus two famous cases of maritime law from the 1290s, Upright *v.* Helemes from 1294 and Mulard *v.* Hobbe from 1294–5, were adjudicated by

---

[16] Marsden, *Select Pleas*, I, pp. xi–xii.

[17] Rodger, *Safeguard of the Sea*, pp. 106–7, 131–2.

[18] Rymer, *Foedera*, I, part 2, pp. 861, 990; *ibid.*, II, part 1, pp. 135, 244, 278, 487, 562, 616; Rodger, *Safeguard of the Sea*, p. 131.

[19] Rymer, *Foedera*, II, part 1, pp. 562, 616; *ibid.*, III, part 1, p. 13.

[20] John Gillingham, 'Richard I, Galley-Warfare and Portsmouth: The Beginnings of a Royal Navy', in *Thirteenth Century England*, VI (1997), pp. 1–15; F.W. Brooks, 'Naval Administration and the Raising of Fleets under John and Henry III', *The Mariner's Mirror*, 15 (1929), pp. 351–90; *idem*, 'William de Wrotham and the Office of Keeper of the King's Ports and Galleys', *Eng. Hist. Rev.*, 40 (1925), pp. 570–9; Bryan Dick, 'Framing Piracy: Restitution at Sea in the Later Middle Ages', Ph.D. thesis,

the king and his Council with the Warden of the Cinque Ports and the bailiff of Sandwich assisting in the former case and the constable of Bristol in the latter, as executive officers. Like their French colleagues, the early admirals' legal powers seem primarily to have been concerned with keeping discipline amongst the mariners impressed for royal service and ensuring that they did not abuse their employment by seeking indiscriminate plunder for their own profit, trying to avoid service, deserting or mutinying.[21]

Maritime law – the so-called Laws of Oléron – and the law merchant had traditionally been administered by the Warden of the Cinque Ports, by town councils and at market courts where the merchant's peers and local authorities presided. The law merchant was an international legal system distinct from the common law in the Middle Ages. It was charged with dealing with pleas of trespass, debt, contract, sale and restitution, but not with serious offences, which were reserved for royal justice.[22] Nevertheless the fourteenth-century sources demonstrate a considerable confusion as to who should adjudicate over such commercial suits and according to what law – not least because the relationship between law merchant, law maritime and common law was unclear. Throughout the fourteenth century most cases seem to have been tried on an ad hoc basis with no English court having absolute and supreme jurisdiction. The Laws of Oléron dealt with the shipmaster's and crew's conduct and responsibilities, discipline, terms and conditions of employment, matters of health and safety, general points of management and seamanship, and with the freightage of merchants' goods on ships.[23] The Laws did not however in any way deal with piracy and neither they nor the law merchant made any provision in regard to that activity. Nevertheless complaints over piracy sometimes request that the case should be judged according to the law maritime and merchant. This is probably because piracy was treated judicially as a commercial transaction of debt and recovery of property unjustly detained by another party. Piracy was in this way transformed from a criminal matter which was the exclusive prerogative of royal jurisdiction into a civil suit which the local courts could handle. Thus the violent aspect of the acquisition of property, sometimes with loss of life – which could only lead to festering hatred and enmity – was left to one side; but it was the only way to solve such quarrels in the international maritime community without involving the royal courts and hence running the risk of individual suits

---

University of Glasgow, 2010, pp. 57–8, 64–71, 185–6; R.G. Marsden, 'Vice-Admirals of the Coast' (cit. in n. 15), pp. 468–77, at 480; Marsden, *Select Pleas*, I, pp. xii–xxvii.

[21] Marsden, *Select Pleas*, I, p. xvi; 12, in Given-Wilson, *PROME*, I: 1275–1294, ed. P. Brand, pp. 75 and 77–8 ('1294 Summer' and '1295 Summer'), and 648–51, and II: 1294–1307, ed. P. Brand, pp. 14–16; Ward, *World of the Medieval Shipmaster*, pp. 27, 31–2.

[22] Ward, *World of the Medieval Shipmaster*, pp. 15–17.

[23] *Ibid.*, pp. 18–23; T.K. Heebøll-Holm, *Ports, Piracy and Maritime War* (Leiden, 2013), pp. 129–31.

becoming subject to royal foreign policy. Here the Crown's political interests often took precedence over the dispensing of impartial justice to the victim.[24]

The *Fasciculus de Superioritate Maris*

The first time that an English king expresses that an English admiral has jurisdiction at sea is in 1297 in the aftermath of the maritime wars between English, Bayonnese, Norman, Flemish and Castilian mariners. However, this was mostly tentative and not until the negotiations at the so-called Process of Montreuil do we see a clear and confrontational English claim to sovereignty over the sea.[25] In 1306 French and English negotiators met in the castle of Montreuil-sur-Mer on the maritime march of England and France in order to settle outstanding and reciprocal claims of restitution due to piracy and naval action from 1292 until 1306. At this meeting the English, both in order to counterbalance the French king's position as the liege lord over the duke of Aquitaine (that is the king of England) and in response to the naval campaign of the French admiral, the Genoese Renier Grimaldi, against Flemish shipping – which had entailed attacks on shipping along the English east coast – formulated a claim of English sovereignty. It was now claimed that English kings had 'since time immemorial been in the <u>peaceful</u> [*my underlining*] possession of the sovereign lordship of the sea of England and the islands in that sea'. More specifically, these seas were stated to encompass the waters from the Pyrenees to Flanders, and the right supposedly dated back to the twelfth-century Angevin kings of England. Furthermore the English claimed that this peaceful (i.e., uncontested) possession of sovereignty was recognised by all nations plying their trade in those waters – except, of course, the French. The supreme officer of justice in this sea was (after the king) the admiral of England.[26] That is to say, the admiral had jurisdiction.

At this point it might be worth mentioning that in the Middle Ages jurisdiction comprised a sort of synthesis of powers, namely *iurisdictio, dominium, imperium* and *potestas*[27] – that is to say, the right to rule, judge and carry out sentences – making it close in meaning to the modern notion of sovereignty. By this definition Grimaldi had usurped English legal prerogatives and had infringed English sovereignty. For this he ought to suffer the penalty of

---

[24] Heebøll-Holm, *Ports, Piracy and Maritime War*, pp. 132, 134, 139, 143–4, 146.

[25] *Ibid.*, pp. 83–98; Sebastian Sobecki, *The Sea and Medieval English Literature* (Cambridge, 2008), pp. 150–1.

[26] Pierre Chaplais, *English Medieval Diplomatic Practice. Part I: Documents and Interpretation*, 2 vols (London, 1982), I, p. 367; G.P. Cuttino, *English Diplomatic Administration, 1259–1339*, 2nd edn (Oxford, 1971); Heebøll-Holm, *Ports, Piracy and Maritime War*, pp. 175–86.

[27] Francesco Maiolo, *Medieval Sovereignty* (Delft, 2007), p. 143.

death; and in any case no English mariner should answer to any other legal authority than the English admiral. However, this claim in truth was merely a bluff and an attempt to enable the English king to negotiate with the French as equals rather than as vassal and lord. The actual legal status of the sea was of little concern to Edward I, and the declaration had no backing in any actual jurisdictional practice or in the formal legal rights of the English admirals. Indeed neither the Montreuil negotiations nor those of 1308, 1309 and 1311 concerning Anglo-French piracy cases were handled by English admirals, being dealt with instead by the royal chancellor.[28]

In the longer run, however, the Montreuil declaration, together with an Anglo-Flemish peace treaty of 1297 and a number of other treaties or diplomatic negotiations over various outstanding claims such as – but not restricted to – piracy and restitution, with France, Flanders, Spain and Portugal, ranging in date from the late thirteenth century to 1339, together came to form the core of the set of documents called the *Fasciculus de Superioritate Maris*.[29] These documents were used by Edward III as part of his renunciation of allegiance to the French king and indeed as part of the *casus belli* against France. In one of the documents – which to my knowledge is otherwise known only from the writings of John Selden in the seventeenth century – it is stated that:

> And finally, that the procedure ordained and instigated by the ancestor of our lord the king and his council for the prosecution of the below-mentioned subjects must be resumed and continued in order to uphold and preserve the old superiority over the sea of England and the rights of the office of admiralty in the same with regard to the reformation, interpretation, declaration and maintenance of the laws and statutes formerly ordained by his ancestors, kings of England, to uphold peace and justice between all people of whatever nation that cross the sea of England, and to learn of any hostile undertakings in that [sea], and to punish delinquents and attain satisfaction for those who have been wronged. Indeed, these laws and statutes were reformed, interpreted and declared by the lord Richard, once king of England, upon his return from the Holy Land, and they were made public on the Isle of Oléron and called in the Gallic tongue [i.e., French] *la ley Olyroun*.[30] (My translation)

---

[28] Marsden, *Select Pleas*, I, pp. xviii–xix; Heebøll-Holm, *Ports, Piracy and Maritime War*, pp. 151, 187–90.

[29] Marsden, *Select Pleas*, I, pp. xxx–xxxv. The extant *Fasciculus* documents are in the National Archives: Kew, TNA, Chancery Miscellanea, C 47/32/19.

[30] 'Item ad finem, quod resumatur et continuetur ad subditorum prosecutionem forma procedendi quondam ordinata et inchoata per avum domini nostri regis et ejus consilium, ad retinendum et conservandum antiquam superioritatem maris Angliæ et jus officii admirallatus in eodem, quoad corrigendum, interpretandum, declarandum et conservandum leges et statuta per ejus antecessores Angliæ reges dudum ordinata; ad conservandum pacem et justiciam inter omnes gentes nationis cujuscunque per mare Angliæ transeuntes, et ad cognoscendum super omnibus in contrarium attemptatis in eodem, et ad puniendum delinquentes et dampna passis

However, there is nothing either in 1306 or in 1339 to show that this in any way reflected reality, either of English power at sea or of the legal powers of the admiral. With Karl-Friedrich Krieger, I would suggest that they had in no sense been given by Richard Lionheart or had any relation to the Laws of Oléron. Rather, the *Fasciculus* was an invention created to enhance English independence from France.[31]

Many historians have nevertheless taken this declaration at face value and have assumed that the English admirals in or shortly after 1340 were vested with formal jurisdictional powers and indeed a court to uphold the English kings' justice at sea. This view rests on three assumptions. The first is a belief in a royal will to shoulder the legal burden stated in the *Fasciculus*, in order to facilitate trade. The second is Edward III's payment, out of his own purse, of restitution in the 1330s and early 1340s to Italian and Flemish merchants for piracy committed by English mariners. These payments of restitution for the piracy of his subjects have been deemed a profound diplomatic embarrassment by some historians,[32] and it is certainly true that in the thirteenth and fourteenth centuries it was fairly exceptional for European kings to pay restitution for their subjects' piracy. These payments have consequently been taken as implicit evidence for the sincerity of the claim to sovereignty over the English seas since Edward was prepared not only to reap the benefits from it but also to shoulder the burdens. The third assumption is that the victory at Sluys in 1340 gave the English lasting naval superiority over the French.[33]

I consider these assumptions, and hence their relation to the dating of the beginnings of the Court of Admiralty, to be mistaken. As regards the restitution cases, the one referred to by historians as evidence for sovereignty concerns the Crown's compensation in 1330 to Italian merchants who had

---

satisfaciendum: quæ quidem leges et statuta per dominum Richardum quondam regem Angliæ, in reditu suo a Terra-sancta, correcta fuerunt, interpretata, declarata, et in insula Oleron publicata, et nominata in lingua gallicana *la ley Olyroun.*' J. M. Pardessus, *Collection de lois maritimes antérieures au XVIIIe siècle*, 6 vols (Paris, 1828–45), I, p. 289. Like Pardessus, I will avoid a discussion of the authenticity of the document. For current purposes it mostly serves as part of a historiographic discussion. Marsden considered the reference to the *ley Olyroun* to be apocryphal: Marsden, *Select Pleas*, I, p. xxxii.

[31] Karl-Friedrich Krieger, *Ursprung und Wurzeln der Rôles d'Oléron* (Cologne and Vienna, 1970), pp. 43–6.

[32] Rodger, *Safeguard of the Sea*, p. 79: 'the empty boast was a source of embarrassment and expense. It was difficult to claim sovereignty and yet avoid all responsibility. So Edward III was driven to pay large sums in compensation for piracy by the subjects he had been unable to control.' See also Graham Cushway, *Edward III and the War at Sea* (Woodbridge, 2011) p. 77.

[33] Rodger, *Safeguard of the Sea*, pp. 79, 97, Cushway, *Edward III and the War at Sea*, p. 77; Marsden, *Select Pleas*, I, pp. xxxv–xxxvi; Anthony Musson and W.M. Ormrod, *The Evolution of English Justice in the Fourteenth Century* (New York, 1999), p. 22; Ward, *World of the Medieval Shipmaster*, pp. 29–30.

been plundered by English sailors of the king's ship, *La Seint Edward*. These were not random Italian merchants, however. Rather, they were of the society of the Bardi, creditors to the English Crown. Accordingly, in order to avoid damaging relations with these bankers and to avert suspicion of Crown collusion in this piracy, Edward III was more or less obliged to pay. A few years later, in 1336, Edward suddenly felt the need to settle a long-outstanding Genoese claim for restitution for piracy committed by Hugh Despenser in 1321 or 1322. Edward offered to pay 14,300 marks sterling to the Genoese in damages, but this payment was not proposed because of a sudden instance of royal remorse or any need to live up to a claim of sovereignty over the seas. Instead it was a clever attempt to foil the French hiring of Genoese fleets. The English proposal to pay restitution made it open to the Genoese to decide whether it was the victims or the Commune of Genoa that should receive the compensation. Thus Edward tried to cause splitting and dissent in the city-state's government by creating a faction in the city with a clear economic interest in not aiding the French. It also formed part of a more general English policy of trying to dissuade or bribe Genoa away from supplying naval assistance to the French.[34] Furthermore, in July 1338, Edward III had sailed to Antwerp to cement his alliance with the rulers of Flanders and the Low Countries. During his stay, in 1338 English ships in royal service attacked neutral ships belonging to the count of Guelders, and in 1340 over 100 named English shipmasters were indicted for the plunder of a large vessel (probably owned by Italian merchants) called a *taryt*. For these assaults Edward again paid restitution out of his own pocket to the victims of his mariners' piracy. The *taryt* case is a particularly thorny one. Craig Lambert has demonstrated that *taryt* indicated a type of ship rather than the actual name of the vessel.[35] To add to the confusion, it appears that from the 1340s to 1353 there were at least five separate court cases concerning piracy or the wreck of a *taryt*: in Bristol, Dartmouth, the Isle of Wight, off Great Yarmouth and finally off Flanders. Only the last of these resulted in Edward paying restitution.[36] However, the royal payment of restitution for these attacks was by no means the expression of an embarrassed monarch failing to uphold his proclaimed protection of the seas, nor was it the signal of a changed royal policy with regard to the sea. It was simply an attempt not to alienate neutrals and allies, and to prevent them from using this as a reason for siding with the French.

---

[34] *Cal. Pat. R., 1327–30*, p. 520; Rymer, *Foedera*, II, part 2, pp. 941, 948, 1185–6; *ibid.*, III, part 1, p. 280; Jonathan Sumption, *The Hundred Years War: Trial by Battle* (London, 1990), p. 162; Rodger, *Safeguard of the Sea*, p. 93.

[35] Craig Lambert, *Shipping the Medieval Military* (Woodbridge, 2011), pp. 18–19.

[36] *Cal. Pat. R., 1338–40*, pp. 491–2, *Cal. Pat. R., 1340–3*, p. 319; *Cal. Pat. R., 1343–5*, pp. 21, 27, 68, 75, 214, 323, 517; *Cal. Pat. R., 1345–8*, p. 68; Reginald G. Marsden, *Documents Relating to the Law and Custom of the Sea*, 2 vols (Navy Records Soc., 49–50, 1915–16), I, pp. 74–5.

Moreover, in the case of the *taryt*, the king managed to turn the demand for those responsible to repay him into two or more months of royal naval service with fully fitted ships and crews at the indicted parties' own expense, albeit in return for a pardon. For instance, Admiral Morley requested a pardon for William Hesoul or Ensoull in 1346 in return for a two-month term of naval service to the Crown with a fully victualled 100-tun *cog*, the *Jon* or *Johan* and an armed crew, all provided at his own expense.[37] Edward in one case even increased his demand for the amount due to him from the £16,527 17s. 1d. of the initial damages, as stated in 1340, to £20,000 in 1341; although in 1342 the amount seems to have been settled at 18,000 marks (i.e. £12,000). While some mariners proved recalcitrant, most cases were settled by their agreeing to do naval service at their own expense in exchange for a pardon. Thus, strictly speaking the king was not paying restitution; he was merely advancing money for the culprits indicted, which he afterwards recovered by converting the money that he was owed into naval service. In these cases, the admirals along with other royal officers were to inquire into the matter and arrest the perpetrators, their ships and/or their goods; but they did not act as judges or were in any way different from previous admirals. The admirals were still regular royal officers competent to try legal cases by common law.[38]

Indeed the whole notion of Edward III making a real claim to sovereignty at sea following the defeat of the French at Sluys in 1340 seems fictitious to me. Throughout the 1340s and 50s the French and their Castilian and Genoese allies continued to pose a significant threat to English shipping and to raid the English coast. Nothing suggests that the French naval threat receded after Sluys. For instance, shortly after it, a new French admiral, Robert Houdetot, attacked the Isle of Wight, the Isle of Portland, Teignmouth and Plymouth. Even on the eve of the peace of Brétigny, in 1359, when France was on her knees, a French fleet still managed to capture and burn Winchelsea.[39]

Accordingly, Edward's payments of restitution for the piracy of English mariners against foreign merchants do not express either a particular English royal embarrassment or a serious effort to protect and uphold sovereignty on the English seas. They were simply actions to buy allies, placate neutrals who were liable to side with the French, and strengthen the naval service.

---

[37] Marsden, *Documents Relating to the Law and Custom of the Sea*, I, pp. 74–5.

[38] Rymer, *Foedera*, II, part 2, p. 1008; *Cal. Pat. R., 1338–40*, pp. 143, 149, 491–2; *Cal. Pat. R., 1340–2*, pp. 319, 358, 469; Sumption, *Trial by Battle*, pp. 260–4. For the traditional interpretations of these cases, see Marsden, *Select Pleas*, I, xxvi–xxix; Rodger, *Safeguard of the Sea*, pp. 92–3, 97, 116. The 'taryt' case and the pardons are documented here: *Cal. Close R., 1341–3*, pp. 499–502, 529, 553–4, 569, 644; *Cal. Pat. R., 1338–40*, pp. 491–2; *Cal. Pat. R., 1340–3*, pp. 319, 469, 477, 483, 491, 513, 513, 538, 541; *Cal. Pat. R., 1343–5*, pp. 21, 27, 119, 323, 517; *Cal. Pat R., 1345–8*, p. 68.

[39] Charles de la Roncière, *Histoire de la marine française*, 6 vols (Paris, 1909–32), I, pp. 457–61; Sumption, *Trial by Battle*, pp. 346–7; Geoffrey le Baker, *Chronicon Angliæ*, ed. J.A. Giles (London, 1847), p. 70; Rodger, *Safeguard of the Sea*, pp. 92–105.

The restitution monies were paid to secure the goodwill of the recipients in the war against France, and Edward's action parallels his buying or bribing of allies in Flanders, the Low Countries and the Rhineland.[40]

Nevertheless, it does seem that the 1340s and 50s saw an increase in the English admirals' legal activity, even though I think it is premature to term what happened as initiating a proper law court. Instead, the admiral seems to have exercised a confusing mixture of ad hoc legal powers which were exercised by regular legal clerks of the Chancery, and by various royal officers as well as by the ports' authorities. While there is an increase in cases where the admiral is involved in the legal prosecution of mariners accused of piracy, the matter is complicated not only by the fact that many of these cases continued to be resolved by the king and Council (especially in cases of major diplomatic importance), by special commissions, and by the Chancery or the common law courts, with the admiral merely functioning as inquisitor and then as executant of the judge's decision. It is also unclear whether the legal activity of the admiral was a genuine reflection of the requirement to police the waters of England in general, or if the increased involvement was due to the fact that Edward III had strained the kingdom's naval resources, thereby causing a significant proportion of the mariners to be impressed for the war against France and thus *de facto* come under the admiral's authority.[41] In other words, it is difficult to tell if the admiral's apparently increased role in the judicial process pertained to his duty to discipline and punish unruly mariners. In addition there seems in general to have been widespread confusion over whether pirates and other transgressors should be judged according to law maritime, law merchant or to common law. The unclear legal status of the admiralty did not help.[42]

The *Fasciculus* should not be seen as being any more genuine in its claim of English sovereignty at sea than was the declaration of Montreuil. Both were simply part of the politico-legal attempts of the English kings to free themselves from French vassalage, and should be viewed a bit like Edward III's claim to the French throne made on 26 January 1340, even though in

---

[40] Sumption, *Trial by Battle*, pp. 242–4.

[41] Murray, *Constitutional History*, pp. 123–4; Ward, *World of the Medieval Shipmaster*, pp. 16–18; Rymer, *Foedera*, I, part 2, p. 328; Cushway, *Edward III and the War at Sea*, pp. 83–4.

[42] Marsden, *Select Pleas*, I, xxxvii–xli; Rodger, *Safeguard of the Sea*, pp. 123–5; Lambert, *Shipping the Medieval Military*, pp. 16–19; Ward, *World of the Medieval Shipmaster*, pp. 32–4. While Ward speculates that a case in 1347 of forfeiture of a ship to the Crown, taken because of the owner's piracy and subsequently given to a Peter Foulke of Winchelsea possibly by order of the admiral, may be the first example of a Court of Admiralty, I consider the source (*Cal. Pat. R., 1345–8*, p. 260), to be inconclusive, and in any event, as Ward himself points out, in 1349–51 a piracy case adjudicated in Bristol raises considerable confusion both over the possible powers of that admiral at this point in time and more generally about the legal status of offences at sea.

1331 he had recognised Philip of Valois as the legitimate king of France and had done liege homage to him.[43] In fact the primary intended audience of the *Fasciculus* may have been the Flemish towns and lords, so as to ensure good maritime and commercial relations between England and Flanders. The Anglo-Flemish alliance of 1297 certainly demonstrates that it was vital for the English to give guarantees of English maritime protection in order to assure the continued trade and prosperity of both countries and also to further cement the Anglo-Flemish alliance against the French. It is in the same vein that the English declaration of sovereignty over the waters of Brittany in 1320 should be understood. Though the text could be read as setting out a universal principle, it in fact served primarily to reassure the Flemish that Edward II would protect them in return for continued commercial relations.[44]

Not until 1357, in the aftermath of the victory at Poitiers and with the contours of a general victory over the Crown of France looming on in the horizon, do we begin to see signs of a court of admiralty with clearer legal prerogatives.

The Peace of Brétigny and the Court of Admiralty

In March 1357, the English and the French agreed to a two-year truce to negotiate both the ransom of John II and the terms of peace between the two kingdoms. In this period of truce the process towards the creation of a court of admiralty with jurisdiction over the waters of the English king's territories seems to have speeded up. Most historians who have looked into the origins of that court assume that it was instituted either in 1357 or in 1358. However, the evidence for either year as pivotal seems unconvincing to me.[45]

By the late 1350s much of the actual naval administration, including cases of arrest, piracy, shipwreck, desertion and other maritime issues, was handed over for investigation by sergeants or knights commissioned by the King's Council. Freed up from the duties of investigating, the admirals could attend to other matters. In 1357 a case of possible restitution to Portuguese merchants for goods that had been taken by French mariners and subsequently captured

---

[43] For a summary of this argument, see Anne Curry, *The Hundred Years War* (New York, 2003), pp. 47–50.

[44] Sumption, *Trial by Battle*, pp. 291–301; Heebøll-Holm, *Ports, Piracy and Maritime War*, pp. 186, 202–3; N.H. Nicolas, *A History of the Royal Navy*, 2 vols (London, 1847), I, pp. 387–9; Rymer, *Foedera*, II, part 1, p. 434.

[45] For instance, Timothy J. Runyan, 'The Rolls of Oléron and the Admiralty Court in Fourteenth-Century England', *American Jnl of Legal History*, 19 (1975), pp. 95–111, at 107–8; Marsden, 'Vice-Admirals of the Coast' (cit. in n. 15), p. 469; R.G. Marsden, 'Early Prize Jurisdiction and Prize Law in England', *Eng. Hist. Rev.*, 24 (1909), pp. 675–97, at 680; Cushway, *Edward III and the War at Sea* (Woodbridge, 2011), p. 163.

as prize by English mariners was referred by the king to the admirals of the North and West fleets for adjudication. In 1358 the admiral of the West Fleet, Guy Brian, certainly had some legal powers to act as judge in a case of restitution to the London merchant Saier Scoef. Both have been recognised by historians as founding cases of the Court of Admiralty, but I think it is premature to claim that these demonstrate the existence of a legal institution. Rather, they seem to have acted on an ad hoc basis, just like bailiffs and other port officials, who enjoyed similar legal powers to the admirals – though the latter certainly were increasingly given the more high-profile cases.[46] As Robin Ward writes:

> When the Council or other courts, with an admiral present, could reach the decision that in several areas of complaint the principles of maritime law should be followed, the stage had been set for the appearance of a specialised admiral's court with, perhaps limited, judicial authority.[47]

To me, the defining moment in the creation of the Court of Admiralty was the signing of the Peace of Brétigny in May 1360. With regard to the sea, this stipulated that the king of England was to enjoy the same rights over all the territories ceded in the treaty as the king of France had previously enjoyed.[48] This I can only see as a French acceptance of English dominion, and hence of sovereignty, over these lands and islands, including the coasts and waters bordering them. In maritime matters Edward III by this treaty came very close to reconstituting the Angevin Empire of Henry II and Richard I, as he now controlled the coastline of France from the Pyrenees to the Loire, with an English ally, the duke of Brittany, controlling the coast from the Loire to Normandy; and finally he was in direct control of the strategically important ports: of Brest, Barfleur and Calais on the French side of the Channel. English sovereignty over these waters, which had been claimed in theory since the beginning of the fourteenth century, could now be enforced in practice.[49] It was only natural that Edward at this point began to contemplate the creation of a court of maritime justice.[50] Two months before the signing of the treaty of Brétigny, John Pavely, Prior of St John of Jerusalem in England, was in March 1360 appointed captain of the all the fleets of England with royally confirmed

---

[46] Cushway, *Edward III and the War at Sea*, pp. 162–3; *Cal. Pat. R., 1354–8*, p. 546; *Cal. Pat. R., 1358–61*, p. 277; *Cal. Close R., 1354–60*, pp. 441, 490–1, 578, 653–4; Marsden, *Select Pleas*, I, p. xli; Marsden, 'Early Prize Jurisdiction', p. 680.

[47] Ward, *World of the Medieval Shipmaster*, p. 34.

[48] Rymer, *Foedera*, III, part 1, p. 515.

[49] Jonathan Sumption, *Trial by Fire* (London, 1999), pp. 458–9; Heebøll-Holm, *Ports, Piracy and Maritime War*, pp. 185–90.

[50] Cushway raises the interesting argument that the peace also permitted a refreshing change in personnel and a reform of the admiralty, as previous admirals had increasingly been drawn into the port's local politics and into quarrels with the shipowners and mariners. Cushway, *Edward III and the War at Sea*, p. 176.

rights to judge and punish, over all the men serving in the royal fleets, according to law maritime. However, he seemingly was not admiral by title, and he was only an interim commander of the English fleets. Furthermore he lacked legal authority over the Cinque Ports. This final aspect was realised a few months later, in July, when all the fleets of England were explicitly united under the command of Admiral John Beauchamp. In contrast to Pavely, he was given full jurisdictional power over all maritime cases – not just those pertaining to the royal fleets. Furthermore he was at the same time appointed Warden of the Cinque Ports and Constable of Dover Castle (henceforth the Warden-Constable).[51]

While the admirals gradually seem to have acquired more jurisdictional powers and duties throughout the 1340s and 50s, England had in fact for some decades boasted of another court of maritime law, the Court of Shepway, presided over by the Warden of the Cinque Ports. The Cinque Ports had since at least the twelfth century enjoyed a special relationship with the English Crown. Due to their geostrategic position and their obligation to furnish fleets for the Crown in times of war, the Ports had acquired a number of privileges and liberties.[52] One of these was the Portsmen's right to be judged in international, maritime affairs by their peers at the Court of Shepway. While it technically was a royal court, and thus was developed to discharge royal business concerning maritime law, coastal defence and naval administration, it also served as a source of unity for the Portsmen as it was presided over by their peers and then, from the thirteenth century onwards, by the Warden of the Cinque Ports. The Warden was appointed by the king, but upon entry into office he had to swear to respect and protect the Portsmen's rights and privileges.[53] In 1268, in the wake of the Barons' Revolt, when the Portsmen had sided with de Montfort, the office of Warden of the Cinque Ports was combined with that of Constable of Dover Castle. The principal royal legal officer with the Ports was now imbued with military might, since he also had at his disposal the castle and garrison of Dover. This gave him the power to prevent future revolts as well as ensuring that this maritime frontier of

---

[51] Rymer, *Foedera*, III, part 1, pp. 495, 496, 499; Simon Phillips, *The Prior of the Knights Hospitaller in Late Medieval England* (Woodbridge, 2009), pp. 48–9.

[52] The latter is a matter of contention: Rodger holds that the Ports' prominent position in the naval sources was not due to an especially large fleet of ships, but rather because in geostrategic terms they were located at the maritime gateway to England. Craig Lambert, however, has recently and very convincingly argued that the naval power of the Cinque Ports has been severely underestimated. Cf. Rodger, *Safeguard of the Sea*, p. 125; N.A.M. Rodger, 'The Naval Service of the Cinque Ports', *Eng. Hist. Rev.*, 111 (1996), pp. 636–51, at 647–8; Lambert, *Shipping the Medieval Military*, pp. 13–15; and Craig Lambert, 'The Contribution of the Cinque Ports to the Wars of Edward II and Edward III: New Methodologies and Estimates', in *Roles of the Sea*, ed. Gorski (cit. in n. 4), pp. 59–78, at 72.

[53] Murray, *Constitutional History*, pp. 60–1, 65, 74, 75.

the kingdom had a military commander who was certain to be loyal to the Crown. By the fourteenth century the Warden-Constable had sole charge of all communication between the central government and the Ports, and he performed all the duties of a sheriff. The Constable-Warden thus came to enjoy total jurisdiction internally and externally in cases regarding the Ports.[54]

The Court of Shepway was mainly occupied with solving maritime and commercial quarrels involving the Portsmen and other mariners, native and foreign alike. By the beginning of the fourteenth century the Portsmen had become exempt from trial in all other courts: according to Elisabeth Murray, the Portsmen were allowed even when being sued by foreigners, e.g. for piracy, to be judged at Shepway alone. This changed in 1314, and from then on it was only in domestic cases that they had the privilege of being exclusively judged at Shepway.[55] The 1350s saw an increase in the court's power, and in 1355 the first Warden for life was appointed (though the title was never allowed to become hereditary). Furthermore in regard to maritime matters, the Portsmen enjoyed rights to wreck which were usually reserved exclusively for the Crown. In cases of wrecks, piracy and prizes concerning the Cinque Ports, the Warden normally held inquests and determined disputes, and he could legitimately contest the jurisdictional rights and authority of the admirals throughout the fourteenth century. He continuously served in trials as expert in maritime affairs, and he had a right to a share of the Portsmen's captures from prizes, wrecks and *findals* (flotsam and jetsam). Hence in 1358, the Portsmen complained about the admiral's claim to a share of their prizes, as they had already paid their due share to the Warden and thus the Crown.[56]

The importance of the combination in one person of the title of admiral of all the English fleets with that of Constable-Warden of the Cinque Ports has been overlooked by historians, but it was politically and legally necessary so as to achieve an independent admiralty. This manoeuvre also ensured that the central government could circumvent the legal immunities enjoyed by the Portsmen and gain a tighter grip on a maritime community which historically had shown a problematic propensity for piracy and independent action which could complicate an English claim to sovereignty and impartial jurisdiction at sea. An admiralty court with quasi-supreme judicial authority could not function without express legal control over the Ports, as it was most likely that the Constable-Warden would contest the jurisdictional power of the admiralty court. In essence, there could be no Court of Admiralty without control over the Cinque Ports.

[54] *Ibid.*, pp. 76–81, 83–5, 102–6; David G. Sylvester, 'Communal Piracy in Medieval England's Cinque Ports', in *Noble Ideals and Bloody Realities*, ed. N. Christie and M. Yazigi (Leiden, 2006), pp. 163–77; Heebøll-Holm, *Ports*, pp. 166–7.

[55] Murray, *Constitutional History*, pp. 70–1.

[56] *Ibid.*, pp. 69–71, 88, 121–4.

Beauchamp died shortly after his appointment, and it fell to his successor as admiral and Warden-Constable, Robert Herle, appointed in 1361, to institute the Court of Admiralty in practice. Herle served as admiral until 1364 when he was succeeded in all his titles by Ralph Spigurnell, the last admiral in the fourteenth century to unite the office of Constable-Warden with the admiralty.[57] As the 1360s progressed, the legal side of the admiral's role grew continuously and the admirals increasingly were expected to formulate maritime law as well as to understand the existing legislation.

It was during the admiralty of Robert Herle that we have what I would term the first official cases of the Court of Admiralty. Both involved the Dartmouth shipmaster and former lieutenant of Admiral Guy Brian, William Smale. In 1361 Smale was involved in two cases before Admiral Herle and the Admiralty Court. In the first, in March 1361, Smale was indicted for a case where West Country ships under his command had attacked and plundered a ship owned by English and Flemish merchants while *en route* from Nantes to Flanders. Initially, Herle was ordered to hear and judge the case according to common law. However by May this commission to proceed by common law was revoked and instead Edward and his Council declared that

> according to the law and custom of our realm, felonies, trespasses, or injuries done upon the sea ought not to be dealt with or determined before our Justices at the common law, but before our Admirals according to the maritime law.[58]

Despite the viciousness of the attack – Smale's men slaughtered 100 people on the ship – Smale was for unknown reasons never brought to justice.[59] While the court here apparently failed to pass a verdict it now possessed an important legal right: to judge by maritime law. This was in many ways a

---

[57] Marsden, *Select Pleas*, I, p. xlii; Rymer, *Foedera*, III, part 1, pp. 479, 505; Rymer, *Foedera*, III, part 2, p. 597; Cushway, *Edward III and the War at Sea*, p. 177; Murray, *Constitutional History*, pp. 123–4. Although William Clinton from 1340 until 4 April 1342 was Constable-Warden of the Cinque Ports and admiral of the fleet from the Thames to Portsmouth, no other admirals carried this double title until 1360 (practical extension of West Fleet). Indeed the three admirals from 1360 to 1369 – John Beauchamp, July 1360 to January 1361; Robert Herle, 1361–4; and Ralph Spigurnell, 1364–9 – not only were each Constable-Warden of the Cinque Ports, but were also (and in contrast to William Clinton) sole admiral of England. The admiral was now both all-powerful over the English fleet and an officer with wide and ever expanding jurisdiction in English maritime affairs. Thus it seems reasonable to see the connection of these two as the finalisation of the English Court of Admiralty.

[58] Marsden, *Law and Custom*, I, pp. 88–9 ('videtur esse consonum dictis legi et consue-tudini quod felonie, transgressiones, seu injurie, supra mare facte, non coram Justiciariis nostris ad communem legem, sed coram Admirallis nostris juxta legem maritimam deducantur et terminentur').

[59] *Cal. Close R., 1360–4*, p. 120; Marsden, *Law and Custom*, I, pp. 84–9; Cushway, *Edward III and the War at Sea*, pp. 177–8.

masterstroke, for it allowed the incorporation in the Court of Admiralty of all the legal privileges that Edward III had already conceded to the mercantile community with the Statutes of the Staple of 1353. In these he had offered extensive protection of the staples and their visitors – domestic as well as foreign – and he had granted to the mayor and ministers of the staple that they enjoyed supreme jurisdiction over all suits except criminal cases and that they could judge according to the law merchant and not the common law. He had also promised that the royal officers would not interfere with or challenge the staple court's jurisdiction. Criminal offences were still to be judged by the king's officers, but, interestingly, pursuance of a suit about robbery at sea was to be treated in accordance with the law merchant.[60] With the Council's Admiralty Court declaration of 1361 these provisions were in principle respected and unharmed, but in practice the admiral now had a competing court with wider jurisdiction than that of the staples. Indeed the admiral could not only pass judgment but also had the means to police the waters: he thereby had a much wider range in his operational jurisdiction.

A few months later, in July 1361, Smale and another Dartmouth shipowner, John Bronde, accused the French shipmaster Johan Houeel of having captured a ship of theirs and slain the crew off Winchelsea in 1359. The ship was later recaptured by another Englishman and taken to Great Yarmouth with its goods. Though Smale and Bronde sought to have the case tried by common law, it was again stressed that the admiralty judged according to equity and maritime law, not common law, especially as Houeel was a foreigner and hence lacking knowledge of the latter. It is surely likely that such a statement, which ran counter to the interests of native Englishmen, will have increased the court's reputation for impartiality abroad.[61] Houeel claimed that the capture happened in time of war and was therefore legitimate prize. Furthermore, according to the Treaty of Brétigny suits pertaining to captures made during war could not be prosecuted after the conclusion of peace. However the plaintiffs were able to prove that the capture had happened in time of truce. Consequently on 4 October the case was adjourned at the Wool Quay, which was later to become one of the two staples of the Admiralty Court, and Houeel was sentenced to pay £1,000 in damages and was handed over to the Marshal's custody until he had paid. However, in accordance with the civil aspects of maritime law, he was not punished for the killing of the

---

[60] *Statutes of the Realm*, I, pp. 332–43; Dick, *Framing Piracy* (cit. in n. 20), p. 200.

[61] Charles Johnson, 'An Early Admiralty Case (A.D. 1361)', in *Camden Miscellany* XV, Camden Third Series, xli (Royal Historical Soc., 1929), pp. 1–9, at 4 ('ceste court qest office damiralle ne serra pas rullez si estroit come serront les autres courtz du roialme qe sont rullez par commune ley de la terre, mes est reullable par equite et ley marine ou chescun homme serra resceu a dire sa verite, et le dit Johan Houeel est alien et nad pas conisaunce des leys de la terre') ; Ward, *World of the Medieval Shipmaster*, p. 36.

crew.[62] Indeed in this case the court appears to have acted impartially and Houeel – though he may in fact have been a prisoner – seemingly did not contest its right to jurisdiction.

In line with my general approach to the origins of the Court of Admiralty I would suggest that it cannot be seen as a durable and institutionalised court of maritime law, charged with administering international maritime law, until 1361. After the signing of the peace treaty of Brétigny in October 1360, the French were forced (albeit only temporarily) to recognise English superiority over parts of the French coastal lands and thus implicitly to recognise an English sovereignty there. With the French acceptance of these terms, the Court of Admiralty acquired international recognition as a court of maritime law. Given that the French had been the primary challengers of this claim, and with Castile locked in civil war, no one could contest the claim and indeed English legal authority (short-lived though it actually turned out to be). Furthermore, by uniting all the fleets of England under the admiral, whose title was both permanent and combined with that of Constable-Warden of the Cinque Ports, all possible jurisdictional disputes of the various courts that had previously dealt with maritime offences were now, at least theoretically, laid to rest.

The Court of Admiralty's jurisdiction over maritime matters was never total, however, and maritime business matters such as wages and general average[63] remained with the traditional courts. The development of the Admiralty Court's authority was a gradual affair with several elements in the process running in parallel. Even the powers acquired by the court in the 1360s proved fleeting and by the 1370s it was coming under severe pressure by a combination of the admirals' mishandling of their role, competing domestic courts of law and the threat posed by the increasing naval power of the French and Castilian fleets. Nevertheless, a new chapter in the history of the jurisdiction of the English Admiralty had opened. It had become a fully recognised court of law. There now commenced a process of defining its legal role and prerogatives more narrowly, as is demonstrated for instance by the commissions that sat intermittently from 1375 to 1403 and which formulated the Inquisition of Queenborough, the new and revised English code of maritime law. While the Court of Admiralty in the following centuries was subject to numerous reforms and a curtailing of its prerogatives, and indeed at its core seems until the seventeenth century to have been little more than

---

[62] Johnson, 'Early Admiralty Case', pp. 1–5; Chaplais, *English Medieval Diplomatic Practice*, I, part 1, p. 370, n. 36; Cushway, *Edward III and the War at Sea*, p. 178.

[63] The law of general average is the legal principle in maritime law that all parties in a sea venture proportionally share any losses resulting from a voluntary sacrifice of any part of the ship or its cargo that is made in order to save the whole in an emergency (as when the crew throws some cargo overboard to lighten the ship in a storm).

a source of profit for the admirals, it had ushered in a slow criminalisation of piracy and something else that is perhaps even more important: after 1361 royal sovereignty was represented by a permanent and specialised legal institution, and admiralty jurisdiction was an established fact both in practice and by royal order.[64]

---

[64] Ward, *World of the Medieval Shipmaster*, pp. 35–6; Simpkin, 'Keeping the Seas' (cit. in n. 4), pp. 88–92; Kenneth R. Andrews, *Elizabethan Privateering* (Cambridge, 1966), pp. 22–31; Marsden, 'Vice-Admirals of the Coast' (cit. in n. 15), p. 469; Marsden, 'Early Prize Jurisdiction' (cit. in n. 45), pp. 681–2; Alfred Rubin, *The Law of Piracy* (Honolulu, 1988), 40–4; Heebøll-Holm, *Ports, Piracy and Maritime War*, pp. 1–13, 229–45; Rodger, *Safeguard of the Sea*, pp. 127–8.

CHAPTER 9

The *Consulate of the Sea* and its Fortunes in Late Medieval Mediterranean Countries*

Lorenzo Tanzini

In this chapter I outline very summarily the long history of the text known as the *Llibre del Consolat de mar* [*Consulate of the Sea*] (in Italian, *Libro del Consolato del mare*), from its very origins in the time of the Aragonese Crown through to its fortunes in the sixteenth century across Europe, especially in the Mediterranean area. Italy will be a crucial focus of analysis: indeed, if we examine the extant manuscripts and printed copies of the *Llibre*, Italy seems to be the most important area of the text's circulation at the end of the Middle Ages. One of the seven manuscripts of the *Llibre* dating from before the *editio princeps* (1484) is preserved at the Biblioteca Universitaria of Cagliari,[1] while another library, in Palermo, has an early manuscript translation into Italian, dating back to 1479.[2] The *Llibre* was printed in eight different Catalan editions, in Barcelona, in the fifteenth and sixteenth centuries; during the same period the text appeared in nine Italian editions, in Rome and Venice.[3] Of these latter, in 1519 an edition was printed in

* I thank Nigel Ramsay for his help with translation and for his suggestions.

[1] It is the starting point of my recent essay, 'Le prime edizioni a stampa in italiano del Libro del Consolato del mare', in *Itinerando senza confini dalla preistoria ad oggi: Studi in ricordo di Roberto Coroneo*, ed. R. Martorelli (Perugia, 2015), pp. 965–78.

[2] First analysed by C. Giardina, 'Una traduzione italiana del "Consolato del mare" del 1479', *Rivista di diritto della Navigazione*, 2/1 (1936), pp. 200–5; but see now S. Corrieri, 'Un manoscritto italiano inedito del "Libro del Consolato del mare"', in *La formazione del diritto marittimo nella prospettiva storica*, ed. G. Camarda, S. Corrieri, T. Scovazzi (Milan, 2010), pp. 81–4.

[3] Germà Colon and Arcadi Garcia, *Llibre del Consolat de mar* (Barcelona 1981–4; reprinted in a single volume, 2001); see vols I–II for the edition, III/1 *Estudi juridic* and III/2 *Diplomatari*, with an interesting selection of late-medieval Catalan sources on trade and navigation. An earlier edition, *Les costums maritimes de Barcelona*, ed. E. Moliné y Brasés (Barcelona, 1914), was based on the Barcelona printed version of 1494. The most complete survey of the manuscript and printed tradition of the *Llibre* is by Aquilino Iglesia Ferreirós, 'La formación de los libros de Consulado de Mar', *Initium*, 2 (1997), pp. 1–372. The latest edition of the Italian version (currrently used by modern scholars) is still Giuseppe Lorenzo Maria Casaregi, *Il*

Rome but with a dedicatory prologue referring to the Florentine merchant community,[4] and this was the first printed translation of the *Llibre* from Catalan. Even the later French edition (1577) depended on an Italian translation. As a consequence, the use and fortune of the *Llibre del Consolat* is, above all, part of the history of economic, political and cultural relations between Italy and the Iberian world,[5] within the general evolution of the western Mediterranean.[6]

Nevertheless, such a history of the text – and this point should be emphasised straight away – must not be seen as an attempt to draw a complete textual genealogy of all the maritime law of the late medieval Mediterranean. Nineteenth- and twentieth-century scholars once tried to trace a coherent line of transmission starting (as they hoped) with survivals of classical law (the *Lex Rhodia*) and coming down to the medieval *Llibre del Consolat*, which was supposed to have been transmitted from the Mediterranean world to the Atlantic *Loi d'Oléron* and finally to the English customs set out in the *Black Book of the Admiralty*.[7] It was a misleading idea, for two different reasons. First of all, there is clear evidence that medieval maritime laws, and particularly those used in Italy, sought to improve their own effectiveness by claiming a very ancient origin: in other words, antiquity was a kind of – more or less conscious – textual strategy. It is well known, for example, that the

---

consolato del mare, ed. G.L.M. Casaregi (Turin, 1719), reprinted by O. Sciolla (Turin, 1911).

[4] *Capitulj et ordinatione di mare et di mercantie* (Rome: Antonio de Bladi, 1519). See above for the dedication. The Florentine community in Rome had a well-established organisation and used the name of Consolato as well: the street just in front of the church of San Giovanni dei Fiorentini in Rome is still known as 'Via del Consolato': cf. Melissa Bullard, '"Mercatores florentini Romanam Curiam sequentes" in the Early Sixteenth Century', *Jnl of Medieval & Renaissance Studies*, 6 (1976), pp. 51–71; Irene Polverini Fosi, 'Il consolato fiorentino a Roma e il progetto per la chiesa nazionale', *Studi Romani*, 37 (1989), pp. 50–70. For Florentine interest in Mediterranean navigation see Michael Mallett, *The Florentine Galleys in the Fifteenth Century* (Oxford, 1967), and Giovanni Ciccaglioni, 'Il mare a Firenze: Interazioni tra mutamenti geografici, cambiamenti istituzionali e trasformazioni economiche nella Toscana fiorentina del '400', *Archivio Storico Italiano*, 167 (2009), pp. 91–125.

[5] According to Riniero Zeno, *Storia del diritto marittimo italiano nel Mediterraneo* (Milan, 1946), the Consulate can be considered for all these reasons to be 'un testo italico di diritto marittimo' (p. 201).

[6] The bibliography of the history of Mediterranean trade and navigation between Italy and Spain is too rich to be listed here; for a recent introduction to the main historical topics see *Navegación institucional y navegación privada en el Mediterráneo medieval*, ed. R. González Arévalo (Granada, 2016).

[7] The starting point is obviously the five volumes of the *Collection de lois maritimes antérieures au XVIIIe siècle*, ed. J.M. Pardessus (Paris, 1831–9). For a good introduction to possible misunderstandings, especially with regard to the meaning of *lex mercatoria* in Mediterranean and English traditions, see *From Lex Mercatoria to Commercial Law*, ed. Vito Piergiovanni (Berlin, 2005).

late-fifteenth-century edition of the *Consolate* included a very strange text, the *Tabula adotionum* or *Cronica de le promulgacions*[8] in which the *Libro* was asserted to have been accepted by the rulers of many Mediterranean cities (Rome, Jerusalem, Tyre, Marseilles and so on) early in the eleventh or twelfth century, more than 200 years before the time when we know that the *Llibre del Consolat* was composed! At the same time, a pretended antiquity was quite a common feature for medieval legislative texts, and in this sense the maritime laws are no exception. The city of Trani in Apulia, southern Italy, used a maritime law text written in vernacular Italian and allegedly dating back to 1063 – a date when no legal text in the whole of Italy was in the vernacular – and which in fact was probably composed only in 1363.[9] That is to say, it would be very dangerous to take seriously the supposed genealogy of maritime legal codes.

The second reason for avoiding any generalised coherent history of maritime law codes in Europe stems from the textual history of the *Llibre del Consolat*. As can be seen from the very accurate survey by Aquilino Iglesia Ferreirós,[10] one cannot speak of a sole text of the *Libro*, or at least not until the first edition in 1484. Earlier manuscripts varied, in fact, according to their different areas of circulation – Barcelona, Valencia, Majorca. In other words, there was not a straightforward history of a text appearing first and then circulating; rather, there was a long process of textual consolidation within a number of different contexts.[11]

Coming back to my intended outline, I would like first of all to approach the history of the *Llibre* in a more pragmatic way. What was the principal aim in composing and copying such a body of maritime law? How did historical circumstances affect the text over the years and prompt its internal changes? And in what sense was the *Llibre del Consolat* actually useful?

---

[8] *Llibre del Consolat de mar*, ed. Colon and Garcia, III, pp. 158–64: the text seems to have been written first in Valencia in the mid-fourteenth century and then reproduced with many variations in the printings.

[9] Antonio di Maggio, *La Puglia nel Medioevo: Trani e gli statuti marittimi* (Bari, 2003).

[10] Aquilino Iglesia Ferreirós, 'Il Libro del Consolato del mare', *Rivista Internazionale di Diritto Comune*, 6 (1995), pp. 81–125; *idem*, 'Il Libro del Consolato del mare: Appendice', *Rivista Internazionale di Diritto Comune*, 7 (1996), pp. 307–409; *idem*, 'De los costums al Llibre de consolat o de la dificultad para escribir la historia', *Studia et Documenta Historiae et Iuris*, 62 (1996), pp. 473–512; and *idem*, 'La formación de los libros'.

[11] 'manuscritos que recogían el Derecho mercantil durante los siglos XIV y XV... no testimonian la existencia de unas compilaciones con un contenido definido que corrían por en Mediterraneo, sino la existencia de manuscrito diferentes que según las necesidades y según los deseos de sus propietarios incorporaban los distintos textos de Derecho mercantil, a medida que éstos iban apareciendo': Aquilino Iglesia Ferreirós, 'El Libro del Consulado de mar', in *Del ius mercatorum al derecho mercantil: III Seminario de Historia del Derecho Privado (Sitges, 28–30 de mayo de 1992)*, ed. C. Petit (Madrid, 1997), pp. 109–42, at 121.

Concerning the first point, it is worth reminding ourselves of the text's internal structure. Sixteenth-century editions (both Catalan and Italian) usually presented a text composed of three different sections. First of all, a short section of 44 chapters, concerning the internal procedure of the *Consolato del Mar* as a maritime legal court in Valencia (*Orde judiciari de València*); in this section the Book reflects the institutional context of just one of the merchant cities that were under the Aragonese Crown in the early fourteenth century. The second and main part of the *Llibre* includes a long section of around 240 chapters, usually entitled 'I buoni costumi di mare' (*Costums de la mar*). Most of these chapters are devoted to the authority and duties of the shipmaster, the right government of the ship, the security of the laded goods, and the practical operations of maritime trade: unlike the first part, this main section makes very little reference to the institutional framework of Catalan courts, and it depends on the long-term accretive development of maritime customs.[12] After the main section, most manuscripts and early printed editions include a short series of privileges granted by the kings of Aragon as well as relevant statutes made by the town council of Barcelona, dating from the late fourteenth or fifteenth century and dealing with specific matters such as marine insurance. Before the first Catalan printed edition of 1484 there are, as we have already seen, many differences in the internal composition of the three parts of the text, such as those between Catalan manuscripts from Barcelona and Valencia. Some manuscripts, including one of 1407 preserved in Valencia and another of around 1385 in Majorca, were not used by the late-fifteenth-century editors, and consequently the printed versions generally followed what the councillors of Barcelona considered to be the *Llibre del Consolat*.[13] For this reason, too, the 'standard' printed text of the consulate started with the judicial procedure of the Consolat court in Valencia but ended with the *Ordinacions de consellers ... sobre fets maritims*, written in Barcelona in 1435.

As a result of the text's development in this way, it is possible to argue that in the Mediterranean world the customary maritime laws, as seen in

[12] This is the most closely comparable part of the text for a general history of medieval navigation. It is possible to find correspondences between the very essence of the *Llibre*, the customary rules or *Costums de la mar*, and the customs witnessed by the Atlantic texts: see, for example, Margarita Serna Vallejo, 'La correspondencia entre los contenidos de los Rôles d'Oléron y el texto más antiguo de la costumes de mar del Llibre del Consolat de mar', *Initium*, 20 (2015), pp. 159–204. On the early versions of the *Costums*, and their relationship with the mid-thirteenth-century *Costums de Tortosa*, see Aquilino Iglesia Ferreirós, 'Costums de mar', in *El dret comú I Catalunya: Actes del V Simposi Internacional (Barcelona, 26–27 de maig de 1995)*, ed. A. Iglesia Ferreirós (Barcelona, 1996), pp. 243–602.

[13] Ferreirós, 'De los costums al Llibre de consolat', pp. 488–9. In 'La formación de los libros', Ferreirós emphasises very clearly the differences between the 'consulate books' of Barcelona, Valencia, Perpignan and Majorca, whose composition depended on the different collections of privileges granted by the king to local consulate courts.

the manuscript tradition, were always related to the institutional rules of the courts and their history;[14] and this institutional link will be seen to have been very significant for the developments that we discuss.

The 1519 edition and its fortunes

Once the text of the *Llibre* began to be known in Italy, its editors or revisers made different choices according to their practical needs. The manuscript copy at Palermo was based on the standard Barcelona version of the text, but it also included the first section, concerning the maritime court of Valencia.[15] Palermo was in fact simply a part of Aragonese territory, and some of the later editions of the *Libro* also included the 'Ordinationi degli consiglieri di Barcellona per il consolato di Sicilia'; such an adherence to the early model is surely significant. By contrast, the 1519 edition which was printed in Rome made a very clear selection.[16] This version was composed by Jaime Gell of Perpignan and was dedicated to Pope Leo X. Despite the personal background of the editor, the historical context and the general purposes of the translation were wholly different :

> la presente opera detta di Consolato, certo alle mie spalle peso non conven-
> iente, ma per la multitudine delle cose, per la varietà et per la perplexità de'
> molti pericoli degna che in luce sia data, parte per illustrare dello Oceano
> tertio elemento la ingenita potentia, parte per più sicuro et expedito praticar
> per esso Oceano summamente opportuna, in mezo adducendo conveniente
> lege a ciaschun dubio per causa de esso fra gli homini surgente come da
> ogne bon autor usar se sole, per magior splendore de' soi libri, così io a
> vostra Sanctità dedicare non dubitai...[17]

---

[14] 'Se puede afirmar que circulaban desde principios del siglo XIV manuscritos de una collección u obra denominada Costums de mar, pero no es posible ni negar ni afirmar que se incluyesen otras obras en esos manuscritos. Puede, sin embrago, afirmarse que nadie ha logrado aportar prueba alguna de la circulación de una compilation de derecho marítimo-mercantil, en el sentido precisado, en este período' (Iglesia Ferreirós, 'La formación de los libros', p. 206, and also 'Costums de mar', especially pp. 274–80): in other words, it is impossible to verify the manuscript tradition of the Costums without or apart from their textual connection with the institutional rules, *ordo* and privileges of the different Consulates.

[15] An edition of the entire 'Sicilian' text is in *Llibre del Consolat de mar*, ed. Colon and Garcia, IV, pp. 979–1152.

[16] On this edition, see Tanzini, 'Le prime edizioni a stampa in italiano'; Ferreirós, 'El Libro del Consulado', pp. 139–42.

[17] 1519 edition, f. 1: the editor wanted therefore to celebrate the majesty of the Ocean, and to provide sailors with the tool to resolve any controversy that might arise, while offering to the Pope a book to add to his library.

More practically, in granting his authorisation for this publication, the Pope emphasised that it might be found useful by the Florentine merchant community in Rome:

> Cum sicut accepimus superioribus diebus non mediocribus diligentia et vigiliis quendam librum in lingua cathalana scriptum statuta ritus et ordinem rerum mercantilium in se continentem et universo fere mundo seu eiusdem mercatoribus deservientem in vulgare italicum reduxisti et ad instantiam dilectorum filiorum nostrorum consulum societatis mercatorum florentin. nuncupat. publicasti, quem ut speramus toti Italie et ydioma ipsum intelligentibus summopere profuturum fore ...[18]

As a result, the Roman–Florentine edition did not include the first section, on the judicial procedure of the court of Valencia – that was too far from the Italian praxis and reflected too much its own particular context to be relevant; the edition was thus shorter than the other versions printed in sixteenth-century Italy, comprising only 247 chapters. At the same time, Jaime Gell chose to include at the end of the text a copy of the list of towns that it was claimed had adopted the *Libro* between the eleventh and thirteenth centuries; this list was not in the Palermo manuscript of 1479, and first appeared in the 1494 Barcelona edition. The decision to include such a strange, even fantastic, reference to the High Middle Ages probably resulted from the fact that Rome appeared at the top of the list, dating back to 1075 – the moment when the Romans, according to the historical claims in the *Llibre*, first adopted the Consolato. One last interesting feature of the 1519 edition is that at the very end of the text the editor included some chapters taken from the Barcelona statutes, about insurance and bills of exchange, dating to 1435–6:[19] even though these statutes related to a particular local context in Barcelona, the mention of an international financial device used by Italian merchants was surely the reason why such a text was selected for the Italian translation.

The editorial choices of the first Italian edition were followed in the first edition to be printed in Venice, in 1539.[20] A few years later, the *Libro del Consolato* was printed again in Italian in Venice, but this time in a different version:[21] now (1549) the text included the first 44 chapters, and thus was

---

[18] *Ibid.*, f. 1: 'A book in the Catalan language concerning laws, customs and procedures of mercantile practice ... useful for the whole world ... translated on behalf of the consuls of the Florentine merchant community ...'

[19] *Les costums maritimes de Barcelona*, ed. E. Moliné y Brasés (Barcelona, 1914), pp. 214–15; Ferreirós, 'La formación de los libros', p. 297.

[20] *Libro di consolato novamente stampato et ricorretto, nel quale sono scritti capitoli & statuti & buone ordinationi, che li antichi ordinarono per li casi di mercantia & di mare & mercanti & marinari, & patroni di nauilii* (Venice, 1539): this edition (like that of 1519) does not include the first forty-four articles of the Valencia Consulate collection.

[21] The text according to the 'Venetian' version is now available in the reprint *Il consolato e il portolano del mare*, ed. L. Guatri, C. De Deo and G. Guerzoni (Milan,

a more 'Catalan' version. In subsequent Venetian editions the same choice was followed, and the original rules on insurance were included as well, as *Ordinationi sopra le sicurtà maritime.*

Before going forward in our survey, we need to ask: what was the relation between the text of the *Libro* and the actual judicial and maritime practice of the period? Here is one of the most striking paradoxes of our history. The *Llibre del Consolat* provided, as is usually said, the legal background for maritime activities; and the mercantile courts in both Valencia and Barcelona each called themselves *Consolato del Mare.* We read at the beginning of the *Llibre* that

> [§ m 41] Les sentències que per los dits cònsols e iutge són donades se donen per les costumes escrites de la mar e segons que en diverses capítols d'aquelas és declarat.[22]

But the lack of judicial records of the consulate courts prevents us from verifying the real impact of such 'written customs' on the daily life of the courts themselves:[23] the textual study of the *Libro* by Aquilino Iglesia Ferreirós shows that the 'costumes escrites' were written alongside the different collections of privileges of the different Consulates,[24] and it was within the practical needs of the different consulate courts that the central section called *Costums de la mar* was gathered and set down as part of the *Llibres del Consolat.* Unfortunately, however, the documentation of the Catalan Consolati is too poor to be able to cast light on such questions about statutory rules and practices. Accordingly, we need to adopt a broader base for comparison, by using the Italian archives and their rich series of mercantile trials.

2007), with a very useful introduction by C. De Deo, 'Il consolato del mare: Storia di un successo editoriale', pp. xi–xxviii. The text edited by S. Corrieri, *Il consolato del mare: La tradizione giuridico-marittima del Mediterraneo attraverso un'edizione italiana del 1584 del testo originale catalano del 1484,* (Rome, 2005) follows another printed version of the Venetian tradition. During the sixteenth century the *Libro del Consolato* was so popular among Venetian merchants that, according to one eighteenth-century scholar, Venetians knew the Catalan maritime laws much better than their own: see F.C. Lane, 'Maritime Law and Administration, 1250–1350', in his *Venice and History* (Baltimore, 1969).

[22] *Llibre del Consolat de mar,* ed. Colon and Garcia, I, p. 418: 'The judgments of the above-mentioned consuls have to be pronounced according to the written customs of the sea and their different chapters...' It is worth recalling that this particular section of the text belongs to the manuscripts of Valencia; consequently it attests to the existence of a written version of the *usus maris* in Valencia but not in other Catalan towns.

[23] But see now, for the Barcelona court, the doctoral thesis of Elena Maccioni, '"Mercadejar simplement et segura en costra senyoria et en altres partes": Il consolato del mare di Barcellona e la difesa degli interessi mercantili nel Quattrocento', University of Cagliari, Ciclo XXIX, forthcoming.

[24] Ferreirós, 'La formación de los libros', pp. 134–44.

The Italian tradition

In late-medieval Italy there are some statutory texts, with elements that are quite similar to the *Llibre del Consolat de mar*; their history is linked to the towns where they are supposed to have been written – Venice, Rimini, Ancona, Bari, Amalfi, Trani. Legal historians have sometimes assumed their dependence on certain chapters of the *Consolato*, but that argument is dangerous because of the extremely doubtful chronology of the texts. At the same time, to consider all the Italian maritime statutes together as a whole, as Pardessus does in his marvellous collection of medieval texts,[25] risks hiding the real features and purposes of many of them. Most maritime statutes in medieval Italy were composed by public officers and rulers in order to assure the safety of their ports and of maritime trade: the best example of this sort is the Venetian *Statuta* of 1255.[26] Usually they were written in Latin, and therefore had to be used in a civil court by a notary or a judge who was able to read that language – and not by merchants themselves. Wholly different is the case of late-medieval vernacular laws,[27] which still survive in a couple of relevant cases.

The *Ordinamenta et consuetudo maris* of Trani purport to have been written in 1063, in spite of internal references in the text to the word 'comune' and to the pilgrimage to Santiago de Compostela, more or less impossible before the twelfth century. The text as we actually know it is a vernacular version, preserved in a printed copy of the early sixteenth century. Despite their uncertain dating and very short form (just thirty-two chapters), the *Ordinamenta* of Trani have many similarities with the *Llibre del Consolat* customs: apart from their specific contents, they use a standard clause to introduce every single chapter: 'Propone dice termina et diffinisce questa infrascripta questione de l'arte del mare. La quale è così facta che se alcuna nave ...' [28] Such a 'hypothetical' form reminds us what we can read in the *Llibre del Consolat*, where most chapters declare that a case 'se nave...'('if a ship') and then set out the rule to be followed in that case. This is the same hypothetical structure that we find in the *Loi d'Oléron*:

---

[25] Pardessus, *Collection de lois maritimes*, vol. V, for the Italian statutes.

[26] The statute of Doge Ranieri Zeno was followed by a very rich series of further statutes during the fourteenth century: Lane, 'Maritime Law and Administration, 1250–1350'.

[27] For the context and consequences of the use of the vernacular in Italian statutory texts in the fourteenth century, see now Francesco Salvestrini and Lorenzo Tanzini, 'La lingua della legge: Volgarizzamenti di Statuti nell'Italia del Basso medioevo', in *Comunicare nel Medioevo: La conoscenza e l'uso delle lingue nei secoli XII–XV*, ed. I. Lori Sanfilippo and G. Pinto (Rome, 2015), pp. 249–301.

[28] ('This clause introduces, describes and resolves the following question about the art of the seamanship, which is: If Di Maggio, *La Puglia nel Medioevo* (cit. in n. 9).

Une nef charge a Burdeux ou aillours et avent chose qe torment la prent en la mer et qe il ne poent echaper saunz gettre darres et des vinc. Le mestre est tenu de dire …[29]

We can imagine that this was exactly the way in which maritime customs were created: a case occurred, a solution was found, and that solution became a rule. The history of the *Black Book of the Admiralty* shows just such a 'practical' building-up of a legal text, starting from particular cases such as the Queenborough Inquest of 1375.[30]

Much more interesting for a comparison with the Consolato are the *Statuti del mare* of Ancona,[31] on the Italian coast of the Adriatic Sea – quite an important free town, whose naval tradition was not completely overshadowed by the Venetian rule of the Adriatic. Here the analogy with the Consolato del mar is very close: the *Statuti*, written in the vernacular in 1397, are quite a long text (87 chapters) with a wide range of subjects, concerning the shipmaster, relations with traders, and daily life on board. Ancona, it may be mentioned, had some dealings with Catalan merchants, and in 1399 the commune agreed the *pacti de li Catalani* with the subjects of the Aragonese Crown.

In two different passages of the *Statuti*, the text refers to the use of written maritime laws to resolve conflicts and controversies on board:

§ 37: Che le nave e li altri navilii porte li capitoli de mare exenplati.
Anchi mo statuto et ordinato è [che] omni scrivano de nave e de omni altro navilio, la quale overo el quale di fuora del porto d'ancona ussirà per

---

[29] ('A ship is loaded at Bordeaux or elsewhere and it happens that a storm catches the ship at sea, and that it cannot escape without casting overboard goods and wine. The master is bound to say …') I quote from the edition by Serna Vallejo, *Los rôles d'Oléron*, p. 198 (MS version in the London *Liber Horn*): the Oléron law is also known as 'la chartre d'Oliron des jugemenz de la mer', referring very clearly to the judicial origin of the text.

[30] I refrain here from mentioning the substantial historiography of the English maritime laws: it is sufficient to refer to the recent book by Robin Ward, *The World of the Medieval Shipmaster: Laws, Business and the Sea c. 1350–c. 1450* (Woodbridge, 2009), pp. 9–47. The same procedural focus is evident in the treatise *Lex mercatoria*, which is copied in the collection known as the Little Red Book of Bristol: see the edition by Daniel R. Coquillette, 'Incipit lex mercatoria, que, auando, ubi, inter quos et de quibus sit: El tratado de Lex mercatoria en el Little Red Book de Brístol (ca. 1280 AD)', in *Del ius mercatorum al derecho mercantil* (cit. in n. 11), pp. 143–228 (edition of the Latin text of the treatise *Lex mercatoria*), and note the edition *Lex Mercatoria and Legal Pluralism: A Late Thirteenth-Century Treatise and its Afterlife*, ed. and transl. Mary E. Basile, Jane Fair Bestor, Daniel R. Coquillette and Charles Donahue (Cambridge, Mass.: The Ames Foundation, 1998).

[31] *Ancona e il suo mare: Norme, patti e usi di navigazione nei secoli XIV e XV, I: Statuti del mare di Ancona – Patti del comune di Ancona con diverse nazioni*, ed. M.V. Biondi (Ancona, 1998); Gruppo di studio di Diritto della Navigazione, 'Aspetti dello Statuto del mare di Ancona (XIV secolo)', *Archivio Giuridico Filippo Serafini*, 201 (1981), pp. 149–232.

navigare en alcuna parte de fuora dal golfo, debia portare li capitoli del
mare exemplati publici, socto pena de cento soldi d'ancontani piccioli, acciò
che ello possa dechiarare li decti capitoli quando bisogna quessi capitoli.
§ 38: Che li consoli de oltramare porte li capitoli del mare exemplati.
Dicemo e statuimo che li consoli de ultramare porte li capitoli del mare
esemplati et sia tenuti de farli exemplare et portarli et averli cum seco,
acciò che segondo quessi possa fare ragione a ciascuno, pena cento soldi a
qualumque contrafacesse. [32]

Such passages have sometimes been interpreted as showing that in late-
fourteenth-century Ancona the Catalan law was used – the 'capitoli del mare'
being, according to some historians, none other than the *Llibre de Consolat*.[33]
Upon closer examination, differences between the Ancona rules and the *Libro*
are much more significant. Almost all the Ancona chapters read like a typical
communal statute: 'statuto et ordenato è che ...': that is to say, the whole
text is intended as a public law of the commune of Ancona, rather than as
a customary law. In this sense, the example of the 1255 statutes of Venice
was very powerful. At the end of the *Statuti*, according to the one surviving
manuscript, there is a very clear reference to the validity of Ancona's own
municipal law:

Statutum et ordinatum fuit quod omnia et singula statuta leges et refor-
mationes dicti comunis Ancone que in aliquo contradicerent supradictis
statutis insertis in hoc volumine statutorum sint cassa et irrita. Et similiter
sint cassa et irrita omnia alia statuta dicti comunis, salvis semper refor-
mationibus dicti comunis loquentibus de reformatione statutorum dicte
civitatis[34]

---

[32] ('§ 37: That every kind of ship has to have on board a copy of the text of the
"chapters of the sea".
It is also decreed that every scrivener of every kind of ship sailing from Ancona
and going anywhere beyond the Adriatic sea has to have on board the text of the
"chapters of the sea" in published form, under pain of a fine of 100 pence of Ancona,
if the aforesaid chapter "in case of necessity" is to be used.
§ 38: That the consuls of the sea must have the text of the "chapters of the sea".
We decree that the consuls of the sea must have the text of the "chapters of the sea"
and have them copied and bring them with them, in order to give justice according
to them, under pain of a fine of 100 pence for each transgression.') It is also stated
that the ships' copies must be 'essemplati publici', i.e., notarially authenticated –
another element of the text's 'public' transmission.
[33] For the lexical overlapping of *capitula et privilegia* with *consuetudines et usus* of the
court, see again Iglesia Ferreirós, 'La formación de los libros', pp. 144–68.
[34] ('It has been decreed and ordered that each and all of the statutes and bylaws of the
commune of Ancona that could be contrary to the abovementioned statutes copied
in this present book must be considered cancelled. And in the same way all the
statutes of the said commune [dealing with the same subject] have been abrogated
except for those statutes on the distribution of public charges'.) *Ancona e il suo mare*,
I: *Statuti del mare di Ancona*, pp. 73–4.

Even within the text we can find many references to the podestà, the commune and the public officials.[35] To conclude: the main section of the *Consolato del Mare*, and in a sense the *Ordinamenta* of Trani too, are customary rules whose application depended on the autonomous practices of the people living on board; the *Statuti del mare*, by contrast, have the general appearance of a law made and operated by public officers according to their own procedures – that is to say, most definitely, corresponding to Roman law. There is an interesting example of such a difference:

§ m 57
Capítol de escrivà a metra en nau o en leyn.
Lo senyor de la nau pot metre scriva en la nau ab consentiment dels personers…Et deu lo fer iurar ab testimoni dels mariners e dels mercaders e dels personers si en loch ne serà que sia suau e fael axi bé al mercader com al senyor de la nau…e que tenga lo cartolari e que ncn y scriva res sino ho ou de cascuna de les parts e él que dó dret a cascu.[36]

On the same subject, the *Statuti del mare* of Ancona of 1397 have:

§ XV De li scrivani de le nave et de li lengni.
Li scrivani de le nave et de li lengni sia tenuti de giurare, ciascuno in comenzamento del suo offitio, ennençi che comença lo suo offitio, de farlo a buona fede, sença fraude et de observare lo presente statuto et tute le altre cose le quali è tenuti de observare per la forma d'alcuno statuto del comuno d'Ancona, sì per li mercanti, sì per li patroni et per li marnari …
Et puoi che lo scrivano averrà giurato lo suo offitio, se è fuora d'Ancona denanti da lo consolo e se è in Ancona denanti a lo giudece de meser lo podestà a li civili deputato, a tucte le sue scripture se creda, e deaseli fede en tutte le cose sì come fosse notario pubblico, non obstante che alcuna sollepnità la quale se de' ponere et agiongere ne li contracti non cie fosse posta.[37]

---

[35] Note in the first passage mentioned above that the copy of the 'capitoli' should be 'essemplati publici', that is to say a notarially authenticated copy: another element of a 'public' transmission of the text.

[36] ('Chapter about the clerk (or scrivener) of the ship.
The managing owner of the ship may appoint a ship's clerk without the consent of the part-owners … and he must make him swear in the presence of the mariners and the merchants and the part-owners if they are present that he will be dutiful and faithful both to the merchants and to the managing owner … and that he will keep the ship's book and that he will write nothing in it except what is true and what he hears from each of the parties and what is right in regard to each party.')
Llibre del Consolat del mar, ed. Colon and Garcia, I, p. 440.

[37] ('Of the clerks (or scriveners) of the ship.
The clerks of the ship must swear at the beginning of their term of office. before starting to exercise it, that they will fulfil it fairly, without any fraud and according to the present statute and according to all other statutes of Ancona, in the interests of the merchants, the mariners and the managing owners. … And once the clerk

As we can see, the main difference is that the scrivener on a Catalan ship has to fulfil his duties according to maritime customs, whereas those bound by the rules of Ancona have to follow the municipal statutes of the commune.

Comparisons and differences

The differences that have been emphasised here need to be taken into consideration for any estimate of the real importance of the fortunes of the Catalan *Llibre de Consolat* in late-medieval Italy. As we have seen, there is evidence for the presence of the *Libro* outside Aragonese lands (Sardinia and Sicily), in Venice and in Rome – but Rome here is really the Florentine community, living around a Florentine pope and using a Tuscan vernacular language, so we can say 'Florence'. It may seem surprising that there is no mention of Genoa. But apart from the fact that Genoa did not have a flourishing printing tradition in the sixteenth century, we should bear in mind that traditionally Genoa was a strong competitor of the Catalan merchants in Mediterranean trade, and therefore Catalan customs may have been ignored deliberately. As regards Venice, there was a very rich tradition of legislation by the doges on maritime matters. But in Venice particular statutes and regulations were not brought together into a general code: accordingly, Venetian rules on navigation and maritime laws are not as full as those of Ancona, despite the enormous importance of the city of San Marco in comparison with the small port of Ancona.

If we focus on the place of maritime and mercantile law in the general legal framework, in Italy the fourteenth century is the great period of the mercantile court, whose role was usually intended as an effective tool for public authorities to improve international trade and to shield it from violent actions – above all, piracy and reprisals.[38] In Genoa, for example, the ducal authority created the court of *Robaria*, which was specifically concerned with cases of reprisals. A very similar function was granted to the Florentine *Mercanzia* – but even though the *Mercanzia* was created in 1308 by the leading guilds of merchants, its judicial competence was directly controlled by the leading members of Florence's government.[39]

has sworn, before the consul if he is far from Ancona, or before the judge of the civil court of the podestà if he is in Ancona, then all his writing shall be considered valid and will be treated as a deed written in public notarial form, notwithstanding the short and simplified form in which it has been written.') *Ancona e il suo mare, I: Statuti del mare di Ancona*, pp. 34–5.

[38] For a recent discussion of the legal framework of late-medieval trade in Italy and Spain, see *Tribunali di mercanti e giustizia mercantile nel tardo Medioevo*, ed. E. Maccioni and S. Tognetti (Florence, 2016).

[39] A short survey of the history of the Italian *Mercanzie* in the fourteenth century is given by Lorenzo Tanzini, 'Tribunali di mercanti nell'Italia tardomedievale tra

In a sense we can say that this was really a widespread European attitude in this period: even the *Black Book of the Admiralty* as a corpus of maritime laws was developed in the context and under the influence of the Admiralty court, the role of which was, above all, focused on the royal oversight and protection of maritime activities against piracy and reprisals. Nevertheless, within such a European context, Mediterranean countries show very significant differences:[40] there is, indeed, a certain paradox or at least irony in Italian maritime law when compared with Catalan examples. Whereas we have a written code of maritime law, presumably as a result of a mercantile tradition – in Aragonese lands – hard facts about actual court practice there are rare. In Italy, by contrast, we have a very rich series of court records (Florence, Venice, Genoa) but there is no maritime legal text such as the *Consolato del Mare*, and consequently the Catalan book was adopted despite the obvious differences of its historical and institutional background from all Italian contexts.[41]

In that sense, it must be emphasised that in the Aragonese lands, the municipal elites and royal power were two different actors engaged in a sharp negotiation. The municipal elites used a distinctive law to emphasise their identity and to bring together the privileges granted by the king:[42] this is the reason why the *Llibre del Consolat* arose in this period as such a key text. The brief reference that has been made above to the legal framework allows us to suppose that such a text was as much (or more) a symbol of autonomy than merely an effective legal base-text. But it was, nevertheless, the book which most fully embodied the identity of the merchantmunicipal elites.

In Italy, by contrast, there was no distinction between the merchant elites of the cities and the political powers: Genoa, Florence and Venice were all governed by merchants. Accordingly, it was the public authority that ruled over the merchants' laws, and there was no need to create a separate or distinct text: the 'maritime' codes here had an ordinary statutory profile without any reference to the customary laws. Such a text (in a 'Consolato del mare' style) appeared in Ancona, but precisely because Ancona was a

economia e potere politico', in *Il governo dell'economia: Italia e Penisola Iberica nel basso Medioevo*, ed. L. Tanzini and S. Tognetti (Rome, 2014), pp. 229–55.

[40] The different roles of mercantile courts in Spain and Tuscany are now outlined by Maria Elisa Soldani and Lorenzo Tanzini, 'Corporaciones y tribunales entre Toscana y Cataluña en torno al siglo XIV', *Hispania*, 76 (2016), pp. 1–36.

[41] Such a paradox has frequently been discussed in Italian historiography: see, recently, Vito Piergiovanni, 'Le regole marittime del Mediterraneo tra consuetudini e statuti', in his *Norme, scienza e pratica giuridica tra Genova e l'Occidente medievale e moderno* (Genoa, 2012), pp. 1231–44, with his suggestion to 'riportare lo studio dei singoli testi alla realtà politica in cui crescono e operano'.

[42] The origins of the consulate jurisdiction, developing from a set of privileges granted by the Crown to merchants, who were allowed to use these to derogate from the ordinary law, are well brought out in Iglesia Ferreirós, 'La formación de los libros', p. 43.

comparatively small town, not able to engage in foreign politics by itself, and without a major 'public' mercantile court. It is not by chance that the typology of 'Consuetudo' as a text was usual not in the city-states of northern Italy, but within the kingdom of Sicily–Naples, where the towns used exactly the same distinctive strategy of a local custom contrasted with royal authority, just as in the Aragonese realm.[43] In such a context was written, for example, the famous *Tabula de Amalfi*, whose similarity with the Consulate of the Sea has been well known since the time of Pardessus.[44]

In the leading Italian towns during the late Middle Ages, municipal legislation paid a great deal of attention to maritime matters, but that was mostly about the external organisation of travel and fleets of ships, while the particular needs of maritime cases were usually left to the free decision of public courts. Genoa in the fourteenth century composed the *Liber Gazarie*, a very detailed code for all that related to navigation,[45] but its focus was principally on the organisation of the fleet, and not the customs of the sea. Even more significantly, in 1421 the Florentine government created the *Consoli del mare*, whose name actually meant a quite different institution from the Catalan one, because the *Consoli* were citizen holders of a public office, entrusted with the government of the public fleet. In any case, in neither the *Mercanzia* nor in the archive of the Consoli del Mare is there any mention of the use of the *Llibre del Consolato*. When the public office-holders of the Consoli del mare and Capitani di parte wrote to the *Capitoli della Nazione fiorentina a Londra* in 1511, the procedure of the Console required the free choices of the local Florentine committee to be followed, and made no reference to written customs.[46]

---

[43] Examples and comparisons are given in Mario Caravale, *La monarchia meridionale: Istituzioni e dottrina giuridica dai normanni ai Borboni* (Rome-Bari, 2008), pp. 167–200.

[44] 'Tavola e Consuetudini di Amalfi', *Archivio Storico Italiano*, 1 (1844), Appendix, pp. 253–89. A 'Consulate of the sea' as a part of customary maritime law also existed in Trapani and Messina during the fourteenth century: Zeno, *Storia del diritto marittimo* (cit. in n. 5), pp. 132–40.

[45] Giovanni Forchieri, *Navi e navigazione a Genova nel Trecento: Il Liber Gazarie* (Bordighera, 1974); Giovanna Petti Balbi, 'Un binomio indisoluble: Navigación comercial y armamento público en Génova en los siglos XIV–XV', in *Navegación institucional y navegación privada*, ed. González Arévalo (cit. in n. 6), pp. 41–76.

[46] *Statuti delle colonie fiorentine all'estero (secc. XV–XVI)*, ed. G. Masi (Milano, 1941), p. 186: 'quando alchuna cosa ocorressi che negli ordini non se fussi fatto mentione, della quale non tornassi né onore né utile della nostra natione, o de' merchanti, che in quello caso il consoli et li consiglieri, con dodici de' giurati che là si trovassino, che fussino eletti per li consoli et consiglieri, et li due terzi d'acordo, possino fare quelle provisione che a loro parrà, a emenda dello detto honore et utile, et anchora provedere a ciaschuna chosa che fussi fuora delle detti ordini, che paressi loro di honore et di utile della nostra communità, o merchanti; et di tutto quello ne facessino si intenda con qualla auctorità che se per li sopradetti ordini fussi ordinato da' detti consoli del mare e chapitani di parte'.

The lack of a general maritime law-book in the principal maritime courts of late-medieval Italy was perhaps part of a strategy of the municipal regimes, in order to be free from strict rules. When the Florentine merchant community in Rome asked Jaime Gell to translate and edit the *Consolato del mar* according to their particular needs, they doubtless wished to provide themselves with an effective and detailed set of rules; but once it arrived (if it ever did arrive) in Florence, it had no effect on the judicial practice of the *Mercanzia*. What happened in Venice was different, but was prompted by the same reasons: nobody believed that the Catalan code could be used as such in Venetian courts, and therefore no attempt was made to adapt it to local context – it was simply reproduced without any relevant change from the Catalan printed editions. In both cases, since the text of the Consulate came from a different institutional background, the recipients remained free to follow their own maritime politics without the limitations imposed by a customary or written law.

Finally, it must be stressed that the printed editions of the *Libro* were above all an aspect of a politics of prestige. The 1519 printing gave an opportunity to praise the Pope and his ambitions to expand papal power across the Oceans; the Venetian editions were mostly dedicated to the Habsburg ambassadors and consuls, whose Iberian dominions were the primary reason for such an 'antiquarian' choice. I think that the final impression of this short survey should be that politics, far more than maritime practice, were fundamental to the laws of the sea in the late-medieval Mediterranean world.

CHAPTER 10

The Admiralty and Constableship of England in the Later Fifteenth Century: The Operation and Development of these Offices, 1462–85, under Richard, Duke of Gloucester and King of England

Anne F. Sutton

It was unusual for the same man to combine the roles of Admiral and Constable, but it was a logical pairing. From 1462 to 1483 Richard, duke of Gloucester, was Admiral and from 1469 to March 1470 and from 1471 to 1483 he was Constable. The two decades were a time of change for both these offices: they were increasingly subordinated to the appointment by king and Council of specific commissions to deal with all matters of disorder and treason, whether on sea or land. When he became king, Richard III's experience in the two posts allowed him to make beneficial changes in the management of the Admiralty and navy and in effect to bring the role of the Constable to an end.

It is surprising that the earl of Warwick, Richard Neville, was not automatically made Admiral on Edward IV's accession, given his achievements as captain of Calais from 1456, and his ownership of a fleet sufficient to ensure that the king hardly needed to think of acquiring his own ships in the 1460s. He remained Keeper of the Seas, however, and was Warden and Admiral of the Cinque Ports and so had little practical need of the title.[1] Edward IV appointed Warwick's uncle, William Neville, Lord Fauconberge and newly created earl of Kent, as Admiral on 30 July 1462, but only during the king's pleasure and coincidental to his command of a fleet to raid the French coast. This was a compliment to that useful and loyal noble and would not have

---

[1] C.F. Richmond, 'Royal Administration and the Keeping of the Seas, 1422–1485', D.Phil. thesis, University of Oxford, 1962; Edward IV's encouragement of ship-building, etc., pp. 384–5, 444–5, 454–6; and see his 'The Earl of Warwick's Domination of the Channel and the Naval Dimension to the Wars of the Roses, 1456–60', *Southern History*, 20–1 (1998–9), pp. 1–19. *Cal. Fine R., 1461–77*, p. 8; A.J. Pollard, *Warwick the Kingmaker* (London, 2007), pp. 131, 229 and nn. 16–18, especially n. 17.

offended Warwick.[2] Richard of Gloucester can be understood to have had the title and profits of the office by 12 August and the formal appointment from 12 October 1462, while Neville went off on Edward's northern campaigns – where he died before the end of the year. The nomination of the ten-year-old Richard was similarly unlikely to offend Warwick, especially if the boy was already in his household (as may have been the case).[3] The appointment was essentially intended to supply Richard with an income from the charges that belonged to the post and the fees of the Admiralty court.[4]

The Admiral was the king's lieutenant in matters of the sea and ships, and the Constable was the king's lieutenant in his army in times of war, with powers to act with severity and dispatch against persons making war on the king in times of peace. The two courts of law, of the Admiral and Constable, had much in common: essentially they were concerned with money and profit on sea and land. They had a similar juridical foundation in the civil law and they were subject to similar control by a lieutenant of the king. The commands were military, but the courts and their specialist civilian judges dealt mainly with commercial cases that concerned merchants caught by piracy or mischance at sea, tied into contracts made abroad or with subjects of other princes, or involved in the infringement of truces and safe-conducts.[5]

The Admiral and the Court of Admiralty

Of the two offices, the Admiralty can be suggested as the more significant, for the sea was England's longest border, over which came trade; and the taxes on trade were a major part of the king's income. A wise king knew his coastline, ports, havens and creeks, and which of their officers he could depend on for service.[6] Ships were always in danger of attack in peace and

---

[2] *Cal. Pat. R., 1461–7*, p. 195. For William Neville, see GEC, *Complete Peerage*, vols V, pp. 281–7 (Fauconberge) and VII, p. 163 (Kent). Spelling of Fauconberge has been adopted from *Complete Peerage*. See also C. Scofield, *The Life and Reign of Edward the Fourth*, 2 vols (London, 1923), I, pp. 258–9.

[3] *Cal. Pat. R., 1461–7*, pp. 197, 214; London, BL, Cotton MS Julius B xii, f. 117. Translation of part of appointment: A.F. Sutton, 'Richard of Gloucester 1461–70: Income, Lands and Associates: His Whereabouts and Responsibilities', *The Ricardian*, 16 (2016), pp. 41–85, at 45; for his seal as Admiral of Dorset and Somerset, see p. 44 and n. 12 and sources there cited.

[4] The office could be lucrative: N.A.M. Rodger, *The Safeguard of the Sea: A Naval History of Britain*, vol. I: *660–1649* (London, 1997), p. 149, including a share of prizes taken at sea.

[5] Sir John Baker, *The Oxford History of the Laws of England*, VI: *1483–1558* (Oxford, 2003): short survey of both courts, pp. 209–19, especially at 211 (predominance of commercial cases); M.H. Keen, *The Laws of War in the Late Middle Ages* (London, 1965), pp. 244–5.

[6] Rodger, *Safeguard of the Sea*, pp. 491–7; and see I. Friel, 'How Much Did the Sea

war. The Yorkist kings knew the value of trade and provided protective convoys: '… yet it shalbe nescessarie that the kynge have alway some ffloute upon the see, ffor the repressynge off rovers, savynge off owre marchauntes, owre ffishers, and the dwellers uppon owre costes, and that the kynge kepe alway some grete and myghty vessels, ffor the brekynge off an armye when any shall be made ayen hym apon the see'. Edward IV and Richard could have written these words of advice as easily as had John Fortescue.[7] They had before them the example of their father, Richard, duke of York, who had spoken out for the maintenance of a fleet and better sea defences,[8] and there was also the splendid example of Warwick as captain of Calais from 1456 which had heartened his countrymen and secured him loyal support along the south coast of England. Throughout the 1460s Edward increased his knowledge and experience while Warwick dominated the sea with his fleet.[9] The experience (and enthusiasm) of Edward IV and Richard III for all matters maritime are crucial to any assessment of the Admiralty under the Yorkists – to quote Colin Richmond on Richard: 'There was no slackening of naval activity during this reign; and with Richard himself taking (as Henry V had done) a personal interest, with John Howard, duke of Norfolk, the new Admiral and with Thomas Rogers as Clerk, that activity was as successfully directed and performed as it ever had been in the reign of Henry V'.[10]

By the mid-fifteenth century the Admiralty worked within laws that had evolved over more than three centuries and were available in custumals and formularies of which one composite volume has become known as the *Black Book of the Admiralty*. This was made and added to in the mid- to late-fifteenth century and kept in the office of the Admiralty for consultation. The court's lawyers had brought these texts together: for example, several old Anglo-French texts were translated into Latin by Thomas Rowghton in the reign

Matter in Medieval England (*c.* 1200 – *c.* 1500)', in *Roles of the Sea in Medieval England*, ed. R. Gorski (Woodbridge, 2012), pp. 167–86, at 169 and *passim*; at p. 175 he tempers Rodger's picture of the lawlessness of the sea.

[7] Sir John Fortescue, *The Governance of England*, ed. C. Plummer (Oxford, 1885), p. 123. The prevalence of this opinion can be shown by the repetition of this advice to Richard III by Lord Dinham in 1483: *BL Harleian MS 433*, ed. R. Horrox and P. Hammond, 4 vols (London and Upminster, 1979–83), II, pp. 22–3. Convoys: A.F. Sutton, 'East Coast Ports and the Iceland Trade, 1483–5 (1489): Protection and Compensation', in *Medieval Merchants and Money: Essays in Honour of James L. Bolton*, ed. M. Allen and M. Davies (London, 2016), pp. 159–76.

[8] C.F. Richmond, 'English Naval Power in the Fifteenth Century', *History*, 52 (1967), pp. 1–15, at 2–4; an excellent, under-used survey of the Yorkist period.

[9] *Ibid.*, pp. 8–10; he emphasises the rise of professional seamen in Yorkist royal service. See also his 'The Earl of Warwick's Domination of the Channel'.

[10] Richmond, 'English Naval Power', p. 11 (quotation). Howard's importance can hardly be over-stated.

of Henry VI.[11] The earliest laws had been generated by the maritime needs of the seamen of southern England and France when these coasts were part of the empire of the Angevin kings of England – and came to be known as the laws of Oléron, an island off Aquitaine.[12] Possibly as early as the reign of Richard I, and certainly by the early 1300s, England, Normandy, Brittany, Gascony, Aquitaine and Castile had accepted their own versions of these laws of the sea, which covered innumerable aspects of shipping, with an emphasis on the all-important wine trade. They were practical laws for working seamen and masters and their importance to commercial ports, such as London and Southampton, is witnessed by the survival of the two earliest Anglo-French copies of the laws among their records: *Liber Horn* of the city of London and in the *Oak Book of Southampton*, both circa 1300.[13] They were among the laws and regulations of England referred to by local coastal courts and by the central Court of Admiralty which came into being about 1340–57, a time when Edward III was claiming sovereignty of the seas and when piracy had become an acute problem. In the 1350s the restitution of goods to merchants despoiled by pirates or in wartime was regularly being settled before the Admiral: restitution and compensation for the innocent, the observance of truces and suppression of piracy by the king's subjects were to remain the major work of the Admiralty court, with the king and his council supreme above, ready to deal with emergencies by special commissions.[14] Important later improvements to these laws for England included the Inquisition of Queenborough of 1375 concerning such issues as conditions of work, wages, the division of prizes, piracy, pillage, felonies, wreck, as well as the shares and charges paid

---

[11] Twiss, *Black Book of the Admiralty*, vol. I. Now Kew, TNA, High Court of Admiralty: Black Book of the Admiralty, HCA 12/1. Rowghton has never been identified.

[12] Under English rule, 1154–1373: R. Ward, *The World of the Medieval Shipmaster: Law, Business and the Sea, c.1350–c.1450* (Woodbridge, 2009), pp. 24–5. The island was able to authenticate a copy of the laws in 1266: *The Oak Book of Southampton*, ed. P. Studer, 3 vols (Southampton Record Soc., x–xii, 1910–11), II, pp. xxxvi–xxxviii.

[13] Twiss had to reconstruct the Black Book as the original was missing in his day, and as a consequence other editions of the text must be consulted: *The Oak Book of Southampton*, II, pp. 54–103, and Ward, *Medieval Shipmaster*, pp. 183–205 (new transcript from *Liber Horn*, with translation and commentary). D. Burwash, *English Merchant Shipping 1460–1540* (reprinted Newton Abbot, 1969), pp. 171–4, appx 1, summarises the editions and theories, as does Ward, *Medieval Shipmaster*, pp. 20–6. See N.R. Ker, *Medieval Manuscripts in British Libraries*, I: *London* (Oxford, 1969), pp. 34, 35, for the date of *Liber Horn* and its copies.

[14] The main sources remain: *Select Pleas in the Court of Admiralty*, ed. R.G. Marsden, 2 vols (Selden Soc., vi and xi, 1894–7), vol. I: *The Court of Admiralty of the West (1390–1400). The High Court of Admiralty (1527–45)*, pp. xiv, xxxiv–xxxvi, xli–xlii; *Select Cases before the King's Council, 1243–1482*, ed. I.S. Leadam and J.F. Baldwin (Selden Soc., xxxv, 1918), pp. xxvi–xlvi *passim* and especially pp. xxviii–xxix; and Baker, *Oxford History of the Laws of England*, VI, especially pp. 191–3, 195–7. For re-dating the formation of the English Court of Admiralty, see the work of Heebøll-Holm, above, ch. 8.

to the Admiral.[15] Another important formulary added to the *Black Book* was a collection of cases and documents of the court during the admiralty of John Holland, duke of Exeter (1443–6), all dealing with the east coast from Norfolk to Essex where Huntingdon's vice-Admiral was Sir Miles Stapleton.[16] These texts provided precedents concerning such matters as the capture of vessels, reprisals, ransoming, breaking of truces, return of cargoes to innocent parties, and the lawful and unlawful conduct of a shipmaster, such as tipping ballast into a creek or the right to search a suspect vessel.

Only two of the *exempla* in the *Black Book* date from the period of Richard of Gloucester: a safe-conduct to English merchants for four years from Louis XI in 1463 (a time of great anxiety over the wine trade and the safety of English ships); and an undated safe-conduct from Richard concerning Bretons allowed to go home to raise ransoms for themselves and their fellows left in custody.[17] Safe-conducts were one of the most ubiquitous and troublesome documents of the period: they might be mutual and of long standing between countries, as for example that between England and Portugal, or that between England and Brittany (which ran from 1464), or limited individual ones obtained by a merchant from a sovereign prince, his Admiral, or a vice-Admiral, of which the terms had to be found to be precise in every particular when subjected to hostile questioning. The responsibility for the safety of the seas lay heavily on the grantors.[18]

The fifteenth-century Admiral and his court operated under the jurisdiction defined in the 1390 and 1392 statutes that had been made after forty years of excessive encroachment by Admirals and their deputies on the rights of others. No power was allowed them over contracts made within the counties of the realm whether on land or water, and this included wrecks (a lucrative right often held by the local landowner). The *Admiral* (not his court) did, however, have authority to adjudicate in matters of murder and mutilation committed on large ships on rivers up to the first bridge away from the sea; he could arrest ships for the king's service, he had judicial powers on

---

[15] Twiss, *Black Book of the Admiralty*, I, pp. xxvi, 133–77, and Ward, *Medieval Shipmaster*, pp. 23, 206–18, with commentary.

[16] Twiss, *Black Book of the Admiralty*, I, pp. 246–75; formulary status illustrated by use of initials for names in a few of the documents.

[17] Twiss, *Black Book of the Admiralty*, I, pp. 276–80, dated 20 Nov. 1463 and *temp.* Edward IV; compare *Harleian MS 433*, ed. Horrox and Hammond, II, p. 83. (This addition to the Black Book has implications for the date and compilation of the volume; see also n. 71 below). The mutual safe-conduct between England and Brittany was affected by the war, Oct. 1483–April 1484; safe-conducts issued during the uncertain period can be found in *Harleian MS 433*, ed. Horrox and Hammond; *Cal. Pat. R., 1476–85*; and Kew, TNA, Chancery: Treaty Rolls, C 76, and Chancery: Warrants for the Great Seal, Series I, C 81 (with some duplication). The subsequent prorogation specified the resumption of free access.

[18] L.A. Boiteux, *La fortune de mer: Le besoin de sécurité et les débuts de l'assurance maritime* (Paris, 1968), pp. 21–6.

these ships during expeditions, and in cases of extreme technical difficulty he could set up arbitration. The Admiral and his court were not to encroach on the franchises of towns, boroughs and lords.[19] Essentially, the Admiral exercised military discipline over any ship in the king's service, with a civil jurisdiction over prizes, shipping and maritime affairs in cases involving both English and aliens; his court operated under the civil or Roman law with reference to the maritime laws as they had evolved; and the court had no general criminal jurisdiction and therefore dealt with complaints over piracy as suits for damages.[20] The sheer complexity of disputes, for example over the infringement of truces, was often so great that the use of juries lapsed during the fifteenth century.[21]

There has been a tendency to depict the central Admiralty court as in decline in the fifteenth century, justified by rather unfair comparison with the period of encroachment before the statutes of 1389–92, and aggravated by the failure of the court records after 1450.[22] Moreover, the central court should not be thought of as a single unit: if the king's justice was working effectively, the king's Admiral and his centralised court worked in tandem with the Admiral's deputies and the various local Admiralty jurisdictions. These last were as essential to the daily life of ports as their ships which tramped the busy coastal routes, using the services of local pilots plying back and forth between a small run of ports. The small courts provided quick local justice for local disputes.

Through the fifteenth century and after, the Admiralty court sat at Orton's or Horton's Quay in Southwark 'by the tideway in a high hall there in the parish of St Olave'.[23] A deputy had been allowed to the Admiral in 1360 and

---

[19] 13 Richard II, stat. 1, c. 5, and 1391–2, 15 Richard II, stat. 1, c. 3, in *Statutes of the Realm*, II, pp. 62, 78–9; Marsden, *Select Pleas*, I, pp. l–li, 1–26; Ward, *Medieval Shipmaster*, pp. 36–40; *A Calendar of Early Chancery Proceedings relating to West Country Shipping 1388–1493*, ed. D.M. Gardiner (Devon and Cornwall Record Soc., New Ser., xxi, 1976), p. xii.

[20] Rodger, *Safeguard of the Sea*, p. 149; Baker, *Oxford History of the Laws of England*, VI, p. 212, includes piracy and murder on sea or the waters under the Admiralty's criminal jurisdiction.

[21] Marsden, *Select Pleas*, I, p. liv. For laws over truces, see Keen, *Laws of War*, pp. 206–17: a truce was an absolute suspension of war and made by the highest authority, and observation of which was crucial, with only small infringements being tolerated. Truces were especially important to merchants.

[22] E.g. Ward, *Medieval Shipmaster*, pp. 5, 46–7, 180; N.J. Williams, *The Maritime Trade of the East Anglian Ports, 1550–1590* (Oxford, 1988), pp. 1–23.

[23] At 'le Key de William Horton a Southwarke' *temp.* Henry IV: Marsden, *Select Pleas*, I, p. li; at 'Orton's Key' in the sixteenth century, A.A. Ruddock, 'The Earliest Records of the High Court of Admiralty (1515–1558)', *Bull., Institute of Historical Research*, 22 (1949), 142; *Cal. Pat. R., 1467–77*, p. 52 (quotation). I am indebted to Graham Dawson's topographical work on Southwark for the information that William Horton was connected to two adjacent properties between the Watergate (a lane)

1361, probably intended to provide 'a judge of the newly erected court', and men learned in the law were expected to be present by early in the fifteenth century.[24] These men were often highly trained civilian lawyers operating in both courts; their careers are, however, often obscure. Dr John Aleyn can be found acting for the Admiral in 1461,[25] and from before January 1468 William Goodyer, DCL,[26] was Richard of Gloucester's deputy and judge in the Court of Admiralty. As the records of the Yorkist court do not survive,[27] Goodyer's level of business can only be gauged from the number of appeals against his judgments: about one a year, the percentage of the total number of judgments unknown.[28] Given the complexity of some issues, it is not surprising that there were a number of appeals, very often brought by wealthy merchants of London. Goodyer was awarded £40 a year for life in 1471 and in 1478,[29] and was appointed to commissions headed by the learned knight Sir John Astley (renowned for his expertise in the laws of war[30]) looking into robberies and infractions of safe-conducts and truces by pirates that were to be punished according to the laws of the Admiralty, in 1475 and 1478.[31] Goodyer can

and a Bridge House tenement on the Bridge-foot *c.* 1400: the quay is probably 230 on Fig. 7, in M. Carlin, *Medieval Southwark* (London, 1996), p. 35.

[24] Marsden, *Select Pleas*, I, p. xlii; Ward, *Medieval Shipmaster*, p. 45.

[25] Aleyn: *Cal. Pat. R., 1461–7*, p. 89, when a sentence of his as commissary general of the Earl of Warwick, 'Admiral of England' [*sic*], was the subject of a commission, 14 Dec. 1461. See below for his later career.

[26] Emden, *Biog. Reg. Univ. Oxford*, II, p. 791: 'Goodyer': DCL by 1466; married by 1467 (whence his move to secular employment). On a commission about treasons (1464), and another concerning the foundering of a carrack near the Isle of Wight (1466): *Cal. Pat. R., 1461–7*, pp. 347, 492. That he was not tied to the Admiralty is indicated by his acting as proxy for the abbot of Eynsham before the bishop of Lincoln in 1475: *Eynsham Cartulary*, ed. H.E. Salter, 2 vols (Oxford Historical Soc., xlix, li, 1907–8), II, p. 204.

[27] Marsden, *Select Pleas*, I, esp. pp. xl–lv (a tendency to miss out the fifteenth century because of the poor records). Ruddock, 'Earliest Records of the High Court of Admiralty', pp. 139–49, emphasises their commercial value, and the use of Chancery for similar suits (see especially p. 140–1), as does Gardiner, *West Country Shipping, passim*.

[28] Complaints 1468, 1469, 1470 (2 appeals), 1475 (2 cases), 1478: *Cal. Pat. R., 1467–77*, pp. 52, 171, 184–85, 201, 488–89, 495, and *Cal. Pat. R., 1476–85*, p. 102. The lawyers appointed to inquire into these alleged miscarriages are hard to identify and have to be classified as notaries rather than university men; an exception was Michael Carvanell, 1440s–1489, on appeals 1468–75 for both courts, who became rector of Farnborough, 1475–89: Emden, *Biog. Reg. Univ. Oxford*, I, p. 365.

[29] *Cal. Pat. R., 1467–77*, p. 278, *Cal. Pat. R., 1476–85*, p. 119.

[30] A.F. Sutton and L. Visser-Fuchs, '"Chevalerie … in som partie is worthi forto be comendid, and in some part to ben amendid": Chivalry and the Yorkist kings,' in *St George's Chapel, Windsor, in the Late Middle Ages*, ed. C. Richmond and E. Scarff (Windsor, 2001), pp. 107–33, at 130–2.

[31] *Cal. Pat. R., 1467–77*, p. 525; *Cal. Pat. R., 1476–85*, p. 112, also with John Fortescu esq., and Alured Cornborough (once).

be assumed to have died before 1482, when Robert Rydon was appointed promoter of civil and criminal cases in both the Admiral's and the Constable's courts – a description of his office which illustrates precisely the overlap of law, cases and expertise between these tribunals.[32] In March 1483 William Lacy was appointed 'chief judge and commissary general' in the principal *'and other courts* of the Admiralty of England' – significant phrasing (present author's italics). This he retained while clerk to Richard III's Council; as he also went on diplomatic missions, he would have had deputies. He acted as an important conduit between the Admiralty and the king. He or his officers could write pointed covering letters for the king to such towns as Hamburg concerning the cases of their erring merchants (German and English), adjudicated with wry exasperation in that court and before the Council.[33]

To take four examples of cases from the Admiralty in this period. In Trinity term 1466 a case of debt against Segar Suterman, a diamond grinder, was described as heard before Richard of Gloucester as Admiral at Southwark. Suterman was apparently successfully sued for £4 by William Hardyngham before William Goodyer (the debt was incurred in Southwark and therefore at sea); Suterman then sued Hardyngham in the Court of King's Bench for contempt of the act of 1389–90 which confined cases in the Admiral's court to events at sea; discussion was allowed and it seems the matter was settled out of court.[34] In May 1467 the mayor of Newcastle and others were on a commission to investigate robberies and breaches of safe-conducts and truces committed by men then in the town's prison and see them punished by maritime law 'at a court of Admiralty'.[35] In December 1473 a letter went in the duke's name to the mayor and bailiffs of Dartmouth to bring into the Admiral's court at Horton Quay a case that had come before the mayor between a merchant of Bristol and a man of Dartmouth on a matter of maritime law – this case brings into relief an example of an important local

---

[32] *Cal. Pat. R., 1476–85*, p. 345. Rydon became judge in the Admiralty Court in or before 1490 and was lieutenant for John de Vere, earl of Oxford, then Admiral; Clerk of the King's Council from 1499: W. Senior, 'The Judges of the High Court of Admiralty', *Mariner's Mirror*, 13 (1927), pp. 333–47, at 334. Rydon was allowed to surmount his service to Richard III via a brief appointment as governor of the Merchant Adventurers in the Low Countries, 1486: A.F. Sutton, *The Mercery of London. Trade, Goods and People 1130–1578* (Aldershot, 2005), p. 321.

[33] Lacy: *Cal. Pat. R., 1476–85*, p. 346, and Senior, 'Judges of the High Court of Admiralty', pp. 332–3. The letter to Hamburg over an assault on an English ship is translated by Sutton, 'East Coast Ports and the Iceland Trade' (cit. in n. 7), p. 176.

[34] Kew, TNA, Court of King's Bench, Coram Rege Rolls, KB 27/823, rot. 68d; I am grateful for this reference to Graham Dawson, who informs me that he has located no other cases during Gloucester's tenure relating to the Admiralty in Southwark.

[35] *Cal. Pat. R., 1467–77*, p. 605; this implies that Newcastle did not have this power. See n. 47 below.

court, that of the water bailiff of Dartmouth.[36] In 1475 a petition to Chancery from a man of Topsham (Devon) complained that he had been wrongly called before the Court of Admiralty at Horton Quay over a case which had nothing to do with the sea.[37]

The Admiralty court was only one part of the business of the sea and ships, the centre of a complex network. The king and the Admiral could appoint local deputies for a stretch of the coast – the importance of John Howard to the Yorkist kings in East Anglia cannot be doubted. At a lesser level, the local water bailiffs, customs officials, mayors of the port or local JPs would hold the local courts of their ports and havens, for example the water bailiff of Dartmouth already mentioned – a port could not operate without jurisdiction over its haven and shore.[38] The Cinque Ports enjoyed the most ancient and closely guarded powers (confirmed in a major charter 23 March 1465).[39] Other leading ports carefully had their ancient local powers confirmed in charters either as Admiralty jurisdiction or as exemptions from the interference of the king's officers during the fifteenth century,[40] for example: Southampton, 1445 and 1447;[41] Bristol secured exemption from the jurisdiction of the king's Admirals and from answering pleas in the court

---

[36] H.R. Watkin, *Dartmouth*, vol. I: *Pre-Reformation* (Devonshire Association, 1935), pp. 403–4. Nicholas Palmer, the water bailiff, was used extensively by Richard III for naval matters; see e.g. *Harleian MS 433*, ed. Horrox and Hammond, I, pp. 204, 271, II, pp. 66, 84, 97, 180.

[37] Gardiner, *West Country Shipping*, no. 87.

[38] Twiss, *Black Book of the Admiralty*, I, pp. 246–75; Baker, *Oxford History of the Laws of England*, VI, pp. 210–11. Gardiner, *West Country Shipping*, p. xi. A useful example is Matthew Andrew, deputy of John Howard, who issued safe-conducts in the south-west: *Cal. Pat. R., 1476–85*, p. 520, with full text in *Documents Relating to Law and Custom of the Sea*, vol. I: *1205–1648*, ed. R.G. Marsden (Navy Records Soc., xlix, 1915), pp. 138–41.

[39] S. Jeake, *Charters of the Cinque Ports* (London, 1728), pp. 51–87 (Richard of Gloucester being among the witnesses). It is intriguing that Gloucester was appointed Warden and Admiral of the Cinque Ports in the reign of Edward V, indicating perhaps a desire to rationalise the post of Admiral; the elderly earl of Arundel, however, regained the post from Richard III: *ibid.*, p. 49; *Harleian MS 433*, ed. Horrox and Hammond, I, p. 126.

[40] See M. Weinbaum, *The Incorporation of Boroughs* (Manchester, 1937), pp. 71, 111, on popularity of this practice; *The Admiralty Court Book of Southampton 1566–85*, ed. E. Welch (Southampton Records Ser., 13, 1968), pp. xiv–xvi, xxxiv. Marsden, *Select Pleas*, II, pp. xix–xxii, refers to these ports as claiming 'exemptions' from the High Admiral's jurisdiction.

[41] Weinbaum, *Incorporation of Boroughs*, pp. 70–2 and nn. According to Studer, *Oak Book*, I, pp. xxi–xxii, courts sat from tide to tide to settle disputes between merchants or seamen swiftly; formal confirmation of Admiralty jurisdiction, 1452, citing *The Charters of the Borough of Southampton 1199–1480*, ed. H.W. Gidden, 2 vols (Southampton Record Soc., vii and ix, 1909–10), I, pp. 92–5; J.S. Davies, *A History of Southampton* (London, 1883), pp. 221–5, 239–42. Map of jurisdiction: Welch, *Admiralty Court Book*, p. xi.

of Admiralty in 1446, confirmed by Edward IV in 1461;[42] Rochester, 1446;[43] Ipswich, 1446, with a confirmation from Richard III;[44] Scarborough's wide-ranging charter of incorporation, 1485, was meant to include Admiralty jurisdiction; Youghal in Ireland received a grant of Admiralty jurisdiction coterminous with the customs jurisdiction from Richard III in 1485, and his charter to Dublin of 1485 implied the same;[45] Hull, 1382, but no exclusion of the Admiral's interference in its main charter of 1442;[46] and Newcastle, 1442.[47] The Admiralty jurisdiction of the small but growing ports of Harwich and Dovercourt was in contrast granted to the duke of Norfolk, 1468.[48] The Admiralty jurisdiction was usually coterminous with the customs jurisdiction of these ports and is a healthy reminder of the dominance and value of coastal trade. A jealous protection of privileges did not exclude cooperation between the local courts and the Admiral, especially if that official was interested and knowledgeable like Richard and the ubiquitous John Howard.

Above the Admiral and the local courts was the king: the king in his Court of Chancery was a regular source of redress and appeal over such issues as truce-breaking at sea, by the time of the Yorkists. The importance of the Court of Chancery was underlined by Richard III's Chancellor in Michaelmas term 1484 bringing disputes over spoil firmly before his court. At the top of the hierarchy stood the king himself and his Council as the ultimate place of appeal and judgment – the king might send out commissions in answer to reports of misbehaviour or in response to petitions from aggrieved persons, and he took a special interest in heinous offences.[49] King and Council decided where the resulting cases should be tried – the courts of the Admiral or the

---

[42] *Bristol Charters, 1378–1499*, ed. H.A. Cronne (Bristol Record Soc., xi, 1946), pp. 71–3: Cronne expands on the annoyance caused when the Admiral infringed the borough court and on the freedom of burgesses from foreign pleas; the mayor and recorder tried cases as they arose; the extent of the town's maritime jurisdiction was settled in 1462; texts, pp. 122–7, 132–6.

[43] Rochester: Weinbaum, *Incorporation of Boroughs*, pp. 75–8 and nn.

[44] Ipswich: *ibid.*, pp. 72–5 and nn.

[45] Scarborough: A.F. Sutton, '"Peace, love and unity": Richard III's Charters to his Towns', in *The Yorkist Age*, ed. H. Kleineke and C. Steer (Donington, 2013), pp.129–32, and Weinbaum, *Incorporation of Boroughs*, p. 27 n.; Youghal and Dublin: Sutton, 'Richard III's Charters', pp. 137–8, and Weinbaum, *Incorporation of Boroughs*, p. 114.

[46] Hull: Weinbaum, *Incorporation of Boroughs*, pp. 65–8, 93–6 (king's officials excluded but Admiral not specified). But see Welch, *Admiralty Court Book*, pp. xiv, xxxiv.

[47] *Cal. Pat. R., 1467–77*, p. 605; Welch, *Admiralty Court Book*, pp. xiv, xxxiv.

[48] Harwich: *Cal. Charter Rolls, 1427–1516*, pp. 223–5.

[49] Marsden, *Select Pleas*, I, p. liv, citing Year Book, Mich. 2 Richard III, case 4 (p. 2). See Baker, *Oxford History of the Laws of England*, VI, p. 210 on these 'concurrent' jurisdictions, and see also pp. 191–3, 195–7; Gardiner, *West Country Shipping*, p. xvii and passim.

Constable or a special commission of royal councillors and local men. A well balanced commission made up of lay and legal experts might provide the best possible answer, and became the regular recourse of both Yorkist kings.

Lastly, it must be noted that the greatest problem for the king and his Admiral was the incidence of attacks between ships, seizure of ships (even while in harbour), reprisals, and the resulting compensation suits (highly expensive for the king as he had undertaken to safeguard the seas, protect his own subjects and ensure they did not attack foreigners whose nations enjoyed peace or truce with England and to whom he had granted safe-conducts). Merchants were the main sufferers – and often not entirely without guilt. The expense of these cases amounted, for example, to 50,000 crowns between England and Brittany in 1476, and both Yorkist kings faced regular petitions for compensation from Spanish merchants whose ships and cargoes suffered from illegal English attack in the Channel.[50] The precise procedure by which compensation was claimed and pursued between nations can be illustrated by a case which was begun in 1482 by John Croft, who was trying to retrieve his ship the *Mary of Newcastle* (owned by the earl of Northumberland) and over £1,500 worth of goods from Breton pirates. He pursued the case through the courts of the duke of Brittany but despite orders from the duke in September 1482 and January 1483 he received no justice from the port of Brest where the ship had been taken. The next procedure (the last resort) was to petition his sovereign, and on 28 July 1483 Richard III ordered his officers in all ports to seize the ships and goods of the six offending Breton towns as and when they came into English ports until the sum owing had been recovered. Ships were seized and dealt with expeditiously and correctly, the several masters gave sureties for the value of their ship and goods in the accepted form and were allowed to depart. It was a civilised procedure but the full settlement of such a claim might take a very long time.[51]

The role of the Constable and the Constable's Court

The office of Constable was more political and potentially more dangerous than that of Admiral and was not suitable for a boy: Richard, now aged seventeen, was appointed following the terms of John Tiptoft (1461–7) and

---

[50] Compare Keen, *Laws of War*, pp. 218–25, for examples on land; pp. 236–8, for the proper process of reprisal and compensation with minimum of violence. Gardiner, *West Country Shipping*, pp xiii, xv; *Foedera*, XII, pp. 22–4 (Brittany), and e.g. Rodger, *Safeguard of the Sea*, pp. 155–6.

[51] Hist. MSS Commn. [18], *Eleventh Report, Appendix*, Part III: *The Manuscripts of the Corporations of Southampton and King's Lynn* (London, 1887), pp. 102–3, and *Cal. Pat. R., 1476–85*, p. 366. *Pace* B.-A. Pocquet du Haut-Jussé, *François II, duc de Bretagne, et l'Angleterre* (Paris, 1929), p. 245, who misinterprets Richard III's standard letter as vengeful; at p. 241 he notes that this case was finally settled years later.

Richard Woodville, Lord Rivers (1467–9; executed 12 August 1469). Richard's patent of 17 October 1469 was the same as that of Rivers and Tiptoft. The patent included the power to try all cases of treason 'summarily and plainly without noise and show of judgment, on simple inspection of fact'.[52] This clause emphasises that from the Constable, the king expected total loyalty. Richard's first term was brief: he was replaced by John Tiptoft on 14 March 1470,[53] and only regained the office after Edward's return from exile.

The position of the Constable was already undergoing change by the time of Richard's first appointment, and what was apparently his first encounter with a treason trial (just before his appointment) is indicative of these changes. Richard was the second highest lord in rank presiding at the commission of oyer and terminer at Salisbury which tried Sir Thomas Hungerford and Henry Courtenay for conspiracy to aid Queen Margaret and her son to enter the realm and depose Edward IV. The most senior noble on the commission was Richard's elder brother Clarence, and also present was the then Constable, Lord Rivers. So important was this trial to the king that it was delayed from November 1468 to January 1469 so that Edward could be present when the verdict was pronounced. Hungerford pleaded not guilty and put himself on the country, Courtenay pleaded a pardon. Henry Sotehill, the king's attorney, acted as prosecutor and put the Crown's case that they were both guilty. A jury was summoned and duly agreed. Sentence followed, presumably pronounced by the senior lord present.[54] It is important to note this was a treason trial not under the current Constable's control, although Rivers was present. It was a commission of oyer and terminer, the increasingly common form for inquiries and trials of a serious nature.

The Court of the Constable was the Court of Chivalry, knighthood and honour, as well as military authority. The original Roman advice on military matters was enshrined for fifteenth-century readers in Vegetius' *De*

---

[52] *Cal. Pat. R., 1467–77*, p. 178. Full text of grant (Rivers's patent had given a remainder to his son Anthony, not put into effect by Edward): L.W. Vernon Harcourt, *His Grace the Steward and Trial of Peers* (London, 1907), pp. 407–11; p. 408: 'audiendum, examinandum et fine debito terminandum etiam summarie et de plano sine strepitu et figura justicii sola facti veritate inspecta'. Translated by R.J. Mitchell, *John Tiptoft, 1427–1470* (London, 1938), p. 85.

[53] Rymer, *Foedera*, XI, p. 654.

[54] Scofield, *Edward the Fourth* (cit. in n. 2), I, p. 482. *Cal. Pat. R., 1467–77*, p. 128 (12 Dec. 1468). Clarence, Rivers, Gloucester *et al.* were on two other such commissions at this time, *ibid.*, pp. 69–70, 126–7; see J.G. Bellamy, *The Law of Treason in England in the Later Middle Ages* (Cambridge, 1970), pp. 164–5, for the significance of the king's presence and the role of the king's attorney (it is only the king's presence that gives some certainty that all the lords were present). *Pace* M. Hicks, 'Piety and Lineage in the Wars of the Roses: The Hungerford Experience', reprinted in his *Richard III and His Rivals: Magnates and their Motives in the Wars of the Roses* (London, 1991), pp. 165–84, at 175.

re militari.[55] The role of Constable and the origins and functions of the Court of Chivalry have been expertly explained by Maurice Keen.[56] The Constable and his colleague, the Marshal, had authority over the army in field, and the latter had special duties within the king's household; their offices went back to the household of Henry I. The laws and regulations were in place by the mid-fourteenth century, mainly drawn together in the work of the civil lawyer John of Legnano with what amounted to a translation into French by Honoré Bouvet known as the *Tree of Battles*,[57] which assisted those laymen, such as Sir John Astley (see above), who sat as judges with the lawyers. The English Constable's jurisdiction, alongside that of the Admiral, was set out in the statute of 1390: 'to the Constable it belongs to have knowledge of contracts touching deeds of arms and war out of the realm, and also of things touching arms or war within the realm which cannot be determined or discussed at common law, with other usages and customs thereunto belonging'.[58] The court was therefore a recognised element in the legal administration of England. Matters adjudicated were treason, deeds of arms against the king, homicides and robberies, ransoms, safe-conducts, and the right to armorial bearings.[59] In campaign conditions, such as the 1475 expedition to France, the Constable was the recipient of petitions for justice from the men of the army.[60] His jurisdiction could be exercised as effectively and appropriately by lawyers learned in the laws of war, by a summary tribunal made up of lords and knights available in an emergency, and by the panoply of a full Court of Chivalry.[61] The punishment of a delinquent was on his body and goods, not on his lands.[62]

The court sat in the White Chamber or Hall of Westminster Palace. The court had an all-important clerk attendant on the Constable from the earliest

---

[55] Keen, *Laws of War*, pp. 56–9. See also A.F. Sutton and L. Visser-Fuchs, *Richard III's Books* (Gloucester, 1997), pp. 77–80: copy made for Richard's son; read by John Howard during Scots campaign.

[56] M.H. Keen, 'Treason Trials under the Law of Arms', *Trans. Royal Historical Soc.*, 5th ser., 12 (1962), pp. 85–103. Also his 'The Jurisdiction and Origins of the Constable's Court', in *War and Government in the Middle Ages: Essays in Honour of J.O. Prestwich*, ed. J. Gillingham and J.C. Holt (Woodbridge, 1984), pp. 159–69 (reprinted in M.H. Keen, *Nobles, Knights and Men at Arms in the Middle Ages* (London and Rio Grande, OH, 1996), pp. 135–48), and his *Laws of War*, esp. ch. 2.

[57] *The Tree of Battles of Honoré Bonet*, ed. and trans. G.W. Coopland (Liverpool, 1949), sets out the connection with Legnano.

[58] Statute 13 Richard II, statute 1, c. 2 (*Statutes of the Realm*, II, pp. 61–2); modernised by Wagner, *Heralds and Heraldry in the Middle Ages*, revised edn (London, 1956), p. 21.

[59] Keen, 'Treason Trials', pp. 96–100, 103; his 'Jurisdiction and Origins', pp. 159–60; his *Laws of War*, pp. 54–5.

[60] Keen, 'Treason Trials', p. 100 and n. 2.

[61] *Ibid.*, pp. 96–7, 99–100.

[62] Keen, 'Jurisdiction and Origins', p. 159.

years of his existence.[63] Men learned in both laws were appointed deputy to the Constable and adjudicated in the court when he was absent or the law needed to be expounded during complex cases which might involve the intricacies of ransoms, safe-conducts and the breaking of truces. The pressure of work may not have been onerous. From 1445 Thomas Kent was the deputy Constable and he may have sat as late as 1466, the end of his term as clerk of the king's Council, an extremely important figure in the development of his profession.[64] Other judges are remarkably obscure, not university men but notaries and proctors, trained in the civil law, law merchant and the laws of the sea and of war.[65] John Aleyn was employed by Edward IV by the early 1460s on matters of Admiralty jurisdiction, and a commission was set up to review a judgment by him as lieutenant of the Constable before 20 April 1469.[66] William Goodyer, already mentioned as a lieutenant in the Court of Admiralty in the 1460s, was also a judge in the Court of the Constable where he was sitting in the White Hall shortly before February 1472.[67] Shortly before, on 8 October 1471, Thomas Appleton had been appointed 'clerk of king's Constableship of England and promoter of business concerning the king's majesty', in succession to a Thomas Brouns.[68] John Aleyn was still deputy Constable in 1475, for in March of that year another commission investigated a judgment of his.[69] In May 1476 William Goodyer reappeared on a commission with two other doctors of laws, John Fox and John Coke, to hear an appeal to the king's audience from John Forster (lately provost of Edward IV's army in France) against a judgment of John Aleyn, deputy

---

[63] *Ibid.*, p. 167. For use of White Chamber and the need for a deputy by the time of Henry IV: Keen, *Laws of War*, p. 27. 'White Hall' used in 1472: *Cal. Pat. R., 1467–77*, p. 307. Audley was tried there in 1497, see n. 90.

[64] Kent: *Cal. Pat. R., 1441–6*, p. 348. Biography: A.F. Sutton, *Wives and Widows of Medieval London* (Donington, 2016), pp. 238–74, and references there to his important bequest of books to the future Doctors' Commons.

[65] Baker, *Oxford History of the Laws of England*, VI, pp. 209–10.

[66] Aleyn: *Cal. Pat. R., 1467–77*, p. 169. He was a graduate of Padua and Bologna and friend of William Hatclyf, secretary to Edward IV: R.J. Mitchell, 'English Law Students at Bologna', *Eng. Hist. Rev.*, 51 (1936), pp. 270–87, at 272–3, 286. John Aleyn and Sir John Howard, as the king's deputies in the office of the Admiralty, tried the validity and extent of the abbot of Ramsey's right over Brancaster haven, Norfolk (and the maritime jurisdictions of neighbours); Ramsey's rights duly confirmed by Edward IV, 1465: B. Cozens-Hardy, 'Havens in North Norfolk', *Norfolk Archaeology*, 35 (1970–73), pp. 356–63. For Aleyn's work in Norwich with Gloucester, see below. He should not be confused with the dean of St Patrick's.

[67] *Cal. Pat. R., 1467–77*, p. 307.

[68] *Ibid.*, pp. 110, 605; he may be the man acting as a pledge in Chancery, 1474–85, and escheator of Essex and Herts., 1466, and who d. 1485: J.H. Baker, 'Lawyers Practising in Chancery 1474–86', *Jnl of Legal History*, 4 (1983), p. 58 (will: Kew, TNA, PROB 11/6, ff. 150v–151). Brouns has not been identified.

[69] *Cal. Pat. R., 1467–77*, p. 511.

and judge of the Constable's court.[70] No records survive for the Constable's court (even though it was a court of record) save for these three appeals between 1469 and 1476. This sequence suggests (without certainty) that the day to day business of this court was comparatively small and certainly less than in the Admiralty court. It is noteworthy that three of the judges and lawyers in the courts of Admiralty and Constableship, 1440s to 1480s (Kent, Lacy, Rydon), became clerk of the king's Council – another proof of the control exercised by the king, his Council and the office of the Privy Seal.

The last appointments for the Constable and his court under Edward IV were those of Robert Rydon, as promoter of civil and criminal cases or crimes of *lèse-majesté* before the king's judges of the Constableship *and* Admiralty of England on 23 October 1482 – again underlining the overlap of the two courts.[71] Hardly a month later on 14 November 1482, the office of Constable was put into commission, no doubt with Richard of Gloucester's agreement, and possibly at his initiative.[72] The commissaries were Sir William Parre,[73] Sir James Harrington and Sir James Tyrell[74] (one of whom in the absence of the other was to be vice-Constable), and Masters John Wallington,[75] William Lacy, William Fuller[76] and George Warde,[77] all Bachelors in Laws; Sir Thomas Grey was to be Vice-Marshal.[78] The number of officers suggests more work

---

[70] *Ibid.*, p. 591; the judgment was presumably made by Aleyn in Picardy (where the offence was committed), so Goodyer may have remained in office in England.

[71] *Cal. Pat. R., 1476–85*, p. 343. The fact that there are three documents concerning the Constable's duties in the *Black Book of the Admiralty* (Twiss, I, pp. lxxiv, 231–344) suggests these were bound in the book when an Admiral was also Constable, or when the same man was acting as judge in both courts.

[72] *Cal. Pat. R., 1476–85*, p. 317. The suggestion (Bellamy, *Law of Treason*, p. 162) that the office of Constable was put in commission because Richard was conducting the Scots war seems unlikely as it was made so near the end of the war, quite apart from the Constable's important duties in the king's army.

[73] Sir William Parre: JP Westmorland, 1461–83, and sheriff, 1475 to death; frequent negotiator with Scots; at Barnet and Tewkesbury (his brother killed at Richard's side at Barnet); at coronation of Richard III; d. 26 Feb. 1484. See W.E. Hampton, *Memorials of the Wars of the Roses* (Gloucester and Upminster, 1979), no. 327, and *The Coronation of Richard III*, ed. A.F. Sutton and P.W. Hammond (Gloucester, 1983), p. 380.

[74] Harrington, *Coronation of Richard III*, ed. Sutton and Hammond, p. 353; Tyrell, *ibid.*, p. 407. And see below for Sir Ralph Assheton.

[75] Wallington not further identified.

[76] Fuller was feoffee or lawyer for Anthony Woodville, *Cal. Pat. R., 1476–85*, p. 223; not further identified.

[77] Warde: at All Souls College, Oxford, 1461–9; BCL; proctor in Chancellor's Court, 1466–9; still alive, 1492: Emden, *Biog. Reg. Univ. Oxford*.

[78] There were several Sir Thomas Greys, of whom Wedgwood created a concoction. For a better analysis, see Hampton, *Memorials*, no. 311: (1) a younger brother of Sir Ralph Grey of Heton, an esquire of Edward IV's body, 1461, knighted at Tewkesbury, on 1475 expedition and at Richard's coronation; or (2) his namesake, knighted by the earl of Northumberland 1480, sheriff of Norham 1483 and 1484

in the court than the evidence already cited, and here again, none would have known better than Gloucester what was needed. Territorial responsibilities for the non-legal officers can be suggested: Grey, the north-east down through East Anglia; Tyrell, Devon, Cornwall and Glamorgan; Harrington, Lancashire and Yorkshire; and Parre the north-west. The oversight of county musters and array can be mooted. The division would also fit in with the territorial responsibilities of the other officers of the Constable, the heralds. Richard would have continued to operate in his capacity as the king's lieutenant and Constable for his army during the remainder of the Scots campaign: keeping order in his host by the law of arms, with summary courts composed of the lords and knights present. Cases would have ranged from minor disputes between men to more serious offences. As Constable he was the man to whom members of his host could appeal for justice and put forward their grievances – and an army included not only knights and men at arms, but artificers, camp laundresses and cooks.[79]

Heralds were the better known officers of the Constable, arbiters of chivalry and honour, of tournaments and matters of coat armour. They carried messages across frontiers (including the Scots border for Richard of Gloucester) and between opposing armies, enjoyed immunity as ambassadors and reported battles and deeds of arms.[80] From 1469 onwards, Richard would have had some say in their appointment. A set of ordinances with thirteen clauses has been conclusively dated to his term, the late 1470s. The key clauses emphasised that they should know all nobles and gentlemen of the realm especially those who ought to bear arms; to hold chapters and discuss matters in doubt and refer them and any complaints to the Constable if necessary; to frequent good company and study books and histories, deeds of knights and the properties of things that might appear on a coat of arms.[81] Under the Yorkist kings the heralds were closely involved in royal pageantry, tournaments and funerals of noble and armigerous persons – Richard's ordinances emphasised their duties to record 'all manner of solemn occasions, solemn acts and deeds of the nobility, those concerned with deeds of arms as well as others, be truthfully and indifferently recorded without favour, without

---

(seven year term), but with activities, says Hampton, mainly in East Anglia as the son-in-law of Lord Scales, d. 1498.

[79] Keen, 'Treason Trials', pp. 100 and n. 2; his 'Jurisdiction and Origins' (cit. in n. 56), pp. 160, 162.

[80] Keen, *Laws of War*, pp. 21–2, 50, 194–5. A.R. Wagner, *Heralds and Heraldry in the Middle Ages*, pp. 34–8, and his *The Heralds of England: A History of the Office and College of Arms* (London, 1967), *passim*.

[81] Wagner, *Heralds of England*, pp. 67–8. Wagner, *Heralds and Heraldry in the Middle Ages*, pp. 136–8 (before the author had redated the ordinances). Sutton and Visser-Fuchs, *Richard III's Books*, pp. 185–6. Full edition of MSS: N.L. Ramsay, 'Richard III and the Office of Arms', in *The Yorkist Age*, ed. H. Kleineke and C. Steer (Donington, 2013), pp. 146–8, 154–63.

partiality or sympathy ...'. Narratives of ceremonies for the Yorkist period survive, and even for the short reign of Richard III there is a substantial number of narratives written up in accordance with Richard's ordinances. It can be said that his ordinances were effective.[82] Visitations also took place while Richard was Constable. One by John More, Norroy King of Arms (1478–91), was of the gentry of the northern counties, a matter of immediate interest to Richard as lord of the North. The other of 'about 1480' by William Ballard, March King of Arms, of his province of the north-west, which has been noted to include a compilation which followed exactly the ordinances of the late 1470s, with its ready instruction to refer matters of doubts to the Constable.[83] Richard apparently reserved time for this duty.

Richard's role as Constable is especially intriguing because of its affinity with his role as Edward IV's lord of the North, and warden of the Western March, which required expertise in the laws of the English–Scots border – different in details perhaps from the laws of war used in the court of the Constable, but close enough for all practicalities under the wardens.[84] As on the sea, England's other border, attacks across this frontier involved the breaking of truces and safe-conducts – with merchants an all-important proportion of those affected. As on the sea, any escalation of reprisals could be disastrous.[85] The situation was controlled on the Scots border in the time of the Yorkist kings by a steady sequence of truces and mutual safe-conducts after 1449 coupled with responsible wardens, regular love days and the kings of England and Scotland consistent in support of this responsible way of government. As on the sea, there was a proper procedure of petition, settlement and compensation between the nations. The Admiral of England and the Scottish Admiral adjudicated on infringements of the truce at sea.[86]

---

[82] Listed, Sutton and Visser-Fuchs, *Richard III's Books*, pp. 185–6. To this list can be added Caxton's dedication to him of the *Order of Chivalry* (ibid., pp. 80–5); the record of the making of a knight of the Bath, the pictures clearly showing the dress of the early 1480s, before the reign of Henry VII (Writhe's Garter Book); the Beauchamp Pageant; and the copy of the Salisbury Roll which includes a crude image of Richard and his queen (co-heiress of the Salisbury line), in their coronation robes, ibid., pp. 296–7.

[83] Discussed in full: Ramsay, 'Richard III and the Office of Arms', pp. 151–3.

[84] Keen, *Laws of War*, pp. 40, 209, 215, finds them to be different, but the similarities of the border conditions – whether in France or between England and Scotland – are more significant.

[85] See n. 50 above.

[86] See C.J. Neville, 'The Law of Treason in the English Border Counties in the Later Middle Ages', *Law and History Review*, 9 (1991), pp. 1–30, at 20–2 and nn. 102–3; her 'Keeping the Peace on the Northern Marches in the Later Middle Ages', *Eng. Hist. Rev.*, 109 (1994), pp. 1–25, at 21–3; and her *Violence, Custom and Law: The Anglo-Scottish Border Lands in the Later Middle Ages* (Edinburgh, 1998), ch. 7, and esp. pp. 156–66; this excellent study has contradictions caused by its effort to accommodate the hostile view of Gloucester held by earlier historians.

Relations between Edward IV and Scotland deteriorated and led to war, 1481–2, and the conditions of truce were only restored by Richard III and James III in mid-1484. In the text of the truce with Scotland, 1484, Richard conceded that if Dunbar should be the subject of local fighting this would not affect the truce – the cessation of war understood by a truce allowed for a certain level of infraction which would not constitute a return to war. Berwick was the castle that was to stay English and Dunbar Richard recognised was likely to return sometime to the Scots. This was similar to his concession on entering Edinburgh in 1482 that the city should not be sacked. Both James III and Richard III and their advisors understood the need for peace on the border and the complex diplomacy of give and take that had to lie behind any truce between such hardened antagonists.[87]

The Constable's duty over treason to the king has to be considered. The Yorkist period has been bedevilled by accusations levelled at Constable Tiptoft (1461–7), in particular that he was acting in a new and unacceptable way, but also at Edward IV and Richard III. This was and is largely 'partisan' opinion, first enunciated by the chronicler Warkworth, repeated by John Rastell and influential nineteenth- and twentieth-century historians (Stubbs and Holdsworth), and not uncommon in the work of more recent historians.[88] It was modified by R.J. Mitchell, Tiptoft's biographer.[89] It is clear, however, that the treason trials of the 1460s to 1483 all followed the accepted formulas of the Court of Chivalry and the law of arms: those of Grey (1464) and Desmond in Ireland (1468);[90] the Southampton executions in 1470 of common sailors, dramatically punished on the judgment of Tiptoft;[91] the

---

[87] C. Ross, *Edward IV* (London, 1974), pp. 278–9. Summary of treaty, 1484: Sutton and Visser-Fuchs, 'Chevalerie ... is worthi forto be comendid' (cit. in n. 30), pp. 119–20, incl. judicial machinery for the Border. And see Neville, 'Keeping the Peace', p. 22, on the 1484 treaty's improvements of procedure between the countries and on the use of heralds. For a definition of truces, see n. 21 above.

[88] Noted as unfair vilification by Keen, 'Treason Trials', pp. 85–93; and see his 'Jurisdiction and Origins' (cit. in n. 56), pp. 159–60. S. Rezneck, 'Constructive Treason by Words in the Fifteenth Century', *American Historical Review*, 33 (1927–8), pp. 544–52, at 544, also deals with the anti-Yorkist slant. Summarised by Bellamy, *Law of Treason*, pp. 158–60; cf. Ross, *Edward IV*, pp. 43, 80, 150.

[89] Mitchell, *John Tiptoft* (cit. in n. 52), finds him beneficent and an equable judge on several occasions, pp. 85–90, 96–102.

[90] The case of Sir Ralph Grey, recorded by Warkworth (John Warkworth, *A Chronicle of the First Thirteen Years of the Reign of Edward IV*, ed. J.O. Halliwell (Camden Soc., x, 1839), pp. 1–27, whose criticism has been taken as 'gospel' for centuries), is compared to the 1497 trial of Lord Audley by Keen, 'Treason Trials', pp. 90–1; and see Mitchell, *John Tiptoft*, pp. 96–9. See also A. Cosgrove, 'The Execution of the Earl of Desmond, 1468', *Jnl, Kerry Archaeological & Historical Soc.*, 8 (1975), pp. 11–27.

[91] This episode is often misreported, again due to Warkworth (p. 9): an attempt in the port of Southampton to seize certain ships, especially the *Trinity* owned by Warwick, involved well-connected instigators as well as common sailors who were engaged to sail the ships. Lord Rivers was instrumental in preventing the coup and

executions after Tewkesbury (1471); and the commission which tried the duke of Buckingham after his treason (1483).[92] There is also remarkably little difference between these cases and the executions of Anthony Woodville and his associates in June 1483 after a summary hearing before Sir Richard Ratcliffe and the earl of Northumberland, and that of William Lord Hastings on 13 June when there were present lords and knights such as Sir Robert Harrington, Sir Charles Pilkington and Sir Thomas Howard, able to form a tribunal to try a case at the command of the Constable, Richard of Gloucester, according to the words of his commission: 'summarily and plainly without noise and show of judgment, on simple inspection of fact'. Such summary trials continued under subsequent monarchs.[93] There is one important aspect of these precise and harsh powers conferred on the Constable – it allowed the king to exercise the divine gift of mercy. In 1465 Constable Tiptoft pronounced the standard punishment on a young esquire St Leger, for the offence of fighting within the king's palace of Westminster, that he should lose a hand. Edward IV chose to pardon him.[94]

In fact, the increasing use of commissions of oyer and terminer through the fifteenth century and certainly under the Yorkist kings, to inquire into and deal with cases of disorder, rebellion and treason, followed by attainder in parliament if the king wished, rendered the Constable unnecessary. Commissions were especially useful in the aftermath of Barnet and Tewkesbury, when Edward IV was not in the mood to be over merciful. Edward's instructions to Richard in 1471 were clearly to make examples of lords and gentry if they were recalcitrant. A commission of July headed by the earl of Essex was ordered to inquire into insurrections in Essex and to turn the offenders over to the Constable for punishment, and Richard was

---

two conspirators were captured by Howard: Sir Geofrey Gate and a man called Clapham. Gate, the ring-leader was pardoned, Clapham (who had assisted Robin of Redesdale in his rebellion) was beheaded, and twenty sailors hanged, drawn and quartered, their bodies impaled and their heads displayed on spikes. This has all the signs of punishment for mutiny, which attracted the strongest reprisals, and it seems likely that Tiptoft was making an example in a port where it would be well advertised. Edward then offered a general pardon to all who submitted before 7 May. Scofield, *Edward the Fourth* (cit. in n. 2), I, pp. 518, 521–2; *The Chronicle of Fabyan* (London, 1542), pp. 450, 451; Davies, *History of Southampton* (cit. in n. 41), p. 472; C. Richmond, 'Fauconberg's Kentish Rising of May 1471', *Eng. Hist. Rev.*, 85 (1970), pp. 673–92, at 674 and n. 6.

[92] Scofield, *Edward the Fourth*, I, p. 588 (Tewkesbury). In 1483 a commission tried Buckingham: Bellamy, *Law of Treason*, pp. 123, 163.

[93] For antecedents and continued use of summary trials, see Keen, 'Treason Trials', pp. 85–103, and his 'Jurisdiction and Origins', pp. 164–5. Baker, *Oxford History of the Laws of England*, VI, pp. 216–17, notes especially the trials of Audley, Warbeck and Tyrrel, 1497–1502.

[94] Mitchell, *John Tiptoft*, pp. 126–7; *Cal. Pat. R., 1461–7*, p. 380.

certainly travelling through the eastern counties at this date.[95] At the same time Edward himself dealt with offenders in Kent, the mayor of Canterbury not escaping execution. Commissions under Lord Dinham, Sir John Fogg and others, ordered to deal with other offenders in the counties of Kent, Sussex and Essex at this time, seem, however, to have been allowed to impose substantial fines, if the egregious Warkworth can be trusted.[96] The crisis of the 1483 rebellion led to Richard's appointment of Sir Ralph Assheton as Vice-Constable *hac vice* while he was moving south-west, at Coventry on 24 October 1483. Assheton was to investigate and hear all cases of *lèse-majesté*. How far or if Assheton acted by himself is not clear. Later commissions also inquired into the treasons that had occurred during the rebellion. Another comparable commission inquired into the treasonable plotting and fomenting of discontent by William Colyngbourne in 1484. The Constable in office during this period, Lord Stanley, was, like his predecessor in the office, not regularly and specifically involved. [97]

Richard of Gloucester's personal career as Admiral and Constable, 1462–83

Gloucester's early personal experience of the sea (as we know it) consisted of his voyage into exile and back in 1460–1; and the same again in 1470–1, the return journey encountering bad weather which drove the ships ashore in Holderness. His subsequent bestowal of a bell upon the guild of seamen and pilots of Holy Trinity, Hull, may have been in gratitude for their skills and help at this time.[98] His first encounter with a treason trial was as a member of the commission of oyer and terminer of January 1469 which tried Hungerford and Courtenay, already mentioned. There are no clear references to him acting personally in the roles of Admiral and Constable before 1471.

As Constable he was involved in the trials and summary executions of as many as sixteen men after Tewkesbury – the details are meagre – in which

---

[95] Bellamy, *Law of Treason*, pp. 149–50; *Cal. Pat. R., 1467–77*, p. 287. For Richard's journey though East Anglia see below.

[96] Scofield, *Edward the Fourth*, II, pp. 1–2, 21–2; Bellamy, *Law of Treason*, p. 175; Warkworth, p. 21.

[97] Assheton: Rymer, *Foedera*, XII, p. 205, and *Cal. Pat. R., 1476–85*, p. 368; he was one of several names in a commission for Kent, 10 Dec. 1483 (*ibid.*, p. 392). Stanley's appointment (Rymer, *Foedera*, XII, p. 209) concentrates on his emoluments. Colyngbourne: Rezneck, 'Constructive Treason', pp. 549–50, gives the indictment in proper detail with comparison to the Bagnall and Scot case of 1494. Bellamy, *Law of Treason*, p. 121.

[98] D. Woodward, 'The Accounts of the Building of Trinity House, Hull, 1465–1476', *Yorks. Archaeological Jnl*, 62 (1990), pp. 153–70, at 169, 170.

he was associated with the Marshal of England, the duke of Norfolk.[99] After Tewkesbury, Richard travelled south from London with part of Edward's victorious army: one of his tasks was, as Admiral, to take charge of the ships surrendered by Thomas Neville, Bastard of Fauconberge, on 26 May, perhaps numbering as many as forty-seven. The king followed and dealt with the punishment of rebels in Canterbury and Sandwich, and it was at Sandwich that Edward received the formal submission of Neville and took him back to London. Neville was duly pardoned on 10 June, received letters of protection and a knighthood and was made a vice-Admiral under Gloucester. He apparently undertook to serve the duke of Gloucester in the north, but it is not certain when he actually went north, for Gloucester was in Westminster on 3 July, as was Lord Howard with whom Richard then travelled to East Anglia. After a visit to Norwich around 23 August in his capacity as Constable (see below), he probably moved swiftly north for by 11 September it was known that the Bastard had taken to his heels. He was swiftly recaptured and executed at Middleham Castle, Yorkshire, it can be presumed after a summary trial before Richard as Constable. His head was put up for display on London Bridge on 27 September; his brother, William, escaped to sanctuary at Beverley, and was duly pardoned in 1477.[100]

As mentioned, Gloucester and Howard travelled through Suffolk, via some of the de Vere estates which Gloucester had been granted. It was important for Howard to cultivate the newly grown-up duke and Admiral and it is intriguing to find Richard as a companion of this sea-warrior on this journey. Their subsequent careers indicate they 'got on' well and their cooperation on matters to do with the sea, about which Howard could teach the duke so much, was to be significant. Richard was also travelling through East Anglia to Norwich in his role of Constable, indubitably on Edward's orders to reassert his authority. For example, a commission of July 1471 headed by the earl of Essex had been ordered to inquire into insurrections in Essex and to turn the offenders over to the Constable for punishment.[101] Norwich was experiencing enough disorder, mostly troublesome talk, to provoke this visit in late August.[102] (A man from Norwich had been accused of publishing articles issued by Robin of Redesdale promoting war against

---

[99] Scofield, *Edward the Fourth*, I, p. 588.

[100] Richmond, 'Fauconberg's Kentish Rising', p. 682 and n. 3; Scofield, *Edward the Fourth*, II, pp. 1–2, 20.

[101] Bellamy, *Law of Treason*, pp. 149–50; *Cal. Pat. R., 1467–77*, p. 287.

[102] A.F. Sutton, 'Richard of Gloucester visits Norwich, August 1471', *The Ricardian*, 7 (1985–7), pp. 333–4. Gloucester travelled to Norwich via Colchester (where on 21 July he was with John Howard), and then via Sudbury, Lavenham, and Bury, visiting his newly acquired de Vere properties. *Pace* J. Ashdown-Hill, 'Yesterday my lord of Gloucester came to Colchester', *Essex Archaeology and History*, 36 (2005) pp. 212–17, which misdates this journey to 1468. Howard left Richard to go to Calais where Hastings was resuming control.

the king in 1469, and such accusations had a habit of giving a city a bad name, however undeserved.[103]) Norwich had sent thirty men on horseback to support the king at Tewkesbury under Captain John Abbot, so the loyalty of its rulers was not really in doubt.[104] The city borrowed £10 from the two sheriffs to give to the duke when he arrived. On 23 August the mayor duly presented him with the £10 in a purse of gold cloth (*bursa aurea*) bought from Alderman John Aubry and gave rewards to the duke's players, a taboret and his footmen. Although the city's record makes no reference to Richard in the role of Constable, this is confirmed by the fact that later in September Dr Aleyn, a judge in the Constable's court, was paid for his counsel by the city in the matter of John Foster, John Tyler, Thomas Hunworth and another unnamed man who were in prison in the Guildhall for speaking ill of Edward IV and his brother, and were to be sent to the Tower of London where the men would presumably be brought before the king's Council.[105] The presence of John Aleyn, the deputy in the Constable's court, shows that this was indeed a tour to exercise the duties of the Constable, but that no trials of treason were to be held in Norwich; the offenders were merely expedited to the next stage. A serjeant at arms of the king had also, at some date, arrested Henry Reynald in St John's church in order to stop his slanderous speech, but no further details are known. Despite incomplete information regarding the precise business transacted during Richard's visit, it can be inferred that this was short and that he was happy to leave matters of the king's peace largely in the hands of the mayor and his brethren.[106]

An inquiry by Richard as Constable, which is better explained in the records than that in Norwich, shows him taking a relaxed attitude towards a situation that had got out of hand and only needed firm local action. At some date after St Dunstan's Day (19 May) 1473, Richard in his role as Constable was instructed by the king to investigate the 'outrageous, heinous and malicious language and also ... assaults and making affrays' of two goldsmiths who were neighbours in the city of London, called Edward of Bowden and Davy Panter. These two men had been quarrelling and shouting insults at each other since 1468 and the Goldsmiths' wardens had proved unable to control them. The disturbance of the peace and a level of abuse which might so easily

---

[103] Bellamy, *Law of Treason*, p. 121: William Belmyn, a Norwich mercer, had been accused of publishing Robin's treasonable articles in May 1469 to stir up war against the king; he pleaded not guilty; verdict unknown.

[104] Norwich, Norfolk Record Office, Norwich Assembly Book 1434–91, f. 26v.

[105] Rezneck, 'Constructive Treason', pp. 544–52, deals with the particular issue of treasonable words as part of a larger narrative of planned treason.

[106] Norfolk Record Office, Norwich City Chamberlain's Accounts 1470–90, ff. 23, 24v. It is interesting to note that Anthony, Lord Rivers, had been staying with John Butt (Mayor from May 1471) after Tewkesbury and the city paid Butt his expenses (f. 24v). Assembly Book 1434–91, f. 89 notes date of visit; see f. 90 for details about Aleyn under 21 Sept and 10 Oct.

touch on treason had reached the king's ears. Edward and Davy were duly brought before the duke of Gloucester 'and there herd declaring their mater in so moche that it was understond the said mater only proceded of rancour and very malice be twene them of olde continuance hanging and no mater groundly founden touching the kings highnesse'. The Goldsmiths' wardens were in a state of anxiety over the possible consequences to their company's authority, and their 'diligent labour' explained everything to Gloucester who duly remitted the case to them. Such domestic matters were not the concern of the Constable, but no doubt the authority of this office made sure that the culprits now obeyed their wardens. A gentleman of Gloucester's was rewarded with 40s. for 'discharging of Edward [and] Davy aforesaid and their suretees a yenst the kyng'.[107] A storm in a teacup but sufficiently irritating for Edward IV to send his Constable to alarm the citizens into proper action.

Richard seems to have visited ports far from the centre of his duties in the north of England: the port of Lydd (Kent) recorded the Admiral's presence in 1472 and spent 59s. upon him, and a further visit may have followed in 1473. As Admiral and Constable during the 1475 invasion of France, he had a vast increase of business. He was presumably in Southampton at some time during the preparations of Edward's great army for the conquest of France and the fleet to sail him there, but perhaps only towards the end – he had deputies enough if representatives of these offices were required. In 1474–5 the town was a hub of military activity: for example, all the brigandine-makers of the town were taken to work for the king; and the army mustered at Portsdown and at Southampton.[108] There was a battle in Southampton Water in June when French ships ventured up river, no doubt to spy out the preparations and in the hope of singeing the king of England's beard. They seized a Portuguese vessel and were then fought off by the town's lieutenant, Richard Gryme. On 20 June he learnt of more French ships off Portland and asked the lieutenant of the Isle of Wight to signal to the king's ships, and sent a messenger to the king himself at Sandwich. Winchester provided some help, and powder was given to Lord Audley's gunners. Shots were apparently exchanged between

---

[107] London, Goldsmiths' Company of London, Minute Book A, pp. 170, 172–5, esp. p. 173 (consulted in 1976); there were further expenses including a supper and a dinner for the aldermen and arbitrators who finally adjudicated the matter. T.F. Reddaway and L.E.M. Walker, *The Early History of the Goldsmiths' Company 1327–1509* (London, 1975), pp. 151–4. Comparable is the acrimonious dispute between two Bristol officials that escalated into an appeal of treason against the king. This went before the king and his council and was referred to the council of the prince of Wales, not the Constable: *Great Red Book of Bristol*, Pt. IV, ed. E.W. Veale (Bristol Record Soc., xviii, 1953), pp. 57–93.

[108] *Records of Lydd*, ed. A. Hussey (Ashford, 1911), pp. 267, 275; Lydd received a letter from the admiralty: p. 273. R. Moffett, 'Military Equipment in the Town of Southampton during the Fourteenth and Fifteenth Centuries', *Jnl of Medieval Military History*, 9 (2011), pp. 167–99, at 190–1, 192, 198; C. Platt, *Medieval Southampton* (London, 1973), p. 138.

the French ships and the town's quays, necessitating later repairs, and the gun called *Thomas of the Beard* apparently broke when it was fired during the successful rescue of the Portuguese ship.[109] Gloucester had several suits in the local courts of Southampton, of which small details survive: all concerned purveyance for ships and perhaps related to the busy period of 1474–5. The transfer of an army across the sea in 1475 was undoubtedly a great experience; it is known Gloucester owned at least one ship, the *Mayflower*, at this time and he had also acquired the *Anne of Fowey* by 1481.[110]

He took more men with him than any other noble and his entourage included officers of the Constable's court, for it was inevitable that disputes would arise within a large army overseas for an unforeseen period. He has been described as not content with the treaty made by Edward with Louis XI and therefore absent from its making in the cramped quarters on the bridge of Picquigny, but in fact he is known to have gone to view the French army 'drawn up in the field' on the day of the treaty. He was shown around by the Admiral of France and other French lords – a highly suitable activity for the English Constable, the king's lieutenant in command of the army and its discipline, while the king was engaged in diplomacy elsewhere. One judge at least of the court of the Constable was with the army: Dr Aleyn, one of whose judgments was appealed against by John Forster, the proctor of the army.[111] In this busy year the Admiral also had routine matters to attend to, such as confirmation of the right to wreck of the abbot of Abbotsbury (Dorset),[112] and in the north there were important investigations into complaints of violations of the truce between England and Scotland including robbery at sea, demanding the attention of the Admirals of both countries.[113]

The Constable's role as an arbiter of chivalrous ceremony and behaviour was called into use at the knighting of men to celebrate the marriage of Richard, duke of York, to Anne, duchess of Norfolk, in 1478. He had to rebuke four of these knights who had refused to pay the fees due to the heralds.[114]

---

[109] The details in the accounts do not allow a full reconstruction: Davies, *History of Southampton*, p. 473. John Roper arrested certain carracks on Gryme's order, *Book of Remembrance of Southampton*, ed. H.W. Gidden, 3 vols (Southampton Record Soc., xxvii–xxix, 1927–9), I, pp. 44–6. Richard Gryme was 'lieutenant' of the mayor through 1474–5 and all through Richard's reign, and he was the son of another Richard Gryme who was steward 1450–1, sheriff 1458 and mayor 1459: *Book of Remembrance*, III, p. 1 n. 3, and p. 2, and Davies, *History of Southampton*, p. 174 (list of officers).

[110] Hist. MSS Commn. [18], *Eleventh Report, Appx, Pt III*, p. 102 (Gloucester's letter). Richmond, 'Naval Power' (cit. in n. 8) lists all Richard's ships.

[111] Sutton and Visser-Fuchs, 'Chevalerie … is worthi forto be comendid' (cit. in n. 30), esp. pp. 117, 121. See above for Aleyn's case.

[112] E.H.T. Atkinson, 'Some Abbotsbury Records', *Proc., Dorset Natural History & Antiquarian Field Club*, xlviii (1927), pp. 70–85, at 73.

[113] Neville, *Violence, Custom and Law* (cit. in n. 86), p. 159.

[114] W.C. Metcalfe, *A Book of Knights* (London, 1885), pp. 7–8, citing London, BL, Cotton MS Claudius C iii.

Overall, Richard of Gloucester's career as Edward IV's Constable confirms how infrequently that officer was required to look into cases of treason: the power of the king's Council to initiate inquiries and decide where cases should be tried, and the increasing recourse to commissions of oyer and terminer were now paramount.

Developments in the Admiralty and Constableship during the reign of Richard III

There is sufficient evidence to suggest that Richard's experience of these offices informed his actions as king. There were important developments in the Admiralty: the appointment of Lacy as chief judge in the 'principal and other courts of Admiralty' on 10 March 1483 was a sign of the unity of the office under the king – it is probably significant that the court of the Constable is not mentioned, sensibly lost under its more active fellow. On 8 April 1484 a precise and wide-encompassing commission for the Admiralty was set up, undoubtedly prompted by the unexpected Breton war (Oct. 1483 – April 1484), which Richard and his officers had conducted with signal success. This had dramatically extended the king's direct experience of naval war, and especially the use of warships to patrol, fight and convoy. This commission[115] was made up of Sir John Wood, treasurer of England, with years of experience of agreeing to and paying for royal ships and convoys for merchant fleets; Robert Brackenbury, constable of the Tower of London, a sound administrator with strong interests in Kent; the lawyers, William Lacy, clerk of the king's Council and therefore a direct link between Admiralty and king; Master William Dawbeney, who had begun life working for another doctor of laws in this field;[116] and Master Robert Rydon. As the king's commissaries general in the office of Admiralty, they had full powers to all matters pertaining to the office, and they were to engage a notary to write up their proceedings. Wood and Brackenbury were to be vice-Admirals and Sir John Norbury to be vice-Marshal.[117] William Biller was presumably this notary – since 10

---

[115] Lacy: *Cal. Pat. R., 1476–85*, p. 346; commission, *ibid.*, pp. 391–2.

[116] 'Mr' William Dawbeney can be assumed to be the notary who in 1455 was the servant of Mr John Wardale, DCL (London Metropolitan Archives, Corporation of London Records, Journal 5, ff. 246v, 247); notary in 1474 (*Cal. Close R., 1468–76*, p. 369); Wardale had been an advocate in the court of Canterbury, 1461, a royal commissioner for appeals from the court of Admiralty, 1447–55, and d. 1472, Emden, *Biog. Reg. Univ. Oxford*, III, p. 1981); Dawbeney witnessed Wardale's will, Kew, TNA, Prerogative Court of Canterbury, Will Registers, PROB 11/6, f. 41v. He is not to be confused with his namesake, the searcher in the port of London, clerk of Edward IV's and Richard III's jewels and friend of Caxton: A.F. Sutton, 'Caxton was a Mercer', in *England in the Fifteenth Century*, ed. N.J. Rogers (Stamford, 1994), pp. 138–41.

[117] *Cal. Pat. R., 1476–85*, pp. 391–92. For Wood etc., see Sutton, 'East Coast Ports and the Iceland Trade' (cit. in n. 7), p. 169 and n. 44.

December 1483 he had held the office of promoter of all the king's causes civil or criminal or concerning crimes of *lèse-majesté* before the king's judges of the Constableship *and* Admiralty of England, with all profits, etc. (present author's italics).[118] The significance of this act of centralisation and organisation cannot be truly evaluated as it died with Richard III; the input of his Chancellor, John Russell, and his Clerk of the Council, William Lacy, may have been considerable. The importance of the non-lawyers is also striking. Above them or alongside was the Admiral, the experienced John Howard, duke of Norfolk. It seems likely they operated individually, as the vice-Admiral, Sir Miles Stapleton, had done in East Anglia under Admiral John Holland, with allotted areas of coastline to supervise: Brackenbury and Norbury, Kent along to Sussex and probably beyond;[119] Howard naturally kept the North Sea coast; and Wood at the Exchequer oversaw convoys and the money.

What was perhaps the most beneficial order made by Richard to do with the sea also followed his brief war with Brittany and his confirmation of truces with all his neighbours except for the ever-problematic, regency-ruled France: on 11 August 1484 he ordered that no man put to sea before he had found sureties and taken an oath before the officers of the port he was leaving that he would attack no other ship sailing under the king's safe-conduct, which comprised all the king's allies: Spain, Portugal, the subjects of the dukes of Austria and Burgundy (i.e. the Low Countries), Italy, Germany; and those who were at present in a state of truce with England, Brittany and Scotland. Port officials were to promulgate this order, report on any failure, and impound any prizes brought into the port pending investigation.[120]

It can be suggested once more that Richard, like Edward IV before him, would have continued to build up a royal fleet to be employed regularly on convoys and patrols. His death and that of his equally committed Admiral, John Howard, destroyed the convoy system in the North Sea, for example, forthwith.[121] A corollary to all the naval activity of Richard's reign concerning convoys and safe-conducts – which always specified the ship to be used – was the reiteration of Edward's 1463 navigation act, which promoted the use of English ships, in the parliament of 1485 (of Henry VII), almost certainly planned for Richard's second parliament. Few specific new-built ships can be found for the Yorkist kings although it is well known Edward encouraged his subjects' building of new ships; the increase of royal-owned

---

[118] *Cal. Pat. R., 1476–85*, p. 411; feodary in honour of Tickhill and feed as promoter, *Harleian MS 433*, ed. Horrox and Hammond, I, pp. 73, 100, vol. 2, pp. 217–18.

[119] Sir John Norbury: Hampton, *Memorials*, no. 300: of Stoke d'Abernon (Surr.); knighted Jan.×June 1483; JP until Bosworth and active against rebels in Kent and Bretons at sea 1483–84; never restored after Bosworth and therefore probably present at the battle; pardoned 1495; d. 1504.

[120] Full text in Marsden, *Documents Relating to Law and Custom of the Sea* (cit. in n. 38), pp. 136–8.

[121] Sutton 'East Coast Ports and the Iceland Trade', pp. 169–75.

ships under both kings is also well known. Purchases were quicker in times of need, as Richard's acquisitions prove. It is intriguing that the Shipwrights Company, by this date at Ratcliffe (down river, on the Thames), was adding to its ordinances and ordering special supervision of work and materials in 1483. Royal awareness of the changes in ship-building techniques can also not be wondered at, as Sir John Howard was building a skeleton-built carvel between 1463 and 1466 and it can be doubted if he, as Admiral 1483–5, would have tolerated the building of a new, prestige ship, Henry VII's *Sovereign* in 1487–8, in the old-fashioned, cheaper, clinker-built style.[122]

No specific changes to the commission for the office of Constable are recorded for Richard's reign and it seems possible that the commission of 1482 remained silently in place. The tie between the Constable's and Admiral's courts was certainly being tightened: on 10 December 1483 Master William Biller, notary, was made promoter of all the king's causes civil or criminal or concerning crimes of *lèse-majesté* before the king's judges of the Constableship *and* Admiralty.[123] Richard's supreme acknowledgement of his past office was his formal incorporation of the heralds of England with perpetual succession and a common seal on 2 March 1484. This was accompanied by a grant to the twelve principal heralds of Coldharbour, a house in the city of London. As Constable, Richard knew they had been holding chapters since 1420 and were using a seal. They were now able to regulate their professional conduct, have offices and hold meetings under their own roof, and above all have a communal library for the preservation of all their books.[124] To this library, Richard gave two large rolls of arms he had owned while Constable.[125] These grants were arguably Richard's acknowledgement that the Constable was superfluous as regards disputes over grants of arms; he could, however, maintain his personal interest in such matters. His appointment of Lord Stanley as Constable – who was to be the last man to hold the office for more than a day or two (for such events as coronations) – was of a piece. The real power of the Constable remained with Richard as king, with specific commissions of oyer and terminer, and with the heralds. Lord Stanley had little to do except preside at the granting of arms or take part in a commission such as

---

[122] *English Historical Documents*, IV, pp. 1040–1 (1463) and stat. 1 Henry VII, c. 8; Richmond, 'English Naval Power', *passim*; A.C. Knight, *Records of the Worshipful Company of Shipwrights*, I: 1428–1780 (London, 1939), p. xi; I. Friel, *The Good Ship: Ships, Shipbuilding and Technology in England 1200–1520* (London, 1995), chs 3, 8, 9, and esp. pp. 153–4, 164–80.

[123] *Cal. Pat. R., 1476–85*, p. 411. Not otherwise identified.

[124] Wagner, *Heralds of England*, pp. 123, 131–2; also licensed to acquire another £20 worth of land to support a chaplain. The College's coat of arms dates from 1484: *ibid.*, p. 133. Ramsay, 'Richard III and the Office of Arms', pp. 148–50.

[125] The rolls now only exist in copies made by copyists, who thoughtfully recorded his ownership: Sutton and Visser-Fuchs, *Richard III's Books*, pp. 143–4; Ramsay, 'Richard III and the Office of Arms', pp. 145–6.

that looking into the treason of William Colyngbourne, when he was one of many and did not act as Constable.[126]

The fate of the heralds under Henry VII reflected their favour under Richard III: their house was given to Henry's mother – her husband Lord Stanley, being in charge of the Office of Arms, would often have seen it. They managed to retain their corporate status, possibly by not drawing too much attention to it. One herald and one pursuivant, those closest to Richard, disappeared: Gloucester King of Arms, Richard Champneys (1483–5) and the pursuivant Blanc Sanglier, who is said to have ridden the horse bearing the dead king to Leicester after Bosworth – his father Norroy, however, transferred to the new king. It was also some time before the elderly Sir Thomas Holme, an accomplished ambassador, who was Clarenceux King of Arms 1476–85, was brought out of retirement.[127] John Writhe, Garter (1478–1504) seems to have been the most adroit in recovering favour. The entire transfer was possibly less fraught than it might have been because of the general acceptance of the immunity of heralds in times of war.

Richard, duke of Gloucester's tenure of the offices of Admiral and Constable was significant and informed his reign. The naval expertise of the country was increased in Richard's reign in the tradition of Edward IV, and the central and local courts of Admiralty were busy under an interested king and an increasingly professional body of seamen–administrators. The heralds were incorporated and given independence of all control except that of the king, while there is every sign that Richard, and Edward before him, realised that the office of Constable was a dead letter.

---

[126] Stanley's appointment was solely concerned with his emoluments: Rymer, *Foedera*, XII, p. 209; *Cal. Pat. R., 1476–85*, pp. 519–20. Baker, *Oxford History of the Laws of England*, VI, p. 216, notes the demise of the Constable's function over armorial disputes.

[127] Ramsay, 'Richard III and the Office of Arms', pp. 144–5, 151, for Richard's personal heralds and their demise. For Champneys see Wagner, *Heralds of England*, p. 135; H.S. London, in Godfrey, *College of Arms*, p. 259, has no reference to him after March 1484 and therefore assumes he died; it is possible that he died or was executed after Bosworth. Blanc Sanglier is usually identified as [–] More, son of John More Norrey, Godfrey, *College of Arms*, p. 238, Wagner, *Heralds of England*, p. 134 and n. 3. For Clarenceux Holme, previously Norroy 1467–76, see Wagner, *Heralds and Heraldry in the Middle Ages*, p. 74; Wagner, *Heralds of England*, p. 135; ambassador e.g. to Denmark, 1477 and 1489; resigned 4 Jan. 1484 and already had a position among the alms-knights of Windsor (he was over 60 years): Godfrey, *College of Arms*, pp. 78–9.

CHAPTER 11

Some Dubious Beliefs about Medieval Prize Law

John Ford

For fifty years now, historians have had at their disposal a coherent account of the law of arms applicable in the Court of the Constable and Marshal to cases concerned with the dividing of spoils and the ransoming of prisoners taken in wars.[1] Disputes over these matters were resolved by reference to any contracts formed between the parties involved, failing which to any regulations issued in relation to the particular conflicts in which they fought, failing which to more general regulations or the customs of warfare.[2] At the more general level especially, the law of arms had an international flavour, for the regulations introduced in one place were often influenced by those already in force elsewhere, and the communities that considered themselves obliged to conform to customary usages were not always nationally defined.[3] It was of course important for the decisions delivered in the courts of one place to appear acceptable in the other places from which those despoiled or imprisoned came, and it was partly to this end that the practice of military tribunals was rationalised in terms of the legal theory expounded in broadly similar terms in universities throughout Europe.[4] The learned doctrine of

---

[1] M.H. Keen, *The Laws of War in the Late Middle Ages* (London, 1965), is still essential reading, partly because it provides the foundation on which later writers have built, and partly because it provides a more balanced view than most later studies, which tend to focus on particular elements in the law of arms to the neglect of others, or to focus less on the law of arms than on the code of chivalry that influenced its application.

[2] The more practical aspects of the law of arms had already been explored in studies like D. Hay, 'The Division of the Spoils of War in Fourteenth-Century England', *Trans., Royal Historical Soc.*, 5th ser., iv (1954), pp. 91–109, and 'Booty in Border Warfare', *Trans. Dumfriesshire & Galloway Natural History & Antiquarian Soc.*, xxxi (1954), pp. 148–66, reprinted in Hay's *Renaissance Essays* (London, 1988), pp. 265–306.

[3] This is not to dispute the insistence in G.D. Squibb, *The High Court of Chivalry: A Study in the Civil Law in England* (Oxford, 1959), pp. 162–90, that the law applied by the Constable and Marshal was 'the English law of arms', but is to insist in turn that the international flavour of that law mattered.

[4] In challenging some aspects of Squibb's thesis, M.H. Keen, 'The Jurisdiction and Origins of the Constable's Court', in *War and Government in the Middle Ages: Essays*

the law schools provided a framework of legitimacy within which courts in different parts of Europe were able to fashion versions of the law of arms that could be expected to receive recognition elsewhere. It follows that to understand the law of arms properly required – and still requires – familiarity with academic theory as well as forensic practice.[5] It was not without cause that advice was taken on the application of the law of arms from 'doctors of law' or 'iurisperiti', a cadre of experts in the civil and canon laws whose advice was relied on in the specialised courts of the Constable and Marshal, the Admiral, and certain other officials.[6] An assumption evident in the literature on the law of arms is indeed that the law applicable in the Admiral's court to cases concerning vessels, cargoes and mariners captured at sea was informed by the same learned theory as the law applicable to captures on land in the Court of the Constable and Marshal.[7] Yet the literature on the Admiral's court and the prize law applied there tends to give a different impression. Beliefs expressed in articles and books written before the law of arms was carefully investigated have never been directly questioned, and these articles and books remain the standard works to which readers turn for an introduction to the history of prize law in England. The aim here is to examine three or four beliefs about how title to captured ships or goods was acquired. First, however, a little more needs to be said about the theory of the law schools and its relationship with the practice of the courts.

Learned foundations of prize acquisition

In a much quoted instruction issued in the early fifteenth century to the Admiral of England, he was informed that his court should decide cases

---

in *Honour of J.O. Prestwich*, ed. J. Gillingham and J.C. Holt (Woodbridge, 1984), pp. 159–69, observed, at p. 168, that the learning of the law schools was used to give the law of arms 'a respectable and coherent legal footing'. A little more than that, perhaps.

[5] At the risk of seeming unfair to an excellent book, it may be suggested by way of illustration that R. Ambühl, *Prisoners of War in the Hundred Years War: Ransom Culture in the Late Middle Ages* (Cambridge, 2013), would have been even more impressive had the learned laws been examined closely. For instance, the attempt to explain, at pp. 19–20, why those who held prisoners to ransom were invariably referred to as 'masters' omits to mention the obvious explanation that the Roman law texts on which the legitimacy of the practice was believed to rest were couched in terms of *domini* and *servi*.

[6] A. Rogers, 'Hoton versus Shakell: A Ransom Case in the Court of Chivalry, 1390–95', *Nottingham Mediaeval Studies*, 6 (1962), pp. 74–108; and 7 (1963), pp. 53–78, at 6, pp. 78–9. On the role of learned lawyers in admiralty cases see W. Senior, *Doctors' Commons and the Old Court of Admiralty: A Short History of the Civilians in England* (London and New York, 1922), pp. 14–34.

[7] Keen and Hay both used maritime examples in the works cited in nn. 1–2 above.

'solonque loy maryne et aunciens custumez de la meer, saunz tener la solempnite du loy, et saunz meller loy syvyle ove loy marine la ou ele poet estre deporte'.[8] As had been observed half a century earlier, the Admiral's court was not intended to be governed 'si estroit come serront les autres courtz du roialme qe sont rullez par comune ley de la terre, mes est reullable par equite et ley marine'.[9] Because foreigners were often involved in litigation before the Admiral's court, it was required to provide 'sommarye et hastive processe de tyde en tyde', and it is generally thought to have been for the same reason that the court followed forms of procedure derived from the civil and canon laws, with which foreign litigants were more likely to feel comfortable.[10] But it was not only the procedure of the court that was modified to meet the needs of strangers.[11] The *ley marine* or *lex maritima*, to which sources constantly refer, contained provisions that were understood to be accepted as law in other places too, and while explicit references to provisions of the civil and canon laws are harder to find, this does not mean that the learned laws had no effect on the determination of substantive issues.[12] The instruction given to the Admiral in the early fifteenth century may seem to minimise the significance of the civil law, by indicating that it should only be turned to when the law and custom of the sea were found unsatisfactory, but this was consistent with the methodological instruction provided in the law schools, where students learned to handle practical problems by moving progressively from the particular to the general.[13] They learned to apply local sources (*ius proprium*) before resorting to their learning (*ius commune*), and to

---

[8] Twiss, *Black Book of the Admiralty*, I, pp. 408–9, where the passage cited is translated: 'according to the law marine and ancient customs of the sea, without observing the solemnity of the law, and without mixing law civil with law maritime there where it may be equitable'.

[9] C. Johnson, 'An Early Admiralty Case, A.D. 1361', in *Camden Miscellany XV*, Camden Third Series, 41 (Royal Historical Soc., 1929), pt 4, at p. 4. This may be translated: 'as narrowly as are the other courts of the kingdom, which are governed by the common law; for it is ruled by equity and the law marine'.

[10] T.L. Mears, 'The History of the Admiralty Jurisdiction', in *Select Essays in Anglo-American Legal History*, ed. E. Freund, W.E. Mikell and J.H. Wigmore, 3 vols (Cambridge, 1907–9), II, pp. 312–64, at 335–6; T.F.T. Plucknett, *A Concise History of the Common Law*, 5th edn (London, 1956), pp. 660–2; J.H. Baker, *An Introduction to English Legal History*, 4th edn (London, 2002), pp. 122–4. For doubts about the extent to which summary and learned procedures were in fact adopted in the admiral's court see J.L. Barton, 'Roman Law in England', *Ius Romanum Medii Aevi*, V 13a (Milan, 1971), pp. 75–7.

[11] *Cf.* Squibb, *High Court of Chivalry*, pp. 164–6, where it is suggested that 'for all practical purposes' it was the procedure of the courts of chivalry and admiralty alone that was governed by the civil law.

[12] On the meaning of the expression 'maritime law' see M.J. Prichard and D.E.C. Yale, 'Introduction', in their edition of *Hale and Fleetwood on Admiralty Jurisdiction* (Selden Soc., cviii, 1993), pp. xv–ccl, at xxxiii–vii.

[13] On the development of the learned methodology see, for instance, P.G. Stein, *The*

examine local sources critically in the light of the higher standard provided by their learning (conceived of as *ratio scripta* or *aequitas constituta*). Whether recourse had to be taken to civil and canon law sources in the handling of prize litigation depended, therefore, on how satisfactory the local sources seemed to be in the light of the learned laws and on how much the learned sources offered that was lacking in the local sources.

The theory of the law schools in this area rested on relatively slender foundations. Several texts in the surviving works on Roman law stated baldly that things taken *ex hostibus* immediately *capientium fiunt* or *occupantium fiunt*.[14] The meaning clearly was that ownership of these *res hostiles* could be obtained through the mode of acquisition known as *occupatio*, for the taking of property from enemies was likened to picking up pebbles (ownerless things or *res nullius*) on a beach. There were complications, however, which the civilian doctors set about untangling by comparing these texts with others. A crucial move was made by drawing attention to texts in which *hostes* were defined as people from any country against which a war (*bellum*) had been publicly declared.[15] The doctors concluded that enemy property was only open to acquisition through *occupatio* in a conflict formally entered into between sovereign rulers.[16] Comparison was also made with a text that not only declared land captured from enemies to be subject to confiscation (*publicatur*), but also associated property subject to confiscation (*publicari*) with everything to be classified as plunder (*praedae loco cedere*).[17] The doctors had no difficulty in concluding that 'immovable things become the property of the country declaring the war', whereas 'movable things taken in war pass into the ownership of those occupying them'.[18] Yet the association of things

---

Character and Influence of the Roman Civil Law: Historical Essays (London, 1988), pp. 83–90.

[14] *Digest*, 41.1.5.7, 41.1.51, 41.2.1.1 and 41.2.3.21, and *Institutes*, 2.1.17, included in the *Corpus Iuris Civilis*, ed. T. Mommsen, P. Krueger, R. Schoell and G. Kroll, 3 vols (Berlin, 1875).

[15] *Digest*, 49.15.24 and 50.16.118.

[16] The point was first made by the glossators in the twelfth and thirteenth centuries, as summed up by Accursius in gl. 'Bello' ad D.1.1.5, gl. 'Bello' ad D.41.2.1, gl. 'Bella' ad J.1.2.2, and gl. 'Ex hostibus' ad J. 2.1.17, printed in the Paris edition of 1559 at *Digestum vetus*, col. 57, *Digestum novum*, col. 402, and *Volumen legum parvum*, pt 3, cols 17 and 128. Once established the point was routinely reiterated by the commentators of the fourteenth and fifteenth centuries. See, for example, Bartolus de Sassoferrato, *Opera Omnia*, 5 vols (Lyons, 1523), II, pt 1, f. 78 (ad D.41.2.1.1), II, pt 2, f. 236 (ad D.49.15.24), and III, pt 1, f. 95v (ad D.28.1.13), Baldus de Ubaldis, *Commentaria super Codicem*, 4 vols (Venice, 1500), IV, f. 9 (ad C.7.14.4), and *Tractatus Universi Iuris*, 18 vols (Lyons, 1549), XII, ff. 159 (Paris de Puteo) and 169v (Ioannes Lupus).

[17] *Digest*, 49.15.20.1.

[18] *Digestum novum*, col. 1678 (gl. 'Si quid bello' ad D.49.15.28); Bartolus, *Opera Omnia*, II, pt 1, f. 76v (ad D.41.1.5.7), and II, pt 2, ff. 236v–237 (ad D.49.15.26 and 49.15.28); Baldus, *Commentaria super Codicem*, IV, f. 158v (ad C.8.53.36); *Repetitiones*,

plundered from enemies with things subject to confiscation was reinforced by several other texts, which seemed to suggest that anything captured in wartime by soldiers or sailors serving in the Roman army or navy became public property, from which commanders were permitted to distribute a certain amount of booty (*spolia*) by way of reward and encouragement.[19] That this was indeed the case is now taken to be confirmed by literary and historical sources, which show that the *res hostiles* acquired by *occupatio* must have been the belongings of foreigners living in Roman territory when war broke out with their nations, at which point recognition of their rights of ownership was withdrawn.[20] However, this was not the conclusion drawn by the medieval doctors, who rarely looked at literary and historical sources, and who had more interest in relating the legal sources they studied to contemporary practice than in recovering an accurate understanding of the operation of the law in antiquity. They instead adhered to their initial conclusion that movable things captured in a public war were acquired through occupation by their takers, but added the qualification that the owners were obliged to assign (*assignare*) them to their commanders for redistribution among all the combatants according to merit.[21] Those who obtained things through occupation, an original mode of acquiring property, might therefore be required to transfer ownership to more worthy recipients, who would receive title by a derivative mode of acquisition.

The teaching of the law schools was naturally more elaborate than any brief outline is able to suggest. There was also discussion of topics like the treatment of prisoners, there was a certain amount of disagreement, and the canon lawyers studied biblical and patristic sources as well as the texts on Roman law.[22] Nevertheless, it is not misleading to remark both that the doctors of the civil and canon laws tended to concentrate their analysis on basic questions of general importance, and that in doing so they mostly came to a consensus. That title could be acquired by seizing things from enemies, subject to any requirement imposed by commanders to transfer them to

---

Disputationes necnon Tractatus Diversorum Doctorum (Venice, 1472), f. 100v (Angelus de Ubaldis); *Tractatus Universi Iuris*, XII, f. 167 (Martinus Garatus Laudensis). Examples could easily be multiplied.

[19] *Digest*, 48.13.15, 49.14.31 and 49.15.28, and *Code*, 8.53.36.

[20] F. de Zulueta, *The Institutes of Gaius*, Part II: *Commentary* (Oxford, 1953), p. 75; W.W. Buckland, *A Text-Book of Roman Law, from Augustus to Justinian* (Cambridge. 1963), p. 208; I. Shatzman, 'The Roman General's Authority over Booty', *Zeitschrift für Alte Geschichte*, 21 (1972), pp. 177–205.

[21] Bartolus, *Opera Omnia*, II, pt 2, ff. 236v–237 (ad D.49.15.26 and 49.15.28); Baldus, *Commentaria super Codicem*, IV, f. 158v (ad C.8.53.36); Bartolomeus de Saliceto, *In Codicis Libros Commentaria*, 4 vols (Lyons, 1549), IV, f. 150 (ad C.8.50.12); *Tractatus Universi Iuris*, XII, ff. 167 (Garatus), 169v (Lupus) and 192 (Franciscus Arias). Examples could again be multiplied with ease.

[22] The intention is to provide a fuller account of the medieval theory of prize law elsewhere.

others, was universally accepted.[23] The doctors confirmed the legitimacy of the practice and identified the questions to be addressed in particular cases as being whether the things seized had belonged to enemies, whether the things had been taken effectively, and whether any redistribution of the things was required. A little guidance was provided on how these questions might be addressed, but in detail their determination was left to be worked out locally. Conversely, local sources tended to deal with matters of detail while barely touching on more fundamental issues. It was typical, for instance, for the articles of war pronounced at the beginning of conflicts to regulate the retention and redistribution of plunder and prisoners, but it was simply taken for granted in these documents that it would be licit for combatants to seize plunder and prisoners in the first place.[24] It would no doubt have been possible for most disputes to be determined on the basis of local sources, and without explicit reference to the teaching of the law schools, but the local sources were developed, interpreted and applied on the assumption that the teaching of the law schools was sound. It is this point that appears to have been neglected in the literature on the development of prize law in England.

Prize acquisition through adjudication

In the opening chapter of his *History of the English Prize Court*, E.S. Roscoe claimed that by the later fifteenth century 'condemnation by a competent court was necessary in order to give a captor a valid title to a ship or goods seized by him'.[25] In doing so he appears to have been influenced by a passing comment made in R.G. Marsden's pioneering study of 'Early Prize Jurisdiction and Prize Law in England', where it was suggested that a treaty entered into with Flanders in 1426 contained 'perhaps the earliest mention of condemnation as a preliminary to captors acquiring the property in prizes'.[26] Roscoe

---

[23] In the early fifteenth century, Bartolomeus de Bosco felt able to remark in his *Consilia* (Savona, 1620), p. 32, that 'istud est notorium apud omnes Christianos et etiam infideles ubique'. Cf. art. 275/6 of the *Consolato del Mare* (*Consulate of the Sea and Related Documents*, transl. S.S. Jados (Alabama, 1975), p. 150).

[24] Examples are given in M.H. Keen, 'Richard II's Ordinances of War of 1385', in *Rulers and Ruled in Late Medieval England: Essays Presented to Gerald Harriss*, ed. R.E. Archer and S. Walker (London, 1995), pp. 33–48, and A. Curry, 'The Military Ordinances of Henry V: Texts and Contexts', in *War, Government and Aristocracy in the British Isles, c. 1150–1500: Essays in Honour of Michael Prestwich*, ed. C. Given-Wilson, A. Kettle and L. Scales (Woodbridge, 2008), pp. 214–49, and 'Disciplinary Ordinances for English and Franco-Scottish Armies in 1385: An International Code?', *Jnl of Medieval History*, 37 (2011), pp. 269–94.

[25] E.S. Roscoe, *A History of the English Prize Court* (London, 1924), p. 8.

[26] R.G. Marsden, 'Early Prize Jurisdiction and Prize Law in England', *Eng. Hist. Rev.*, 24 (1909), pp. 675–97 (a survey carried forward in later issues of the same journal), at 682.

explained further that it became necessary for 'adjudication' to be sought from a court 'in order to divest the owner of a ship or goods of his property and to give a captor a valid title to his prize'.[27] Although he did not say so, it is clear that Roscoe was not using the term 'adjudication' here in the broad sense of any judicial ruling, but in the specific sense of a ruling that conferred new rights on litigants. Instead of a court being asked to identify and uphold the rights that claimants already enjoyed, as would normally be expected, it was asked to alter their legal position by conferring new rights upon them. In its specific sense, adjudication was another concept derived from Roman law, where it had been developed in relation to a small class of actions used to dissolve common ownership or to settle boundary disputes.[28] In Roman law *adiudicatio* was another original mode of acquisition of property, distinct from *occupatio*. It was never mentioned in any of the texts concerned with the acquisition of property *ex hostibus*, nor was it connected with these texts by the medieval doctors. The doctors might have supposed that the occupation of enemy property gave rise to common ownership, which then needed to be dissolved by adjudication, but they do not appear to have done so.[29] In any case, what Roscoe had in mind was clearly that the enemies from whom ships and goods were captured would retain title until it was conferred by a court order on the captors, who would only then acquire any sort of ownership. His theory of prize acquisition thus revolves around a Roman law concept and yet is consistent neither with that law nor with the learned theory fashioned from it.

Particular weight was attached by Roscoe as well as Marsden to the 1426 treaty with Flanders, which provided that 'biens, prins sur le mer', should not be divided up or passed on until 'le conseil du roy, ou le chanceller d'Engleterre, l'admirall d'Engleterre, ou son depute general pur le temps esteant, soient certifiez du dit prinse, et duement enformez (a savoier) si les biens ainsi prins seront des amis ou des enemis'.[30] Further support was

---

[27] Roscoe, *History of the English Prize Court*, p. 11.

[28] H.J. Roby, *Roman Private Law in the Times of Cicero and of the Antonines*, 2 vols (Cambridge, 1902), I, p. 422, and II, p. 355; F. Schulz, *Classical Roman Law* (Oxford, 1961), pp. 47–8; H.F. Jolowicz, *Historical Introduction to the Study of Roman Law* (Cambridge, 1972), pp. 156 and 205.

[29] Bartolus, *Opera Omnia*, II, pt 1, ff. 76v–77r (ad D.41.1.5.7), did say that anything captured from an enemy 'does not become ours but is placed in common ownership and is assigned to the commander', which if intended literally would have implied that some form of adjudication by the commander was needed. This was not made clear, however, nor did Bartolus adhere to this position elsewhere, and nor was it assumed by anyone else. The passage from Saliceto, *In Codicis Libros Commentaria*, IV, f. 150 (ad C.8.50.12), quoted by Keen, *Laws of War in the Late Middle Ages*, p. 144, explained the assignation and redistribution requirement in terms of *commodum et periculum commune*, but not common ownership, and no other commentator has been found to come closer to developing Bartolus' remark.

[30] Rymer, *Foedera*, X, pp. 367–8, also outlined in *Documents Relating to Law and Custom*

claimed from other sources: an order found in the *Black Book of the Admiralty* requiring those who captured vessels 'amener devant ladmiral illecques de prendre et receyvoir ce que la loy de mer veult et demande'; an agreement made with certain mariners in 1442 that any goods in captured ships would not be 'disperbled ne divided into the tyme that it be duly knowen wheder it be enemyes goodes or freendes goodes'; and a treaty entered into with France in 1498 in which it was provided that captured ships and goods would not be distributed until the captors sought a ruling (*decretum et permissio*) from the 'admiraldum, viceadmiraldum seu eorum officiarios illius portus a quo egressi sunt'.[31] Reference might also have been made to a statute passed in 1414, apparently under the influence of a similar ordinance enacted in France in 1373, which provided for the appointment of a 'conservator' in each port and required mariners to return to their home port with any ships and goods captured and 'make full Information to the said Conservator, before that they thereof make Discharge or Sale'.[32] The only other support actually cited by Roscoe or Marsden was an undertaking given in 1433 that those seeking 'restitution' of goods found on board Scottish or Breton vessels would be required to provide 'sufficeant suerte devaunt l'admirall pur le temps esteant, a le value de lour biens et chatelx'.[33]

The evidence adduced in support of the adjudication theory of prize acquisition shows beyond doubt that judicial supervision of the activity was considered desirable, and also that the Admiral's court came eventually to be regarded as the appropriate forum for the provision of the desired supervision. But does it follow that prize acquisition was understood to turn on a judicial act of adjudication in the technical sense outlined above?

---

of the Sea, ed. R.G. Marsden, 2 vols (Navy Records Soc., xlix–l, 1915–16), I, p. 117, and *Cal. Close R., 1422–9*, pp. 263–4. The longer passage quoted may be translated as follows: 'the king's council, or the chancellor of England, the admiral of England, or his deputy general for the time being, are given notice of the said seizure and duly informed (to be precise) whether the goods thus seized pertain to friends or to enemies'.

[31] Twiss, *Black Book of the Admiralty*, I, pp. 30–1; Given-Wilson, *PROME*, XI: *Henry VI, 1432–1445*, ed. A. Curry, pp. 373–5, no. 30 (also in Marsden, *Law and Custom of the Sea*, I, pp. 130–2); Rymer, *Foedera*, XII, pp. 690–4. The first passage quoted was rendered into English as 'hee ought to bring the same before the admirall there to take and receive what the law and custome of the sea requires'. The third may be translated as 'the admiral, viceadmiral or their officers, of the port from which they departed'.

[32] *Statutes of the Realm*, II, p. 180 (also in Twiss, *Black Book of the Admiralty*, I, pp. 417–18). For the French ordinance see Antoine Fontanon, *Les edicts et ordonnances des roys de France*, 2 vols (Paris, 1584), II, pp. 845–8 (also in *Black Book of the Admiralty*, I, pp. 430–42). See too *Cal. Close R., 1413–19*, p. 19.

[33] Given-Wilson, *PROME*, XI: *Henry VI*, ed. Curry, p. 132, no. 46. This passage may be translated as 'a sufficient guarantee before the admiral for the time being, as to the value of their goods and chattels'.

The references in the earliest evidence to 'certification' and 'information' are indicative of a process that seems less judicial than administrative, and although by the end of the fifteenth century more formal rulings or decrees seem to have been envisaged, there is no compelling reason to believe that these were expected to take the form of acts of adjudication. The concern was with the division or distribution of ships and goods before it was established that they had been captured from enemies and that the captors were entitled to retain them without transferring shares to others. What was required was identification of the rights the captors had acquired, which might best have been provided by an exercise in adjudication in the broad and normal sense, but need not have involved an exercise in adjudication in the narrow and exceptional sense.

As a matter of fact, no examples of acts of adjudication in prize cases have been found from an earlier time than the late sixteenth century, when they came to be mandatory, for reasons that will have to be discussed elsewhere.[34] One explanation for the absence of earlier examples could be that records of the Admiral's court do not happen to have been preserved until a later period, as seems indeed to be the case; yet even in the continuous records that do survive from the 1520s onwards, acts of adjudication do not begin to appear until the 1590s.[35] Moreover, it is not without significance that when proceedings before the Admiral's court in earlier centuries are mentioned in other records, they tend to be described as claims for restitution, of the type envisaged in the 1433 undertaking. In the first known reference to an action before the court, the king of Portugal was informed in 1357 that an action for restitution of goods seized from his subjects had been correctly decided by 'admirallus noster (coram quo bona huiusmodi fuerant ab occupatoribus ipsorum iudicialiter repetita)'.[36] Since the goods had been found to belong to the king of England's enemies, the Admiral had rightly permitted the *occupatores* summoned to retain them, and he had done so simply by dismissing the action raised by the Portuguese claimants. There is no suggestion in the king of England's letter, or in any other source that has so far come to light, that mariners who captured goods ever petitioned the Admiral's court for a decree conferring title upon them.[37] They defended themselves in actions

---

[34] Marsden admitted as much, in 'Early Prize Jurisdiction and Prize Law in England', p. 681.

[35] A.A. Ruddock, 'The Earliest Records of the High Court of Admiralty', *Bull. Institute of Historical Research*, 22 (1949), pp. 139–51.

[36] Rymer, *Foedera*, III, pt 1, p. 354 (also in Marsden, *Law and Custom of the Sea*, I, pp. 81–4, where the translation is provided, 'our admiral, before whom the claim for restitution of the goods was in legal form made').

[37] For evidence from another court see *Select Cases in Chancery, A.D. 1364 to 1471*, ed. W.P. Baildon (Selden Soc., x, 1896), pp. 90–1, and *A Calendar of Early Chancery Proceedings Relating to West Country Shipping, 1388–1493*, ed. D.M. Gardiner (Devon & Cornwall Record Soc., new ser., 21, 1976), pp. 7, 15–16 and 67.

for restitution by arguing that they had made legitimate acquisitions from enemies in wartime, but even then they felt no apparent need to request acts of adjudication in their favour, probably because – as the language used in the earliest records touching on prize litigation suggests – they were understood to have become owners already 'occasione captionis'.[38] If increasing pressure was placed on mariners in the fifteenth century to obtain court orders before dividing and distributing their prizes, the lack of evidence that they did so is easier to understand if it is supposed that obtaining court orders was still not a condition of prize acquisition, and that the orders envisaged would have served merely to confirm that title had already been acquired.

Prize acquisition through royal grant

Roscoe's own explanation for the lack of evidence of adjudication was that the procedure was often found superfluous, since 'sometimes the king gave to shipowners before they set sail the right to their prizes or to a proportion of them'.[39] Roscoe shared with Marsden and others the belief that since the thirteenth century, English mariners had understood that 'they could only enjoy their prizes by grant from the Crown', so that acts of adjudication would only have been a particularly solemn way in which title could be acquired from the king or those acting under his authority.[40] 'According to English constitutional doctrine', as a later author has expressed the point, 'all prize is a *droit* of the crown and can become the property of the captors only by a royal grant'.[41] That this belief has entered the mainstream of historical opinion is apparent from the inclusion of the following statement in the *Oxford Companion to Ships and the Sea*: 'In its strict and original legal definition, prize in Britain is entirely a right of the Crown, and no man may share in prize except through the gift of the Crown'.[42] If use of the term 'Britain' here were taken to reveal a concern with the 'original' position in 1707, the statement would be accurate enough, but if, as seems likely, the intention

[38] Johnson, 'Early Admiralty Case', pp. 2–5; Marsden, *Law and Custom of the Sea*, I, pp. 12–18, 42–4, 94–6, 102–4 and 124–6; *Cal. Pat. R., 1385–9*, pp. 323, 342; *Cal. Close R., 1385–9*, p. 92, and *1409–13*, p. 376.

[39] Roscoe, *History of the English Prize Court*, pp. 8–9.

[40] Marsden, 'Early Prize Jurisdiction and Prize Law in England', p. 675, influenced by N.H. Nicolas, *A History of the Royal Navy*, 2 vols (London, 1847), I, p. 140, and in turn influencing W.S. Holdsworth, *A History of English Law*, 16 vols (London, 1922–66), I, p. 562, B.E.R. Fermoy, 'A Maritime Indenture of 1212', *Eng. Hist. Rev.*, 41 (1926), pp. 556–9, at 556–7, and other sources, some of which are noted immediately below or in the next section of this chapter.

[41] A doctrine again said to date from the thirteenth century, in G. Schwarzenberger, 'International Law in Early English Practice', *British Yearbook of International Law*, 25 (1948), pp. 52–90, at 81.

[42] *The Oxford Companion to Ships and the Sea*, ed. P. Kemp (Oxford, 1976), p. 670.

was to regard Britain as an enlargement and continuation of England, the question would arise whether it is any less dubious to believe that before the late sixteenth century, prize acquisition was dependent on royal grant than it is to believe that it depended on acts of adjudication.[43] The royal grant theory of prize acquisition is itself independent of the adjudication theory, for the belief is that long before adjudication became a condition of acquisition, a royal grant was already considered necessary for any property in captured ships or goods to be acquired by the captors. On this theory, the position in medieval England would have been broadly similar to the position in ancient Rome, but it would not have been consistent with the theory derived from the Roman law texts by the civil and canon lawyers in the medieval universities.

The evidence cited in support of the royal grant theory is quite extensive, but falls into three main types, of which it may suffice to consider representative examples. To begin with, reference is made to half a dozen letters describing gifts (*dedimus*) of ships or goods captured (*capta*) from the king's enemies to various people he wished to reward for services rendered or to recompense for costs incurred.[44] No indication is provided in the letters cited or in any others so far found that the recipients were being rewarded for their part in the capture of the things granted, nor is it made clear how the things came to belong to the king.[45] Some of the letters actually describe the things as forming part of the king's share of captured ships or goods, which tends to suggest that he had not become the owner of everything captured.[46] The second type of evidence cited sometimes gives the same impression. A considerable amount of evidence that has been or could have been cited shows that the distribution of captured ships and goods among shipowners, masters, mariners and others, often including the king himself or his Admiral, was subject to regulation by the king or those acting under his authority.[47] Reference has often been made, for example, to a set of regulations recorded in the *Black Book of the Admiralty* in which it is stipulated *inter alia* that if goods are captured at sea by ships in the king's service, 'then the king shall have and

---

[43] Cf. D.M. Walker, *The Oxford Companion to Law* (Oxford, 1980), p. 1000, written by a Scots lawyer who did confuse Britain with England.

[44] *Rotuli de Liberate ac de Misis et Praestitis Regnante Iohanne*, ed. T.D. Hardy (London, 1844), p. 227; *Rotuli Litterarum Clausarum in Turri Londinensi Asservati*, ed. T.D. Hardy, 2 vols (London, 1833–44), I, pp. 117–18 and 120; *Cal. Pat. R., 1385–9*, pp. 216, 253. One other letter is being left aside for discussion in the next section.

[45] See too *Cal. Pat. R., 1242–7*, p. 73, *1337–9*, pp. 88 and 228, and *1385–9*, pp. 302, 308, 338 and 364.

[46] The significance of some of these letters is closely examined in T.K. Moore, 'The Cost-Benefit Analysis of a Fourteenth-Century Naval Campaign: Margate/ Cadzand, 1387', in *Roles of the Sea in Medieval England*, ed. R. Gorski (Woodbridge, 2012), pp. 103–24.

[47] Marsden, *Law and Custom of the Sea*, I, pp. 36–8 (also summarised in *Cal. Pat. R., 1292–1301*, p. 130); Twiss, *Black Book of the Admiralty*, I, pp. 20–3, 134–5, 144–7, 15–1, 172–3 and 356–7; *Cal. Close R., 1323–7*, pp. 412–13.

take the fourth part of all manner of the said goods, and the owners of the shipps another fourth part, and the other halfe of the said goods shall belong to those whoe took them, which halfe ought to be shared equally between them'.[48] It is notable that the king is to 'have and take' (in the French version of the text, 'aura et prendra') a quarter share, not 'retain and keep' or anything similar. Another document informed the mariners of the Cinque Ports in 1217 that the king had appointed representatives to ensure that those 'qui inimicos nostros nuper in mari spoliaverunt, habeant inde quod habere debent, et ad arestandum de lucro illo id quod ad nos de iure spectat habendum'.[49] Again, the implication would appear to be that the king was entitled to no more than a share in the goods taken, and although the expression 'quod habere debent' fails to make clear the nature of the mariners' rights, a letter from 1295 goes further. It records the settlement of a dispute between the masters and sailors of ships from Bayonne 'super participacionem rerum et bonorum que super inimicos nostros sibi adquicierant supra mare inter eos'.[50] Here there would seem to be more than a mere implication that the masters and sailors had acquired the things and goods 'for themselves'. That the king was understood to be responsible for, and to have the power to regulate, the distribution of prizes must be beyond doubt, but it does not follow that those entitled to shares received title from the king.

The third type of evidence cited consists of licences authorising mariners to arm ships and put to sea against the king's enemies, some of which specified the proportions they were to be allowed of any prizes captured.[51] For example, in the earliest licence cited the crews of galleys in the king's service in 1205 were declared to have been granted (*concessimus*), along with payment for their labours, 'medietatem lucri sui quod facient super inimicos nostros'.[52] This was the type of evidence that Roscoe had in mind when he

---

[48] Twiss, *Black Book of the Admiralty*, I, pp. 20–1. Cf. *Cal. Close R., 1323–7*, pp. 412–13, where it is stated that a quarter of the goods 'thus acquired by the said masters and mariners on the sea' should be 'converted to the king's use'.

[49] Marsden, *Law and Custom of the Sea*, I, pp. 5–6, with the translation: 'who have lately spoiled our enemies at sea, have what they ought to have, and to arrest so much of the spoil as ought of right to belong to us'.

[50] *Ibid.*, I, pp. 36–8, with the translation: 'touching the sharing amongst them of the things and goods that they have captured at sea from our enemies'. Reading 'sibi adquicierant' as 'they have captured' is, to say the least, rather relaxed. The summary in *Cal. Pat. R., 1292–1301*, p. 130, instead uses the phrase 'acquired by them'.

[51] *Rotuli Litterarum Patentium in Turri Londinensi Asservati*, ed. T.D. Hardy (London, 1835), p. 51; *Cal. Pat. R., 1232–47*, pp. 328 and 362, and *1385–9*, pp. 339 and 342; Rymer, *Foedera*, I, pt 1, p. 248, and II, pt 1, p. 640; *Fifth Report of the Royal Commission on Historical Manuscripts* (London, 1876), appx, p. 501. In addition to the licences cited see *Cal. Close R., 1237–42*, p. 467, and Marsden, *Law and Custom of the Sea*, I, pp. 8–10, 35–6, 109–10 and 114–15.

[52] *Rotuli Litterarum Patentium*, p. 51 (also in Marsden, *Law and Custom of the Sea*, I, pp.

sought to explain the absence from the fifteenth-century records of acts of adjudication, and licences like the one granted in 1205 certainly do explain why mariners would have felt little need to obtain judicial approval of their seizures. Yet the language used in these licences does not seem especially supportive of either the adjudication theory or the royal grant theory of prize acquisition. In the licence mentioned the crews were granted or allowed a half not simply of the gains made but of 'their' gains (*lucri sui*). The expression is not particularly precise, but a licence issued in 1294 allowed crews from Oléron who were not in the king's service 'omnia bona que sibi per se adquirere poterunt', which seems rather to emphasise the point that the crews would acquire goods for themselves through their own efforts.[53] Any suspicion that they might have been expected to acquire possession rather than ownership of the goods is laid to rest by the terms of a general licence issued in 1326 to the people of Bayonne, who were granted everything that 'conquirere et occupare possetis'.[54] While the terminology of the learned laws was not used with any great frequency or consistency in these documents, its appearance here may be taken to confirm that mariners were understood to acquire title for themselves in the ships or goods they captured by way of occupation, subject to an obligation to transfer shares to others as required by their superiors. The king was able to regulate the distribution of prizes, which meant that he could both claim shares for himself and thus make gifts to others, and also encourage mariners to put to sea against his enemies by granting them particular shares. All this was consistent with the theory of the law schools, as was the language used in all the documents considered so far, none of which provides clear support for the royal grant theory, and not all of which seem consistent in their terms with that theory. However, there is another document, cited by one author, which does seem more consistent with the royal grant theory. It has so far been neglected and needs now to be considered carefully.

Droits of the Crown or admiralty

The document in question is a letter sent in 1337 to the bailiffs of Great Yarmouth, instructing them to have a ship delivered to one of its captors, to

---

1–2, where the translation is offered, 'one half of the gains which they may make in captures from our enemies', with 'sui' ignored).

[53] Marsden, *Law and Custom of the Sea*, I, pp. 35–6, where the typically relaxed translation is offered: 'all goods that they may be able to capture'.

[54] Rymer, *Foedera*, II, pt 1, p. 640. Basically, in civilian theory 'possession' meant actually having something, whether or not the possessor was entitled to have it, whereas 'ownership' meant being entitled to something, whether or not the owner actually had it.

whom it had been given (*dedimus*) as a reward by the king.[55] Not only is a gift specifically made here to a captor, but the document also specifies that it belongs to the king 'racione forisfacture inimicorum nostrorum'. Shortly afterwards the king laid claim to the goods taken in the ship as well, which prompted a reply from the mariners that they were entitled to the goods 'secundum legem maritimam hactenus usitatem et approbatam'.[56] The reply brings to mind a more general complaint made in 1406 by certain 'marchauntz, mariners et possessours' that things taken from enemies in war ought to be distributed 'en manere accustumez' by the Admiral and his deputies, 'ascune prerogative ou privilege nostre dit seignour le roy, sez admiralx ou ascuns autres nientcontresteantz'.[57] It may be, therefore, that prerogative rights of the king or his Admiral were sometimes asserted in conflict with the customary rights of mariners under *lex maritima*. If so, awareness of this conflict would place limits on the extent to which the *lex maritima* regime may be understood to have operated but would not affect any understanding of the regime itself. Yet it may instead be that mariners who had become familiar with the operation of the *lex maritima* regime in other countries were asserting rights under it in conflict with the approach traditionally taken under the common law. The use of the language of forfeiture or confiscation in 1337 was unusual but not unique. In 1296 and 1297, for instance, a whole series of gifts was made of ships that were declared to have been acquired by the Crown through forfeiture from enemies.[58] At one point the king asked the bailiffs of Ravenser to investigate an objection that one of these ships had been taken before war had commenced with its owners' country, acknowledging that if so it would have to be returned since 'navis illa dici non potest nobis forisfacta'.[59] In this case at least the understanding clearly was that if a state of war had existed the ship would have been acquired by the king through forfeiture, and would thus have been available to be given to a deserving subject, as it had been.[60]

---

[55] Marsden, *Law and Custom of the Sea*, I, pp. 66–7 (also summarised in *Cal. Close R., 1337–9*, p. 172, and cited by Schwarzenberger, 'International Law in Early English Practice', p. 81). Perhaps Marsden omitted to cite the document in his 'Early Prize Jurisdiction and Prize Law in England' because he only discovered it between 1909 (when his article appeared) and 1915 (when his *Law and Custom of the Sea* began to appear). Alternatively, he may have appreciated that the document does not really support the royal grant theory, as is about to be argued here.

[56] Marsden, *Law and Custom of the Sea*, I, pp. 69–74.

[57] Given-Wilson, *PROME*, VIII: *Henry IV, 1399–1413*, ed. C. Given-Wilson, p. 333, no. 22. This passage may be translated as 'any prerogative or privilege of our said lord the king, his admirals or any others notwithstanding'.

[58] *Cal. Close R., 1288–96*, pp. 497–8, and *1296–1302*, pp. 11, 26, 31, 34 and 42.

[59] Marsden, *Law and Custom of the Sea*, I, pp. 44–5.

[60] On the difference between acquisition by forfeiture and occupation see A. Bossuat, 'La règlement des confiscations sous le règne de Charles VII', *Comptes-Rendus des Séances de l'Académie des Inscriptions et Belles-Lettres*, 91 (1947), pp. 6–16.

One question in need of consideration is therefore how far the prerogative rights of the Crown to enemy property were taken to extend.

The answer generally provided by historians of English law is that the Crown enjoyed prerogative rights or 'droits' in all 'great fish (such as whales or porpoises), deodands, wreck of the sea, flotsam, jetsam and lagan, ships or goods of the enemy found in English ports or captured by uncommissioned vessels, and goods taken or retaken from pirates'.[61] Statements that enemy ships or goods seized in English ports or by uncommissioned vessels are droits of the Crown or admiralty can also be found in works dealing with the legal position today.[62] In these works reliance is placed on court decisions delivered at the end of the First World War, which in turn placed reliance on decisions delivered by Sir William Scott, later Lord Stowell, during the Napoleonic Wars.[63] For his part, Stowell placed reliance on documents associated with the admiralty practice of Sir Leoline Jenkins in the 1660s, by which time it had become necessary for privateers to obtain commissions before they could legitimately acquire enemy ships or goods.[64] But is there any evidence that before this time enemy ships or goods taken by uncommissioned vessels belonged to the Crown, or to the Admiral as representative of the Crown? If enemy ships or goods taken by uncommissioned vessels were treated like enemy ships or goods taken in English ports, what exactly was the relationship?

An early modern source that makes a connection between these types of seizure is Sir Matthew Hale's treatise on the royal prerogative, written after the restoration of the monarchy in 1660. Hale first observed that 'goods of enemies within the kingdom not taken by force do belong to the king as confiscate', noting in support that 'it was one of the articles of eyre, *de catallis inimicorum domini regis retentis, et quis illa habeat*'.[65] He then added that 'the ancient custom of the realm' had been to allow those who captured

---

[61] Holdsworth, *History of English Law*, I, pp. 559–60; Mears, 'History of the Admiralty Jurisdiction', pp. 318–19; F.R. Sanborn, *Origins of the Early English Maritime and Commercial Law* (New York, 1930), p. 295. For a more circumspect and reliable definition of 'droits' in this period see J.H. Baker, *The Oxford History of the Laws of England*, vol. VI: *1483–1558* (Oxford, 2003), pp. 211–12.

[62] *Halsbury's Laws of England*, ed. Lord Mackay, 103 vols (London, 1990–2010), vol. XXXVI(2), pp. 441–2, and vol. 93, p. 142; Viscount Tiverton, *The Principles and Practice of Prize Law* (London, 1914), p. 2; C.J. Colombos, *The International Law of the Sea* (London, 1967), p. 814.

[63] *The Rebeckah* (1799) 1 Ch. Rob. 227; *The Melomane* (1803) 5 Ch. Rob. 41; *The Maria Francoise* (1806) 6 Ch. Rob. 182; *The Roumanian* [1916] 1 AC 124; *The Abonema* [1919] P 41; *The Feldmarschall* [1920] P 289; *The Anichab* [1921] P 213 and [1922] 1 AC 235.

[64] How this came about will also have to be discussed elsewhere. For Stowell's role see H.J. Bourguignon, *Sir William Scott, Lord Stowell, Judge of the High Court of Admiralty, 1798–1828* (Cambridge, 1987), pp. 115–242.

[65] *Sir Matthew Hale's The Prerogatives of the King*, ed. D.E.C. Yale (Selden Soc., xcii, 1976), p. 131.

ships or goods from enemies to keep a share for themselves, citing some of the evidence considered earlier of the royal regulation of the distribution of prizes. It has been argued already that evidence of this type does not justify the belief that captors acquired title to prizes by gift from the Crown. The other evidence cited in Hale's treatise is the article of eyre 'de catallis Francorum, vel Flandrensium, vel aliorum inimicorum domini regis retentis, qui illa habeat', which had first been introduced in 1208.[66] This article, however, related to enemy property that was seized (*arestata* is the word used in another version of the article) in England, and had no bearing on captures made at sea or overseas.[67] No other article seems to have been concerned with prizes taken by force at sea, nor was there any mention of the acquisition of prizes in the pseudo-statute *De Prerogativa Regis*, nor does prize acquisition appear to have been a topic dealt with in treatments of the royal prerogative before the seventeenth century.[68] Ships and goods taken by uncommissioned vessels appear to have been assimilated to ships and goods taken in English ports only after the basis of prize acquisition changed at the close of the sixteenth century.[69]

Like the adjudication of prizes to their captors, then, the forfeiture of prizes to the Crown was a feature of the later law that has been read back into the medieval evidence. It remains the case, however, that references to forfeiture appear in medieval sources, and these still need to be explained. In fact,

---

[66] *Statutes of the Realm*, I, pp. 233–4; *Rotuli Litterarum Clausarum*, II, p. 214; *Munimenta Gildhallae Londoniensis*, ed. H.T. Riley, 3 vols in 4 (Rolls Ser., 12, 1859–62), I, p. 118. There was another article, 'De catallis extraneorum captis de potestate regis Franciae existencium dum rex fuerit in Vasconia: quo devenerunt, et qui habent ea' (*Annales Monastici*, ed. H.R. Luard, 5 vols (Rolls Ser., 36, 1864–9), I, p. 332, *The Eyre of Kent, 6 & 7 Edward II, A.D. 1313–1314*, ed. F.W. Maitland, L.W.V. Harcourt and W.C. Bolland (Selden Soc., xxiv, xxvii and xxix, 1910–13), I, p. 32, and *The Eyre of Northamptonshire, 3–4 Edward III, A.D. 1329–1330*, ed. D.W. Sutherland, 2 vols (Selden Soc., xcvii–xcviii, 1983), II, p. 778), which was combined with the one which Hale seems to have had in mind in *Historia et Cartularium Monasterii Sancti Petri Gloucestriae*, ed. W.H. Hart, 3 vols (Rolls Ser., 33, 1863–7), II, p. 278.

[67] The origin of the article is discussed in H.M. Cam, *Studies in the Hundred Rolls: Some Aspects of Thirteenth-Century Administration* (Oxford, 1921), pp. 19–20 and 93, and the article 'De catallis extraneorum' is discussed in *Crown Pleas of the Wiltshire Eyre, 1249*, ed. C.A.F. Meekings (Wilts. Archaeological & Natural History Soc., Records Branch, xvi, 1961), p. 32.

[68] *Statutes of the Realm*, I, pp. 226–7; *John Spelman's Reading on Quo Warranto*, ed. J.H. Baker (Selden Soc., cxiii, 1997), pp. 26–42; *Prerogativa Regis: Tertia Lectura Roberti Constable de Lincolnis Inne, Anno 11 H. 7*, ed. S.E. Thorne (New Haven, Conn., 1949); Sir William Staunford, *An Exposicion of the King's Prerogative, Collected out of the Great Abridgement of Justice Fitzherbert* (London, 1567).

[69] At that time an inquest 'De officio admiralitatis quinque portuum' listed a large number of matters in which the Admiral had acquired an interest, including payment of his shares in prizes, but there was no instruction to discover which ships and goods were forfeit (British Library, Add. MS 34150, ff. 153–162).

part of the explanation is provided by the article of eyre cited by Hale, for it happens that all the ships distributed by royal gift in 1296 and 1297 had been arrested after being forced into ports in the north-east by severe weather.[70] As property of the king's enemies seized in England, it is now apparent, they were forfeit to the Crown under the common law and were not covered by the maritime law of prize.[71] The same reasoning does not apply to the ship given to one of its captors in 1337, however, which was said to have been taken by force while sailing between Zeeland and Scotland. According to several chroniclers, it was a 'navis Scottorum', and was richly laden, as official records confirm.[72] The seizure attracted and has continued to attract attention because it was a significant event in the preliminaries to the Hundred Years War.[73] The ship was carrying supporters of the exiled David II back from the court set up for him in Normandy so that they could continue their struggle against Edward Balliol with aid from the king of France. But war had not yet broken out with France, and the king of England did not regard David II as a sovereign prince.[74] With aid from the English king, Edward Balliol had managed to be crowned at Scone in 1334, and he had promptly paid homage for his kingdom to the English king. From Edward III's perspective, the Scots whose ship was captured were not the subjects of a fellow sovereign against whom a war was being waged but were 'rebels' against the authority he exercised through his vassal.[75] From the perspective of any doctor of law, the

---

[70] Marsden, *Law and Custom of the Sea*, I, pp. 21–31.

[71] The position in medieval England, in other words, was the reverse of the position in ancient Rome, for enemy property taken at home would be confiscated, whereas enemy property taken abroad could be privately acquired. The irony is of course that the latter point rested on a misreading of Roman law by the civilians and canonists.

[72] *Chronicon de Lanercost*, ed. J. Stevenson (Edinburgh, 1839), p. 291 (also *The Chronicle of Lanercost*, transl. H. Maxwell (Glasgow, 1913), p. 305); *Thomae Walsingham, quondam Monachi Sancti Albani, Historia Anglicana*, ed. H.T. Riley, 2 vols (Rolls Ser., 28(1), 1863–4), I, p. 198; *Chronicon Henrici Knighton*, ed. J.R. Lumby, 2 vols (Rolls Ser., 92, 1889–95), II, p. 2 (also *Knighton's Chronicle*, ed. and transl. G.H. Martin, Oxford Medieval Texts (Oxford, 1995), p. 5); *Chronicon Domini Walteri de Hemingburgh*, ed. H.C. Hamilton, 2 vols (English Historical Soc., 1848–9), II, p. 314; *Cal. Close R., 1337–9*, pp. 331–2; *Cal. Pat. R., 1334–8*, pp. 513, 579.

[73] H.S. Lucas, *The Low Countries and the Hundred Years War, 1326–47* (Ann Arbor, Mich., 1929), p. 235; A. Saul, 'Great Yarmouth and the Hundred Years War in the Fourteenth Century', *Bull., Institute of Historical Research,* 52 (1979), pp. 105–15, at 108; J. Sumption, *The Hundred Years War: Trial by Battle* (London, 1990), p. 195; M.A. Penman, *David II, 1329–71* (Edinburgh, 2004), pp. 65–6; G. Cushway, *Edward III and the War at Sea: The English Navy, 1327–77* (Woodbridge, 2011), p. 69.

[74] E.W.M. Balfour-Melville, *Edward III and David II* (London, 1954), pp. 5–8; G. Templeman, 'Edward III and the Beginnings of the Hundred Years War', *Trans. Royal Historical Soc.,* 5th ser., ii (1952), pp. 69–88, at 81; C.J. Rogers, *War Cruel and Sharp: English Strategy under Edward III, 1327–60* (Woodbridge, 2000), pp. 110–15.

[75] *Cal. Pat. R., 1334–8*, p. 579. See too M. Prestwich, 'England and Scotland during

ship was not a *res hostilis* open to acquisition by *occupatio* because it was not seized in a *bellum*.[76] Like the ships arrested in English ports in 1296, although for different reasons, the ship captured in 1337 was thus subject to forfeiture, and was not covered by the maritime law of prize. It would seem, in other words, that the records declaring ships and goods forfeit to the Crown are exceptional not only in the sense of being relatively uncommon but also, and more importantly, in the sense of dealing with cases excepted or excluded from the coverage of the prize law applicable in the Admiral's court.[77] If this is correct, a proper understanding of that law will have to be based on examination of the types of evidence considered in previous sections of this essay, which, it has been argued, are more consistent with the theory of prize acquisition taught in the medieval law schools than with the theories encountered in modern writing on the subject.

Prize acquisition under royal licence

Not all modern writing is equally misleading. For example, in an exploration of 'The History of Belligerent Rights on the High Seas in the Fourteenth Century', D.A. Gardiner began by accepting the theory that prize acquisition was dependent on grants from the Crown but then acknowledged that it was difficult to reconcile with the evidence of legal practice surviving in the records he had been examining, in which mariners were frequently found to have acquired title to ships or goods captured at sea without any allegation being made that they had received a gift from the king.[78] Gardiner's solution to the problem was to suggest that the practice of making grants to particular mariners gave rise to expectations among the maritime community which

the Wars of Independence', in *England and Her Neighbours, 1066–1453*, ed. M. Jones and M. Vale (London, 1989), pp. 181–97, at 196; C. Given-Wilson and F. Bériac, 'Edward III's Prisoners of War: The Battle of Poitiers and Its Context', *Eng. Hist. Rev.*, 116 (2001), pp. 802–33, at 809–11; A. King, '"According to the Custom Used in French and Scottish Wars": Prisoners and Casualties on the Scottish Marches in the Fourteenth Century', *Jnl of Medieval History*, 28 (2002), pp. 263–90, at 281–2.

[76] The point may well have been lost on the mariners of Great Yarmouth, but since the record of their objection to the confiscation of the cargo uses the term *guerra* rather than *bellum*, it may be that they were trying to assert rights they believed they had in a less formal type of conflict. This point will have to be neglected here, but on the practices of mariners engaged in *guerrae maritimae* in this period see T.K. Heebøll-Holm, *Ports, Piracy and Maritime War: Piracy in the English Channel and the Atlantic, c. 1280 – c. 1330* (Leiden, 2013).

[77] Why ships or goods were forfeit to the Crown may not always be obvious, but the point is that an explanation must be sought in the common law as opposed to the maritime law of prize.

[78] D.A. Gardiner, 'The History of Belligerent Rights on the High Seas in the Fourteenth Century', *Law Quarterly Review*, 48 (1932), pp. 521–46, at 523–8.

gradually hardened into customary rights. Relying on the types of evidence already examined here, he suggested that before the mid-fourteenth century the particular grants made by the king 'were giving place to a custom claimed by the mariners and not disputed by the sovereign', and that 'by the end of the century captured enemy vessels and goods had come to be regarded as the property of the captors who, when they were receiving the king's wages, were answerable to him for some portion of the gains'.[79] That captors were regarded as the owners of any prizes taken seems the obvious conclusion to draw from the evidence available, and the explanation of how the royal grant theory could have given way to this view is ingenious and, on the face of it, plausible enough. What is not explained, however, is how the view that is understood to have emerged in practice could have been justified in a way that would have been acceptable to those who were deprived of their ships and goods. Presumably the idea is that the English king was understood to make implicit grants to mariners when explicit grants were lacking (as they usually were in Gardiner's experience).[80] Yet even if English mariners were understood to be licensed in one way or another to sail against the king's enemies, this would not explain why foreign mariners and merchants could have been expected to recognise the legitimacy of the capture and acquisition of their ships and goods. It has not been suggested, let alone established, that forfeiture of property to an enemy sovereign was commonly believed to be a consequence of the outbreak of a war. In contrast, it is well established that in the theory of the law schools *res hostiles* were thought to be open to acquisition by *occupatio* as soon as a war began. The theory that implied licences were granted on the outbreak of a war – if this is what Gardiner had in mind – is neither sufficient nor necessary to account for prize acquisition.[81]

Whatever Gardiner intended, the theory that some sort of royal licence was necessary to render the seizure of ships and goods legitimate underpins the widely expressed belief that 'privateers' differed from 'pirates' in being authorised to attack and despoil their victims.[82] On the assumption that

---

[79] Reference is also made to the *Cal. Close R., 1327–30*, p. 319, which is another exceptional record framed in the language of forfeiture. The significance Gardiner attached to this is not made clear.

[80] Gardiner, 'History of Belligerent Rights', p. 528.

[81] The focus throughout Gardiner's informative and interesting article is on English sources.

[82] C.L. Kingsford, *Prejudice and Promise in XVth Century England* (Oxford, 1925), pp. 78–9; J.C. Appleby, 'Devon Privateering from Early Times to 1688', in *The New Maritime History of Devon*, vol. I: *From Early Times to the Late Eighteenth Century*, ed. M. Duffy et al. (London, 1992), pp. 90–7, at 90; D.J. Starkey, 'Voluntaries and Sea Robbers: A Review of the Academic Literature on Privateering, Corsairing, Buccaneering and Piracy', *Mariner's Mirror*, 97 (2011), pp. 127–47, at 130; M. Pitcaithly, 'Piracy and Anglo-Hanseatic Relations, 1385–1420', in Gorski, *Roles of the Sea in Medieval England*, pp. 125–45, at 125; S. Rose, *England's Medieval Navy, 1066–1509: Ships, Men and Warfare* (Barnsley, 2013), pp. 140–1.

something fitting the description existed in the fourteenth century, one writer has remarked that 'privateering, as a legal concept, entailed some authorization by a higher authority'.[83] 'The line between pirate and privateer is clear', another writer has observed, for whereas the pirate was 'a free-enterprise thief', the privateer was 'licensed by a government to attack the vessels and towns of an enemy on whom war was declared'.[84] More precisely, it has been supposed that privateers were 'authorised by states to participate in armed commercial warfare by virtue of "letters of marque"'.[85] When privateering *stricto sensu* developed in the seventeenth century it certainly did become a condition of prize acquisition that licences to seize enemy property were first obtained in the form of letters of reprisal or marque. It is also well known that medieval governments issued documents known as letters of reprisal or marque to authorise seizures of property in peacetime.[86] The final question for consideration here is whether the acquisition of prizes in wartime was dependent before the early modern period on the existence of some such licence or commission.

An interesting contribution to the discussion can be found in a doctoral dissertation on 'Restitution at Sea in the Later Middle Ages' by B.D. Dick, whose survey of the practice of prize acquisition is all the more impressive in its acute and accurate reading of the evidence for being written with minimal reference to the underlying legal theory.[87] Correctly arguing that piracy will not be properly understood unless historians are able to distinguish its occurrence from the situations in which it was considered legitimate for ships and goods to be taken, the writer shows that it was not only in England that issues of prize acquisition tended to arise in the course of actions for the restitution of property despoiled at sea.[88] However, in making the crucial observation that no case has been found to turn on the existence of a licence, he adds, unnecessarily and misleadingly: 'the principle that such commissions were

---

[83] W. Sayers, 'Chaucer's Shipman and the Law Marine', *Chaucer Review*, 37 (2002), pp. 145–58, at 157. The term 'privateering' certainly did not exist in the fourteenth century. Whether the 'legal concept' later designated with this term existed before the early-modern period is what is at issue here and will be returned to elsewhere.

[84] W. Urban, *Medieval Mercenaries: The Business of War* (Barnsley, 2006), p. 189.

[85] W.G. Grewe, *The Epochs of International Law*, transl. M. Byers (Berlin, 2000), p. 305.

[86] G. Clark, 'The English Practice with Regard to Reprisals by Private Persons', *American Jnl of International Law*, 27 (1933), pp. 694–723; P.-C. Timbal, 'Les lettres de marque dans le droit de la France médiévale', *Recueils de la Société Jean Bodin*, 10 (1958), pp. 109–38; M.-C. Chavarot, 'La pratique des lettres de marque d'après les arrêts du parlement (XIIIe–début XVe siècle)', *Bibliothèque de l'École des Chartes*, 149 (1991), pp. 51–89.

[87] B.D. Dick, '"Framing Piracy": Restitution at Sea in the Later Middle Ages', Ph.D. thesis, University of Glasgow, 2010.

[88] Gardiner, 'History of Belligerent Rights', p. 530, also notes that instances of adjudication in the proper sense are not found in the medieval records.

implied is asserted in a case before the Parlement of Paris in 1358'.[89] The action in question was raised by merchants in Bruges, who claimed that their goods had been taken from a vessel by 'pirates, pilatores seu robatores de Bolonia'.[90] In response the mariners of Boulogne maintained that, as a matter of law, whenever a state of war existed 'inter aliquos principes', their subjects were entitled to any 'bona inimicorum' they could lay hands on, and that, as a matter of fact, the merchants in Bruges were Englishmen, who had chosen to reside there. In consequence, they reasoned, there was no requirement to restore the goods taken. No mention is made at any point in the recorded pleadings of an implied licence from the king of France.[91] The reasoning was rather that the subjects of the king of France, like the subjects of any other prince, were entitled to seize and retain enemy property as soon as their prince entered into a war with another prince. The mariners did not claim to have been licensed to sail against the king's enemies, nor need it be supposed that they had an implied licence silently in mind, for the reasoning that they presented makes perfect sense as it stands in terms of the civil law, which was referred to in the pleadings as *ratio scripta*. After it was proved that the goods taken had indeed belonged to English merchants, the Parlement dismissed the action and ordered the claimants to pay the defendants' expenses.

In reaching their decision the judges of the Parlement were aware that the reasoning of the mariners had already been accepted in the court of the Admiral of France.[92] The same kind of reasoning, it is suggested, would have been accepted in any similar case brought before the court of the Admiral of England. In the seventeenth century Sir Matthew Hale wrote that 'no man can acquire *iure belli* but he who hath power *indicere bellum*, or such as have a derived authority under him; therefore a rebel, a pirate &c., can not acquire any property *iure belli*'.[93] This reasoning – that since enemy goods could only be acquired if a sovereign had entered into a war, therefore enemy goods could only be acquired with the sovereign's authorisation – has a certain cogency, and by the time Hale was writing, express authorisation was a requirement of prize acquisition. But it was not a requirement in the theory of the medieval law schools, nor is there convincing evidence that it had come

---

[89] Dick, '"Framing Piracy"', pp. 25–7 and 85–6.

[90] *La Guerre de Cent Ans vue à travers les Registres du Parlement, 1337–1369*, ed. P.-C. Timbal et al. (Paris, 1961), pp. 260–4.

[91] There was a subsidiary argument 'de racione et ordinacione regia'. It was argued that if the merchants were found to be Flemish, by trading with the king's enemies they would still have 'forfeited themselves in body and in goods'. As the king was permitting the Flemings to continue trading with England this was not a compelling argument, and while it would, if successful, have meant that the goods did not need to be restored, it would not necessarily have followed that the mariners of Boulogne were allowed to keep them.

[92] Timbal, *La Guerre de Cent Ans*, p. 262.

[93] *Hale's Prerogatives of the King*, p. 129 (slightly adjusted).

to be regarded as a requirement in England in the Court of the Admiral – any more than in the Court of the Constable and Marshal – before the later sixteenth century. The surviving texts on Roman law were taken to show that it was necessary for one sovereign ruler formally to enter into a war with another, and also that officers authorised by sovereign rulers could then direct the redistribution of any goods acquired, but they were not taken to show that the acquisition of the goods depended on authorisation by sovereign rulers. In practice, mariners did sometimes obtain licences declaring that they had been authorised to sail against their ruler's enemies, especially if the licences spelled out their entitlement to retain a proportion of any goods they seized, but it was not until the later sixteenth century that obtaining a licence before sailing became a condition of prize acquisition, along with obtaining an act of adjudication after returning to port. How this came about will need to be explained elsewhere.

INDEX

Abbotsbury (Dors.), abbey, 69, 210
Abingdon, Nicholas of, 62
Acton, Laurence, 113–14
adjudication (*adjudicatio*), 24, 141, 149,
    154, 164, 220–5, 227, 230, 236
admirals, 2, 4, 6, 9, 11, 140, 149–59,
    161–170, 187–97, 199, 201, 203, 206–7,
    209–14, 216–17, 221–3, 225, 228–30,
Admiralty, Court of, 2, 4, 6, 9, 11, 13
advocates, 9
Agincourt, battle of, 25, 26
Alard, Gervase, Admiral, 155
Albini, William of, monument, 54
Aldermaston (Berks.), manor house
    chapel, 62–3
Alexandria, assault on, 98, 107, 110, 120
Aleyn, Dr John, 9, 193, 200–1, 208, 210
Allostock (Ches.), 82, 84, 91
Amalfi (Campania, Italy), 178; *Tabula de
    Amalfi*, 184
Ambühl, Rémy, 216 n. 5
Ancona (Italy), sea-laws of, 178, 179–81,
    182, 183–4
Anlaby, Thomas of, 58
Annandale (Scotland), chevauchée in,
    105; lordship of, 102
antiquity, 3, 5, 33 n. 13, 58, 73, 172, 173,
    219
Antwerp, 160
Appleton (Ches.), Bradley cross, 47
Appleton, Thomas, 200
Aquitaine, duchy of, 157
Aquitaine, Eleanor of, queen of England,
    18
Aragon, admiral of, 152; kings of, 174
archers, 99, 103
archives: abbey muniments,
    92; 'Chaunterie Rolles', 57; 'livere de
    terres', 57; Hungarian royal archive,
    111; and *see* cartularies; Chancery,
    charters; deed of entail; papal bulls;
    register of church ornaments
armour, 123–7, 129–30; bascinet, 126, 127,
    130; besagew, 127, 130; bevor, 126,
    130; breech (or brayer or brayette),
    124, 129; couter, 126; cuirass,
    125; cuisse, 124; gauntlet, 126,

127; greave, 124, 129; gusset, 125,
    129; haubergeon, 124, 125; leg
    harness, 124; mail sleeves, Plate
    VII; poleyn, 126; protection of
    torso and groin, 124–5; rerebrace,
    126, 129; rondel, 127 and Plate
    XI; sabaton, 123, 124, 129, 132;
    tunicle, 132; vambrace, 124, 126, 129,
    130; visor, 126, 130, 131; voider, 124,
    125, 129, 130; field harness (whole
    armour), Plates VIII-X
armour, 3, 12, 55, 68–9, 85, 121–7, 145
armourers, 7, 9, 10, 122, 123 n. 11, 124–5,
    127
armourers, linen, 122
arms, coats of, 25, 29–32, 63–4, 65
    and Plates I, III-V; of friends, 65;
    display of, 87; display banned
    from Carthusian houses, 69; grants
    of, 3, 10, 26, 31, 32, 34, 45, 90;
    interpretation of displays of, 71–3;
    knowledge of, 80, 103; law of (*jus
    armorum*), 3, 4, 8, 11, 31, 41–2, 132,
    145, 193, 199, 202, 215–16; public
    disgracing of (*subversio armorum*),
    3, 32–3, 40–3; rolls of, 19–20, 22,
    23, 57, 213; (sur)coat of arms, 130;
    and *see* banners; Berkeley; Burnell;
    cadency, marks of; crest, heraldic;
    Grosvenor; Mascy; Morley; Scales;
    Scrope; *Wapenbroek*
Ashley, Hamo, 92
Assheton, Sir Ralph, Vice-Constable of
    England, 206
Astley, Sir John, 193, 199
Audley, Sir Nicholas, of Helegh (Ches.),
    81
authenticity, 3, 52 n. 77, 80, 158–9 n. 30
Auxerre (Burgundy, France), arms at, 38
Aylsham (Norf), church, 52, 59
Ayton, Andrew, chapter by, 95–120; and
    see 3, 8, 64–5, 78

bailiffs, 40, 114, 137, 141, 146, 152–3, 155,
    156, 164, 194, 195, 227, 228
Ballard, William, March King of Arms,
    203

Nicopolis (Bulgaria), 111
nobles, 2, 8, 12, 22, 26, 41, 42, 57, 79, 110
    n. 73, 145, 187, 198, 202, 210
Norbury, Sir John, 211, 212
Normandy (France), 118, 120
Norrois, Andrew, herald, 17, 19
Norrois', Henry 'le, 17
Norton (Ches.), priory, 84
Norwich, Augustinian friary, 56
Norwich, cathedral priory, arms near
    rood, 72; monks, 50; Lenten veil, 55;
    screen, 59; stained glass window,
    Plate I
Norwich, disorders in, 207–8
notaries public, 193
Nuremberg (Germany), 111

occupation (*occupacio*), 219, 221, 227, 228
    n. 60
Oléron, Laws of, 12, 156, 158–9, 172,
    178–9, 190
Orde, Alice (née Graper), *see* Sabraham
ordinances, royal, 2, 6, 18, 20, 26, 32, 131
    n. 27, 135–6, 140, 143–4, 146, 153,
    202–3, 212, 222,
Osney, by Oxford, abbey, heraldry at, 68
Over Alderley (Ches.), 82
Oxford, Augustinian friary, 6, 56, 60–2,
    63, 64, 68; Osney abbey, 51, 5

Painting(s) and painted objects, 20,
    43 n. 47, 51; on bedstead, 55; on
    graveyard cross, 53–4; on hall
    roof, 85; of members of chivalric
    Orders, 44; mural, 51, 72, 120; panel
    painting, 54; on roadside cross, 48
    n. 6; on sign hanging in public, 51;
    imagery, 49–50, 62–3; on tombs, 37,
    60–2, 66, 67; and *see* Walsingham
Palermo (Sicily), 175
Panter, Davy, 208
papal bull, 57, 67
Pardessus, Jean-Marie, 178, 184
pardon, 39, 95, 103, 144, 161, 198, 205,
    207, 212 n. 119
Paris, Chambre des comptes, 135, 136,
    138; Marble Table (*Table de Marbre*) in
    the Palais de la Cité, 9, 139–40, 141,
    146, 153; siege of (1360), 107, 120
Paris, college of arms, 25
Paris, Matthew, 19
Parlement de Paris, 141, 153, 235;

jurisdiction over heraldic disputes,
    36, 40–2, 135, 137, 138, 146;
    jurisdiction over prize litigation,
    153; parlements, provincial, 40
parliament, *see* England, parliament
Parre, Sir William, 201, 202
Pavely, John, captain of English fleets,
    164–5
Pavia (Lombardy, Italy), 116
Peasants' Revolt (1381), 26
pedigrees, 57
Peebles, 105, 119
Percy, Henry (d. 1489), earl of
    Northumberland, 205
Percy, Sir Henry, 97, 105 n. 33
Peter, king of heralds, 16–17
Peterborough (Northants.), abbey, 55
    n. 36
Philip IV, king of France, 20
Philip V, king of France, 18, 137
Philip VI, king of France, 163
Philip the Good, duke of Burgundy, 19
Picardy (France), campaign in, 106
Picquigny, treaty of, 210
Pilkington, Sir Charles, 205
piracy, 4, 10, 149–50, 153–63, 166, 170,
    182–3, 188, 190, 192
pirates, 2, 149, 162, 190, 193, 229, 233–5;
    Breton, 197; Genoese, 149
Pizan, Christine de, *Livre des faits d'armes*,
    7, 35, 137
Plymouth (Devon), 96, 99, 117
Poitiers (France), Augustinian convent,
    37; battle of, 163
Polignac, Armand IX, vicomte de, 145
Polychronicon, 56
Ponta Delgada (Azores), church, 63
Portsdown (Hants), 209
Portugal, negotiations, agreement or
    alliance with, 158, 191, 212; king
    of, 223; Portuguese merchants,
    restitution to, 163, 223
Pot, Philippe, Steward of Burgundy, 44
Poynings, Sir Michael, 23
Poyntz, Sir Hugh, 23
Prestwich, Michael, 78
prisoners, 2, 42 n. 45, 114, 116, 145, 147,
    169, 215, 216 n. 5, 219–20,
privateering, 234; privateers, 152–3, 229,
    233–4
prize, law of, 4, 153–4, 168, 216, 218, 219
    n. 22, 220–4, 227, 231–2,